THOMAS HEYWOOD
Playwright and Miscellanist

Frontispiece:
Portrait of Thomas Heywood *by* Thomas Cecill,
enlarged from the frontispiece of The Hier-
archy of the Blessed Angels (see page 144,
note)

Electi

THOMAS HEYWOOD

Playwright and Miscellanist

By Arthur Melville Clark

*M. A., D. Phil., D. Litt., Reader Emeritus in English Literature
in the University of Edinburgh, sometime Scholar of
Oriel College, Oxford*

NEW YORK / RUSSELL & RUSSELL

PATRI MATRIQVE MEAE
JACOBO ET MARGARETAE MOYES CLARK
A. M. C. ORIELENSIS
MCMXXXI

CONTENTS

PREFACE

IN this book I have tried to reconstruct the life of Thomas Heywood more fully than has been done before, and to correct many old errors about him or about his work. I have necessarily devoted more space to biographical, historical, or literary-historical topics; but I have not ignored the critical aspects of the subject, and may refer those whose interest in Heywood is mainly critical to Chapter IX on *Heywood the Dramatist*, to the discussions in earlier chapters of the longer non-dramatic works, and to the appendices. My annotated *Bibliography of Thomas Heywood (Oxford Bibliographical Society's Proceedings and Papers*, vol. i, pt. ii), and another, without notes but containing a list of selected material on Heywood, for the forthcoming *Cambridge Bibliography of English Literature*, may be regarded as supplements to the present work. Among the points on which I have been able to throw light are the following: Heywood's parentage and Lincolnshire home, his Cheshire ancestry and his family arms, his relatives, marriage(s), and descendants; his education at Emmanuel College, Cambridge; his friends and patrons (including Robert Carre, Earl of Somerset), and his enemies; his relations with Shakespeare, Jonson, Webster, Dekker, James and Henry Shirley, William Rowley, Richard Brome, and William Prynne; the dating of his plays and other works; wrong identifications of plays with entries in Henslowe and, in Appendices VI and VII, many misattributions, dramatic and non-dramatic; the circumstances which made Heywood an apologist for the theatre and thrust on him the championship of women in Γυναικεῖον and elsewhere; his lost works and unfulfilled projects, especially *The Lives of all the Poets*; his excursions into witch-lore, pageantry, and miscellaneous journalism, and his editing, particularly works by Sir Richard Barckley, Marlowe, William Rowley, and Henry Shirley; his connexion with the Navy; contemporary and posthumous allusions, plagiarisms by one Austin, Edward Phillips, and others; adaptations and modern revivals; and lastly Heywood's politics and his surprising emergence in his last years as a puritan satirist of Laud, Finch, and the monopolists.

My additions to the canon are numerous, but I beg to assure the reader that my conclusions were neither hasty nor ill-considered. Some of the additions will not be questioned: e.g. *Love's School*, *A True Discourse of two . . . Prophets*, *A True Relation of . . . Purser and Clinton*, *The Rat Trap*, and portions of five other pamphlets; I should also mention here, *The Phoenix of these late Times*, *A Curtain Lecture*, *The Wonder of this Age*, *Machiavel's Ghost*, and *Reader, here you'll plainly see*, which have never been properly recognized as Heywood's. The evidence for other new ascriptions is, I believe, no less sound, though more circumstantial. Among these are a number of pamphlets: *The Life and Death of Queen Elizabeth*, *Brightman's Predictions*, *A Revelation of Mr. Brightman's Revelation*, and *A Dialogue or Accidental Discourse*; the internal evidence for these is rather better than for three other pamphlets: *The Famous . . . History of Sir Richard Whittington*, *The New Year's Gift*, and *A Certain Relation of the Hog-faced Gentlewoman*. Secondly, there are several plays in which I trace Heywood's hand: *Appius and Virginia*, *Dick of Devonshire*, *The Jew of Malta*, *The Martyred Soldier*, and *A Yorkshire Tragedy* with the associated *Miseries of Enforced Marriage*. These dramatic ascriptions are discussed in Appendices I–V. I have also briefly set forth my reasons for assigning Heywood a small share in *Sir Thomas Wyatt*, which along with *If You Know Not Me*, part i, and scenes from part ii, made up *Lady Jane*; the rest of *If You Know Not Me*, part ii, is all that remains of *The Life and Death of Sir Thomas Gresham*. Heywood's claim to *How a Man may Choose a Good Wife from a Bad* has long been accepted, and a very plausible case has been made out for his participation in *Sir Thomas More*. As for *The Fair Maid of the Exchange* and *Nobody and Somebody*, I have withheld the two essays I had prepared on these plays and admitted only in general terms Heywood's probable connexion with them. I have not seen the unique copy of *Oenone and Paris*, by T. H., sold at Sotheby's on March 23, 1925.

I should like to express my sincere thanks to the University of Oxford for the offer of a considerable sum towards the publication of this work and to the Carnegie Trust for the Universities of Scotland for a further guarantee. I would also express my great appreciation of the help and advice I have received from Mr. Percy Simpson, Professors F. P. Wilson and H. J. C. Grierson, Dr. W. W. Greg, and Mr. Bruce Dickins, and from the staffs at the Bodleian Library and the British Museum.

ARTHUR MELVILLE CLARK.

EDINBURGH.

ADDENDA

P. 4, note 3: Sir Nicholas Raynton was the son of Robert Raynton of Highinton, Lincolnshire; p. 9, note 1: *Fast Bind Fast Find*, in Harvey's *Pierce's Supererogation*, 1593 (ed. Grosart, ii. 311), was not a play by Thomas Heywood as *Biographia Dramatica* guessed, but part of John Heywood's 283rd Epigram (Bates, xiii); p. 10, note 2: *Sir Thomas More* was performed by students of Birkbeck College at the College, December 1922, and at Crosby Hall, March 24, 1926; p. 14, note 2: Malone attributed the 'Three Bold Beauchamps' to Nicholas Breton (manuscript note cited by Miss U. M. Ellis-Fermor in Professor R. H. Case's *Marlowe*, ii. 14); p. 24, note 8: *The Three Famous London Apprentices*, mentioned in Edmund Gayton's *Festivous Notes on Don Quixote*, 271, was probably Heywood's play; p. 67, note 1 (cf. p. 14): Gayton, *ibid.* 271, gives *Greeks and Trojans* as another favourite show for holidays; p. 198, note 7: *The Black Box of Rome opened*, 1641, and *A New plot discovered*, 1641, seemed so similar in style and matter to *The Rat Trap* as to warrant a tentative ascription to Heywood in my *Bibliography*, 135, 137; p. 207, note 1: there are posthumous allusions to Heywood in Thomas Allen's burlesque praise of James Strong's *Joanereidos: or, Feminine Valour*, 1645, and in Joshua Poole's *English Parnassus, or A Help to English Poesy*, 1657, 1677, preface, and to *A Revelation of Mr. Brightman's Revelation* in Izaak Walton's *Life of Sanderson*, 1678 (ed. Keynes, 489–90); p. 210: by 'first surviving play' I mean in composition, not publication; p. 288, note 1: see also Mr. H. S. Bennett's introduction to his edition for Professor R. H. Case's *Marlowe*, iii; p. 289, note 3: *The Jew of Malta* is said by Gayton, *op. cit.* 271, to have been one of the stock pieces demanded by the audience on public holidays.

ABBREVIATIONS

Apology. An Apology for Actors, ed. J. P. Collier.

Bates. *A Woman Killed with Kindness* and *The Fair Maid of the West*, part i, ed. Katharine L. Bates.

Captives. The Captives, or the Lost Recovered, ed. A. C. Judson.

Chambers. *The Elizabethan Stage*, by Sir E. K. Chambers.

C.H.E.L. Cambridge History of English Literature.

Chetwood. *The British Theatre. Containing the Lives of the English Dramatic Poets; with an Account of all their Plays*, by W. R. Chetwood.

Courthope. *A History of English Poetry*, by W. J. Courthope.

C.S.P.D. Calendar of State Papers: Domestic Series.

D.N.B. Dictionary of National Biography.

Fleay, i and ii. *A Biographical Chronicle of the English Drama, 1559–1642*, by F. G. Fleay.

Fleay, *Shakespeare. A Chronicle History of the Life and Work of William Shakespeare*, by F. G. Fleay.

Fleay, *Stage. A Chronicle History of the London Stage, 1559–1642*, by F. G. Fleay.

Fleay, *Anglia* viii. *Annals of the Careers of James and Henry Shirley*, by F. G. Fleay, *Anglia* viii.

Genest. *Some Account of the English Stage, 1660–1830*, by J. Genest.

Hazlitt, *Handbook. Handbook to the Popular and Dramatic Literature of Great Britain*, by W. C. Hazlitt.

H.D. Henslowe's Diary, ed. W. W. Greg.

Herbert. *The Dramatic Records of Sir Henry Herbert*, ed. J. C. Adams.

Hist. MSS. Com. Reports of the Historical Manuscripts Commission.

H.P. Henslowe Papers: being Documents supplementary to Henslowe's Diary, ed. W. W. Greg.

Hunt. *Thomas Dekker: A Study*, by M. L. Hunt.

Kirkman. *A True . . . Catalogue of all the Comedies, Tragedies . . . published, till . . . 1661* [by Francis Kirkman].

Langbaine. *An Account of the English Dramatic Poets*, by G. Langbaine.

M.L.N. Modern Language Notes.

M.L.R. The Modern Language Review.

M.P. Modern Philology.

Murray. *English Dramatic Companies, 1558–1642*, by J. T. Murray.

N. & Q. Notes and Queries.

Pearson. *The Dramatic Works of Thomas Heywood now first collected,* [ed. R. H. Shepherd] for J. Pearson.

Pleasant Dialogues. Pleasant Dialogues and Dramas, ed. W. Bang, *Materialien zur Kunde des älteren englischen Dramas,* iii.

P.M.L.A.A. Publications of the Modern Language Association of America.

R.B. Roxburghe Ballads, ed. J. W. Ebsworth.

S. in Ph. Studies in Philology.

S.R. *Transcript of the Register of the Company of Stationers, 1554–1640,* ed. E. Arber; *continued from 1640–1708,* ed. G. E. B. Eyre.

Tatlock. *The Siege of Troy in Elizabethan Literature, especially in Shakespeare and Heywood,* by J. S. P. Tatlock, *P.M.L.A.A.,* xxx.

T.L.S. Times Literary Supplement.

Ward. *History of English Dramatic Literature to the Death of Queen Anne,* by A. W. Ward, 2nd ed., 1899.

Ward, *C.H.E.L. Thomas Heywood,* by A. W. Ward, *C.H.E.L.,* vi.

CHAPTER I

1573/4–1593: BIRTH, PARENTAGE, AND EDUCATION

THOMAS HEYWOOD was a native of Lincoln-shire, as he himself tells us five separate times.[1] It has been assumed, perhaps from the persons whom he mentions,[2] that he, too, belonged to a gentle Lincolnshire family, though the skilled investigators of whom the county has had no lack have been unable to trace it. We must conclude, then, that since they do not appear in any of the Visitations or in the pedigrees of families with landed property the Heywoods of Lincolnshire

[1] *Londini Artium*, etc., dedication to Lord Mayor Nicholas Raynton; *English Traveller*, dedication to Sir Henry Appleton, friend of 'my countreyman Sir *William Elvish*'; *Pleasant Dialogues*, 252, &c., elegy on Sir George St. Paul; *Phoenix of these late times*, second issue, sig. E 3 verso; and 'To my Friend and Countrey-man James Yorke, Concerning *his Booke of Heraldry*'. Cf. Γυναικεῖον, 262–3, for an anecdote of 'a countrey woman of mine' and *Three Wonders of this Age* for 'one *Robert Wainman*, who served M. *Willoughby* in Lincoln-shire'.

[2] Sir George St. Paul, b. 1562, son of Sir Thomas and Faith, daughter of Vincent Grantham of Lincoln; d. Nov. 28, 1613. See J. Wilford, *Memorials and Characters*, 179, &c., for Dr. John Chadwick's funeral sermon for St. Paul, Dec. 9, 1613, which Heywood seems to echo in his elegy. Sir William Helwysse, whose timely encouragement Heywood gratefully remembers in the dedication of *The English Traveller*, was the obscure son of the better known Sir Gervase, Lieutenant of the Tower at the time of Overbury's murder. He married Sir George St. Paul's niece Martha, daughter of Sir Edward Tyrwhit and Faith St. Paul. Sir George St. Paul's uncle and aunt, John and Mary St. Paul, married about the middle of the sixteenth century Elizabeth and John, children of Sir Richard Thimbleby. Elizabeth, left a widow in 1560, married Thomas Welby of Moulton, a cousin more or less near of the eccentric recluse Henry Welby, the subject of Heywood's *Phoenix of these late times*. Sir Henry Appleton, an Essex landowner, was connected with Lincolnshire by the marriage of his son, also Sir Henry, to Sarah, daughter of Sir Thomas Oldfield. Mr. Willoughby (see note 1) was probably William Willoughby, of Little Coates by his marriage to Elizabeth, daughter and heiress of Sir Chris. Hildyard of Little Coates. James Yorke, the herald-blacksmith, was almost certainly a native of the city of Lincoln.

origin, whom an examination of parish registers all over the county shows to have been a numerous race, had no pretensions to gentility. Yet Thomas Heywood refers with pride to his uncle 'that good old Gentleman'[1], whom from his will we know to have been a person of very considerable means; and the dramatist himself claimed and was accorded the rank of gentleman.[2] The provenience of this gentle family and the proof of its gentility are fortunately established by the application of Heywood's uncle Edmund for a grant of arms as a descendant of 'the ancient family of Heywood of Mottram, co. Chester'.[3] A sketch of Edmund's arms, impaled with those of his wife, a Cheshire lady by name Magdalen Wibonbury or Wiburbury, sister and co-heiress of Roger Wibonbury, appears in MS. Stowe 677[4] as ratified and confirmed in June 1616 by William Camden Clarenceux; they are Argent, two bendlets gules, in chief trefoil sable, all within a bordure of the second; impaled a greyhound statant sable, collared or, with crest on the stump of a tree eradicated and couped at the top vert, a hawk rising proper beak and belled or, on the breast a trefoil of the last.[5] Here, then, is the explanation of the absence of the gentle Heywood and his kin from the Visitations of Lincolnshire. Though he was himself a native of that county, the connexion of his family with it goes back only one generation; in short Heywood's father must have been a migrant from Cheshire at a date previous to the dramatist's birth, and it is more than probable that, like Jonson's parent, he was a clergyman.

We believe that we have found him in the Reverend Robert Heywood, rector of Rothwell and of Ashby-cum-Fenby, two livings in the deanery of Grimsby. Robert

---

[1] *English Traveller*, dedication.

[2] Edmund Howes (Stowe's *Annals*, ed. 1615, 811) numbers 'M. Thomas Heywood gentleman' among the English poets; Thomas Brewer ranks him '*Gent.*' in his lines before *The Exemplary Lives*; and Heywood signs his verses for Holland's version of Xenophon's *Cyropaedia* 'Thomas Heywood, Gen.'

[3] *Grants of Arms*, 95; see also *Grantees of Arms*, 118, 123.

[4] Fol. 7; see another sketch as confirmed Jan. 1616/17 in MS. Harl. 6059, fol. 34; and cf. *Genealogist*, 1900, 278–9.   [5] See 101–3 *infra*.

Heywood was born in 1543[1] and was ordained priest by
the Bishop of Chester on September 7, 1562.[2] He com-
pounded for the firstfruits of the rectory of Ashby-cum-
Fenby on November 15, 1564.[3] A Robert Heywoode
matriculated as a pensioner from Magdalene College,
Cambridge, at Easter, 1567.[4] 'Sir Robert Haywood,
clerk,' was admitted by Thomas Cooper, Bishop of
Lincoln, to preach within the deanery of Grimsby on
July 31, 1573.[5] On July 26, 1575, at Lincoln, Sir Robert
Heywood, clerk, was admitted rector of Rothwell by the
presentation of June 10, 1575, of Richard Bolles, patron
of the living,[6] then vacant by the death of Sir William
Sargeant. Robert Heywood who took up his residence
at Rothwell, was mentioned in 1579 and in 1585,[7] and
in a Subsidy of Armour of 1590 was put down for a light
horse in respect of Ashby-cum-Fenby.[8] He signed the
bishop's transcripts of Rothwell's register at Michaelmas
1586 and 1588. The living of Ashby was vacant by death
in 1593,[9] and the will of 'Robert Haywoode clerk parson
of Ashbye', made in his last sickness, is dated February 13,
1592 (i.e. 1593).[10] Its careful allusions to his few books,

[1] *Liber Cleri*, 1576, fol. 17d (*Lincoln Record Soc.* ii. 178), gives his age
as 33 in 1576. The Rev. S. J. Bastow makes Robert Heywood 33 in 1574.
[2] *Lincoln Record Soc.*, ii. 178. *Liber Cleri*, 1585, fol. 16, says Sept. 20.
[3] *Compositions for Firstfruits*, Public Record Office.
[4] Venn, *Book of Matriculations and Degrees*, 335; Messrs. Venn (*Alumni
Cantabrigienses*, ii. pt. i. 343) would identify this person with our clergyman.
[5] *Lincoln Record Soc.* ii. 178; cf. 109.
[6] *Presentation Deeds*, 1575, 47 (*Lincoln Record Soc.* ii. 14).
[7] *Ibid.* ii. 178, and *Liber Cleri*, 1585, fol. 16d. On July 6, 1576, the
Bishop relaxed the sequestration of the rectory to the extent of 10s.
[8] Fol. 4d.
[9] *Presentation Deeds*, 1593, 17.
[10] Probate Registry, Lincoln. The annual value of the living of Rothwell
was £7 10s. with tenths payable to the crown of 15s. 1d. and procurations
of 5s.; the crown living of Ashby was of the annual value of £14 10s.
with tenths of 24s. 1d. (*Valor Ecclesiasticus*; iv. 66). Rothwell, some two
miles from Caistor and ten from Grimsby, is still a very small village.
Near the ancient Norman church, dedicated to St. Mary Magdalen, is a
cottage referred to in documents as 'the ancient homestead of the Rectory'.
Ashby-cum-Fenby consists of two hamlets six and a half miles from

'my Booke called the poore mans Librarye[1] and my gilded
Testament', bear out the *Liber Cleri's* statement that he
'understands Latin', is 'well versed in sacred learning . . .
performs the holy [mysteries] prescribed by public
authority' and was a 'preacher'.[2] In fact he appears to
have been a conscientious country parson, rather an
exceptional figure at the time. But his faithfulness brought
him no wealth; indeed he seems to have been in very
narrow circumstances, if we may judge from the bequests
he makes, 'twoe ewes and twoe Lambes', 'the Quye with
calfe', 'my new freese coate' and 'my gray ambling nagge'.
He speaks of his 'pore children', grouping them after
their mother, and, which is of supreme importance, makes
a bequest of ten shillings to 'my brother Edmund Heywood'. The localities of the Lincolnshire families with
which Heywood was acquainted do not help us to prove
this paternity.[3] But the fact that Robert Heywood was a
descendant of the Cheshire clan who went to Lincolnshire,
was married and the father of children of the same generation as the dramatist, and who, so far as the evidence goes,
was a scholar, probably a graduate of Cambridge, and a
conscientious and indigent parish priest—exactly what we
should expect Heywood's father to have been—and that
he had a brother Edmund seems to us conclusive enough.
His death in 1593[4] would explain very satisfactorily the
probable cutting short of Thomas Heywood's academic
career and other facts in his subsequent history.

It is probable, therefore, that we must regard either

Grimsby. The church, dedicated to St. Peter, is only a little less venerable
than that of Rothwell; in 1871 an old plate, bearing the date 1584 and so
pertaining to the incumbency of Robert Heywood, was discovered; the
same date is carved on the front of the pulpit. The old rectory belongs to
the same period.

[1] Πτωχομυσεῖον. *The poor man's Library.* By William Alley, Bishop of
Exeter, 1565, 1570, and 1571.

[2] *Lincoln Record Soc.* ii. 178.

[3] The St. Paul estates were at Snarford, Carlton, Melwood Grange near
Epworth, and Lissington. The Helwysses were settled at Worlaby, the
Tyrwhits at Stainfield, the Thimblebys at Irnham near Stainfield, and the
Welbys at Gedney and Coxhill.

[4] Buried at Ashby, Feb. 19, 1593.

'the ancient homestead of the Rectory' of Rothwell or the old and still inhabited rectory of Ashby as the birthplace of Thomas Heywood. Unfortunately the children of Robert Heywood born before 1578 are not recorded in the register of Rothwell; the register of Ashby goes back no further than 1723, about which date a legendary church-warden, Cortis by name, allowed his wife to use the precious pages 'to keep her pies from burning at ye bottom in ye oven',[1] and the Bishop's transcript begins at 1580. The Christian name of Robert Heywood's wife and, as we suppose, of the well-loved mother[2] of him who so often and so heartily wrote of the great Queen is appropriately discovered to have been Elizabeth by the register of Rothwell. A number of children, younger than the dramatist, were born and baptized there, Elizabeth on February 17, 1577/8, Margaret on February 19, 1578/9, who was buried on March 4 following, Sara on January 4, 1580/1, and Vexeynte (? Vincent) on March 5, 1581/2,[3] who was buried on March 7, 1587/8, as 'Vis the sonne of Robert Heywood'.[4] Sara was buried at Ashby on February 23, 1592/3, only four days after her father. Other children of Robert and Elizabeth Heywood were baptized at Ashby, Robert on October 30, 1585, William on March 13, 1587/8, Mary on August 30, 1589, Hester on November 11, 1590, Benjamin on December 3, 1591, and Humfrey on March 17, 1592/3.

Whether this paternity for the poet be accepted or not, it is clear that the researchers have been looking for the ancestry of Thomas Heywood at the wrong side of England altogether. Our Heywood seems to have maintained some slight connexion with Cheshire and to have had several Cheshire friends. In 1618 he wrote verses for Matthew Mainwaring's romance *Vienna*, and in the sixteen-thirties dedicated two plays to Matthew's son

[1] Information of the Rev. G. F. Boissier.
[2] The old lady mentioned in Γυναικεῖον, 428–9, may have been a relative: 'Amongst others I might instance one, now of a great age . . . Felicitie she is called on Earth, Eternall Felicitie may she inioy in Heaven.'
[3] On the same day 'Dorothie Hey farrow' (*sic*) was baptized.
[4] In this entry 'baptized' is deleted.

Thomas. In *Pleasant Dialogues* he included an acrostic on an anagram of Sir Ranulph Crew, once Lord Chief Justice, who was related both by his father John Crew of Nantwich and by his mother Alice, daughter of Humphrey Mainwaring, to the above-mentioned Matthew. John Weever, the collector of epitaphs, for whose tomb in St. James's, Clerkenwell, Heywood probably wrote the inscription, belonged to a Cheshire-Lancashire family, and Dr. Stephen Bradwell, like Weever a Clerkenwell neighbour of Heywood, and a writer of verses for *The Exemplary Lives*, may have been one of the Bradwalls of Bradwalls.

The dramatist was probably born after July 31, 1573, when his father, as we take Robert Heywood to have been, was licensed to preach within the deanery of Grimsby, and before 1575. He would thus be practically the coeval of Middleton, Dekker, and Jonson, a decade younger than Shakespeare and Marlowe, and a few years older than Tourneur and Marston. He is more likely to have been the Thomas Heywood who entered Emmanuel College, Cambridge, the stronghold of Puritanism,[1] as a pensioner about 1591,[2] when he was sixteen or seventeen, than the Thomas Heyward, pensioner at St. John's from Lent 1584/5.[3]

There is a persistent tradition, however, that Heywood was a fellow of Peterhouse,[4] originating apparently with William Cartwright, an actor turned bookseller in the hard times of the Commonwealth, who in 1658 republished *An Apology for Actors* as *The Actors' Vindication* and, omitting the original dedication, rededicated it to the Marquess of Dorchester. The single statement of Cartwright deserves to have its credibility tested, as has never

[1] Founded in 1584 by Sir Walter Mildmay, great-uncle of Sir Henry Appleton's mother. Dr. Alex. Nowel (cf. *If you know not me*, Pearson, i. 263) was one of the benefactors.

[2] Venn, *Book of Matriculations and Degrees*, 335.

[3] Venn, *Alumni Cantabrigienses*, vol. ii. pt. i. 343.

[4] A passage in *The Wise Woman of Hogsdon* (Pearson, v. 321) has been adduced in support: cf. Fleay, i. 292.

been done, by the trustworthiness of the context, which
is as follows:

My Lord,

The Authour of this ensuing Poem, not long before his Death,
discovering how undeservedly our Quality lay under the envious
and ignorant, made our Vindication his Subject, which he hath
asserted with such Arguments of Reason and Learning, that the
judicious will no doubt rest satisfied of the lawfulness and (indeed)
necessity of it: the gentleman was a Fellow of *Peter*-house in
Cambridge; I should think it a high part of ingratitude to let so
illaborate a Piece lye buried with him. And therefore to pay the
Duty he Ow'd your Honour, to undeceive the World, and to
revive his memory, I beseech your Lordship, give me leave to
pursue his Intention, by the humble Dedication of this his so
Genious a Work.

But 'this his so Genious a Work', 'this . . . Poem', instead
of having been written 'not long before his Death', was in
print in 1612, twenty-nine years before its author's death;
so far as we know, Heywood owed no duty to the Marquess of Dorchester, probably did not even know him,
and could have had no intention to dedicate to him what
had already been dedicated to the Earl of Worcester. But
though never a fellow of Peterhouse, Heywood speaks
with evident familiarity of the university, the studies and
the way of life there. His remarks, for example, on
academic plays and the information that he incidentally
gives of the attitude of the university authorities to
dramatic performances are of great value. We may
assume from them that not only did he see 'tragedyes,
comedyes, historyes, pastorals and shewes, publickly
acted, in which the graduates of good place and reputation have bene specially parted',[1] but that he himself had
some practice in the profession he was later to adopt.

[1] *Apology*, 28.

CHAPTER II

1594–1599: LITERARY AND DRAMATIC APPRENTICESHIP

FROM Cambridge we guess that Heywood went straight to London to make as soon as possible a living in the only way open to men with some talent and education but without any particular training, the means to acquire one, or, in the indecent jostle for favour, a patron to secure them a parish, chaplaincy, tutorship, or grammar-school. It must have been to those early years in London that Heywood was referring in his *Funeral Elegy on James I*:

> Henry, *Southamptons* Earle, a Souldier proved;
> Dredded in warre, and in milde peace beloved.
> Oh give me leave a little to resound
> His memory, as most in dutie bound,
> Because his servant once.[1]

Though there is no evidence at this time or later of any company of actors in Southampton's patronage, it was most likely in this capacity that Heywood 'served' him.[2]

He no doubt gained his first experience of the London stage as an actor rather than as a jobbing dramatist, for the theatrical manager, though ready enough to welcome talented young men from the universities, would require of them a knack in taking the popular fancy which the mere study of 'that writer *Ovid* and that writer *Meta-*

[1] Sig. B 4 verso; Southampton is mentioned in *The Three Wonders.*

[2] *Oenone and Paris* (S. R. May 17, 1594), by T. H., the unique copy of which was sold at Sotheby's on Mar. 23, 1925, may have been Heywood's earliest attempt to catch the reading public, and prior to his taking to the stage. The author, whose poem is a close imitation of *Venus and Adonis* of the previous year, offers to the reader 'the first fruits of my indevours, and the Maiden head of my Pen'. Heywood later translated the Ovidian epistles of Paris and Helen for *Troia Britannica* and introduces a short scene between Paris and Oenone in *The Iron Age* (Pearson, iii. 271–3).

morphoses'[1] did not impart. But from a supernumerary to 'a cobler of Poetrie called a play-patcher'[2] would be an easy step for one so adaptable as Heywood. One of his very first jobs appears to have been a share in the revision of Munday's *Sir Thomas More*, probably for Shakespeare's company.[3] The evidence is entirely palaeographical; but so striking is the resemblance between the crabbed hand B of the manuscript[4] and Heywood's undoubted autograph dramas[5] that, since Dr. Greg pointed this out without, however, committing himself,[6] palaeographers have more or less cautiously accepted the proposition.[7] The passages in question consist of an elaboration of the cancelled but still extant scene iv, revised merely to drag in the clown; brief marginal additions for the same character; sixty-seven lines of an apparently original supplement to scene ix; and the rough draft of a speech, transcribed in its proper place by the writer of hand C.[8] How much more, if any, of the latter's script is a fair copy of hand B we cannot say, but Dr. Greg takes B to have had the literary, and C the dramatic revision under his charge.[9] This is just the sort of work which might be entrusted to a tiro; and while there is on the whole nothing to distinguish B's contribution from Munday's, his revised

---

[1] *The Return from Parnassus*, iv, 5.

[2] Dekker's *News from Hell*, ed. Grosart, ii. 146.

[3] Both the date of the play and the company for which it was written are very problematical; cf. Chambers and authorities cited, iv. 33–4; A. W. Pollard, *Shakespeare's Hand in the Play of Sir Thomas More*, 12, 17, &c.; W. W. Greg, *English Literary Autographs, 1550–1650*, pt. i, xi; L. L. Schücking, *Shakespeare and Sir Thomas More*, G. R. Harrison, *The Date of Sir Thomas More*, and A. W. Pollard, *Verse Tests and the Date of 'Sir Thomas More'*, *R.E.S.* i; and S. A. Tannenbaum, *'The Booke of Sir Thomas Moore'*.

[4] B.M. MS. Harl. 7368.   [5] B.M. MS. Egerton 1994.

[6] *Shakespeare's Hand in the Play of Sir Thomas More*, 44, note 1; cf. *English Literary Autographs, 1550–1650*, pt. i, xxii, and *Shakespeare's Hand Once More*, *T.L.S.*, Nov. 24, Dec. 1, 1927.

[7] S. A. Tannenbaum, *op. cit.*, and Charles Sisson, review of last, *M.L.R.* xxiii. 231 &c.

[8] Cf. W. W. Greg, ed. of play, xvii, &c., and *Shakespeare's Hand in the Play of Sir Thomas More*, 42, &c.   [9] Ed. of play, xviii.

scene iv is nearer than the cancelled scene to the mob scenes in *Edward IV* [1] and *Sir Thomas Wyatt*.[2]

Play-patching was evidently still Heywood's line in the autumn of 1596 when he was first mentioned by Henslowe in

> A note of Suche money as J haue
> lent vnto thes meane whose names
> folow at severall tymes edward alleyn
> martyne slather Jeames donstall & Jewbey
> all this lent sence the   1596   14 of octob3 . . .
>   lent vnto them for hawodes bocke   xxx[s] [3]

Little consideration seems to have been given to the name of this 'bocke', which may have been a cautious trial order at the end of the off season. Undoubtedly in the fortnight or more that elapsed between the purchase of the play and the resumption of performances there had been rehearsals, and one or other of the new pieces was pretty certainly Heywood's. The first new production, 'valteger', on December 4, 1596,[4] is generally taken to be the basis of *The Mayor of Quinborough*. Heywood's name has been tentatively but unconvincingly linked with the second, 'stewtley', acted on December 11(10).[5] 'nabucadonizer' of December 19(18)[6] was evidently an old-fashioned Biblical play, the sort of thing that might be safely entrusted to a novice. But perhaps the next piece, 'that wilbe shalbe', given on December 30,[7] is more suggestive of Heywood, who had a weakness for proverbial titles.

---

[1] Pearson, i. 8, &c.

[2] The identification of Heywood and the writer of hand B would alone dispose of Professor Schücking's argument (*op. cit.* 157–9; cf. A. W. Pollard, *op. cit.* 14) for Heywood's authorship of the scenes in *Sir Thomas More* ascribed to Shakespeare. The play was given at Birkbeck College in Dec. 1922 and at Crosby Hall 1922.

[3] *H.D.* i. 45.   [4] *H.D.* i. 50; cf. ii. 181.

[5] *H.D.* i. 50; ii. 181; see 213, and 433 *infra*.   [6] *H.D.* i. 50; ii. 181.

[7] *H.D.* i. 50; ii. 181. Dr. Greg (*H.D.* ii. 86, 88) suggested Heywood's part authorship of *The Isle of Dogs*; Nashe's collaborator has since been shown to have been Jonson (see Herford and Simpson's *Jonson*, i. 15–16, 217–18).

More than a year after this Henslowe records the next certainty in Heywood's history:

'm^r that this 25 of marche 1598 Thomas hawoode came & hiered hime seallfe wth me as a covenante searvante for ij yeares by the Receuenge of ij syngell pence acordinge to the statute of winshester & to begine at the daye a boue written & not to playe any wher publicke a bowt london not whille these ij yeares be expired but in my howsse yf he do then he dothe forfett vnto me by the Receuinge of thes ij^d fortie powndes & wittnes to this   Antony monday   w^m Borne
                                    gabrell spencer   Thomas dowton
                                    Robart shawe   Richard Jonnes
                                    Richard alleyn'^{1}

As Heywood had had dealings with the Admiral's men before and, so far as we can discover, with no other public troupe, this agreement was probably a formal re-engagement. But his status in the company is uncertain. It is true that no wages are specified and on the two occasions on which Heywood's name appears in the *Diary* during his covenanted term Henslowe calls him Mr. Heywood,[2] which addition Fleay believed the mark of a sharer.[3] But the diarist's use of 'Mr.' was governed by other considerations; nor does it appear to have been his custom to mention wages in his agreements, though when hiring Thomas Hearne, who was not a sharer, he did so.[4] As, however, during part of Heywood's engagement to act only at Henslowe's play-house, he was writing for another company, it may be reasonably inferred that he had no share in the Admiral's. It could not have been a very prosperous time for him when, like the other 'very hyerlings of some of our players' he was forced to live on 'a reversion of vi.s. by the weeke',[5] as the wages were in 1579. Indeed the lot of the hireling, a not very elevated

---

[1] *H.D.* i. 204.   [2] *H.D.* i. 102.
[3] *Stage*, 143.
[4] *H.D.* i. 201; for an examination of these agreements see *ibid.* ii. 99 &c., and Chambers, i. 308, &c., 348, &c.; ii. 151, &c.
[5] *School of Abuse*, ed. Collier, 29.

rank in a not very respectable calling, had become harder,
for Henslowe agreed with Hearne for 'fyve shellynges a
weacke for one yeare & vj[s] viij[d] for the other yeare',[1] on
the average rather less than the wages of twenty years
before.

After the drawing of this contract Heywood again
retires into obscurity, and it is not until December 6,
1598, when Henslowe lent Richard Shaa, as representative of the company, three pounds 'to bye a Boocke called
ware wth owt blowes & love wth owt sewte of Thomas
hawodes'[2] that we hear of him again. When the transaction was completed by the payment of an additional two
pounds on January 26, Henslowe renamed the play 'ware
wth owt blowes & love wth owt stryfe'.[3] The five pounds
in all proved that Heywood had no collaborator, but it is
slightly under the usual figure. Apparently the dirtier
work of Henslowe's dramatic factory was still falling to
the juvenile Heywood, from whom a play might be had
on lower terms than his elders would accept. In this very
year, however, Heywood was included by the comprehensive Meres in his *Palladis Tamia* among 'the best for
Comedy',[4] and when Henslowe notes Heywood's next
play he has a little more respect for him; for, although
the total was again but five pounds, three pounds on
February 10, 1598/9 and the rest two days later,[5] the
dramatist on both occasions is Mr. Heywood. The only
surviving fragment of the piece, 'Jonne as good as my
ladey', may be a song in Γυναικεῖον with the burden 'What
care I how faire she bee',[6] our evidence being a ballad in
the Pepysian collection entitled *Joan is as good as my Lady.
To the tune of What care I how fair she be.*[7] Heywood was
probably thinking as much of his comedy as of the pro-

---

[1] *H.D.* i. 201.   [2] *H.D.* i. 100.

[3] *Ibid.* i. 101; cf. *English Traveller*, Pearson, iv. 24: 'Love in these kindes
should not be compel'd'; and *Philocothonista*, 81–2. The secondary title
of *Edmund Ironside* is *War hath made all friends.*

[4] 283 verso.   [5] *H.D.* i. 102.

[6] Γυναικεῖον, 288–9 : see *H.P.* 118, 121, for 'Black Jonne'.

[7] Cf. Hazlitt, *Handbook*, 350. For Fleay's identification with *A Maidenhead Well Lost* see 128–9 *infra*.

verbial phrase when he quoted it in *If you know not me*, part II:

HOBSON. Bones-a-me, *John*, is not this a lady?
JOHN. No, by my troth, master; such as be in the garden-alleys.
     Joan's as good as this French lady.[1]

The Admiral's men did not begin to act at the Rose apparently until April 2, 1598, but from then on with short breaks[2] they played regularly till July 13, 1600.[3] But by that time Heywood's bondage had come to an end. There had been nothing in his agreement obliging him to write only for Henslowe, though normally an actor-playwright would provide his own, rather than another, company with his plays. If, however, he had quarrelled with his fellows or was dissatisfied with his remuneration and was desirous of improving his position, there was nothing in the contract to prevent his taking his goods to another market; and it is perhaps significant that, while Derby's men by whom *Edward IV* was produced opened their season, probably at the Curtain, in the spring of 1599, Heywood ceased to write for the Admiral's company in February.

But from Heywood's share in *Edward IV* and from his supposed share in *The Bold Beauchamps* and *The Trial of Chivalry*, only the first and the last of which we know to have been acted by Derby's men, we can hardly assume that on the termination of his contract with the Admiral's company a year after *Edward IV* had been produced he joined Derby's. The latter were not the retainers of Ferdinando, Lord Stanley, known as the Earl of Derby from September 1593 till his death in April 1594, but of his brother William who succeeded to the title and before September 1594 had given his patronage to the cry of players under discussion. From that time till 1618 they appear repeatedly in provincial records, but their

---

[1] Pearson, i. 314.   [2] *H.D.* ii. 94.
[3] *Ibid.* i. 108; for their court and other private performances see Chambers, iv. 111, &c., 165, &c.

only burst of success was in 1599 when they secured the
services of Heywood.[1]

The evidence, however, for attributing the authorship
of *The Bold Beauchamps* to Heywood about this time and
its performance to Derby's men is very slender. The
spurious second part of *Hudibras*, 1663, does indeed yield
Heywood the doubtful honour:

> The Ancient Poet *Heywood* draws
> From Ancestors of These his Laws
> Or *Dramma*, to fill up his Sceanes
> With Souldiers good, to please *Plebe'ns*,
> And in those famous Stories told
> The *Grecian* Warrs and *Beauchamps* bold.[2]

But the earlier allusions to the play throw no light on

---

[1] They were probably 'the common players' for whom in June 1599
Derby was 'busy penning comedies' (*C.S.P.D.* 1598–1601, 227; cf.
Hatfield MSS. xiii. 609). See Murray, i. 293, for Derby's interest in
other players.

[2] 15; cf. Drayton's *Poly-Olbion*, xviii:

> That brave and godlike brood of Beauchamps . . .
> 　　　　　　　　　　　　so hardy, great, and strong,
> That after of that name it to an adage grew,
> If any man himself advent'rous happ'd to shew,
> Bold Beauchamp men him term'd if none so bold as he;

Suckling's *Goblins*, iv. 4:

> Let me see—the author of the 'Bold Beauchamps'
> And 'England's Joy';

Davenant's *Play-house to be let*, i:

> in the times of mighty *Tamberlane*,
> Of conjuring *Faustus*, and the *Beauchamps* bold,
> You poets us'd to have the second day;

and the Earl of Dorset's *Epilogue on the revival of 'Every Man in his
Humour'*:

> The three bold Beauchamps shall revive again
> And with the London 'prentice conquer Spain.
> All the dull follies of the former age
> Shall find applause on this corrupted stage.

its author. The first in date is in *A Mad World, my Masters* of 1606:

> We sing of wandring Knights, what them betyde,
> Who nor in one place, nor one shape abide,
> They're here now, & anon no scouts can reach 'em
> Being every man well horst like a bould Beacham.[1]

Apparently this romance of 'wandring Knights' was old-fashioned before Middleton wrote, though, if we judge from *The Knight of the Burning Pestle* where it is mentioned along with *Edward IV*—

> I should have seen *Jane Shore* once,
> And my Husband
> Hath promised me any time this Twelvemonth,
> To carie me to the *Bold Beauchamps*,
> But in truth he did not—[2]

it may still have held the boards at the Red Bull, which had a reputation for such melodramas, as late as 1607.[3] The company which produced it, however, still remains a mystery; Fleay's guess that it was 'probably acted by the same company as *Guy, Earl of Warwick*',[4] the adopted ancestor of the Beauchamps, whose *Tragical History*[5] we have John Taylor's authority for inserting in the Derby repertoire,[6] has nothing to commend it. That Heywood was responsible for this lost and obviously worthless effort we are not prepared to urge or to deny.

But we can have no hesitation in accepting *Edward IV* as at least in part his.[7] Whoever his collaborator may have

---

[1] v (prologue to the play within the play).   [2] i. 1.

[3] Or even later; cf. Jonson's *Speech according to Horace*:
>   In the stead of bold
> *Beauchamps*, and *Nevills*, *Cliffords*, *Audley's* old:
>   Insert thy *Hodges*.

[4] i. 287.

[5] *The Tragical History, Admirable Achievements and various events of Guy Earl of Warwick. A Tragedy . . . Written by B. J.* 1661, but probably the same as Dekker and Day's '*life and Death of GUY of Warwicke*', S.R. Jan. 15, 1619/20.

[6] *Penniless Pilgrimage*, 1618.

[7] But see Fleay, i. 288–9 (cf. i. 142; ii. 393) and Oliphant, Problems of Authorship in Elizabethan Dramatic Literature, *M.P.* viii, 427-8.

been, if he had one, and from whatever earlier dramatic sources—*The Siege of London*, or *The Tanner of Denmark* (? Tamworth)—they may have derived certain scenes, it is manifest that the pathetic Jane Shore episodes, to say nothing of the rest, could have come from the hands of only one of the popular dramatists. These two plays, the first by Heywood to receive the dignity of print (S.R. August 28, 1599), appeared in 1599 and were reprinted in 1600, 1605, 1613, 1619, and 1626. Their popularity is attested not only by these repeated issues and the scarcity of modern exemplars but by contemporary literature. It was this currency that brought down on them Beaumont's genial satire and led to their ranking with *Pericles* as great theatrical draws:

> Amazde I stood to see a Crowd
> Of *Civill Throats* stretchd out so lowd:
> (As at a *New-play*) all the *Roomes*
> Did swarme with *Gentiles* mix'd with *Groomes*.
> So that I truly thought, all These
> Came to see *Shore*, or *Pericles*,
> And that (to have themselves well plac'd)
> Thus brought they victualls (they fed so fast).[1]

Christopher Brooke attacked the sentimental and flabby ethics of Heywood's play in his *Ghost of Richard the Third*, 1614:

> And what a peece of *Iustice* did I shew
> On Mistresse *Shore*? when (with a fained hate
> To unchast *Life*) I forced her to goe
> Bare-foote, on penance, with deiected *state*?
> But now her Fame by a vild Play doth grow:
> Whose Fate, the Women so commisserate,
>> That who (to see my *Iustice* on that Sinner)
>> Drinks not her Teares; & makes her Fast, their dinner?[2]

---

[1] *Pimlico or Run Redcap*, 1609, sig. C; see 38 *infra* for a play on Shore and his wife by Chettle, Day, and perhaps Heywood; and E. Hertz (*Englische Schauspieler und englisches Schauspiel zur Zeit Shakespeares in Deutschland*, 98) for the performance of a similar drama by English actors at Gräz, Nov. 19, 1607.

[2] Ed. Grosart, 94; though the address says the subject of Jane Shore was '*made so common in* Playes', Brooke was clearly alluding to *Edward IV* in the body of his poem.

It may even have been the undeserved success of *Edward IV* in Jonson's opinion that provoked his sarcasm—

> I had rather die in a ditch with mistress Shore,
> Without a smock, as the pitiful matter has it—

in *The New Inn* fifteen years later.[1]

Had Fleay not dogmatically declared 'that any criticism of any play bearing as date of production one of the three years 1599 to 1601 which does not take account of' the stage quarrel 'must be imperfect and of small utility',[2] we would gladly have avoided all mention of *'that terrible Poetomachia'*.[3] It is, however, something to be thankful for that Heywood's attitude to the libellous war, in which he does not seem to have been directly involved, may be noticed very briefly. Though his sympathies would naturally lie with the Dekker faction, his only undoubted expression of opinion is an entirely impartial reproof, made years after the dust of the Poetomachia had blown past and in more immediate reference to the indiscretions of the company of the Queen's Revels, of all who put into the mouths of children satirical reflections on 'the State, the Court, the Law, the Citty, and their governements, with the particularizing of private mens humors (yet alive) Noble-men, & others'.[4] When the literary warfare opened, Heywood was occupying a very humble position with the Admiral's men at the Rose. If in the early stages

---

[1] v. i. The 'pitiful matter' was more probably a ballad. Chetwood, 19, was informed by the 'late Mr. *Bowman*', who 'was very well assured by Mr. *Cleveland*, a Poet of the last Age', that 'this double play was performed on two succeeding Nights and had a very great Run (a Theatrical Term)'. Rowe had probably read Heywood's play before writing his *Jane Shore*, but it is by no means a plagiarism, as his *Fair Penitent* is of Massinger's *Fatal Dowry*. Francis Waldron's *King in the Country. A Dramatic Piece, In Two Acts. Acted at the Theatres-Royal, at Richmond and Windsor*, 1788 (published in 1789 and in Waldron's *Literary Museum*, 1792), consists of the Tanner of Tamworth scenes of *Edward IV*, part i, practically without change. Cf. R. Dodsley's *King and the Miller of Mansfield. A Dramatic Tale. As it was Acted at the Theatre-Royal in Drury-Lane*, 1778, and *Sir John Cockle at Court. Being the sequel of the King and the Miller of Mansfield. A Dramatick Tale*, 1797.

[2] *Stage*, 119; cf. *Shakespeare*, 138.   [3] *Satiromastix*, preface.
[4] *Apology*, 61.

of the quarrel he directed some of his very mild satire at
Jonson, the provocation was not enough to tempt the
latter, ever a hearty enemy and a good hater, to waste his
arrows on such small game as Heywood was in 1599.[1]
So far as we can judge, his attitude to Jonson reveals
neither personal friendship nor open enmity. Twice later
he glances at Jonson's 'Works', of which the second
volume began to be issued *in numerous sheets* about
1631.[2] Twice in *A Challenge for Beauty*, *c.* 1634, Heywood alludes quite neutrally to *Cynthia's Revels*.[3] It is
not impossible that in *Love's Mistress* of the same year
Jonson, who after his final rupture with Jones in 1631
no doubt extended the scope of his personalities to include
all Inigo's associates in the fashioning of masques, is
gently chided. But in *The Hierarchy of the Blessed Angels*,
1635, we find an admiring couplet on

> famous *Johnson*, [who] though his learned Pen
> Be dipt in *Castaly*, is still but *Ben*,

in the well-known passage on the nicknames of the
dramatists;[4] and in *Annalia Dubrensia*, 1636, Heywood's
Panegyric to the worthy Mr. Robert Dover generously
recognizes his fellow contributor's eminence:

> But when *Ben: Iohnson*, and brave *Draytons* name
> Shall be Inscrib'd; I dare proclame the same
> To be a work ennobled: For who dare
> With them (and these here intermixt) compare.[5]

But if *The Fair Maid of the Exchange* (S.R. April 24,
1607), 1607, 1625, and 1637, in which we can discover
but few traces of Heywood's hand, be in the main his, it
would follow that he must have taken a more lively interest
in contemporary personalities than would otherwise appear. There is no evidence by whom or where this very
puzzling comedy was acted; but as the publisher in 1607

---

[1] Diogenes Scriben in *The Tale of a Tub*, though probably not meant
for Heywood, may be taken to indicate what Jonson's attitude to such a
nobody as Heywood would have been.

[2] See *Fair Maid of the West*, part i, preface, and *English Traveller*,
preface.

[3] Pearson, v. 8, 13.   [4] 206.   [5] Sig. K.

was silent on these points, we may assume that it had not been very recently presented. It must date in its present form from the very end of the stage-quarrel; there are rather echoes of the fray than any actual attacks launched in its impartial and somewhat judicial remarks on literary characters and foibles of the time. It may very well be, however, that these critical passages are later insertions in the text which has obviously undergone much revision and not very intelligent cutting. Certainly an unquestionable allusion to Nashe as dead must be dated after 1601:

> there liv'd a Poet in this towne,
> (If we may terme our moderne Writers Poets)
> Sharpe-witted, bitter-tongd, his penne of steele,
> His incke was temperd with the biting iuyce,
> And extracts of the bitterst weedes that grew,
> He never wrote but when the elements
> Of Fire and Water tilted in his braine:
> This fellow ready to give up his ghost
> To *Lucaies* [*sic*] bosome, did bequeath to me
> His Library which was iust nothing,
> But rooles and scrolles, and bundles of cast wit,
> Such as durst never visit Paules churchyard:
> Amongst them all, I happened on a quire
> Or two of paper filled with Songs and Ditties,
> And heere and there a hungry Epigramme,
> These I reserve to my own proper use
> And Pater-noster-like have kon'd them all.[1]

Many of the Cripple's dicta are imitations of Jonson's vein:

> FRANK. Faith thou hast rob'd some Sonnet booke or other,
>   And now wouldst make me thinke they are thine owne.[2]
> CRIPPLE. What think'st thou that I cannot write a letter,
>   Ditty, or Sonnet with judiciall phrase,
>   As pretty, pleasing, and patheticall,
>   As the best *Ovid*-imitating dunce
>   In all the towne . . .

---

[1] Pearson, ii. 46. The song (*ibid.* ii. 33) is imitated from a lyric in Breton's *Bower of Delights*, 1597.

[2] Cf. Frank's other remark on sonneteers, Pearson, ii. 39.

> sirra, I could conny-catch the world,
> Make my selfe famous for a sodaine wit,
> And be admir'd for my dexterity,
> Were I dispos'd.

For he has memorized all the cast wit of Nashe, and

> could now when I am in company,
> At alehouse, taverne, or an ordinary,
> Vpon a theame make an extemporall Ditty,
> (Or one at least should seeme extemporall)
> Out of th' aboundance of this Legacy,
> That all would judge it, and report it too,
> To be an infant of a sudaine wit,
> And then I were an admirable fellow.[1]

The Cripple of Fanchurch, too, like Amorphus in *Cynthia's Revels*, would

> make enquiry
> Where the best witted-gallants use to dine,
> Follow them to the taverne, and there sit
> In the next roome with a calves head and brimstone,
> And over heare their talke, observe their humours,
> Collect their jeasts, put them into play,
> And tire them too with payment to behold
> What I have filcht from them. This I would doe:
> But O for shame that men should so arraigne
> Their own feesimple wits, for verball theft!
> Yet men there be that have done this and that,
> And more by much more than the most of them.[2]

The closest parallel to this is in *Satiromastix* where Horace-Jonson is the confessing plagiary.[3] But of this we can be sure, that this youthful attempt at smartness is unexampled in Heywood's authentic work. His collaborator, or, as we think more likely, some drastic and ill-natured reviser, can alone be held responsible for the sour Cripple and his sharp tongue.

[1] Pearson, ii. 46.   [2] Pearson, ii. 47.
[3] Pearson's *Dekker*, i. 212.

CHAPTER III

1600–1606: DRAMATIC JOURNEYWORK

AT the termination of his contract with Henslowe, Heywood had had enough experience as one of the 'mercenary soldiers', one of the '*Switzers* to players (I meane the hired men)' who 'make but a hard and hungry living of it by strowting vp and down after the Waggon' from town to town.[1] The first information we have of him as a sharer in a theatrical company is the record in the Pipe Rolls of a payment to Kempe and him on behalf of the Earl of Worcester's players for court performances during the Christmas festivities of 1601/2.[2] Their patron, Edward Somerset, who as Lord Herbert had given his protection to a company of small importance, on his accession to the earldom on February 22, 1588/9, took his father's players into his service as well. Thereafter his company appear regularly in provincial records. Heywood may have been with them at York in April 1599, and at Coventry between November 20, 1600, and December 2, 1601; and that he was acting with them at Coventry again between the latter date and December 20, 1602, and at Leicester at some time between April 3, 1602, and August 18, 1603,[3] perhaps before their opening at the Rose in August or September 1602, is all but certain. From the very sudden success of Worcester's company, it would appear that some time in the second half of 1601[4] it was completely reorganized, and that the original

---

[1] Dekker and Wilkins, *Jests to make you Merry* (ed. Grosart, ii. 358).

[2] Pipe Rolls, 543, fol. 83; the performances were on Jan. 3, and Feb. 14; no payees are given for the latter. See *H.D.* ii. 106; Sir E. K. Chambers (ii. 225, iv. 114, 167) gives only the Jan. 3 performance.

[3] For the details of the history of Worcester's company see *H.D.* ii. 106, &c., Murray, i. 43, &c., and Chambers, ii. 220, &c., and for the visit of some or all of the company to Germany and the Netherlands see Murray, i. 49, &c., ii. 120–1, and Chambers, ii. 270, &c. Several of them entered the service of Count Moritz von Hessen; cf. Heywood's *Apology*, 40.

[4] Cf. Murray, i. 52, &c., and Chambers, ii. 225, &c.

members, probably Thomas Blackwood, John Thayer, John Lowin, Cattanes, Richard Perkins, and Robert Lee, none of whom is found with any other company immediately before 1602, wooed to them Heywood from a company unknown, and Kempe, John Duke, Christopher Beeston, and Robert Pallant, more or less directly from the Lord Chamberlain's men. Underell and Lee seem to have been hired men, and such also was probably Dick Syferwest's status.[1] All the others mentioned above appear to have been sharers. That Heywood, whose history now escapes somewhat from speculation, besides supplying his company with a play or more a month, acted as well, is clear from the patent issued to Worcester's men on their entering Queen Anne's service, and from the loan to him by Henslowe of half a crown to buy 'a payer of sylke garters' on September 1, 1602,[2] when he was overhauling his wardrobe before the company began acting under Henslowe's auspices.

It was, however, probably before Worcester's men had shifted to the Rose and when they were still in occupation of the Boar's Head in Eastcheap with the Earl of Oxford's troupe, 'beinge ioyned by agrement togeather in one companie',[3] that Heywood wrote for his fellows the very *Pleasant conceited Comedy* of *How a Man May Choose A Good Wife from A Bad*. It underwent slight revision before it was printed in 1602 as it had been 'sundry times Acted by the Earle of Worcester's Servants'. This was the beginning of its popularity in print; six other quartos, all anonymous like the first, followed in 1605, 1608, 1614, 1621, 1630, and 1634, with title-pages copied from that of 1602 long after Worcester's men were dispersed.[4]

---

[1] Sir E. K. Chambers, ii. 226, includes an unnamed tireman, but not Lee who may have joined the company later, though before they were taken into Queen Anne's patronage.

[2] *H.D.* i. 178; the year is not given.

[3] Chambers, ii. 224; iv. 335.

[4] As Heywood was intimate with the Okes, whose partner was John Norton, the printer of the last two quartos, and acted as a kind of literary

Though Henslowe opened the new account with Worcester's men on August 17,[1] everything had not yet been settled, for four days later he disbursed, as a picturesque but business-like entry records, nine shillings towards a supper 'for the company at the mermayd when we weare at owre a grement'.[2] There were great preparations for this grand new start to dazzle the Londoners; now it is 'tafetie & other stuffe to macke ij wemens gownes' that are purchased, then 'buckram to macke a payer of gyente hosse', 'a clocke of chamlett lined wth crymsen tafetie pinked' and 'a sewte for w^mkempe'.[3] The first play may not have been given till the middle of September or even a little later, but thereafter acting was continuous

---

gent for them in the sixteen-thirties (see 166–8 *infra*), it is possible that Heywood made some profit out of the editions of 1630 and 1634. The play was alluded to in *A Discourse of Marriage and Wiving and of The greatest Mystery therein contained: How to choose a good Wife from a bad* by Alex. Nicholes, 1615, 1620; cf. chap. 4, '*How to choose a good wife from a bad*', and chap. 12, '*The patterne of a bad husband and a good wife*'. A ballad entitled *A Good Wife is a Portion every day Or a Dialogue discovering a good Wife from a bad. And happy is that man that hath such a one* was printed by A. Brooks between 1672 and 1695. Cf. Riche's *My Lady's Looking-Glass*, 43, 'rules how to distinguish betweene a good woman and a bad'. Fuller's verse anecdote, sig. G2–G3, appears in a modified form in *Merry Drollery, Complete. The First Part*, 1661 (ed. Ebsworth, 77), in *The Rump: or an exact collection of the Choicest Poems and Songs relating to the Late Times*, 194–5, and in *Loyal Songs*, i. 122. The theme was also treated by the author of another song in *Choice Drollery. To which are added the extra songs of Merry Drollery*, 1661 (ed. Ebsworth, 195–6), and in *The Character of a Mistress*. The Dutch poet, J. J. Starter, who was an Englishman by birth, had already adapted the subject for his *Menniste Vryagie*, which appeared in his book of airs, *Friesche Lusthof*, 1621.

[1] *H.D.* i. 179; cf. ii. 100. Less than a month after, Henslowe lent 15*s*. to Perkins 'to bye thinge for thomas hewode playe & to lend vnto dick yferweste to Ride downe to his felowes' (i. 178). If Syferwest was not a member of the company (cf. *ibid.* ii. 107, 314; Murray, i. 52; and Fleay, *Stage*, 138) why did Henslowe advance the money for Syferwest to Perkins who was a Worcester man ? Worcester's men or most of them may have been still on tour and Syferwest may have joined them somewhere in the provinces. It does not seem to have been noticed that though the entries in the account are almost of daily occurrence from Aug. 17 to Sept. 10 (i. 179–81) there is a gap thereafter till Sept. 19 (i. 181).

[2] *Ibid.* i. 179.   [3] *Ibid.* i. 179–80.

till the middle of March 1602/3,[1] by which time Elizabeth's last illness had practically closed the theatres.
Worcester's men had no doubt a few old pieces to be
going on with in August 1602, and at first they were in
no haste to acquire many fresh ones. The very first item
in their account, it is true, is on August 17 for a play, or
rather for Dekker's 'new a dicyons to owldcastelle';[2] on
August 24 Chettle received earnest money for an unnamed tragedy,[3] and three days later Dekker received
his first instalment for 'medsen for a cvrst wiffe'.[4]

The mention of a fourth play, though somewhat per-
plexing, is more to our purpose:

> Layd owt for the company the 3 of septemb3 ⎤
> 1602 to bye iiij Lances for the comody   ⎬ viij[s][5]
> of thomas hewedes & m[r] smythes some of ⎦

The 'thinge for thomas heywode playe'[6] and the 'iiij clothe
clockes layd wth cope lace for iiij[li] a clocke',[7] bought on
September 4 and December 6 respectively, may, despite
the time that elapsed before the latter purchase, have been
for the same piece. We suggest diffidently that the play
in question may have been *The Four Prentices of London*,
a very immature attempt which could not have been new
in 1602 and may have belonged to Heywood, or have
been in the repertoire of Worcester's men before their
reorganization.[8] On Heywood's excuse in the preface for
publishing this play, '*written many yeares since, in my
Infancy of Iudgment in this kinde of Poetry, and my first
practise ... That as* Playes *were then some fifteene or sixteene*

---

[1] *H.D.* i. 190; on Mar. 14 Henslowe totalled the moneys due to him
from the company and on the 16th Blackwood, Lowin, and Perkins
borrowed small sums to go with their fellows on tour (*H.D.* i. 177–8).

[2] *Ibid.* i. 179; bought apparently from the Admiral's men.

[3] *Ibid.* i. 179.   [4] *Ibid.* i. 179.

[5] *Ibid.* i. 180.   [6] *Ibid.* i. 178.   [7] *Ibid.* i. 185.

[8] So Dr. Greg (*H.D.* ii. 230; cf. ii. 312), though he is doubtful if the
'comody' was the same as *The Four Prentices*, and reluctantly identifies
it, as do Sir E. K. Chambers, iii. 341, and Mr. L. W. Payne, in his edition,
49–50, with the next play by Heywood in the *Diary*, 'albetre galles'
(i. 180). Cf. Glapthorne's *Wit in a Constable*, 1640, iii. 2, 'the Ballad oth'
famous *London Prentice*'.

yeares agoe it was then in the Fashion', along with the further remark that its appearance in print was opportune at a time when '*they have begunne againe the commendable practice of long forgotten Armes*', Fleay established to his own satisfaction the comedy's date.[1] He asserts that as the revival of drilling in the Artillery Garden was in 1610 there must have been an edition in that year, deriving support for his assumption from the advice in *The Knight of the Burning Pestle*, acted first, he thought, in 1610—1607 is a more likely date[2]—to 'read the play of *The Four Prentices of London*'. Now fifteen or sixteen years before 1610 takes us back to 1594/5 and from July 19, 1594, onwards the '2 pte of godfrey of bullen' was acted by the Admiral's men at the Rose,[3] while an interlude entitled '𝐆𝐨𝐝𝐟𝐫𝐞𝐲 *of Bulloigne with the Conquest of Jerusalem*' was registered on June 19. But this could only have been the first part of *Godfrey*, that is probably 'Jerusallem', acted on March 22, 1591/2,[4] and yet it contained the grand finale of Heywood's play. Moreover the Artillery Company was moribund from 1605 till 1611 (not 1610), when an attempt was made to revive drilling. In 1612 the numbers were limited to 250 and in 1614 increased to 500.[5] More important still is Jonson's *Speech according to Horace*, dated March 24, 1624, but written 'these ten yeares day' after the revival of Artillery practice in March 1614.[6] Other evidence of public interest in the revival is Markham's '*schoole for yonge schollers contayning a breife table to teach and learne to trayne and to be trayned*' (S.R. September 23, 1613), Dekker's '*Artillery Garden*' (S.R.

---

[1] i. 282–3; cf. *H.D.* ii. 166.   [2] Cf. Chambers, iii. 221, 340.

[3] *H.D.* i. 18–25, ii. 166.

[4] *Ibid.* i. 13–14; cf. ii. 155, and Chambers, iii. 340.

[5] Cf. *A brief historical account of the Hon. the Artillery Company*, ii. xx, &c., and *The Ancient Vellum Book of the Hon. Artillery Company*, viii. 21, 58.

[6] A phrase from it is quoted in *The Devil is an Ass*, iii. 2. Cf. Howes's continuation of Stowe, 1615, 936. Heywood's lines in reply to a '*base and infamous Ballader*' who had made some fun of the artillery practice (*Pleasant Dialogues*, 283) must have come hot from his pen in 1637: cf. *Londini Sinus Salutis* (Pearson, iv. 295) and *Porta Pietatis* (Pearson, v. 263).

November 29, 1615), and R. N.'s *London's Artillery*, 1616
(S.R. January 3, 1615/6). In any case the first edition,
'As it hath beene diverse times Acted at the Red Bull, by
the Queenes Maiesties Servants', appeared in 1615 in
spite of the ridicule heaped on it by Beaumont in *The
Knight of the Burning Pestle*. The edition of 1632 was
quite falsely declared 'newly revised' by Heywood. It is
impossible now to determine what Wentworth Smith's
share in *The Four Prentices* may have been; his *Hector of
Germany, or the Palsgrave, Prime Elector* shows at least
that he knew it well. When Heywood published the play
he mentions no helper nor does the printed version betray
many signs of double authorship, though there are signs
of revision, especially the mature and Jonsonian induction. But Smith's contribution may never have been more
than the plotting or have disappeared in some later and
unrecorded renovation.

On the next occurrence of Heywood's name in the
Diary he is again associated with Smith, six pounds being
paid to them on September 4, 1602, for 'albe[*t*]re galles'.[1]
That the money was paid in one sum, considerable as that
sum is, may conceivably point to a revival of an older
play; Henslowe, however, unfamiliar with the name, left
a space too long for the subsequent entry, spelt it wrongly
for even his unfastidious taste and achieved in the end an
unintelligible result.[2] Nevertheless the title, odd as it is,
recalls vaguely the Archigallo of *Nobody and Somebody*,
which may conveniently be noticed here. That comical-
historical-moral was given to the world in an undated
edition (S.R. March 12, 1605/6) as *Nobody and Somebody*.

---

[1] *H.D.* i. 180.

[2] ? *Albiō regalis.* Collier, in his ed. of *H.D.* 239, suggests that the subject was Albertus Wallenstein, then, as Dr. Greg notes (*H.D.* ii. 236),
nineteen and a pupil of the Jesuits at Altorf. Fleay is not much happier
in interpreting Henslowe's bungle as *Archigalle's three sons*, i. 294, inas-
much as Archigallo had three brothers but no sons. His other guesses are
Archigallus, i. 290, and *Archigallo, Stage*, 338. Dr. Greg, *H.D.* ii. 230,
believes the entry to refer to *Nobody and Somebody* before its final
revision. For 'the 4 kynges' (*H.D.* i. 104) see Fleay, *Stage*, 107, ii.
296, and Chambers, ii. 167, 169.

With the true Chronicle History of Elydure, who was fortun-ately three several times crowned King of England. The true Copy thereof, as it hath been acted by the Queen's Majesty's Servants, sold by John Trundle 'at his shop in Barbican, at the signe of No-body'.[1] Quite clearly the extant play is an unskilful recension, made after James's accession and not necessarily the first, of a much older piece, written originally in the early nineties of the sixteenth century when *Locrine* and *King Leir* and other histories of mythical kings of Britain were popular. Little can be deduced from the remark 'It shal go hard, but I the shrew will tame',[2] or from allusions to the disrepair of St. Paul's,[3] which was an old story and a continuing. The other abuses were of as old a standing, and the tedious Nobody and Somebody business was antique by 1590 even in England. The phrase '*somebody* once pickt a pocket in this Play-house yard, Was hoysted on the stage, and shamd about it'[4] is puzzling; the only other mention of the prac-tice, if it was a practice, is in Kempe's *Nine Days' Wonder*, 1600.[5] Besides the hypothetical revision for Henslowe there must have been another after James's accession. The dramatist glances at the king's wholesale knightings and perhaps alludes in the same scene to the serious outbreak of the plague in 1603–4.[6] Whether the indiscriminate use of both 'England' and 'Britain' has any connexion with James's assumption of the title of King of Great Britain on March 19, 1604, we hesitate to decide.[7] But it is clear that the satire of Lord Cobham as Lord Syco-phant must date from after his fall in 1603.[8] The ancient *Nobody and Somebody* seems to have been taken to the Continent by certain players from the Earl of Worcester's company who were touring abroad in the autumn of 1590

[1] See S.R. Jan. 8, 1605/6, for Trundle's registration of '*The picture of No bodye*', referred to in the play, sig. D 4, F 2, and in *The Tempest*, iii. 2.
[2] Sig. F 4.   [3] Sig. D 3; but cf. Simpson's *School of Shakespeare*, i, 270–2.
[4] Sig. I verso.   [5] Camden Soc. ed., 6.   [6] Sig. B 4.
[7] Cf. Fleay, i. 293.
[8] Cf. *ibid.* and Chambers, iv. 37. ''Tis a mad world Maister' (sig. D 3) need not refer to Middleton's comedy, as Fleay supposed (i. 294); the phrase was proverbial when used as the title of Breton's dialogue in 1603.

and again from early in 1592 till August 1593 when they left some of their number behind. It was freely translated into German as *Niemand und Jemand* and printed in 1620 in a collection of *Engelische Comedien und Tragedien*.[1] It was, perhaps, as a consequence of the hypothetical revival in 1602 that on the third afternoon of Queen Anne's and Prince Henry's visit to Althorp on June 27, 1603, Jonson introduced a character who '*by reason of the throng . . . could not be heard*' . . . '*in the person of* No-body . . . *attired in a paire of Breeches which were made to come up to his neck, with his armes out at his pockets, and a Cap drowning his face*'.[2] But the vitality and success of the play to which Jonson is not the only witness must have been due to factors we can only guess at, perhaps to the gags of a succession of clowns or to the satiric intention which now almost completely escapes us. The play itself is nearly valueless and Heywood and Smith, if they were the revisers, left it pretty much as they found it, attempting no new episodes, doing nothing to turn the inhuman abstractions into characters, and contenting themselves with a slight modernization of the diction and verse.

Heywood's next job was another revision or at least 'new a dicyons of cuttyngdicke', for which he received a

---

[1] It was performed at Gräz in 1608 before the Archduke Maximilian to whom 'Joannes Grün Nob. Anglus' (i.e. John Green) dedicated the MS. of it now in the Rein Library. Cf. Chambers, ii. 273–5, 278–9, 281–2, 285; iv. 37.

[2] Cf. *Cynthia's Revels*, 1601, iv. 3:

Phantastes. Why popular breeches?
Philautia. Marry, that is, when they are not content to be generally noted in court, but will press forth on common stages and brokers' stalls to the public view of the world.

The well-spoken Nobody, c. 1600, is a reprint cᶠa ? 1585 pamphlet. Day's *Humour out of Breath*, 1608, has a punning address to Signior Nobody, and in *The Noble Soldier*, 1634, probably in part Day's, is a character Signor No. Taylor has an epistle to Nobody in *Sir Gregory Nonsense his News from Nowhere*, 1622. Nemo is one of the speakers in Anthony Nixon's *Scourge of Corruption or a Crafty Knave needs no Broker*, 1615, which exposes many of the same abuses as the play. *Nobody his counsel to choose a wife*, c. 1626, is a two-part ballad. According to Mr. C. E. Andrews, *Richard Brome* 111, Horatio in Brome's *Queen and Concubine* is probably imitated from Lord Sycophant in *Nobody and Somebody*.

reward of one pound on September 30.[1] The eponymous hero of the cobbled piece was a veritable highwayman, Evans by name, 'a notable robber in Wiltshire', who, according to Dudley Carleton's letter of December 29, 1601, to John Chamberlain, was just then 'taken and like to be hanged'.[2] But the original dramatist may have put Dick Evans on the stage some time before, for the robber was notorious and almost proverbial early in 1600.[3]

On the very day on which Heywood was paid for his renovation of *Cutting Dick*, his old collaborator, Smith, received three pounds for 'marshalle oserecke';[4] ten days later Heywood, who seems to have been otherwise engaged in the interval, was handed his equal share for work on the same play.[5] The company were so long rehearsing it that the 'sewte of oserocke' was not paid for till November 3.[6] Fleay's theory that *The Royal King and the Loyal Subject*, 1637 (S.R. March 25), is the *Marshal Osric* of Heywood and Smith, revised after the 1633 revival of Fletcher's *Loyal Subject*, is attractive.[7] But there seems to be as much reason to date the recension not long after the first production of *The Loyal Subject* in 1618. The transference, too, of the Persian story of Artaxerxes and his seneschal Ariobarzanes to an English court would be more likely before 1603 than after, when plays were more often set in unfamiliar localities, as was Fletcher's *Loyal Subject*, while

---

[1] *H.D.* i. 181.　　　　　　　[2] *C.S.P.D.*, 1601–3, 136.

[3] Cf. Kempe's *Nine Days' Wonder* (S.R. April 22, 1600), ed. Camden Soc. 14:

> And now a man is but a pricke;
> A boy, arm'd with a poating sticke,
> Will dare to challenge Cutting Dicke.

There are other allusions to Cutting Dick in *The London Prodigal*, 1605, ii. 2; *Work for Cutlers*, 1615 (ed. Sieveking, 42, 62); Wither's *Abuses Stript and Whipt*, 1613, sig. P; Freeman's *Rub and a Great Cast*, 1614, pt. ii. no. 24; *The Wise Woman of Hogsdon* (Pearson, v. 297); and *The Fair Maid of the West*, pt. i (Pearson, ii. 291). See S.R. 1568–9 for a ballad of '*Desperate Dycke*'; Feb. 17, 1595, for '*Cutting George, and his hostis beinge a Jigge*'; and May 24, 1632, for a ballad *Roaring Dick of Dover*, by R. C. (Pepys's Ballads, i. 434).

[4] *H.D.* i. 181.　　　　[5] *Ibid.* i. 182.　　　　[6] *Ibid.* i. 184.

[7] i. 300; in *Stage*, 155, 341, the revival is dated 1625–36.

the weakness of the character delineation and a general insecurity and vagueness, features which revision could not entirely remove and in which the play is strikingly similar to *Nobody and Somebody*, are clear indications of early composition in Heywood's career. Unfortunately for Fleay's theory, not only is Osric an important character in *A Knack to Know a Knave*, but the Admiral's men had an old piece 'oserycke', acted by them on February 3 and 7, 1596/7.[1] Thus are we put to doubt and ignorance again. Certainly Heywood's fictitious history had received its present name by 1622, for William Rowley's *All's Lost by Lust* seems to allude to the antithesis of the title.[2] That *The Royal King and the Loyal Subject*, which was printed as it had been played by 'the Queenes Maiesties Servants', i.e. Queen Henrietta's men, had been revised is proved from its state to-day, and we have the epilogue's warrant '*That this Play's old*', as antique apparently as doublets with '*stuft bellies and bigge sleeves*', or trunk-hose and rhymed dialogue.[3] The absence of Smith's name from the title-page is sufficiently explained by the one or more revisions which, while not entirely removing his contribution, would give Heywood the right after his colleague's death to claim the play for himself.

About a fortnight after Heywood had done with *Marshal Osric*, Henslowe on October 15 paid to Chettle, Dekker, Smith, Webster, and Heywood, fifty shillings 'in earneste of a playe called Ladey Jane',[4] and six days later the play was finished and the remainder of their fee,

[1] *H.D.* i. 51; ii. 182; cf. Fleay, ii. 301–2, and *Stage*, 100.
[2] ii. 1:

> Malena.   Ye're belov'd lady, and which is more,
> Yea most, of a king belovde.
> Jacinta.   A good induction; and all this
> I may deserve, being a loyall subject.
> Malena.   Your loyalty may be mixt with his royalty.

Cf. S.R. July 23, 1639 '*The Duty of all loyall subiectes &c.*', and Thomas Jordan's *Rules to Know A Royal King from a Disloyal Subject*, 1642. Ashmole liked 'the royall King & Loveing subiect' well enough to copy passages out in Bodley MS. Ash. 420, 11–12.
[3] Cf. the very similar address before *The Roaring Girl*, 1611.
[4] *H.D.* i. 183.

five pounds ten shillings, was handed to Heywood for distribution among the collaborators.[1] There may have been some reason for such haste apart from the satisfaction of London's demand for new plays; but it is scarcely possible that this first part of *Lady Jane* could have been rehearsed, staged, and so enthusiastically received by October 27, that Henslowe on that day paid five shillings by John Duke to Dekker 'in earneste of the 2 pt of Lady Jane'.[2] In the normal course a play does not seem to have been performed for some weeks after the final payment for it. It is, therefore, possible that 'the playe of the over-throwe of Rebelles', for which a 'sewt of satten' was required on November 6,[3] may have been for one or other part of *Lady Jane*, delayed, despite the haste to have it written. But it is much more likely that *The Overthrow of Rebels* dramatized the revolt of the Earls of Northumberland and Westmorland in 1569. We believe rather that *Lady Jane* was indeed staged as an offset to an historical play by some other company on events of the sixteenth century.[4] It has generally been admitted that Dekker's and Webster's contributions to *Lady Jane* survive in *The Famous History of Sir Thomas Wyatt. With the Coronation of Queen Mary, and the coming in of King Philip*, 1607 and 1612.[5] But no one has ever suggested, what we believe to be just as certain, that in *If you know not me, you know nobody*, part I, which is very much shorter than most Elizabethan plays, and in three irrelevant scenes of

---

[1] *H.D.* i. 183; on Oct. 15 Henslowe left a blank which was filled in later, but on Oct. 21 it was 'ther playe of ladye Jane'.

[2] *H.D.* i. 184; Dr. Greg (*ibid.* ii. 232, 252; cf. 312) suggests that the 10s. paid to Smith and the 3s. to Chettle on Nov. 12 (i. 185) were also in earnest of this second part; but he is justifiably suspicious of second parts in earnest of which Chettle especially was in the habit of extracting small sums from Henslowe.

[3] *H.D.* i. 184; again Henslowe left a blank to be filled in later.

[4] For Richard Vennar's *England's Joy*, billed for Nov. 6, 1602, see Chambers, iii. 500–3. The Admiral's men bought properties for 'the earlle of Harfurd' in Sept. 1602 (*H.D.* i. 170).

[5] The coronation of Mary and the landing of Philip, however, do not occur; both incidents are dramatized in *If you know not me*, part I.

part II we have Heywood's share.[1] For some reason, perhaps to provide an obituary drama immediately after Elizabeth's death, the play of *Lady Jane* was dismembered, and Heywood's portion comprising the early history of the late queen was acted separately. *If you know not me*, part II, is in the main a different play with a good text in all but the scenes suspected as extraneous, longer than the average length, not mentioned by Henslowe, and of uncertain date, but apparently the same as the biographical drama of 'the Life and Death of Sir Thomas Gresham with the building of the Royal Exchange' referred to in *The Knight of the Burning Pestle*.[2] The death of Gresham was cut off, perhaps by the actors but more probably by the printer, and the episode of Doctor Parry's treason (1584/5) and the equally independent and corrupt scenes of the Armada (1588) clapped in the place of the original termination. The former seems to have made room for itself by thrusting out the death of Sir Thomas Ramsey, Lord Mayor during the building of the Exchange. The second is clumsily linked to what is now the last scene of the Gresham plot, by a chorus obviously intended to join the last scene of *If you know not me*, part I (the accession of Elizabeth), to the inappropriate finale of part II (the defeat of the Armada):

> From fifty eight, the first yeare of her raigne,
> We come to eighty-eight, and of her raigne
> The thirtieth yeare. This Queen inaugurated,
> And strongly planted in her peoples heart,
> Was in her youth solicited in marriage
> By many princely heires of Christendom, &c.[3]

The astute Nathaniel Butter had part I licensed on

---

[1] Twenty-three scenes in all, the same number as in *Edward IV*, part I.

[2] Induction. See Bodley MS. Tanner 207 for J. Rickets's Latin play, *Byrsa Basilica sive Regale Exambicum in honorem Thomae Greshami, militis*, 1570. The 'phillipe of spayne', bought for the Admiral's men on Aug. 8, 1602 (*H.D.* i. 169) and registered on Sept. 14, 1605, cannot be *If you know not me*, part II, as Hazlitt suggested, for Philip appears only in part I; cf. *H.D.* ii. 224.

[3] Pearson, ii. 332; cf. also the epilogue really answering to the prologue to part I.

July 5, 1605, under the title of *If you know not me*, which really belongs to the Gresham play,[1] and had it printed in a very corrupt copy with prose as verse, and verse as prose, clipped speeches and disjointed scenes; an injury against which Heywood did not protest till about 1623, when for a revival by the Revels Company he declared in a prologue that the play,

> ill nurst,
> And yet receiv'd, as well perform'd at first,
> Grac't and frequented, for the cradle age,
> Did throng the Seates, the Boxes, and the Stage
> So much; that some by Stenography drew
> The plot: put it in print: (scarce one word trew:)
> And in that lamenesse it hath limp't so long,
> The Author now to vindicate that wrong
> Hath tooke the paines, upright upon its feete
> To teach it walke, so please you sit, and see't.[2]

Yet Butter found a good sale for his pirated hash, which was issued again in 1606, 1608, 1610, 1613, 1623 (probably after the Red Bull revival), and 1639. All of these editions were anonymous, corrupt, and quite unrevised; and in the last Butter, with shameless impudence and many mistakes, printed the very prologue that exposes his piracy together with the corresponding epilogue from *Pleasant Dialogues* (the prologue before part I, and the epilogue at the end of part II).[3] The so-called second part of *If you know not me* (S.R. September 14, 1605) appeared in 1606 in a much more correct state, except in the suspected scenes, than the first, and again in 1609, 1623 (probably with part I), and in 1633, on this last occasion with the

---

[1] Pearson, i. 317; cf. *Mucedorus*, 1598, i. 4. Heywood himself called part I *The Play of Queen Elizabeth* (*Pleasant Dialogues*, 248).

[2] *Pleasant Dialogues*, 248–9.

[3] The epilogue says Elizabeth appeared both as a princess and as a queen, which proves it was not the printed play that was acted. Collier (ed. for the Shakespeare Soc. vi–vii, xx–xxi) dates the prologue just before 1632, and Fleay, i. 292, proposes c. 1631. But Thomas Drue's *Duchess of Suffolk*, licensed Jan. 2, 1623/4 (Herbert, 18, 27), which very obviously imitates Heywood's play, may have been written in consequence of a 1623 revival of *The Play of Queen Elizabeth*.

Armada scenes much enlarged. Some help in dating the composition of *The Life and Death of Sir Thomas Gresham*, which we have been compelled to take out of its proper place in Heywood's story, is supplied by a passage in *Eastward Ho*, c. 1604/5: 'I hope to see thee one o' the monuments of our city, and reckoned among her worthies to be remembered the same day with Lady Ramsay and grave Gresham, when the famous fable of Whittington and his puss shall be forgotten, and thou and thy acts become the posies for hospitals; when thy name shall be written upon conduits, and thy deeds played i' thy lifetime by the best company of actors, and be called their get-penny.'[1] This and perhaps the show of 'The Shippe Called The Royall Exchange' in Munday's *Triumph of Reunited Britannia*, 1605, indicate a recent success for Heywood's bourgeois drama in 1604.[2]

Four of the collaborators in *Lady Jane*, Webster, Heywood, Chettle, and Dekker, were soon again at work together. The first two received earnest money of three pounds on November 2 for the play 'cryssmas comes bute once ayeare'.[3] On November 23 two pounds

[1] iv. 2.

[2] Glapthorne's *Wit in a Constable*, 1640, iii. 2, alludes to 'the Ballad . . . [of] the building Of *Britaines* Burse'. Though *If you know not me* is one of the dullest of the chronicle-histories, scenes from both parts were presented at the King's Playhouse after the Restoration as 'Queen Elizabeth's Troubles and the History of Eighty Eight'. Thither went Pepys on Aug. 17, 1667, and found 'the house extraordinary full', and the King and the Duke come to see the new play. 'I confess', he says, 'I have sucked in so much of the sad story of Queene Elizabeth, from my cradle, that I was ready to weep for her sometimes; but the play is the most ridiculous that sure ever come upon the stage; and, indeed, is merely a shew, only shews the true garbe of the Queene in those days . . . but the play is merely a puppet play, acted by living puppets. Neither the design nor language better; and one stands by and tells us the meaning of things: only I was pleased to see Knipp dance among the milkmaids, and to hear her sing a song to Queen Elizabeth; and to see her come out in her night-gowne with no lockes on.' W. C. Hazlitt (*Manual for the Collector of Old Plays*, 113) attributes the revival to the excitement following the recent Dutch raid in the Thames. £10 were paid for the command performance (Allardyce Nicoll, *Restoration Drama*, 306).

[3] *H.D.* i. 184.

were paid by John Duke to Chettle and Dekker, and on the 26th Chettle, apparently the head partner, received through Heywood another two pounds to complete the bargain.[1] Nothing more is known of the play, but it may have been a Christmas show for the holiday season, over which Henslowe proved more lavish than usual.[2] Heywood, however, was given only six pounds for his unaided work on 'the blinde eates many a flye', three pounds on November 24 and twice thirty shillings on December 15 and January 7.[3] We may derive perhaps some idea of the comedy, which Fleay obscurely relates to *The English Traveller*,[4] from a ballad *The Blind eats many a Fly: Or, The Broken Damsel made whole*.[5] At the same time as Heywood was working single-handed at the above-mentioned comedy for Worcester's men, he and Chettle were writing 'a playe called london florenten' for the Admiral's men, though we might have thought Heywood sufficiently occupied with his own company's affairs. Chettle's first ten shillings on December 17 were only in earnest, but by the 22nd he had finished his share of

---

[1] *Ibid.* i. 185.

[2] The properties bought on Nov. 2, 6, and Dec. 9 (*ibid.* i. 184, 186) were perhaps for this play. Cf. *Nobody and Somebody*, sig. B 4; *English Traveller*, Pearson, iv. 15:

> Keepe Christmasse all yeere long, and blot leane Lent
> Out of the Calender;

the prologue and epilogue '*spoken at the right Honourable the Earle of* Dovers *house in* Broadstreet, *at a Play in a most bountifull Christmas hee kept there; the Speaker Hospitality a frollick old fellow: A Coller of Brawne in one hand, and a deepe Bowle of Muscadel in the other*' (*Pleasant Dialogues*, 242); and Nashe's *Piers Penniless* (ed. McKerrow, i. 166). T. H. published in 1647 *A Ha! Christmas, This Book of Christmas is a sound and good persuasion for Gentlemen, and all wealthy men, to keep a good Christmas.*

[3] *H.D.* i. 185–6.   [4] i. 291; cf. *Stage*, 341.

[5] S.R. Apr. 12, 1627; *R.B.* viii. 684. The phrase occurs in the refrain 'Bewar therefore: the blinde et many a fly' of Lydgate's *Balade warning men to beware of deceitful women* (Skeat's *Chaucer*, vii. 295); see *H.D.* ii. 233–4. Cf. *The Golden Age*, Pearson, iii. 19:

> What cannot womens wits? they wonder can
> When they intend to blinde the eyes of man;

The Brazen Age, Pearson, iii. 239; and *Englishmen for my Money*, 1616, ii. 1.

the piece and pocketed three pounds more.[1] On the 20th
of the same month Heywood was handed two pounds and
another pound on January 7.[2] A second part was at least
talked of and a pound paid to Chettle in earnest thereof
on March 12.[3] It may have been one or other part which
was licensed as *The Florentine Friend* to Richard Marriott
between 1653 and 1660.[4] The same two collaborators
had undertaken a new play for Worcester's men on
January 14, 1602/3, when Heywood was given two
pounds earnest money for division with Chettle.[5] But
either the journeymen had not settled the title or Henslowe did not know it, for he left a blank.[6] The very
evidence that the play was finished is slight; but if it was,
there is little likelihood that it was the unnamed tragedy
for which Chettle was paid at the end of August and the
beginning of September,[7] and none whatever that they
or either of them could have been *Hoffman*, which was
an Admiral play.[8]

No sooner was the last of these four lost plays off
his hands than Heywood began his masterpiece. The
notorious gown of black velvet for Mistress Frankford,
for which Henslowe gave thirty-five shillings [9] more than
for *A Woman Killed with Kindness*, was purchased before
the dramatist was paid his first instalment of three pounds
on February 12.[10] The payment of another three pounds is
noted by Henslowe on March 6,[11] and on the next day

---

[1] *H.D.* i. 172.   [2] *Ibid.* i. 173.

[3] *Ibid.* i. 174; cf. ii. 232, 252. For the possibility that the 5*s.* paid to
Chettle on Dec. 9 for a prologue and epilogue for the court was for part I
see *H.D.* i. 173, ii. 226; Fleay, i. 171 and *Stage*, 124; and Murray,
i. 138, &c.

[4] Cf. *A Curtain Lecture*, 49, &c., for the story of the Florentine merchant
Fulgotius.

[5] At first in the Admiral account but cancelled and re-entered (*H.D.*
i. 173, 187). It was, therefore, not *The London Florentine*, pt. II.

[6] In both entries. Collier in one of his lapses inserted 'Like quits Like'
in the Admiral account; see *H.D.* i. xliii–xliv.

[7] *H.D.* i. 179, 181; Dr. Greg, ii. 234, thinks it might have been the play
'wherein shores wiffe is writen'; see 38 *infra*.

[8] See 330–2 *infra*.   [9] Feb. 4 and 5, *H.D.* i. 188.

[10] *Ibid.* i. 189.   [11] *Ibid.* i. 189.

ten shillings more were spent on 'the blacke satten sewt
for the woman kyld wth kyndnes',[1] or more correctly for
her husband. Let us hope that it proved, in spite of its
having been obviously second-hand,

> a well-made suite,
> In which the Tailor hath us'd all his art:
> Not like a thicke Coate of unseason'd frieze
> Forc'd on your backe in summer.[2]

The success of the tragedy was immediate and lasting;
in *The Black Book*, 1604, it is coupled with *The Merry
Devil of Edmonton* as a late dramatic success.[3] This, the
most characteristic of Heywood's plays, was the first to
bring his name on its title-page before the reading public.
But few examples of the 1607 issue are known; a second
edition was so well-thumbed as to have disappeared
entirely. The third edition of 1617, 'As it hath beene
often-times Acted by the Queenes Maiest. Servants', is
common enough.[4]

---

[1] *Ibid.* i. 190.   [2] Pearson, ii. 95.

[3] Sig. E 3. The title of the play is proverbial; cf. Whetstone's *Hep-
tameron of Civil Discourses*, ed. 1582, sig. T 4; *The Taming of the Shrew*,
iv. 1; *The Trial of Chivalry*, 1605, iii. 2; and the play itself, Pearson, ii. 141,
157. The phrase in *The Taming of the Shrew* is echoed in *The Woman's
Prize*, c. 1604, iii. 4. *The Wise Woman of Hogsdon*, Pearson, v. 316, pretty
certainly, and *The Case is Altered. How? Ask Dallio, and Millo*, 1604,
probably, allude to the play; but Dekker in *The Raven's Almanac*, 1609 (ed.
Grosart, iv. 243, 245, 257), Bunyan in *Mr. Badman*, and Farquhar in *Love
and a Bottle*, were thinking of the proverb. Mr. E. H. C. Oliphant
(*Captain Thomas Stukeley*, N. & Q. 10 Series, iii. 302), not knowing
that the words were proverbial, finds allusions to Heywood's play in *The
Taming of the Shrew* and *The Woman's Prize* which, together with *A
Woman killed with Kindness*, *Patient Grissel*, and Dekker's *Medicine for a
Curst Wife*, he declares contemporaneous in one form or another and rival
productions.

[4] Benjamin Victor was so struck by the 'several fine strokes of nature'
in the tragedy that he attempted to rewrite and make more plausible
the main plot in *The Fatal Error*, 'where the husband's forgiveness and
renew'd affection, will, I hope be thought by the reader to be founded on
humanity' (*Original Letters, Dramatic Pieces and Poems*, 1776, ii. 81).
Ingratitude: or the Adulteress, another adaptation by Joseph Moser, appeared
in the *European Magazine*, 1810. Heywood's own play, revived by the
Dramatic Students' Society at the Olympic Theatre on Tuesday, Mar. 8,

The number of plays on which Heywood was engaged
during the eight months from August 1602 to March
1603 is not necessarily exhausted by those with which he
is associated in Henslowe's *Diary*. There is a presumption
that he, as principal playwright for and a sharer in the
Earl of Worcester's company, would have the oversight
of most of the plays produced, and, though his fellow-
dramatists may have carried out slight revisions never
entered in the *Diary*, the burden of modernizing and
making petty additions would fall on the industrious and
indefatigable Heywood. We are, therefore, curious about
'the Booke of Shoare, now newly to be written for the
Earle of worcesters players at the Rose';[1] and since he
wrote once for the Admiral's men, may he not have been
concerned with the revival of 'the 4 sonnes of amon',[2]
which, in giving us a sketch of the plot, he tells us was
performed at Antwerp by English actors?[3] But the data
in the *Diary* are staggering enough and show Heywood
to have had a greater or less share in at least nine plays
between the beginning of September 1602 and the following March 6. If the entry on January 14 refers, as is most

1887, was 'acted intelligently' from a bowdlerized acting version by
Frank Marshall and warmly received; 'The audience was moved to
tears by the revenge of Frankford and the penitence of the erring wife'
(Frank Wedmore, *The Athenaeum*, Mar. 19, 1887; see also Mar. 5). It
was again revived under special conditions at New York in 1914, and
before a popular audience with some measure of success by the Birmingham
Repertory Company in the spring of 1922. But a much greater compliment was paid to the memory of Heywood by Monsieur J. Copeau, who
translated the play as *Une Femme tuée par la douceur* and presented it at
the Vieux-Colombier in Oct. 1913 (*Journal des Débats*, Oct. 27, 1913).

[1] *H.D.* i. 160; an unsigned acquittance in Chettle's hand for earnest
money and on May 9, the entry of 40s. paid at the appointment of Heywood and Duke to Chettle and Day (*ibid*. i. 190). Dr. Greg (*H.D.* i.
234-5) would identify the nameless play by Chettle and Heywood, mentioned by Henslowe on Jan. 4, 1602/3 (*ibid*. i. 173, 187; cf. xliii, xliv),
with *Shore*, which he thinks was possibly, even probably, based on earlier
work.

[2] *Ibid*. i. 173; see also i. 176, and ii. 227, Fleay, ii. 308-9, and S.R.
Feb. 22, 1599, and Feb. 23, 1625/6. The play was re-licensed by Herbert
for Prince Charles's men on Jan. 6, 1623/4 (Herbert, 27).

[3] *Apology*, 58-9.

likely, to a new play, we reach a total of ten, and to this we should perhaps add the second parts of *Lady Jane* and *The London Florentine*. When we remember that he acted regularly as well,[1] his industry must appear prodigious; it is little wonder that he was their 'industrious' Master Heywood to his friends, and became the English Lope de Vega to succeeding generations. With the evidence before us of such steady work as Henslowe supplies, Heywood's boast in the address to the reader of *The English Traveller*, 1633, that that tragicomedy was 'one reserved amongst two hundred and twenty, in which I have had either an entire hand, or at the least a maine finger' need not seem an exaggeration. There is no reason to reduce with Fleay[2] the number of plays to forty in which Heywood had an 'entire hand' and suppose that in the rest, pieces in which he had acted, he had merely inserted 'gag' or recommended alterations. The privilege of 'gagging' could in the nature of things pertain only to the clown, and 'a maine finger' obviously means collaboration such as the *Diary* indicates. Nor can we conclude, as some have done, that Heywood's share in many of the two hundred and twenty was confined to the plotting. That he held his plays in small esteem accounts for the failure of most of them to survive and for the fact that some are badly mutilated, even among Elizabethan and Jacobean quartos, or are masquerading under others' names, or are anonymous. Though it is unlikely that he wrote at the stretch from 1596 to 1633, yet if he could continue for seven months at the rate of a play and a half a month, he might easily have reached the grand total of two hundred and twenty by 1633, and had as well comfortable periods of leisure for *Troia Britannica* and his other non-dramatic work.

[1] Kirkman, 1671, who adds, 'he not only acted almost every day, but also obliged himself to write a sheet every day for several years together; but many of his playes being composed loosely in taverns, occasions them to be so mean, that, except his *Love's Mistress*, and, next to that, his *Ages*, I have but small esteem for any others'. Many of the plays were written 'in the taverns on the back-side of Tavern Bills' (Winstanley).

[2] i. 282.

Despite the labours of these months, it must have been a season of prosperity for Heywood, who combined, as but few did, the professions of actor and dramatist, and drew as well his share of the company's profits. Unlike Greene who, though 'famozed for an Arch-plaimaking-poet', had a purse which 'like the sea sometime sweld, anon like the same sea fell to a low ebbe',[1] Heywood as an actor-sharer had a considerable but now indeterminable income, which, if variable, was never cut off altogether. As the hirelings in 1597 received five shillings a week the first year and six shillings and eightpence the second,[2] the sharers cannot have received less than ten shillings. Acting, however, was not continuous; there were weeks of idleness due to plague or Lenten inhibitions; whole summers were spent in the provinces, where, if expenses were reduced by economizing in new plays and dresses, profits also were small; and though the hired men received their wages without deduction, the sharers were liable to all kinds of extraordinary expenses and had incomes varying with the circumstances which governed theatrical attendances. Nevertheless their incomes seem to have been comfortable. As a dramatist Heywood earned twenty-eight pounds two shillings in the seven months September to March 1602–3. His rapidity of production, though it was often fatal to the literary quality of his plays, did not greatly diminish their price, and must have put him in a much more favourable position than Jonson, whose slowness of composition was notorious. Heywood was not one of those favoured with exceptional prices by Henslowe: he received generally six pounds, the average reward for a play about 1600. It was rather as a result of the steady depreciation in the value of money that Henslowe's usual payment to Heywood had risen from five pounds in 1597, than because his fame had won it. On special occasions, however, when a play was urgently required, Heywood enjoyed his share of the increased disbursements. Fleay calls Dekker's the saddest story in

[1] *A Groatsworth of Wit*, ed. Grosart, xii. 134.
[2] *H.D.* i. 201.

his book.[1] The position of Chettle, still more of Day and Daborne, in the clutches of circumstance and Henslowe, must have been wretched in the extreme. From the correspondence of Daborne with Henslowe in 1613–14[2] we get a vivid impression of the precarious existence of a minor dramatist. The letters run in a sequence with few breaks and in rapid succession; on one pressing occasion, if one can be so called when all were, he wrote twice on the same day. He beseeches Henslowe's help with protestations of industry and promises of instalments of plays; he writes from prison, he writes from a sick bed, he sends his wife as an additional advocate, he hopes for a small sum to tide him over the week-end; he pleads, he expostulates, he even threatens to sell his work to another company and gets Field to corroborate him.[3] Heywood was spared these indignities; and on the whole his life now and later appears to have been fortunate, when contrasted with that of his fellow playwrights who were neither sharers nor even hirelings in one of the theatrical companies. His industry provided him with a competence, and his character protected him from the vagaries of fortune that afflicted his dramatic contemporaries.

When *A Woman killed with Kindness* was first produced, theatrical affairs in London were much disorganized by the Queen's illness, and it was probably for this reason that Worcester's men went on tour in the middle of March. But they were back in London soon after the death of Elizabeth on March 24, 1602/3, and

---

[1] i. 120; cf. M. L. Hunt, *Thomas Dekker*, 79.

[2] At Dulwich; summarized by Fleay, i. 75.

[3] Cf. the wife's remonstrance to her poetic husband in *Divers Crab-tree Lectures*, 1639: 'what hath your pen purchast?', she demands, 'or your goose-quill got you? . . . unlesse to be the Printers' Packe-horse, the Stationers' Iournyman, and the Players' Drudge: the Players . . . have the wit to keepe you poore, that they themselves may pranke it in Plush . . . I have found it by observation, and so have others, that the first steppe to beggarie, is to write to the Stage. I speake not of all, but of your poore Poets, who have made them your Idols, who ought rather to have falne downe and worship't you, who have put Oracles into their mouthes, who would eate the bread out of yours'.

Henslowe opened a new account with pomp and circumstance:

> In the name of god amen
> Begininge to playe agayne by the kynges licence
> & layd owt sense for my lord of worsters men
> as folowethe 1603 9 of maye.[1]

Only one entry, however, follows, and Worcester's men, like their rivals, were constrained to travel in the provinces by the plague which closed the theatres from before May 17[2] till at least December 22, 1603.[3] We hear of them at Leicester, Coventry, and Barnstaple,[4] but back they seem to have come to the capital in the autumn, for their famous clown, Kempe, was buried at St. Saviour's, Southwark, on November 2.[5] They must have had a most successful season with Henslowe, to be accorded the second place among the dramatic companies when the royal family took the leading troupes into their patronage. In the splendid Christmas festivities of 1603/4, which promised a renewal of the best days of Elizabeth, Queen Anne's men, as they had recently become, played before Prince Henry on January 2, 1603/4, and again on January 13.[6] On December 20, 1604, they played before the King 'How to Learn of a Woman to wooe by Hewood',[7] which Fleay would identify with *The Wise Woman of Hogsdon*.[8] They were at court again on Decem-

---

[1] *H.D.* i. 190.

[2] F. P. Wilson, *The Plague in Shakespeare's London*, 110.

[3] Murray, i. 55–6, ii. 185; but cf. Fleay, *Shakspere*, 149. Mr. Murray (i. 55) has suggested another and less likely reason for their departure (perhaps to the Boar's Head, mentioned in an undated draft licence to the Queen's men as one of their usual theatres), an uncertainty about their tenure of the Rose. Cf. *H.D.* i. 178, ii. 55, 303; Fleay, *Stage*, 149; and Ordish, *Early London Theatres*, 200.

[4] Murray, i. 55, ii. 199, 243, 308.   [5] Chambers, ii. 327.

[6] Chambers, iv. 118, 168.

[7] *Ibid.* iv. 119, 171; cf. iv. 136, &c.

[8] i. 291–2, 293, ii. 386; see 165 *infra*. Fleay, i. 34, thinks this play may be alluded to in Brewer's *Lovesick King, c.* 1607, at the end of i and in ii. *A way to woo a pretty wench* (S.R. July 16, 1658) is reprinted in *R.B.* viii. 245.

ber 27, 1605,[1] when they gave an unspecified play before
the King. In the first of the three lists of the Queen's men
extant, an undated draft of a patent of late in 1603 or
early in 1604,[2] Heywood's name stands third after
Thomas Greene and Christopher Beeston;[3] the same
place is assigned him in the patent of April 15, 1609,
authorizing Queen Anne's men to play 'at theire nowe
usual houses called the Redd Bull, in Clarkenwell, and
the Curtayne, in Hallowell', as well as in the provinces.[4]
It was at the Curtain they began to act after the long
visitation of the plague in 1603–4,[5] but probably in 1605,[6]
certainly before 1608, when Heywood's *Rape of Lucrece*
was printed as it had been played at the Red Bull, they
had acquired the latter theatre as well.

To this period belongs *A Yorkshire Tragedy*; we have
put forward in an appendix Heywood's claim to this
specimen of domestic tragedy.[7]

[1] Chambers, iv. 120, 173.
[2] During the plague and while they were still at the Boar's Head. Sir
E. K. Chambers, ii. 229–30, dates it in 1603–4; cf. Fleay, *Stage*, 191, and
H.D. ii. 100.
[3] Chambers, ii. 229–30; for the authenticity of the draft see *H.D.* ii.
107, 144. See Murray, i. 186 and Chambers, ii. 229 for a list of the
Queen's men, including Heywood, to whom were issued lengths of red
cloth for cloaks for James's coronation, Mar. 15, 1604. From Aug. 9–
27, 1604, Greene and ten of the Queen's men 'groomes of the Chamber'
attended 'vppon Countye Arrenbergh and the reste of the comyssioners
at Durham howse' (Chambers, iv. 170). Heywood was no doubt one of
the ten, and may have acted in the same capacity during the two visits of
Christian IV of Denmark, July 17–Aug. 11, 1606, and July 22–Aug. 1,
1614 (Chambers, iv. 121, 129).
[4] Chambers, iv. 230, &c.
[5] Murray, i. 149, ii. 171, 185. The Queen's men are named in the
Privy Council's letter of Apr. 9, 1604, instructing the Lord Mayor and the
Justices of Middlesex and Surrey to permit the resumption of playing
(Chambers, iv. 336).
[6] Cf. Chambers, ii. 445, &c.
[7] See 301–28 *infra*.

CHAPTER IV

1607–1614: MODEST FAME AND LITERARY AMBITIONS: MARRIAGE: FRIENDSHIPS

PERHAPS the success of several of his plays on the stage and after publication may have encouraged Heywood to work more definitely literary than in his own estimation he had yet undertaken. At any rate the first book which he prepared for the press [1] was not a play but an excellent translation of Sallust. *The Two most worthy and notable Histories which remain unmaimed to Posterity: (viz.) The Conspiracy of Catiline, undertaken against the government of the Senate of Rome, and The War which Jugurth for many years maintained against the same State,* 1608 (S.R. February 15, 1607/8),[2] a small and excessively rare folio, does not bear the translator's name on the title-page. For all his modesty, however, if indeed that was the reason for omitting his name from the title-page, and his pedagogic insistence on the worth of the histories '*Both written by C. C. Salustius*', he does not make clear the fact that his very interesting introduction 'Of the choice of History, by way of Preface, dedic-/*ated to the Courteous Reader, upon occasion of the frequent* Translations of these latter times' is a translation of Bodin's *Methodus ad Facilem Historiarum Cognitionem,* a document of Renaissance criticism well deserving attention, or that the historical tracts of Sallust were rendered from the French version of Lois Meigret Lyonnois. That the dedicatee, Sir Thomas Somerset, third son of the Earl of Worcester, deigned 'to accept of this unpolisht Translation' we feel sure: but 'eyther Time or better iudgment' did not furnish Heywood 'with the more desertfull proiect' he meant to have submitted to Sir Thomas's approbation, unless we suppose that *Troia Britannica* or

---

[1] But see 8 *supra,* note 2, for *Oenone and Paris* by T. H.

[2] The separate title-page of the *Jugurthine War* is dated 1609.

An Apology for Actors, both dedicated to the Earl of Worcester, was the fulfilment of the promise. But the submission by Heywood of his first literary venture to one of the younger Somersets implies a considerable familiarity with them, and certain phrases in the dedication appear to mean that Sir Thomas had been a powerful friend to Queen Anne's company, which in spite of its royal patroness had lost favour at court.

'Sir', says Heywood, 'having no fitter occasion to manifest my duty to your Worthinesse (though I have often wisht matter more expressive both of my love & zeale) I have adventured rather to tempt your acceptance in this small presentment, worthy (no man will denie) in its proper Ornament, of an Honourable Patronage: Then by perpetuall neglect to incur the imputation of Ingratitude . . . Herein therefore (right Generous) let me in lieu of all my friends, make confession of your many and extraordinary favours, from time to time vouchsafed to us. In acknowledgment wherof, sithence we want power to deserve, yet give us leave with thankfull overtures to remember.'

The friends for whom Heywood spoke could only have been his fellow-actors, to whom Sir Thomas Somerset may have been either a protector in certain bouts with the magistrates or an advocate at court. At any rate, in April 1609 the Queen's men were given another patent[1] and were called five times to court during the Christmas holidays in 1608 after two years' exclusion.[2]

When the patent of 1609 was issued, however, the Queen's men and their rivals were inhibited from acting by the return of the plague. There had been a discouraging year by reason of the infection in 1607, and now from July 28, 1608 till December 7, 1609, or even later, the theatres were apparently closed.[3] The lot of both players and dramatists, who lived at the best of times from hand

---

[1] Murray, i. 188–9; Chambers, ii. 230–2.
[2] Chambers, ii. 232, iv. 123, 175.
[3] F. P. Wilson, *The Plague in Shakespeare's London*, 124–5; Murray, ii. 186–7; and Chambers, iv. 350–1. The company's wanderings in the provinces are difficult to trace on account of the appearance of a secondary company in the Queen's service; cf. Murray, i. 202, &c., ii. 244, 343, 400; and Chambers, ii. 233.

to mouth, must have been hard indeed. 'There Comedies', says Dekker in the middle of the epidemic, 'are all turned to Tragedies, there Tragedies to Nocturnals . . . Think you to delight yourselves by keeping company with our poets? Proh dolor! their Muses are more sullen than old monkeys now that money is not stirring; they never plead cheerfully but in their term times when the two-penny clients and penny-stinkards swarm together to hear the Stagerites.'[1] It is not surprising, then, that in the threatening month of June 1608 Heywood, authorized by the company which was itself impoverished by the diminished receipts, decided to turn his plays to a second account by the press, instead of suffering the stationers to issue corrupt or anonymous copies from which he benefited not at all. Accordingly in 1608 he published with an interesting preface his recent success, *The Rape of Lucrece*, as it had been performed by Queen Anne's men at the Red Bull (S.R. June 3). Heywood's tragedy was not the first on Lucrece's story, for as early as 1594 Drayton in his *Legend of Matilda* speaks of Lucrece

> Lately reviv'd to live another age, . . .
> Acting her passions on our stately stage,[2]

and in *Cynthia's Revels* Jonson has the phrase, 'He makes a face like a stabb'd Lucrece',[3] that looks like a reminiscence of a play. From another allusion in *Saint Mary Magdalen's Conversion*, 1603–4, to 'Tarquins lust and lucrece chastitie', Mr. Tatlock would date the first performance of Heywood's play in 1603,[4] though there is no reason for supposing that the author of *Saint Mary Magdalen's Conversion* was referring to plays at all. That Heywood's quaint, farcical tragedy was written, as Rupert Brooke thought,[5] in 1604, or in 1605, as Fleay believed,[6] is not established merely by the song '*The Gentry to the Kings head*',[7] which in fact does not appear in the first

---

[1] *Work for Armourers*, ed. Grosart, iv. 96–7.
[2] Taken by Collier (*New Particulars regarding the Works of Shakespeare*, 28) as referring to Heywood's play or to Shakespeare's poem. Cf. *Edward III*, ii. 2.   [3] v. 4.   [4] *P.M.L.A.A.* xxx. 736.
[5] *John Webster*, 130.   [6] i. 292.   [7] Pearson, v. 198.

edition. For a clue to the date we are therefore thrown back on other evidence, especially on parallels to Shakespeare. It seems clear, for example, that in sketching his Tarquin and Tullia the 'prose Shakespeare' was imitating his poetic contemporary's *Macbeth*. A date, then, for his play in 1606 or 1607 seems likely, and is corroborated by the fact that in 1607 Nicholas Okes issued another edition of Shakespeare's *Lucrece* to which Heywood was very considerably indebted. In the 1609, 1614, 1630, and 1638 quartos, four new songs are thrust in; in the 1638 edition five more were added and some attempt made to link the songs to the dialogue. Only in the 1638 quarto is the revision noticed, but the slight changes made in the second, and all subsequent editions, indicate that Heywood retained some sort of interest in the book. Most of these very rude ditties were by Heywood himself,[1] but in all the editions there is an appendix with two jingling catches 'by the stranger that lately acted *Valerius*', 'Because we would not that any man's expectation should be deceived in the ample printing of this booke'. No doubt, therefore, some of the less edifying and apparently extemporary verses were by the same merry stranger, to whom the tragedy, a serious but outrageous parody of the classics, appears to have owed not a little of its popularity.[2] The singing senator even suggested to Beaumont the equally jolly Master Merrythought in *The Knight of the Burning Pestle* who actually sings one of the songs in Heywood's appendix.[3] After

---

[1] Two of the better lyrics, '*The* Spaniard *loves his ancient slop*' (Pearson, v. 216) and the pleasing '*Packe cloudes away, and welcome day*' (*ibid.* v. 227), are also found respectively in *A Challenge for Beauty* (Pearson, v. 65) and as *A song at the marriage of James and Anne Waade* in *Pleasant Dialogues*, 262–3 (see 156 *infra*).

[2] It is impossible to say who this actor was: no new name appears in the patent of Apr. 1609. He may have rejoined the company after a foreign tour, since Valerius is said to have 'been in the German warres' and to 'have bin germanis'd' and sings 'after the Dutch fashion' a 'Dutch' song (Pearson, v. 205–6).

[3] iii. 1. It was not 'the confutation of Saint Paul' that the citizen's wife saw on the arras, but '*Ralph* and *Lucrece*', ii. 1.

the dissolution of Queen Anne's company, who played
'Lucrecia' in conjunction with the King's men at Greenwich before the Queen and Prince Henry on January 13,
1611/12,[1] the Roman chronicle seems to have passed
through the agency of Heywood or Beeston to the Lady
Elizabeth's men. Certainly after the transfer of most of
that company to the patronage of Queen Henrietta, *The
Rape of Lucrece* was in the Queen's men's repertoire, and
was performed by them at the Cockpit on August 7, 1628,
in the presence of the Duke of Buckingham before his
departure for La Rochelle.[2] It was later one of the forty-
five plays resigned by Queen Henrietta's men to Beeston's
Boys, perhaps because they were the property of their late
manager, and from some time before February 7, 1636/7,
manager of the recently constituted company of boy-
actors.[3]

A play almost exactly similar, *Appius and Virginia*, was
accepted without dispute as Webster's until Rupert
Brooke, than whom Webster never had a more sympathetic critic, assigned the tragedy in the main to Heywood, a reattribution so sensible that we can only wonder
it was never made before.[4] The present writer continued
the proof from the point of view of likeness to Heywood
rather than of disagreement with Webster.[5] Though he
still regards Webster as only a reviser, not as a collaborator, he feels compelled to assign him much more of the
play than Brooke would concede. One of the minor
objections to Webster's authorship is the difficulty of
giving it a plausible date in his dramatic career. But it
fits neatly into Heywood's history a year or two after he

---

[1] Chambers, iv. 126, 178.

[2] *Autobiography and Correspondence of Sir Simond D'Ewes*, ii. 210.

[3] Murray, i. 367–9; the anonymous author of *Tiberius*, 1607, was not unin-
fluenced by Heywood's much inferior play. See E. Hertz (*Englische
Schauspieler und englisches Schauspiel zur Zeit Shakespeares in Deutschland*,
98) for a play on the subject in Germany in 1619.

[4] *The Authorship of the later 'Appius and Virginia'* (*M.L.R.* 1913) and
in *John Webster and the Elizabethan Drama*, 161, &c.

[5] *The Authorship of Appius and Virginia* (*M.L.R.* 1921). See 252–75
infra.

had written *The Rape of Lucrece.*[1] The change in tone is very easily accounted for by the intermediate production of *Coriolanus.* We conclude, therefore, that it was staged by Queen Anne's men in 1608, and as it was confirmed to Beeston's Boys in August 1639 its subsequent history seems to have been exactly the same as Heywood's other Roman tragedy. It was printed for the first time in 1654 (S.R. May 13), some copies bearing the publisher's name on the title-page and some not; remainders of this edition were issued with fresh titles in 1659, and, after Betterton's revival, in 1679.[2]

Perhaps *Fortune by Land and Sea* was another of Heywood's essays during the plague of 1608–9. From time to time the public interest in pirates was reawakened by reports of their daring, and 1609 appears to have been a year of unusual excitement. *The Seaman's Song of Captain Ward* and its sequel in honour of Ward's fellow, Danseker the Dutchman, were licensed on July 3; and not long after was issued Andrew Barker's *True and Certain Report of the Beginning, Proceedings, Overthrows, and now present Estate of Captain Ward and Danseker, the two late famous Pirates* (S.R. October 24), which was hastily dramatized by Daborne in his *Christian Turned*

---

[1] The heroines of both plays are mentioned together in *Appius and Virginia*, ed. Lucas, iii. 224:

> Two fair, but Ladies most infortunate,
> have in their ruins rais'd declining *Rome*,
> *Lucretia* and *Virginia*, both renown'd
> for chastity.

[2] As *Appius and Virginia, Acted at the Duke's Theatre under the name of The Roman Virgin or Unjust Judge, A Tragedy*, to deceive the unwary; it misled even the elect Malone who, following Langbaine's statement on Cartwright's authority that the play had been altered by Betterton before his revival of it, pronounced his copy of the 1679 ed. (Bodley: Malone, 72) to be this recension. Downes dates the revival in 1666. Pepys was present at a performance on May 12, 1669, at the Duke's Theatre; 'there in the side balcony, over against the musick, did hear, but not see, a new play, the first day acted, "*The Roman Virgin*", an old play, but ordinary, I thought'. The play, however, had a fair run of eight successive nights with Betterton = Virginius, Harris = Appius, and Mrs. Betterton = Virginia, and was frequently acted later (Downes).

Turk. Daborne, too, has been credited with a pamphlet account, '*Newes from the Sea*', of Ward and his Dutch ally.[1] Others in the piratical line were celebrated in *The Lives, Apprehensions, Arraignments, and Executions of the 19 late Pirates*, ?1609/10. Both Ward and Danseker were mentioned by Dekker in 1610 in *If it be not Good*,[2] and Ward by Jonson in *The Alchemist*[3] of the same year. But Heywood, ever ready with topicalities, had a thief as good, or rather two of them, whom he alludes to in *Troia Britannica*,

> *Purser* and *Clinton* Pyrats, that denaide
> allegiance to the Queene, [and] at length were tane
> By *William Barrowes*,[4]

either in anticipation or in reminiscence of his play. It will certainly be convenient to notice now this posthumously published tragicomedy, though we shall have to refer to it again later. The publication of it, 'As it was Acted with great Applause by the Queen's Servants', in 1655 in the most slovenly quarto of the Heywood canon, was of course an entirely unofficial transaction.[5]

It may be that Heywood's first original non-dramatic venture, *Troia Britannica: or, Great Britain's Troy. A Poem Divided into XVII several Cantons, intermixed with many pleasant Poetical Tales. Concluding with an Universal Chronicle from the Creation, until these present Times*, which falls to be noticed now, was of earlier composition than the last-mentioned play. For no obvious reason Mr. Tatlock supposes from the modern instances in the poem, to which Heywood was partial, that it may have been begun not earlier than 1602, but decides that it was really published soon after it was written.[6] Certainly there was ample time for Heywood, whose Γυναικεῖον was written

---

[1] S.R. June 2; identified by Arber with Barker's pamphlet.

[2] Pearson's *Dekker*, i. 352.   [3] v. 2.   [4] Sig. Qq 5.

[5] See 179–82 *infra*. It was revived with strange liberties 'for the Annual Theatricals of the Harvard Chapter of Delta Upsilon' in 1899 from an acting version by Miss J. E. Walker. The title of the play was probably proverbial; cf. *Jew of Malta*, ed. Tucker Brooke, 245: 'Thus trowles our fortune in by land and Sea'; and *Eastward Ho!* iv. 2: 'Sir Flash . . . sent her to seek her fortune by land, whilst himself prepared for his fortune by sea.'

[6] *P.M.L.A.A.* xxx. 688–9.

and printed in seventeen weeks, to have thrown off a work three times as long as his mythological chronicle in the months between the appearance of the 1607 edition of Caxton's *Recueil of the Histories of Troy*, on which *Troia Britannica* is mainly based, and December 5, 1608, when William Jaggard entered it at Stationers' Hall. The unusual proviso in the licence to the printer, 'that yf any question or trouble growe hereof. Then he shall answere and discharge yt at his owne Losse and costes', could not have been made in anticipation of any official objection to Heywood's innocuous poem, which duly appeared in 1609 as a small folio, though full of misprints and with the pagination hopelessly muddled. But to Heywood's righteous anger Jaggard turned a deaf ear, refusing to publish a table of *errata* to expose his own 'disworkman-ship'.[1] Heywood dedicates *Troia Britannica* in rather obscure terms to the Earl of Worcester:

> To you, whose Favour gave my Muse first breath,
> To try in th' Ayre her weake unable wing,
> And soare this pitch, who else had tasted death
> Even in her byrth, from the Castalian spring
> >   She dedicates her labours (as they are)
> >   Though as you see, poore, featherlesse, and bare;

insisting on his Muse's 'Penlesse Age', 'Her Cradle', 'her Infant grave', and 'her nonage Art'. The graces of 'her Patron-Lord', manifested over a long period, had encouraged Heywood to regard himself as Worcester's *protégé*. Indeed in one of the preliminary stanzas with which in Spenser's fashion he opened every canto he appears to infer that Worcester himself had suggested the poem:

> >   Your favour and protection decke my phrase,
> >   And is to me like *Ariadnes* clew,
> >   To guide me through the labyrinthine Maze,
> >   In which my brain's entangled: Tis by you,
> >   That every vulgar eye hath leave to gaze
> >   And on this Proiect takes free enter-view.[2]

[1] Letter to Nicholas Okes in *An Apology for Actors*. Heywood, however, wrote an execrable hand and himself excused the compositor for mistakes in reading the MS. of *The Exemplary Lives*, sig. Ff4 verso.   [2] Sig. Ee 4.

It is possible, of course, to read into these complimentary phrases meanings which they were never meant to convey, and no doubt Heywood was making graceful, but larger acknowledgements, than he need have done of the earl's favour to himself or his company. Yet his continuing till Worcester's death to address all but one of his non-dramatic efforts to him implies that there was more than a merely formal patronage. With the true pamphleteer's touch, Heywood had promised the reader more if *Troia Britannica* was well received. But we find no contemporary references from which to judge of its welcome, and Heywood, when he had turned the matter in it to the uses of the stage with such success in his *Ages*, did not consider it profitable to write more in the same vein. The poem was sufficiently obscure in 1612 for Jaggard, as we shall see, to filch several hundred lines from it and publish them under Shakespeare's name in the third and enlarged edition of *The Passionate Pilgrim*.[1]

Though *Troia Britannica: or, Great Britain's Troy* is by far the best of Heywood's non-dramatic works and a poem of true beauty, it has remained by reason of its rarity practically unknown. The deceptive title has misled not a few with respect to the contents and style of the book; and the epistle to the reader is not very encouraging in its promise that we '*shall finde included ... a briefe memory or Epitome of Chronicle, even from the first man, unto us, this second time created* Britons, *with a faithfull Register, not onely of memorable thinges done in* Troy *and this Island, but of many, and the most famous accidents happening through the World, In whose raigne and what yeare of the world they chanced (with which we have conferred the Histories of the Sacred Byble) & truth of the times so eeven, that whosoever will daigne the perusall of these, shall not onely perceive such things were doone, but bee also satisfied in whose Raigne (then successively governing in the kingdome of Britaine) they happened*', to which Heywood with unconscious candour adds '*In all which I have taskt my selfe to such succinctnesse and brevity, that in the iudiciall perusall of these few Cantons*

---

[1] See 82–3, *infra*.

(with the Scolies annexed) as little time shall be hazzarded, as profite from them be any way expected'. But in fact the book is not at all an historical manual. Except the prose proem which gives the posterity of Noah, the establishment of the monarchies of Assyria, Persia, Alexander, and Rome, and a few of the usually accepted parallels from sacred and profane history to classical mythology, canto 16 which is

> *A Genealogie exactly found,*
> *From the first man, to* Norman Williā *crownd,*[1]

and canto 17,

> *From* Norman William *a true note collected,*
> *Of al the kinges and Queenes that here protected,*[2]

the book relates the classical myths from the rivalry of Saturn and Titan to the death of Hercules *'with many pleasant Poeticall Tales'*[3] and other digressions, and secondly the tale of Troy from the establishment of Priam's kingdom to its destruction. At the end of every canto are observations for the benefit of the less erudite reader. We can hardly regret the curtailment of the historical matter; such as there is, boiled down to a quintessence of chronicles, does not suggest that, had it been less hurriedly written and less condensed, it would have rivalled *Albion's England*, and a collector of gems of versified ineptitude would be well advised to search here. But we are unwilling to be severe for a little dullness at the end on one who has been so generally entertaining through fifteen cantos and who pleads so disarmingly in his preface: *'Let that which pleaseth, mittigat the harshness of the other. He that speaks much, may (excusably) speake somewhat Idely, and he that in unknown Climats travayles farre, may (by misadventure) wander out of the way: but where the mayne intent and purpose is honest and good, it is pardonable to expect the best. And in that hope I prostrate these my barraine industries to your kindest and gentle Construction'*.

Troia Britannica is, then, in the main a versifying of

---

[1] Sig. Mm 3.   [2] Sig. Oo 3.   [3] Title-page.

the most popular myths of the ancient world. Many
factors had contributed to make the matter of Troy the
best loved of all the classical stories, the romance *par
excellence*. It has occupied some of the greatest figures in
literature and it has been told and restd in the noblelot
as well as in the baldest of narratives. The very grandeur
and fame of it attracted to it hosts of satellites until the
majority of the myths of the classical theogony rotated
around it. The obscuration of Homer and Virgil, the
authority of Dares and Dictys, the great additions of
Benoît de Sainte-More, the plagiarizing from Benoît by
the Latinizing Guido delle Colonne, the sentiment of
Boccaccio, the realism of Chaucer, the chronologica
method of Lydgate, the compilation of Lefevre, and his
translation into English by Caxton as *The Recueil of the
Histories of Troy*, all these fall outside our survey. With
the Renaissance and the restoration of Homer and Virgi
to their places as the prime sources and true founts o.
Trojan lore, the cycle's popularity rather increased thar
diminished. The great corpus of romance was butchered
for plays, poems, romances, and ballads. But though
under classical influence the tone was somewhat modified
the medieval and chivalric dominant remained: the love
interest still outweighed the epical, the supernatural was
still minimized and the classical deities rationalized, the
heroes were still knights and the women were still medie
val ladies and matrons; the characters in the medieva
accretions to the cycle were as prominent as ever; in shor
the emphasis was still on the same elements as in Caxton'
Recueil and Lydgate's *Troy-Book*. The old pedigree of the
British from Brutus, grandson of Aeneas, which Geoffrey
of Monmouth had drawn, met with practically no criticism
till the seventeenth century, and in fact Heywood's poem
was written to versify the whole apocryphal descent. I
is interesting to find in Heywood the retention of what
we may call the Trojan prejudice and the medieval con
viction of the partiality of Homer.[1] At the same time
there is an attempt to adopt the more classical point o

[1] Sig. Cc 2.

view; but it is needless to say that his poem achieves but a remote resemblance to the classics, less indeed than do his very unclassical *Ages*, for *Troia Britannica* in matter is pure Caxton with additions in a similar style.

Except in the verse dedication to the Earl of Worcester in sixains and in most of cantos 9 and 10 which contain translations into heroic couplets of Paris's epistle to Helen and her reply,[1] Heywood uses throughout the *ottava rima* which had already established itself in England for 'a type of narrative-poem somewhat rambling, long, varied, romantic, warlike, sentimental, and pseudo-historical'.[2] It suited Heywood's digressive and wordy style. The couplet, which he manages tolerably well when he translates from so strict a measure as the elegiac couplet of Ovid, would have been as much distorted as in *The Hierarchy*; but the *ottava rima* allowed him just the liberty and the restraint he needed. On the whole Heywood carries his story through the eleven thousand odd lines of stanzas very successfully, though he breaks down in the additional eighteen hundred of the last two cantos. There is something of the muscular pulse of Drayton in places, and flashes of imagination which make us wish the author had had time to spend on the polishing of his romance. The following stanzas illustrate fairly well the movement and style of the whole:

> His knotted beard was as the *Porphir* blacke,
> So were the fleecy lockes upon his crowne,
> Which to the middle of his armed backe,
> From his rough shaggy head discended downe,
> His fiery Eie-bals threaten *Saturnes* wracke,
> Sterne vengeance rous'd her self in *Cæous* frowne,
>   His sheild, a broad iron dore, his Lance a beame,
>   Oft with his large strides he hath Archt a streame.
>
> *Typhon* in skins of Lyons grimly clad,
> Next his too Brothers in the march proceeds,
> The hides of these imperious beasts he had,
> From th' *Erithmanthian* [*sic*] forrest, where his deeds

---

[1] *Heroides*, xvi–xvii.   [2] Tatlock, *P.M.L.A.A.* xxx. 684.

Live still in memory, like one halfe mad
The Gyant shewes in these disguised weeds,
   The Lyon iawes gnawing his Helmet stood,
   And grinning with his long fangs stain'd in blood.

Hiperion in an armor all of Sunnes,
Shines like the face of *Phœbus* o're the rest:
This Gyant to his valiant Brothers runs,
Crying to Armes, base lingering I detest,
Damn'd be that Coward soule that damage shuns,
Or from apparent perill shrinkes his brest,
   Behold where *Saturne* mongst his people crownd,
   His hornes and Clarions doth to battell sound.[1]

This stanza describing Diana,

Her weapons are the Iavelin, and the Bow,
Her garments *Angell-like*, of Virgin white,
And tuckt aloft, her falling skirt below
Her Buskin meetes: buckled with silver bright:
Her Haire behind her, like a Cloake doth flow,
Some tuckt in roules, some loose with Flowers bedight:
   Her silken vailes play round about her slacke,
   Her golden Quiver fals athwart her backe,[2]

has a delicacy and fancy that we scarcely expected to find
in Heywood at all. These passages will serve to display the
strength of Spenser's influence on *Troia Britannica*. The
reader is constantly meeting, not Spenserian archaisms,
which are rare, but Spenserian turns of expression and
modes of narration and description, modern instances,
digressions, and long decorative similes. Of the Spen-
serians Heywood is not the least readable, for he was
not enslaved by a tedious moral allegory; he was writing
a straightforward story, and his own haste, together with a
more or less prescribed plan, kept him from too great
divagation. The derivation of the romance through
medieval authorities from Ovidian sources could hardly
be expected to result in anything very austere, but any
one familiar with the 'reverent misunderstanding of the
classics' in the Middle Ages and later will accept with
pleasure what Heywood has to give. Without being

---

[1] Sig. G 3.   [2] Sig. E 3.

pedestrian, he has all the qualifications of the competent story-teller in verse, and without being high-imaginative, he carries the reader on through description and myth, digression and comment. Nothing is too decorative, nothing too epical; he is as successful with the love escapades of Jupiter or the beautiful legend of Proserpine as in the Wars of the Giants or the combat of Hector and Ajax. He even shows a surprising felicity in phrasing, a sense of the melody of words that his plays hardly ever exhibit:

> The all-dispoyled Virgin in a Trance,
> Wayling her ruine on the bryny Strand; [1]

> Fame that hath undertooke your name to blaze,
> Plaid but the envious Huswife in your praise; [2]

> Downe drops his sonne towards earth, and falling, past
> Through al the Planets, by *Apollo* hier
> Then all the rest. So by the Moone at last,
>   Twixt heaven and earth, who can describe the way?
>   When he was falling a long Summer's day. [3]

This poem, then, is of all Heywood's miscellaneous work the one most deserving of republication.

So far we have had but few glimpses of Heywood's private life, a fact the more to be deplored in one so tenderly domestic. No doubt on his first coming to London he took up his abode near the Rose,[4] and remained on the Bankside till the Queen's men migrated to the Curtain in Shoreditch, whither he and his fellows would shift their properties, domestic and theatrical, in 1603 or soon after.[5] After a fairly thorough search through the London parish registers for Heywood's marriage, we have discovered only one likely entry. On

---

[1] Sig. P.   [2] Sig. V 4.   [3] Sig. M 5.
[4] We have been unable to prove the authenticity of Collier's citation (Bodl. MS. 29445; cf. Chambers, iii. 338) of a Thomas Heywood's name from 1588–1607 in the token books of St. Saviour's, Southwark, or the baptisms of children of Thomas Heywood, 'player' in the same parish, June 28, 1590–Sept. 5, 1605.
[5] In Γυναικεῖον, 1624, 414, Heywood states that he had known a woman in Clerkenwell over twenty-four years.

June 13, 1603, at St. Antholin's, a 'Thomas Hayward' was married to 'Aenn Buttler servt. to Mr. Venn'.[1] Another entry in the register of St. James's, Clerkenwell, for the marriage of 'Thomas Hayward & Jane Span: lic. from the Facul.' on January 18, 1632/3, may record the dramatist's second venture. There is something appropriate in his long association with Clerkenwell, a centre for theatrical performances from the fourteenth century.[2] It was a district, however, like all the suburbs, of rather doubtful repute. But it had its respectable residents as well; Oliver Cromwell set up his sign in Clerkenwell Close; Sir Thomas Chaloner lived at the Priory, and Sir Roger Wilbraham at St. John's Gate; and the Earl of Aylesbury had a country house in the vicinity. Heywood had more literary neighbours in Thomas Dekker, William Rowley, John Weever the epigraphist at Clerkenwell Close,[3] and Izaak Walton. He was himself a decent householder 'neare Clarkenwell Hill',[4] and a friend of the most substantial residents. Dr. Stephen Bradwell, a physician in the parish distinguished enough to have written medical treatises, composed intimate commendatory verses for The Exemplary Lives of his 'learned, loving Friend'.[5] Sir Philip Woodhouse, and probably his son Sir Thomas at whose request apparently Heywood wrote his Epitaph upon the death of Sir Philip Woodhouse, Knight Baronet,[6] had a mansion in Clerkenwell. Sir Henry

---

[1] 'Ann Hayward, a maid-servt.', buried according to the same register on Jan. 12, 1621/2, was more likely to have been the dramatist's daughter than his wife. He had a wife alive in 1625; see 102 infra. The 'Thomas Haward' married to 'Joane Henwarde' at St. Martin's in the Fields on Jan. 23, 1604/5, was probably the person of the name buried there on Jan. 3, 1615/16.

[2] Apology, 40.

[3] Weever's monument on a pillar at the west end of the church bore an epitaph almost certainly by Heywood.

[4] See C. W. Wallace, Gervase Markham, Dramatist, Shakespeare Jahrbuch, xlvi. 347, where a number of Heywood's associates in a wager with Gervase Markham are mentioned.   [5] See 6 supra, 183 infra.

[6] Pleasant Dialogues, 255; see also 256 for an epitaph on a gentlewoman called Patience or Grizel (perhaps Sir Thomas Woodhouse's daughter Grizel, buried at Clerkenwell on Aug. 27, 1614; see 154 infra, note 3).

Appleton's second wife, Alice, was the daughter of William Riplingham of St. James's,[1] and John Witt, gentleman, who was at the expense of plate 4 of *The Hierarchy of the Blessed Angels*, buried his wife Rose in the chancel of the church, where only a few months later Heywood himself was laid. Presumably, too, Katharine Skip, for whose monument Heywood wrote an epitaph and on whose scholarly husband an epigram,[2] were relatives of the Robert Skip married to Sarah Muckley at St. James's on February 19, 1665/6.[3] Still another family of some position with a Clerkenwell connexion and friends of Heywood were the Littleboys of Sussex; not only did the poet write on her death at the age of twenty[4] *A Funeral Elegy upon the death of Mistress Mary Littleboys, Daughter to Master George Littleboys of Ashburnham in Sussex*, full of 'classical allusions from the pagan authors', but also a more religious inscription for her tomb in St. James's.[5] The William Toomes whose name is found in the parish register, and who paid for plate 2 of *The Hierarchy*, was one of the cashiers of the fabulously wealthy Sir Paul Pindar, and so conscientious an executor of his will that in 1655, five years after Pindar's death, discouraged by the embarrassment of the estate, he committed suicide. Samuel King, whose praise of Heywood is printed at the end of *The Wise Woman of Hogsdon*, was one of the Clerkenwell Kings,[6] and probably the Frances Long(e), for whom Heywood wrote *An Epithalamium or Nuptial Song upon a young sweet virtuous Gentlewoman. F. L. An Acrostic upon her name*,[7] was a

---

[1] See 1 *supra*, notes 1 and 2, and 101, 119 *infra*.
[2] *Pleasant Dialogues*, 256.   [3] See 155 *infra*, note 1.   [4] Mar. 8, 1635–6.
[5] *Pleasant Dialogues*, 257–9; see 155–6 *infra*, note 1.
[6] Married Aug. 12, 1601, to Margaret Hoye.
[7] *Pleasant Dialogues*, 260. George Long, esq., third son of John Long of Holmhall in Chesterfield, died aged 73½ on Feb. 1, 1654/5, and was buried on the north side of St. James's 'in a kind of Chapel leading into a gallery' (Pointer, *New View of London*, 291), where his monument gave the names of his three wives, the first being Frances Lollyman. A William Long and his wife Frances had several children baptized in the fifties of the seventeenth century.

member of another family of the parish. An interesting
unknown is the 'woman of good credit and reputation,
whom I have knowne above these foure and twenty yeares
and is of the same parish where now I live'; it would be
unjust at this date to impugn her veracity because of the
marvellous tale she often related 'upon her credit with
manie deepe protestations' of her strange adventures with
a flying witch of Amsterdam.[1] He had of course friends
in the actor colony, Christopher Beeston, Thomas
Greene,[2] John Blaney, Richard Perkins, John Sumner,
Hugh Clark (the dashing Bess Bridges in *The Fair Maid
of the West*), Christopher Goad, Robert Axell, and no
doubt others belonging to Queen Anne's, the Lady
Elizabeth's, and Queen Henrietta's companies. We hope
that these associates conformed to Heywood's idea of
what was proper to the quality:

'I also could wish', he says, 'that such as are cōdemned for their
licentiousness, might by a generall consent bee quite excluded our
society: for, as we are men that stand in the broad eye of the world,
so should our manners, gestures, and behaviours, savour of such
government and modesty, to deserve the good thoughts and reports
of all men, and to abide the sharpest censures, even of those that are
the greatest opposites to the quality. Many amongst us, I know, to
be of substance, of governement, of sober lives, and temperate
cariages, house-keepers, and contributory to all duties enioyned
them, equally with them that are rank't with the most bountifull;
and if amongst so many of sort, there be any few degenerate from
the rest in that good demeanor, which is both requisite & expected
at their hands, let me entreat you not to censure hardly of all for the
misdeeds of some, but rather to excuse us, as Ovid doth the generality
of women,

> *Parcite paucarum diffundere crimen in omnes,*
> *Spectetur meritis quaeque puella suis.*[3]

---

[1] Γυναικεῖον, 414–15; cf. 'a very reverent Matron on *Clarkenwell-
Green*, good at many things' (*Wise Woman*, Pearson, v. 292). Other
picturesque acquaintances are mentioned in *Philocothonista*, 71, 75, and
perhaps in Γυναικεῖον, 103.

[2] Described in his will as of the parish of St. James, Clerkenwell. Heywood was both a witness to the will and one of Greene's 'fellowes of the
house of the redd Bull' to whom he left 40s. to buy gloves.

[3] *Apology*, 43–4.

We cannot say whether any children were born to the dramatist and his wife before his removal to Clerkenwell, but on March 30, 1608, 'Isbell d. of Thomas Haywood' was christened. On September 16, 1609, his child Mary, christened on the previous March 8, was buried. A son Nicholas was christened on December 29, 1611, another son Robert on June 18, 1613, and a daughter Anne on March 26, 1615. A certain Henry Heywood, son of Thomas Heywood and christened on March 26, 1615, may have been a twin to Anne. There is no sign in Clerkenwell till 1639 of a second Thomas Heywood, perhaps the dramatist's son.[1] Edmond Hayward, buried at St. James's on September 1, 1636, may be another son, named after his great-uncle, and born like the just mentioned Thomas before their father's residence in Clerkenwell. There were two Henry Heywoods, one already noticed and another, son of Walter, christened on January 6, 1614/15; one or other married a certain Frances and had several children between 1647 and 1661.[2]

By 1608–9 the Queen's men had lost their place as the second company in London and were more and more forced to appeal to a less sophisticated, less refined, and less generous civic audience than the companies under the patronage of the King and Prince Henry; and even from the beginning of James's reign they were not favourites at court.[3] A year or two after their occupation

[1] Or of Richard Heywood, christened Dec. 3, 1615. His children by his wife Elizabeth were Susanna, Thomas, John, Jane, Richard, and Elizabeth, christened respectively on Mar. 31, 1639, Dec. 6, 1640, Mar. 30, 1645, Oct. 22, 1648, May 29, 1651, and July 14, 1654.

[2] A male child buried Sept. 4, 1647, and Frances, Henry, Andrewe, and Katherin, christened respectively on Aug. 16, 1648, Sept. 11, 1650, May 23, 1656, and July 7, 1661. In view of Heywood's acquaintance with artists—Peacham, the Christmas family, Gething the calligraphist, Paine, Glover, and perhaps William Marshall—it may be noted that an obscure artist, Heywood by name, in 1650 made a portrait of Fairfax, once in the possession of Brian Fairfax; a draft of it by James Hulet 'was produced to the Society of Antiquaries by Mr. Peck in 1739' (Horace Walpole, *Works*, ed. 1793, iii. 279).

[3] Their court appearances were as follows: Jan. 2 and 13, 1603/4, before Prince Henry; Dec. 30, 1604, before the King (*How to Learn of a Woman*

of the newly built Red Bull began,[1] that is from 1608 on,
their fortunes seem to have mended a little. They were
summoned to court again in 1608 after an absence of
three years, and Webster wrote for them *The White Devil*,
probably the year after. On its publication in 1612
Webster added a preface in which he approves 'that full
and haightned stile of maister CHAPMAN, the labor'd
and understanding workes of maister Johnson, the no
lesse worthy composures of the both worthily excellent
maister Beamont and maister Fletcher; and lastly (without wrong last to be named), the right happy and copious
industry of m. Shake-speare, m. Decker, and m. Heywood'. Of these, if we include Webster himself, the eight
most eminent in the dramatic brotherhood, the Queen's
men retained three, Heywood, Webster for a time, and
Dekker, who continued to write with unabated zest for
his 'loving friends and fellows',[2] till his weary imprisonment in 1613. Another notable success in these brief
years of prosperity was Cooke's *City Gallant*, or *Greene's
Tu Quoque* as it was renamed in honour of 'the lean fool
of the Bull',[3] Thomas Greene, who played the part of
Bubble.[4]

But it was Heywood himself who seems to have contributed most to his company's success at this time. *The
Rape of Lucrece* was a palpable hit, but along with *Appius
and Virginia* only a preliminary exercise in the classics
before the elaborate cycle of *The Ages*. This statement
runs counter to practically all works since Fleay's *Biographical Chronicle*[5] which have touched on the sequence

to Woo, by Heywood); Dec. 30, 1605, before the King; Christmas 1608/9,
five times before the King and Prince Henry, Dec. 27, 1609, before the
King; Dec. 10, 1610, three plays before Prince Henry; and Dec. 27, 1610,
before the King'(Chambers, iv. 120, &c., 173, &c.).

[1] Chambers, ii. 232, 445–7.
[2] Dedication of *If It be not a Good Play*.
[3] W. Turner, *A Dish of Stuff or a Gallimaufry*, 1662, quoted by Fleay,
Stage, 375.
[4] Played by the Queen's men at court before the King and Queen on
Dec. 27, 1611, and Feb. 2, 1611/12 (Chambers, iv. 125–6, 178).
[5] i. 284–5.

and dates of Heywood's plays. Fleay supposed that *The Golden, Silver, Brazen,* and *Iron Ages,* were originally written between 1595 and 1597 and are to be identified with plays mentioned during these years by Henslowe.[1] The evidence in refutation of this theory is so overwhelming that we are forced simply to assert here that *The Ages* are, beyond the shadow of a doubt, dramatizations of Heywood's own *Troia Britannica,* 1609 (S.R. December 5, 1608). As the theatres were closed continuously from the middle of 1608 till the end of 1609, it is possible that the grand reopening of the Red Bull was with the first of the series. Heywood had just time to legitimize the edition of it in 1611 (S.R. October 14) as *The Golden Age: or The Lives of Jupiter and Saturn, with the defining* [in some copies '*deifying*'] *of the Heathen Gods. As it hath been sundry times acted at the Red Bull by the Queen's Majesty's Servants.* He was not seriously annoyed by the forced publication, for in 1612 he gave Nicholas Okes, who probably printed it for William Barrenger, peculiar praise as a craftsman and continued on friendly terms with him to the end of his life. The address had concluded with a promise to publish the rest of the series then written, provided that a sufficiently encouraging reception was accorded to *The Golden Age,* 'the eldest brother of three Ages, that have adventured the Stage'. After an interval of two years appeared with the full authority of the dramatist *The Silver Age. Including The Love of Jupiter to Alcmena: The birth of Hercules, and the Rape of Proserpine, concluding with the Arraignment of the Moon.* He had now determined to give the whole series to the world: 'Though wee begunne with *Gold,*' he says, 'follow with *Silver,* proceede with *Brasse,* and purpose by God's grace, to end with *Iron,* I hope the declining Titles shall no whit blemish the reputation of the Workes.' The next member of the series, *The Brazen Age. The First Act containing the Death of the Centaur Nessus. The Second the tragedy of Meleager: The Third the Tragedy of Jason and Medea. The Fourth Vulcan's*

[1] i. 284–7.

Net, The Fifth The Labours and Death of Hercules, followed
the same year. But the two parts of *The Iron Age* were
probably still too popular and were withheld till 1632,
when the first appeared as *The Iron Age: Containing the
Rape of Helen: The Siege of Troy: The Combat betwixt
Hector and Ajax: Hector and Troilus slain by Achilles:
Achilles slain by Paris: Ajax and Ulysses contend for the
Armour of Achilles: The Death of Ajax, &c.*, and the second
with the no less sanguinary title, *The Second Part of the
Iron Age: Which containeth the Death of Penthesilea, Paris,
Priam, and Hecuba: The Burning of Troy: The Deaths
of Agamemnon, Menelaus, Clytemnestra, Helena, Orestes,
Aegisthus, Pylades, King Diomed, Pyrrhus, Cethus, Sinon,
Thersites, &c.* In recalling them to the light of day, for
they may not have been acted since the dissolution of
Queen Anne's company soon after 1619, Heywood refers
to the first three *Ages* and adds '*This* Iron Age . . . *beginneth
where the others left . . . I desire thee to take notice that these
were the Playes often (and not with the least applause,)
Publickely Acted by two Companies, uppon one Stage at once,
and have at sundry times thronged three severall Theatres,
with numerous and mighty Auditories*'.[1] Fleay's assumption
was that records of performances of *The Iron Age*, to
which alone he understands Heywood's words to apply,
by the Admiral's and Lord Pembroke's companies in
1597, were made by Henslowe on pages now missing
from the *Diary*. But it is incredible that, even if these
elaborate plays had been in existence at the time, they
should have been presented in a partnership that lasted
only from October 11 to November 5.[2] It is as absurd
to limit Heywood's boast to the last two pieces of the
pentalogy; he had been speaking of the whole series,
every member of which would require more actors and
properties than one company could muster. Professor
J. Q. Adams, who takes the statement as referring to all
The Ages and assumes that they were written between

[1] Address to pt. i.
[2] See Fleay, i. 284–5, and *Shakespeare*, 222–3, Chambers, ii. 132–3,
156, and Murray, i. 68–70, 125, for the Admiral-Pembroke combination.

1610 and 1612, more plausibly argues that the 'three severall Theatres' were not, as Fleay held, the Rose, the Curtain, and the Red Bull, but the Red Bull, the Curtain, and either the Globe or the Blackfriars.[1] In any case we know that on Sunday and Monday, January 12 and 13, 1611/12, the combined King's and Queen's companies presented *The Silver Age* and *Lucretia* (i.e. *The Rape of Lucrece*) before Queen Anne and Prince Henry.[2] It is practically certain that these plays had been performed in public by the two royal companies before their appearance at court; and it is not unlikely that the other *Ages* were staged in the same way. In commending part II of *The Iron Age* to the reader Heywood showed himself conscious that the taste of the Carolines was rather for 'Satirica Dictaeria, *and* Comica Scommata'; but he was in no doubt of the real merits of his work '*long since writ*', for he looked forward to the fulfilment of his printer's promise to publish all *The Ages* together in '*an handsome Volume*' to be illustrated '*with an Explanation of all the difficulties, and an Historicall Comment of every hard name, which may appear obscure or intricate to such as are not frequent in Poetry*'.[3] We have been spared[4] what would no doubt have been a long, garrulous, mythological miscellany of the kind Heywood loved, either because of the public's lack of support or because the poet was

[1] *Shakespeare, Heywood, and the Classics. M.L.N.* xxxiv. 336, &c. Sir E. K. Chambers (iii. 345) thinks that Heywood referred only to *The Iron Age*, and that the three theatres were the Red Bull, the Curtain, and the Cockpit.

[2] Cunningham, *Extracts from the Accounts of the Revels at Court*, xli. 210, and Chambers, iv. 126, 178, from *Audit Office Account*, Various, 3, 907. These accounts have been suspected as forgeries; see Chambers, iv. 136, &c., for a *résumé* of the controversy. Fortunately we discovered a piece of evidence, hitherto overlooked, in Bodley: Malone 248, no less than the unimpeachable authority of a note by Malone that *The Silver Age* at least was played before the King and Queen at Greenwich by the King's and Queen's players on Jan. 7, 1611/12 (*sic*) 'as appears in Sir George Buc's accounts'.

[3] Cf. *Hierarchy*, 31.

[4] Cf. Langbaine, 259, and *Momus Triumphans*, 11.

diverted from his editing by the anti-theatrical explosion
of Prynne. Old as *The Iron Age* was in 1632, Heywood
considered the two parts as not unworthy tributes to
dedicate to two personal friends, and inscribed the first
to his 'Worthy and much Respected Friend, Mr. *Thomas
Hammon*, of Grayes Inne Esquire'[1] and the other to
'Mr. *Thomas Mannering* Esquire'.[2] Complacent phrases
in the prefaces to the earlier plays of the pentalogy show
that he had looked on his work and decided that it was
good. In *An Apology for Actors* he is even more enthusiastic
and declares that the representation on the stage of the
antique heroes might well make the moderns heroes too;
'to see a *Hector* all besmered in blood, trampling upon the
bulkes of kinges. A *Troylus* returning from the field in
the sight of his father *Priam* as if man and horse . . . had
bene together plunged into a purple Ocean. . . . To see as
I have seene, *Hercules* in his owne shape hunting the
Boare, knocking downe the Bull, taming the Hart, fighting
with Hydra, murdering *Gerion*, slaughtring *Diomed*,
wounding the Stimphalides, killing the Centaurs, pashing
the Lion, squeezing the Dragon, dragging *Cerberus* in
Chaynes, and, lastly, on his Pyramides writing *Nil ultra*,
Oh these were sights to make an *Alexander*'.[3] These
classical figures were still running through his brain
when in distinguished company he contributed verses to
the *Minerva Britanna*, 1612, of his Cambridge contemporary, Henry Peacham, and in 1613 when he lamented
with Trojan parallels for most of the royal family the
death of Prince Henry, and again the next year when he
celebrated the marriage of the Lady Elizabeth. The same

---

[1] Thomas Hammon[d] 'of Ashe, Suffolk, gent.' admitted to Gray's Inn
on Oct. 29, 1611, was probably the son of Thomas Hammond who became sergeant-at-law in 1589; the son was called to the bar on June 26,
1617, and became an ancient on May 4, 1638. We have traced the following Thomas Hammonds in Suffolk: (1) 1583–1640 (will dated Aug. 31,
1638, and proved at Sudbury on Aug. 31, 1640) m. Susan, daughter and
coheir of Francis Asty of Market Weston, and buried at Hawkstead;
(2) of Hawkedon; (3) of Wetherden; (4) of East Bergholt; (5) of Great
Wallingfield.

[2] See 5-6 *supra* and 85 *infra*.   [3] 19–20.

year Thomas Freeman[1] seized the epigrammatist's chance
in the discrepancy between the precious titles of the first
two *Ages* and the poet's actual poverty, in the lines '*To
his Worthy friend Maister* Heywood, *of his Gold and
Silver Age*':

> So wrote the ancient Poets heeretofore,
> So hast thou lively furnished the stage,
> Both with the golden and the silver age,
> Yet thou as they, dost but discourse of store,
>> Silver and gold is common to your Poet,
>> To have it, no; enough for him to know it.

Though the time was auspicious for further essays,

---

[1] He left Oxford for London (Wood's *Fasti*, ed. Bliss, i. 341) and a literary
career when Heywood's *Ages* were being staged. His ambitions, however,
issued only in his book of passable epigrams, *Run and a Great Cast*. The
quotation is from pt. II, *Run and a Great Cast*. Cf. Mennes and Smith's
Choice Drollery, 1656, ed. Ebsworth, 6:

> Haywood, sage, . . .
> Well of the Golden age he could intreat,
> But little of the Mettall he could get.

Callisto or The Escapes of Jupiter, consisting of scenes from *The Golden*
and *Silver Ages* but differing considerably from the quartos, appears in
B.M.: MS. Egerton 1994; see W. W. Greg, '*The Escapes of Jupiter*':
an autograph play of Thomas Heywood, Anglica (*Palaestra*, cxlviii) and
91 *infra*. Sir E. K. Chambers (ii. 286, iii. 345) thinks an *Amphitryo*,
presented by English actors at Dresden in 1626, may be *The Silver Age* or
be based on it. Davenant in the prologue to *The Unfortunate Lovers*, 1643,
may be alluding to *The Iron Age*:

> with what delight
> They would expect a jig, or target fight,
> A furious tale of Troy, which they ne'er thought
> Was weakly written, so 'twere strongly fought.

The following *Age* ballads appear in S.R.: Nov. 16, 1621, '*The silver Age*'
(or *The World turned backward*, Pepys ballads, i. 154) and '*the brasen age*'
(Rollins, *Pepysian Garland*, 234); Dec. 14, 1624, and Aug. 4, 1626, '*The
age of the world*'; May 24, 1632, '*The honest age*' (by Laurence Price, to the
tune of *The Golden Age or An Age of Plain-dealing*, Rollins, *op. cit.* 406);
and Jan. 11, 1633/4, '*The Phantasticke Age*' (R.B. iii. 147). *The wiving age*
by John Cast, to the tune of *The Golden Age* (Chappell, *Popular Music*, i.
208) was printed at least as early as 1625 because the second part was from
the press of John Trundle. Cf. Fletcher's *Coxcomb*, ii. 2, 'This is the iron
age the ballad sings of'. See also S.R. July 26, 1658, for '*Greece & Troy*',
i.e. *The Greeks' & Trojans' Wars* by H(umphrey) C(rouch) of Mar. 1,
1674/5 (*R.B.* vi. 543).

now that Heywood had become a figure of some little importance in the literary world, yet it was not a desire for literary reputation that induced him to undertake a defence of the stage but some pressure from circumstances at which we can only guess. He whose 'pen hath seldom appeared in presse till now'[1] would much rather have committed to the senior members of the profession the task of attacking its adversaries, yet 'a kind of necessity', he adds, 'enjoyned me to so sudden a businesse'.[1] Probably he was strongly persuaded to overcome his apologetic modesty by the solicitations of his 'good Friends and Fellowes, the Citty-Actors', to whom he addressed a prefatory letter and with whom he proudly associates himself; they were no doubt the 'well qualified favorers' whose persuasions were an equal inducement with his desire to stop 'the envious acclamations of those who chalenge to them-selves a priviledged invective, and against all free estates a railing liberty'.[2] But the situation is obscure, for though no doubt the preachers preached and the civic authorities grumbled, there was no literary campaign in 1612 for the suppression of the theatres. Heywood's casual allusion to 'any succeeding Adversary'[3] suggests that the pamphlet was issued to anticipate the breaking of puritan vials; and Sir E. K. Chambers very reasonably argues that the treatise was originally composed in 1607 and retouched in 1608,[4] when indeed the enemies of the quality were more threatening; we may supplement his argument with the following considera-

---

[1] To the reader.   [2] 16–17.

[3] To the reader. He hints at 'lavish and violent' criticism of governmental control of the stage, 16. Webster's lines suggest fear of new exactions and severer plague inhibitions.

[4] iv. 250: 'Since (*a*) the series of actors named as dead ends with Sly, who died in Aug. 1608; (*b*) the Revels Office is located at St. John's, which it lost about Feb. 1608; (*c*) the frustrated Spanish landing in "Perin" in Cornwall "some 12 yeares ago" is probably the abortive Spanish attempt to burn Pendennis Castle on Falmouth Harbour, 3 miles from Penrhyn, which appears from *S.P.D. Eliz.* cclvi. 21, 40, and Dasent, xxv. 15, to have taken place in the autumn of 1595, probably in connexion with the better-known landing of July 22, 1595, in Mount's Bay.' Sir E. K. Chambers notices earlier raids in 1595–6.

tions. That the Queen's men in 1608 owed something to the countenance of Sir Thomas Somerset, their late patron's third son, perhaps in a brush with the authorities or in securing their return to court after having been passed over in the festivities of 1606–7 and a new patent dated April 15, 1609, we gather from Heywood's words in his dedication of his translation of Sallust; and we may perhaps suppose that the 'second worke', which Heywood in *Troia Britannica* [1] says he was dedicating to the Earl of Worcester, was no other than *An Apology for Actors*, though he delayed its publication for three years. Heywood's condemnation at the very end of his pamphlet of those who commit 'their bitternesse, and liberall invectives against all estates, to the mouthes of children' was much more appropriate in 1608, when after a series of indiscretions the Children of the Queen's Revels at Blackfriars, partly no doubt because of two plays representing respectively James I and the Queen of France on the stage, surrendered their theatre to the King's men about August. Whenever it was written, Heywood's *Apology* has the tone of a work produced in anticipation of, not in retaliation for, a new attack on the position and privileges of his class. For, though he avows himself to be 'Moved by the sundry exclamations of many seditious sectists in this age, who, in the fatnes and ranknes of a peacable commonwealth, grow up like unsavory tufts of grasse', [2] and strives 'to make good a subiect, which many through envy, but most through ignorance, have sought violently (and beyond merit) to oppugne', [3] yet neither in 1612 nor in 1608, unless we except William Crashaw's *Sermon preached at the Cross, Feb. xiiii. 1607* (i.e. 1607/8), [4] nor indeed since the end of the previous century had there been any danger to the theatres from puritan agitation. In fact the improved status of the actors, resulting largely from their reception

---

[1] Sig. Ee 4.   [2] 16.   [3] Dedication.

[4] Printed in 1608 and again in 1609; cf. Chambers, iv. 249. Sir Edward Coke, in his *Charge at Norwich*, 1607, complained of the manner in which the country was troubled with players, and denounced them from the bench.

into the patronage of the royal family, the greater literary worth of their plays, the increased decorum of their performances, and lastly the more effective control exercised over the theatres by the Master of the Revels removed many causes of offence and gave the civic authorities, who may have fomented puritanic attacks on plays and players in the past, less cause to complain. The theatre both gained and lost by the direct patronage of the crown and the extended authority of the Master of the Revels; for while on the one hand the wealthier citizens and still more their wives looked with a more favourable eye on the now fashionable and therefore respectable theatres, the stage was ceasing to be a national institution and was becoming more and more dependent on the court, more restricted in its appeal, and in reality no more acceptable to an ever-increasing body of puritans. But for the moment the actors occupied an impregnable position and in consequence Heywood's pamphlet, though he deliberately widened the issue, is a little old-fashioned in its answers to arguments that had in 1608 or 1612 little force or novelty.

It is, therefore, rather surprising to find Heywood at the very flourishing of the drama in England open his treatise with a melancholy vision of Melpomene, 'Her heyre rudely disheveled, her chaplet withered, her visage with teares stayned, her brow furrowed, her eyes deiected, nay her whole complexion quite faded and altered'.[1] So far as the characters of the plays and the status of the actors were concerned, Heywood was practically the first advocate of the stage to have a really good case; to which advantage he added a thorough knowledge of the theatrical conditions. Lodge's *Honest Excuses* was by one probably still unacquainted with the theatre from within, and certainly writing in the still untutored infancy of the drama. Sidney had a genial contempt for the plays of his own day and admits that they were 'not without cause cried out against'.[2] Greene was too much concerned with

[1] 17.   [2] *Defence of Poesy*, ed. Shuckburgh, 63.

the enormities of certain players,[1] and with jealousy of
Shakespeare,[2] to spare more than a few words in praise
of the stage,[3] while Sir John Harington,[4] Gager,[5] and
Gentili,[6] were defending the academic drama. Only
Nashe appears to have had any idea that the contemporary
drama was literature. His epistle *To the Gentlemen
Students of Both Universities*, prefixed to Greene's *Menaphon*, 1589, praises several 'sweete gentlemen' for their
plays;[7] but it was three years later, three years during
which the English drama really burst its chrysalis, that
Nashe anticipated the most interesting passages of Heywood's *Apology*. His *Piers Penniless his Supplication to
Devil* adds to the usual moral plea the patriotic argument
that the subject was '(for the most part) . . . borrowed out
of our English Chronicles, wherein our forefathers valiant
acts (that have line long buried in rustie brasse and
worme-eaten bookes) are revived, and they themselves
raised from the Grave of Oblivion, and brought to pleade
their aged Honours in open presence: than which, what
can be a sharper reproofe to these degenerate effeminate
dayes of ours?'.[8] Coincidentally the stage was acquiring
respectability, and Nashe can boast 'Our Players are not
as the players beyond Sea, a sort of squirting baudie
Comedians', but such as Alleyn, Tarlton, Knell, and
Bentley. Heywood, however, had witnessed still greater
triumphs of the drama. It was, therefore, natural that he
shifted the debate a little from the question of the lawfulness and propriety of the drama to a justification of the
profession with which he was proud to identify himself,
and to express the wish 'that such as are cōdemned for
their licentiousnesse, might by a generall consent bee
quite excluded our society: for as we are men that stand

[1] e.g. *Francesco's Fortunes*, ed. Grosart, viii. 132; *A Quip for an Upstart
Courtier*, ix. 289; and *A Groatsworth of Wit*, xii. 131.

[2] *A Groatsworth*, &c. To his quondam acquaintance.

[3] e.g. *A Quip*, &c., ed. Grosart, xi. 289.

[4] *Apology for Poetry*, prefixed to his *Ariosto*.

[5] *Th' Overthrow of Stage Plays*.   [6] *Ibid*.

[7] Ed. McKerrow, iii. 323; cf. 315 and Chettle's preface to *Kind
Heart's Dream*.   [8] Ed. McKerrow, i. 261.

in the broad eye of the world, so should our manners, gestures, and behaviours, savour of such government and modesty, to deserve the good thoughts and reports of all men, and to abide the sharpest censures, even of those that are the greatest opposites to the quality'. In words that recall Gosson's admission[1] he adds, 'Many amongst us, I know, to be of substance, of governement, of sober lives, and temperate carriages, house-keepers, and contributory to all duties enioyned them, equally with them that are rank't with the most bountifull; and if amongst so many of that sort, there be any few degenerate from the rest in that good demeanor, which is both requisite & expected at their hands, let me entreate you not to censure hardly of all for the misdeeds of some'.[2]

Besides the advantages which he derived from the fact that he wrote when the drama had become literature and the profession of acting respectable, Heywood had personal qualifications which made him an ideal apologist. An experienced dramatist and a shareholder in a royal company, he was also university-bred, a student, a writer unlike Lodge and Nashe of unblemished character; he was both in origin and in sympathies essentially middle-class; his common sense and culture, his humour, and his modesty, completely absolved him from the temptations which beset disputants, while his humanity, his timidity, and his persuasive friendliness, make his essay a remarkable document in the debate. Except in the contributions of Sidney who was studiously vague and of Lodge whose generosity to Gosson was perhaps a wise measure to disarm a strong enemy, the controversy had been as acrimonious as most disputes of the day. Though Heywood had himself introduced general strictures on the puritans, he sincerely echoed the complaint of the printer of Th' Overthrow of Stage Plays that some 'have not bene afraied of late dayes to bring upon the stage the very sober countenances, grave attire, modest and matronelike gestures & speaches of men & weomen to be laughed at as a scorne and reproch to the world', when he reproved

---

[1] *School of Abuse*, ed. Collier, 29. [2] 43–4.

those who inveighed 'against the State, the Court, the Law, the Citty and their governements, with the particularizing of private mens humors (yet alive), Noble-men, & others' and committed their railing to the mouths of children.[1] Yet there is no dubiety in Heywood over the rights of his case: it is only the nature of the man that keeps his pamphlet kindly. As for his acquaintance with dramatic history, he shows an impressive off-hand knowledge. From Stowe he derives details of royal patronage back to the reign of Richard II. He knows, perhaps from provincial tours, that 'there be townes that hold the priviledge of their faires, and other charters by yearely stage-playes, as at Manningtree in Suffolke [*sic*], Kendall in the north, and others'.[2] He has collected as an offset to the puritanical list of divine judgements other anecdotes which tell how

> guilty creatures sitting at a play
> Have by the very cunning of the scene
> Been struck so to the soul that presently
> They have proclaimed their malefactions:
> For murder, though it have no tongue, will speak
> With most miraculous organ;

and tells how the drums of a theatrical company in Cornwall terrified a party of marauding Spaniards.[3] Like Nashe he singles out for special praise among English actors Alleyn, Tarlton,[4] Knell, and Bentley, to whom he adds Tobias Mils, Robert Wilson,[5] Crosse, and John Laneham, all but Alleyn being before his own time, and Kemp, Gabriel Spencer, Singer, Pope, Phillips, and William Sly, his contemporaries.[6] He alludes to the English actors in the pay of the Cardinal and Archduke Albert, Governor of the Spanish Netherlands, about 1608–12,[7] Frederick II of Denmark (father of Queen

---

[1] 61.   [2] 61.

[3] *Ibid.* 58: cf. Chambers, iv. 250.

[4] The praise of Tarlton immediately after that of Roscius suggests that Heywood knew John Case's *Sphaera Civitatis*, vii. caput 17.

[5] See Chambers, ii. 349–50 for the identity of this Wilson.

[6] 43.   [7] 60.

Anne, patroness of Heywood's company), whose company
was 'commended unto him by the honourable the Earle
of Leicester', Henry Julius, Duke of Brunswick-Wolfen-
büttel, and Maurice the Learned, Landgrave of Hesse-
Cassel.[1] Certain remarks even indicate some slight
acquaintance with theatrical conditions in Italy, France,
and Spain.[2]

Though Heywood obviously knew well the earlier
pamphlets, he mentions none of the theatrophobes by
name, and of the theatrophils only *famous* Scalliger,
learned Doctor Gager, *Doctor* Gentiles';[3] and though he
says he has altogether omitted the latter *'because I am
loath to bee taxed in borrowing from others'*,[4] yet *An Apology
for Actors* is largely a repetition or a refutation of arguments which had been advanced by one side or the other
in the prolonged debate. If he leaves untouched the problem of Plato's opposition to poets which Sidney had
sufficiently solved, he tries, not very successfully, to dis-
credit Marcus Aurelius,[5] whose enmity to shows had been
interpreted from the time of Gosson's *Plays Confuted*[6] as
proof positive of his contempt for the stage. Like Northbrooke,[7] he mentions the fame of Roscius, his approval
by Cicero, and his princely pension, though he turns these
facts to a very different use,[8] and boldly tranfers to his
side with the same hazardous quotation from the *De Arte
Amandi* the anecdote of the founding of the theatre in
Rome by Romulus.[9] From Munday he may have drawn
an allusion to the antiquity of the theatre and perhaps
defended the players from Munday's accusations of loose-
ness and immorality.[10] Lodge, too, insists on the antiquity
of the drama and etymologizes the words 'tragedy' and
'comedy' after Donatus, whose attribution to Cicero of

---

[1] 40.   [2] 40, 60; cf. prologue to *A Challenge for Beauty*.
[3] 4; he quotes Harington's *Apology* without naming him, 55.
[4] 4.   [5] 26.
[6] 24, 32; cf. Northbrooke, *Treatise*, ed. Collier, 28.
[7] 29.   [8] 42.
[9] 21–3; cf. Northbrooke, 31, and *School of Abuse*, ed. Collier, 19.
[10] 43–4: cf. *A second and third blast of retreat*, 151.

the famous definition of comedy as 'imitatio vitæ, speculum consuetudinis et imago veritatis' Lodge quotes,[1] Gosson questions,[2] Shakespeare paraphrases,[3] and Heywood repeats with the afore-mentioned etymologies in a passage obviously from Lodge.[4] The stock objections to the dressing of men in women's garments,[5] the advantages of academic plays which the earlier humanists had admitted and only such stubborn opponents of the theatre as Gosson[6] and Rainolds[7] had disapproved, the praises of Terence and Plautus,[8] the moral uses of the stage, all the usual authorities, texts, and theatrical commonplaces were at Heywood's finger-ends.[9] He could make even more than Nashe of the contemporary drama, the 'many famous histories . . . from *William* the *Conqueror*, nay from the landing of *Brute* untill this day',[10] the stories of Midas, and Nero, Sardanapalus, Ninus, Pompey, Horatius, Phæton, Narcissus, Belphœbe, Rosamund, Matilda, the Countess of Salisbury, and 'M. Kid's' *Spanish Tragedy*.[11] With pardonable pride he even alludes to his own success: 'to see a *Hector* all besmered in blood, trampling upon the bulkes of kinges. A *Troylus* returning from the field in the sight of his father *Priam* as if man and horse even from the steeds rough fetlockes to the plume of the champions helmet had bene together plunged into a purple Ocean . . . To see as I have seene, *Hercules* in his own shape hunting the Boare, knocking downe the Bull, taming the Hart, fighting with Hydra, murdering *Gerion*, slaughtring

---

[1] Sig. C 2–C 3; cf. prologue to Richard Edwardes's *Damon and Pythias*.

[2] *Plays Confuted*, sig. C 4.

[3] *Hamlet*, iii. 2.   [4] 49–50.

[5] Northbrooke, 36; and *Plays Confuted*, sig. E 5, &c.

[6] *Plays Confuted*, sig. D 8; for the humanists see Chambers, i. 239.

[7] *Passim*; Northbrooke admits school plays but is doubtful of the academic drama, 37.

[8] Cf. Erasmus's *Epistolae*, xxxi; Vives's *Commentary on St. Augustine's De Civitate Dei*, viii. 27; Elyot's *Governor*, ed. Croft, i. 123; Ascham's *Schoolmaster*, ed. Wright, 238, &c.

[9] His knowledge of English literature apart from the theatrical dispute was extensive; see 44, 55.

[10] 52–3.   [11] 45.

Diomed, wounding the Stimphalides, killing the Centaurs, pashing the Lion, squeezing the Dragon, dragging *Cerberus* in Chaynes, and lastly on his high Pyramides writing *Nil ultra*, Oh these were sights to make an *Alexander*': [1] there are, too, 'the destruction of *Troy* in the lust of *Helena*', 'the falle of the *Tarquins*, in the rape of *Lucrece*', '*Appius* destroyed in the ravishing of *Virginia*', and the fate of Mistress Shore. [2]

As Sir E. K. Chambers remarks, 'however much the Puritans and the humanists might disagree, they were at one in referring their judgement of the drama to purely ethical standards of value, and . . . the conception of aesthetic value, which means so much for modern thought, was in the main beyond the scope of Elizabethan criticism'. [3] For Heywood, as for such profounder critics as Sidney and Jonson, literature was primarily an affair of didacticism. He counters the arguments of Gosson and his kind with others no less loyal to the neo-classic conception of the function of literature. When Heywood defends literature on other grounds he is unconsciously straining the bonds of a narrow creed, but usually he makes no complaints in his theory. Thus in the blank-verse speech of Melpomene he gives a summary of the standard moral arguments for the stage, [4] and so far as he argues from moral grounds later he does little more than expand and illustrate with ancient saws and modern instances, concluding that 'there is neither Tragedy, History, Comedy, Morrall or Pastorall, from which an infinite use cannot be gathered'. [5] It is of course just because both parties to the dispute were puritans in the modern sense of the word and concerned primarily with the ethical side of the question that the strife appears to us so unreal.

---

[1] 20–1.   [2] 56–7.   [3] i. 259–60.

[4] Cf. e.g. William Bavande's *Work of Joannes Ferrarius Montanus touching the good ordering of a Commonweal*, 100 verso, which first laid down in English the main ethical lines of defence; Whetstone's dedication of *Promos and Cassandra*; Sidney, *Defence of Poesy*, ed. Shuckburgh, 44; and Webbe, *Discourse of English Poetry*, ed. Arber, 42.

[5] 54.

'No one can pretend that Shakespeare and his fellow playwrights troubled themselves about theories of conduct. The defenders of the stage made pitiful attempts to justify their craft upon moral principles; but, in admitting the subordination of art to ethics, they had yielded their whole position. Had puritans only studied the theatre more and the early fathers less, they might, starting with the premisses which their antagonists gave them, have made out a much better case for prosecution. They had all the logic on their side. On the side of the apologists was all the commonsense—if they could only have seen it.' [1]

Heywood needed less space for the defence of the academic stage since he had convinced himself that it was 'none of the gravest, and most ancient Doctors of the Academy, but onely a sort of finde-faults' [2] who opposed it. But he takes the opportunity to digress from the confidence and self-control which acting gives to a discussion in Hamlet's vein on the qualifications of an actor.[3] The task of deducing the stage *from more then two thousand yeeres agoe* [4]—one may doubt the validity of some of the examples—was almost a moral argument for an age which regarded a string of authorities as cogent as a syllogism; so Heywood leaves his record of antiquity, the sumptuous theatres and the noble patrons, 'to the favourable consideration of the wise, though to the per-verseness of the ignorant, who had they any taste either of Poesie, Phylosophy, or Historicall Antiquity, would rather stand mated at their owne impudent ignorance, then against such noble, and notable examples stand in publicke defiance'.[5]

But in one or two of Heywood's pleas for toleration he almost forgets to moralize. Once indeed he seems to catch a glimpse of the joy which art can give:

'To speake my opinion with all indifferency, God hath not enioyned us to weare all our apparel solely to defend the cold.

---

[1] Dover Wilson, *The Puritan Attack upon the Stage*, C.H.E.L. vi. 409.
[2] 30.   [3] 29–30; cf. 43 and John Case, *Sphæra Civitatis*, v. cap. 8.
[4] 4; cf. 34, &c., with Whetstone's dedication to *Promos and Cassandra*
[5] 36; cf. Lodge, *Honest Excuses, passim*, and also the dedications of *The Iron Age*, pt. I, and *The English Traveller*, and a prologue written soon after Prynne's *Histriomastix* (*Pleasant Dialogues*, 235–6).

Some garments we weare for warmth, others for ornament . . .
That purity is not look't for at our hands, being mortall and humane,
that is required of the Angels, being celestiall and divine. God
made us of earth, men; knowes our natures, dispositions and
imperfections, and therefore hath limited us a time to reioyce, as
hee hath enioyned us a time to mourne for our transgressiõs. And
I hold them more scrupulous then well advised, that goe about to
take from us the use of all moderate recreations. Why hath God
ordained for men, varietie of meates, dainties and delicates, if not
to taste thereon? why doth the world yeeld choyce of honest
pastimes, if not decently to use them? Was not the Hare made to
be hunted? the Stagge to be chaced; and so of all other beasts of
game in their severall kindes? since God hath provided us of these
pastimes, why may wee not use them to his glory?' [1]

The same commonsense appears in his reply to those who
objected on Scriptural grounds to the dressing of boys as
women.[2] He very neatly turns the tables on his Bible-
quoting adversaries by noting also that though 'the
spacious Theatres were in the greatest opinion amongst
the Romans; yet neither Christ himselfe, nor any of his
sanctified Apostles, in any of their Sermons, Acts, or
Documents, so much as named them, or upon any abusive
occasion, touched them'.[3] It was as novel an argument
that states prosper when theatres flourish. Still more so
was the triad of arguments towards the end of the pamphlet. The first of these, already alluded to, was that
'playes have made the ignorant more apprehensive, taught
the unlearned the knowledge of many famous histories,
[and] instructed such as cañot reade in the discovery of
all our *English* Chronicles'.[4] In the first he boldly declares
that 'playing is an ornament to the Citty, which strangers
of all Nations, repairing hither, report in their Countries,
beholding them here with some admiration: for what
variety of entertainment can there be in any Citty of
Christendome, more then in London?' [5] It is greatly to
Heywood's credit that he had the penetration to adduce

    [1] 25; cf. *Plays Confuted*, sig. G, and Jos. Wibarne's *New Age of Old
Names*, 125-6.
    [2] 28; cf. Selden to Ben Jonson, Feb. 28, 1615/16, *Works*, ed. 1690, ii.
    [3] 24.   [4] 52.   [5] 52.

the remaining argument; 'our *English* tongue,' he says, 'which hath ben the most harsh, uneven, and broken language of the world . . . is now by this secondary meanes of playing, continually refined, every writer striving in himselfe, to adde a new flourish unto it; so that in processe, from the most rude and unpolisht tongue, it is growne to a most perfect and composed language, and many excellent workes, and elaborate Poems writ in the same, that many Nations grow inamored of our tongue (before despised). . . . Thus you see to what excellency our refined *English* is brought, that in these daies we are ashamed of that *Euphony* & eloquence which within these 60 yeares, the best tongues in the land were proud to pronounce'.[1] The improvement of English is occasionally referred to by others, but Heywood is the only critic who rightly attributes it in large measure to the drama. Great as were the services to the language of the non-dramatic writers, the dissemination of a rich and fluent vernacular which occurred in all countries at the Renaissance was in England due not least to the popular stage; to the constant experiments and freedom of the drama from hampering conventions we owe much of the sinewiness, the resourcefulness, the variety and vigour of our language.

After its long incubation the tract was published without licence[2] in 1612 as *An Apology for Actors. Containing three brief Treatises. 1 Their Antiquity. 2 Their ancient Dignity. 3 The true use of their quality*, with a familiarly respectful dedication to the Earl of Worcester. Heywood's friends rallied to his support with commendatory verses: *Aλ. Π.*, perhaps Alexander Preston, who may also have written the lines signed 'Anonymus, sive pessimus omnium Poëta', Ar. Hopton,[3] Richard Perkins, Christopher

---

[1] 52.

[2] Which led Prynne to say it was published by stealth, see 140 *infra*.

[3] Assumed to be Arthur Hopton (?1588–1614), a member of a Shrewsbury family, a writer on astrological and kindred subjects and a minor poet. He is confused by Wood (*Athenae Oxonienses*, ed. Bliss, ii. 151–2) with Sir Arthur Hopton (?1588–1650), who may quite well have been Heywood's admirer. He was the fifth son of Sir Arthur Hopton of Witham, Somerset, and Rachel, daughter of Edmund Hall of Gretford, Lincs.

Beeston, Robert Pallant, John Taylor, and Webster. The pamphlet sufficiently provoked the Puritans to call forth *A Refutation of the Apology for Actors. Divided into three brief Treatises. Wherein is confuted and opposed all the chief Grounds and Arguments alleged in defence of Plays: And withal in each Treatise is deciphered Actors,* 1. *Heathenish and diabolical institution.* 2. *Their ancient and modern indignity.* 3. *The wonderful abuse of their impious quality* in 1615, 'a Bundle of *Scolding Invectives,* and Railing, instead of *Reasoning*'.[1] But J. G.,[2] though he parodied Heywood and sneeringly referred to 'mr. Actor' and his abominable profession, had no scandal to publish of his antagonist.[3]

Such puny blows as J. G. could deliver were all in the game, but a few years earlier Heywood, in view of his budding reputation, was forced to protest against two literary thefts of which he was the victim. The expostulation in the preface to *The Brazen Age* was the second in point of time but may refer to an earlier offence. There Heywood accuses

[1] Langbaine, 270; cf. Baker, *The Theatre Vindicated,* 17.

[2] Usually expanded to J. Greene, but by Oldys (MS. note in Langbaine, 270: B.M.: C. 28. g. 1) to Gager, i.e. William Gager. J. G. could not have been one of the dedicators of *The Masque of Flowers,* 1614, to Bacon, but was probably the J.G. whose ' *booke of prayers and meditacons called steps of Ascension vnto GOD* ' was registered on Dec. 22, 1624. A J.G. in 1630 published *The Christian's Profession* and in 1643 *The First Man.*

[3] During the Commonwealth, William Cartwright, driven by the times from acting to bookselling, published the *Apology* as *The Actors' Vindication, Containing, Three brief Treatises,* &c. Cartwright, besides inserting a passage on Alleyn (29; cf. Oldys, MS. note in Langbaine, 256: B.M. : C. 28. g. 1.), substituted for the dedication to the Earl of Worcester, an extraordinarily mendacious one to the Marquess of Dorchester (see 6–7 *supra*), and to pass his farrago of nonsense gave only the initials of the writers of commendatory verses and omitted Heywood's letter to Nicholas Okes. Fleay (i. 279) seems to have believed that this edition appeared about Oct. 1633—the B.M. copy (E. 948 [4]) is dated in ink June 15, 1658—in fulfilment of the promise in the dedication of *The English Traveller* to vindicate the quality; and that there was a third edition in 1658. In *Theophilus Cibber to David Garrick with Dissertations on Theatrical Subjects,* 1759, is a passage of some length paraphrased without acknowledgement from Heywood's *Apology.*

'a Pedant about this Towne, who, when all trades fail'd, turn'd *Pedagogue*, & once insinuating with me, borrowed from me certaine Translations of *Ovid*, as his three books *De Arte Amandi*, & two *De Remedio Amoris*, which since, his most brazen face hath most impudently challenged as his own, wherefore I must needs pro-claime it as far as *Ham*, where he now keeps schoole, *Hos ego versiculos feci tulit alter honores*, they were things which out of iuniority and want of iudgement, I committed to the view of some private friends, but with no purpose of publishing, or further com-municating them. Therefore I wold entreate that *Austin*, for so his name is, to acknowledge his wrong to me in shewing them, & his owne impudence and ignorance in challenging them.'

The object in this instance of one of Heywood's rare bursts of anger, who has been given on scanty evidence the Christian name Henry, seems to have been a kind of literary jackal of the early seventeenth century, combining with his scholastic duties at (? West) Ham the procuring for booksellers such stray manuscripts as he could borrow or appropriate. Though Dr. Grosart may be right in identifying the modest editor H. A. of *The Scourge of Venus*, 1613, 1614, and 1620, with the impudent, plagiarizing pedagogue of Ham,[1] we have no evidence for doing so but the insignificant fact that both were publishers of others' work. *The Scourge of Venus* was not, however, as Grosart supposed, the obnoxious publication, of which we have found no less than eight editions.[2] What was probably the first was issued without imprint or date from some press in the Low Countries, most probably in Middelburg or Amsterdam, and with the title *Publii Ovidii Nasonis De Arte Amandi, Or, The Art of Love*. Another edition was printed by Nicholas Iansz Visscher at Amsterdam[3] as *Love's School*.[4] *Publii Ovidii Nasonis De*

[1] *Occasional Issues of Unique and Extremely Rare Books*: see also *D.N.B.*, article *Henry Austin*. In the 1620 ed. the initials are reversed.

[2] Originally reported in *Thomas Heywood's 'Art of Love' Lost and Found* (*Library*, 1922).

[3] In business from 1597–1637 (*Alfabetische Lijst der Boekdrukkers, Boek-verkoopers en Uitgevers in Noord-Nederland* ... door A. M. Ledeboer, 180).

[4] Cf. *How a Man*, &c., sig. C 2:

Never was such a trewant in Loves schoole,
I am asham'd that ere I was his Tutor.

Arte Amandi, or The Art of Love. Still another issue—
the apparently unique copy lacks a title-page—would
seem to have been printed abroad, if the misprints in
it are any criterion. The earliest extant edition printed
in England is contained in *Ovid De Arte Amandi, and The
Remedy of Love Englished. As also the Loves of Hero and
Leander, A Mock Poem. Together with Choice Poems, and
rare pieces of Drollery*, 1662.[1] The second part of the
miscellany had appeared before in 1651 and 1654, and
the whole was reissued in 1672, 1677, 1682, and 1705.
The proof of Heywood's authorship of *Love's School* lies
in his *Troia Britannica, An Apology for Actors, Γυναικεῖον*,
and *The Hierarchy of the Blessed Angels*, together with odd
couplets in *The Brazen Age* and other works; in them
will be found between five and six hundred lines translated
from the *Ars Amatoria* and, except for author's corrections,
identical with *Love's School*. The Ovidian translation was
certainly in existence before *Troia Britannica* and was most
likely an academic exercise.

Heywood's other remonstrance was made in his letter
to his friend Okes at the end of his *Apology for Actors.*
After animadverting on Jaggard's villainous printing of
Troia Britannica and contrasting his conduct with Okes's,
'so carefull, and industrious, so serious and laborious to
doe the Author all the rights of the presse', he refers to
another 'manifest iniury done me in that worke, by taking
the two Epistles of *Paris* to *Helen*, and *Helen* to *Paris*,
and printing them in a lesse volume, under the name of
another, which may put the world in opinion I might
steale from him; and [that] hee to doe himselfe right,
hath since published them in his owne name: but as I
must acknowledge my lines not worthy his patronage,
under whom he hath publisht them, so the Author I know
much offended with M. Iaggard (that altogether un-
knowne to him) presumed to make so bold with his

---

[1] The separate title-page of *The Loves of Hero and Leander* is dated 1667;
apparently, therefore, sheets of a 1662 edition remained when another was
required in 1667. *The Remedy of Love Englished* is not Heywood's and
quite obviously dates from at least the fourth or fifth decade of the century.

name'. The 'lesse volume' alluded to is *The Passionate Pilgrim. Or Certain Amorous Sonnets, between Venus and Adonis, newly corrected and augmented. By W. Shakespere. The third Edition. Whereunto is newly added two Love-Epistles, the first from Paris to Helen, and Helen's answer back again to Paris,* 1612. Heywood's claim is moderate, for not only are the two epistles his, but seven other passages from the notes to *Troia Britannica*, six from the translated *Ars Amatoria*, and one from the version of the *Remedium Amoris*. His complaint at the theft must have appeared when the third edition of *The Passionate Pilgrim* was being printed off, for Jaggard issued a second title-page which omitted Shakespeare's name but still advertised the added 'Love-Epistles'.[1]

In the winter of 1612–13 our poet had a chance of appealing for royal notice through two events, the death of the popular and able Prince Henry, and the marriage of the Lady Elizabeth. It was not a great chance: the odds were one to fifty or a hundred against making any impression when nearly every one of note in the world of letters besides many unknown were in the competition. The death of the Prince on November 6, 1612, plunged the nation in grief undoubtedly sincere despite the exaggerated phrases thought proper for its expression. The press as if in expectation of the event at once went into the deepest mourning. It was not, however, till December 23 that the joint effort of Tourneur, Webster, and Heywood, *Three Elegies on the Most Lamented Death of Prince Henry* (1613), was registered, a sombre book in appearance as well as in theme, with blackened pages lavishly scattered throughout. Heywood's contribution to this volume is dedicated to the Earl of Worcester, and has, like the others, a separate title-page, *A Funeral Elegy*,

---

[1] Dr. Farmer, in his *Essay on Shakespeare's Learning,* 1766 (*Eighteenth Century Essays on Shakespeare,* ed. Nichol Smith, 203), was the first to point out Heywood's authorship of the 'Love-Epistles' in *The Passionate Pilgrim.* Nevertheless, Heywood's verses, including the passages from the *Ars Amatoria* and the *Remedium Amoris,* were printed in editions of Shakespeare's poems down to 1804.

Upon the late most hopeful and illustrious Prince, Henry, Prince of Wales.[1] Three months later, in the exceptionally mild spring that had followed the inclement winter, when preparations were being pushed forward in indecent haste for the marriage of the Lady Elizabeth, Heywood was busy on his *Marriage Triumph. Solemnized In An Epithalamium, In Memory of the happy Nuptials betwixt the High and Mighty Prince Count Palatine And the most Excellent Princess the Lady Elizabeth* (S.R. February 15, 1612/13, the day after the marriage on St. Valentine's day), which he addressed to the bride and bridegroom in hope no doubt of the usual largess. The basis of *A Marriage Triumph* was Ausonius's *Cento Nuptialis* from which eleven years later in Γυναικεῖον Heywood with characteristic economy inserted a long extract in translation closely parallel to his epithalamium.[2]

It was probably Heywood's having published his *Marriage Triumph* by John Trundle, together with his membership of the Queen's company, that induced Trundle to ask him in 1614 to edit Jo. Cooke's *Greene's Tu Quoque or The City Gallant*.[3] 'I could not choose,' he kindly remarks, 'being in the way just when this play was to be published in print, but to prefix some token of my affection' both for the author[4] and for Thomas Greene, who had contributed so much to the play's success by his appearance in it as Bubble. In the same year Heywood was the subject of two allusions, the first in Freeman's collection of epigrams, and the second in his friend Richard Brathwaite's *Scholar's Medley*, which mentions for the first time Heywood's 'Generall (though summary)

[1] Heywood calls Worcester 'My Mecaenas', him who 'gave my Muse first wing, And from [whose] bounty shee had voyce to sing'; it was thence 'I grew' and 'first receiv'd my being'. Nichols, *Progresses, etc. of James I*, ii. 507, probably wrongly infers that the three elegies were also issued separately. [2] 333–6.

[3] Other editions in 1622 and n.d. (? 1628). It was presented before the King and Queen on Dec. 27, 1611, and Feb. 2, 1611/12 (Chambers, iv. 125–6, 178). Either by Heywood or Beeston it passed to the Lady Elizabeth's men who on Twelfth Night, 1624/5, performed it before Prince Charles (Herbert, 52). [4] See Chambers, iii. 269.

description of all the Poets lives' [1]; and in Edmund Howes's continuation of Stowe's *Annals*, 1615, 'M. *Thomas Heywood* gentleman' is included among 'Our moderne and present excellent Poets which worthily flourish in their owne workes'.[2] Heywood himself perhaps prepared his *Four Prentices* for publication in 1615. Three years later, in 1618, he wrote prefatory verses for his friend Matthew Mainwaring's romance, *Vienna*, and in 1620 he was given an honourable place in John Taylor's *Praise of Hempseed* with those 'living at this day [who] doe in paper their true worth display'.

[1] See 98–9 *infra*.   [2] 811.

CHAPTER V

1615–1630: VICISSITUDES: RETIREMENT FROM THE STAGE

THE fortunes of Queen Anne's company had never been very bright and were now dark indeed. They could no longer command the services of Dekker and Webster. Even more serious was the loss of their celebrated clown Thomas Greene by his death on August 12, 1612,[1] for by the dead hand of his will and the living hand of his widow they were completely ruined. In the Christmas festivities of 1613/14 they made their last appearances at court.[2] After Greene's death their manager was Christopher Beeston, a man of some means but of doubtful honesty. His duplicity involved them in November 1619 in a suit of John Smith, 'Citizen and ffishmonger', who through Beeston had supplied the company with 'diverse tinsell stuffes and other stuffe' to the value of £46 5s. 8d. between June 27, 1612, and February 23, 1617, after which the troupe had 'fallen at variance and strife amongst themselves and separated and devided themselves into other companies'.[3] They were brought, too, unpleasantly before the notice of the authorities by certain rowdy incidents in the neighbourhood of the Red Bull.[4] With the other companies they may have been fined for playing in Lent 1616.[5] About this time they fell into arrears in

---

[1] Greene soon after his return from abroad made his will, Heywood being one of the witnesses, on July 25, 1612. See Brathwaite's *Remains after Death*, 1618, sig. G 5 verso, and I verso for epigrams on Greene, his creditors, and fellow-actors.

[2] Before the King on Dec. 24 or 28, 1613, and Jan. 5, 1613/14 (Chambers, iv. 128, 182). See Murray, ii. 340, 341, 343, for visits by the Queen's men to Norwich in 1615–16–17.

[3] C. W. Wallace, *Three London Theatres of Shakespeare's Time*, 29, &c., and Chambers, ii. 238, &c.

[4] *Middlesex County Records*, ii. 64–5, 86, 165, 175.

[5] See Fleay, *Stage*, 309.

the upkeep of the streets near their theatre. The matter was raised in October 1616, and on October 2, 1617, when Beeston, Heywood, Perkins, Drue, Harrison, and Worth, representing the shareholders, petitioned the Sessions of the Peace. They met with a favourable hearing,[1] perhaps on account of the expense they had been at after the apprentices' Shrovetide riot on March 4, 1616/17, which had partially wrecked their new private house, the Cockpit.[2] It seems to have been quickly restored, for on June 3, 1617, according to the Baskervile papers,[3] they were 'now comme, or shortlie to come [perhaps from their temporary re-occupation of the Red Bull] ... to the Playhouse in Drurie Lane called the Cockpitt', where the payments to Susan Baskervile were to be made. On their separation from Beeston, apparently its owner, they returned to the Red Bull, perhaps after the death of their patron on March 2, 1618/19.[4] Heywood celebrated her death in *A Funeral Ode*, more like a light

[1] *Middlesex County Records*, ii. 235. They seem, however, to have done nothing for the repair of the 'footewaies' by Oct. 3, 1622, when 'Proces de Novo' was awarded against them upon the former presentments, *ibid*. ii. 170.

[2] Chambers, ii. 241. The ballad in Collier (i. 386–8) 'in praise of London Prentices, and what they did at the Cockpitt Playhouse in Drury Lane' is probably spurious; two of the stanzas are as follows:

> King Priam's robes were soon in rags,
>   And broke his gilded scepter;
> False Cressid's hood, that was so good
>   When loving Troylus kept her.
> Besse Brydges gowne, and Muli's crowne,
>   Who would full faine have lept her:
> Had Thesus seene them use his queene
>   So ill, he had bewept her.
>
> Books olde and young on heap they flung,
>   And burnt them in the blazes,
> Tom Dekker, Haywood, Middleton
>   And other wandring crayzes.
> Poor Daye that daye not scapte away;
>   And what still more amazes,
> Immortall Cracke was burnt all blacke,
>   Which every body praises.

[3] See 89–90 *infra*.   [4] Cf. Chambers, ii. 240.

lyric than an elegy. But he may have been so discouraged by the general disappointment with the poor show at the funeral, delayed till May 2 'for want of money to buy blacks',[1] that he withheld it from the press and inserted it in Γυναικεῖον;[2] it came in useful with slight modifications for *A Funeral Elegy upon a virtuous Maid, who died the very day on which she should have been married* in *Pleasant Dialogues*.[3] At the Queen's funeral Heywood walked with his fellows in her London and her provincial companies of actors, each clothed in his four yards of black cloth which had somehow or other been bought after all.[4]

Heywood, now approaching his fiftieth year, had probably retired from the boards, though he may still have supplied his late fellows with plays.[5] It may have been for the Red Bull company, as they were called after the Queen's death, or for the Children of the Revels, as they became on July 8, 1622, that Heywood wrote a prologue and epilogue for '*A young witty Lad playing the part of Richard the third: at the Red Bull: the Author because hee was interessed in the Play to incourage him, wrot him this Prologue and Epilogue*'.[6] *Callisto or The Escapes of Jupiter*[7] may also

[1] Nichols, *Progresses, etc. of James I*, iii, 534–5.   [2] 123–4.
[3] 254.   [4] Chambers, ii. 240, and Murray, i. 196.
[5] Fleay's supposition (*Stage*, 273, &c., and i. 296; cf. Bates, xxxii) that Heywood acted for the Lady Elizabeth's men in 1623–4 is based on a misreading of a passage in the Baskervile papers as referring to 1623–4 instead of to 1617. The advice in *Wit's Recreation*, 1640, which commends *The Hierarchy*, was to

> Fly that way still, it will become thy age
> And better please than groveling on the stage.

It may refer simply to his play-writing and in any case is scarcely a proof that the old man was acting in 1640.

[6] *Pleasant Dialogues*, 247; on July 27, 1623, the Palsgrave's men at the Fortune received a licence for 'a Tragedy of *Richard the Third, or the English Profit*, with the Reformation, written by Samuel Rowley' (Herbert, 24; cf. 64). G. Chalmers (*Supplemental Apology for the Believers in the Shakespeare Papers*) assumes that Heywood wrote a play on Richard III, and Fleay (i. 305) dates the prologue in 1635; Shakespeare's play was acted by the King's company at St. James's on Nov. 16 1633 (Herbert, 64).   [7] See 67 *supra*, note 1.

have been prepared for them, and it was almost certainly
their revival of *If you know not Me* in 1623, that Thomas
Drue echoed in his *Life of the Duchess of Suffolk*, played
by the Palsgrave's men at the Fortune.[1]

But the remnant of the company succumbed under
ever-increasing difficulties and broke soon after May 10,
1623.[2] Accordingly on May 23, Ellis Worth, John
Cumber, who died within a few weeks, and John Blaney,
petitioned Lord Keeper Williams to free them from their
engagements. At Greene's death in 1612 the company
was in his debt £37, and by his will, dated July 25, 1612,
to which Heywood, Beeston, and Perkins were witnesses,
his share in the company, estimated at £80 by his widow,
Susan, who became Mrs. Baskervile within a year, passed
to her. The above petitioners asserted that Susan by
indirect means induced Beeston to persuade the company
—Beeston, Heywood, and five others—to pay to her and
her son Francis Baskervile for life and during the sur-
vivor's life 2s. and 1s. 8d. respectively on each of the six
days a week any four of them acted together. On Francis's
death five years later, Susan, say the petitioners, bribed
Beeston to continue the reversion to William Browne,
Susan's son by her first marriage, and, by a bond which
she had drawn for greater security, the money was to be
paid to William Jordan in trust for herself and her son.
What was the company's astonishment, then, to find in
the bond a clause binding them to find new members to
take the place of those who left them and thus to per-
petuate the conditions? On the reassurances of Susan,
however, some of them signed the indenture in 1617 and
bonds of a hundred marks apiece for its performance.
But now in May 1623, when all who signed and were
bound had died or departed to other companies, the
petitioners thought it hard to pay £60 or more a year,
especially since Susan had received £500 already. Moreover, Jordan was now dead and Mrs. Baskervile was
threatening them with arrest if all their agreements were
not fulfilled to the letter. The rejoinder, however, of

[1] After Jan. 2, 1623/4 (Herbert, 18, 77).   [2] Herbert, 23.

Mrs. Baskervile and her son Browne on June 16 puts a different complexion on the affair. It appears that the original debt in 1612 totalled £117, that the company had refused then to discharge it, and that Viscount Lisle, Queen Anne's Lord Chamberlain, had directed them to pay 'without further troubling of him'. Thereupon they did undertake to pay a full half-share of their profits until both the sum of £37 and that of £80 for the whole share were discharged. By June 1613 only £6 had been paid. Baskervile in his wife's interest then took part in the dispute and various complicated arrangements were made by which the Queen's men, through repeated failures to carry out their bonds, were brought into arrears of a sum between £100 and £200. It was then that, to free themselves from these complications, Beeston, Heywood, Worth, Cumber, Francis Walpole, Blaney, William Robinson, and Thomas Drue, with the consent of the rest of the company, made the agreement on June 3, 1617, to pay William Jordan 3s. 8d. per day for six days a week in which any four should act together in or about London, and to fill up vacancies in their number with new-comers prepared to carry out the bond. The case dragged on till June 23, 1626, when the court, as it was bound to do, found for the defendants but refused them costs.[1]

In the same year, 1623, Heywood was more directly concerned in yet another law-suit. Some five years before, he and thirty-eight others, mostly actors at the Red Bull, the Fortune, and the Globe, guaranteed to Gervase Markham[2] 'of London gent.' various small sums—Heywood's stake was five shillings—if he walked from London to Berwick, crossing streams only with 'an ordinarye Leape staffe' and neither swimming nor sailing. Though the journey was punctually performed in October 1622,

[1] Greenstreet printed the documents in the *New Shakspere Soc. Transactions*, 1880–6, 48, &c. For Beeston's finance see C. W. Wallace, *Three London Theatres of Shakespeare's Time*, 29, &c.; and Chambers, ii. 236, &c.

[2] For the identity of this Markham and for the documents see C. W. Wallace, *Gervase Markham, Dramatist, Shakespeare Jahrbuch*, xlvi. 345, &c.; J. Q. Adams, *Every Woman in her Humour and the Dumb Knight, M.P.* x. 427, &c.; and Chambers, iii. 417.

Markham's guarantors failed him, and on May 16 (?13), 1623, his affidavit was lodged in the Court of Requests for a writ of the Privy Seal to summon the defaulters to answer before the court. Apparently all but seven paid up soon after, for in the statement on January 29, 1623/4, of the messenger, only the seven, of whom Heywood was not one, were summoned on May 23, 1623, to appear on the 25th.

We next hear of our dramatist writing for the Lady Elizabeth's men at the Cockpit, for whom on September 3, 1624, his *Captive(s), or the Lost Recovered* was licensed.[1] The manuscript of this, the most pleasant of all the plays recovered for Heywood, was discovered by Bullen in B.M.: MS. Egerton 1994, a codex of thirteen dramatic pieces including *Callisto or The Escapes of Jupiter*, like *The Captives* in Heywood's own illegible scrawl, and *Dick of Devonshire*, also we submit by Heywood but of later composition.[2] His employment by what was now easily the second company in London may be taken as a sign of returning prosperity after seven lean years.[3]

Heywood, ever the admirer of women, loud in their praises, tender to their faults, and after Shakespeare and before Greene the dramatist whose women, in spite of the sketchiness with which they are drawn, seem to us the most lovable, natural, and human of all the Elizabethans' female characters, conceived at the turn of the tide of his fortunes and hastily executed in 1624 an encyclopaedic work that was to win for him the title of 'historian of women'. This was his Γυναικεῖον *or Nine Bookes of Various History Concerning Women; Inscribed by the names of the*

---

[1] Herbert, 29. H. C. Hart (*Notes on Bullen's Old Plays, Academy,* xxxiv. 240–1) argues for a date twenty years earlier.

[2] See 103, 376 *infra.*

[3] Heywood pretty certainly did not transfer to the Lady Elizabeth's men at the same time as Beeston; but see Fleay, *Stage,* 273, and i. 296, and cf. Murray, i. 257. Fleay (i. 295–6) saw an allusion in *The Fair Maid of the West* (Pearson, ii. 324, 393) to Andrew Cane whom Herbert in 1622 assigns both to the Lady Elizabeth's and to the Palsgrave's companies (Herbert, 63; cf. Murray, i. 215–16, 218, 266, table). The glowing panegyric of the Princess in Γυναικεῖον, 125, perhaps indicates that Heywood had found a new market for his plays with her company.

Nine Muses.[1] It was an '*Opus Excogitatum, Inchoatum, Explicitum, Et a Typographo excusum, inter septemdecem septimanas*'.[2] So hurried indeed had the author been to see it published that he waited for no licence and asked no friends for commendatory verses, explaining instead that as his labours were not communicated to any, there was nobody who could truly commend them; '*Neither doe I thinke I am so little knowne,*' he adds, '*or ill beloved amongst them, that any one would have denyed me so small a courtesie.*' This haste was due perhaps to the poet's straitened circumstances, and in his dedication to his old patron he frankly admits his need.[3] He alludes to the length of time which had elapsed since his last address to the earl and declares that he would have been unwilling to have appeared before him 'at this present, did I not bring the Nine Muses, with an Armie of Goddesses and Women, to mediate in my behalfe'. 'I was (my Lord),' he continues, 'your creature, and (amongst other of your servants) you bestowed me upon the excellent Princesse *Q. Anne* (to whose memorie I have celebrated in these Papers the zeale of a subiect and a servant) but by her lamented death your Gift (my Lord) is returned againe into your hands, being stil yours, either to keepe unto your selfe, or to conferre where your noble disposition shall best please.'[4]

[1] Heywood calls it *The History of Women* twice (*Hierarchy*, 231, *Exemplary Lives*, address); see also George Estoutville's lines in *Exemplary Lives*. Γυναικεῖον was freely plagiarized in *Elogium Heroinum: or, The Praise of Worthy Women* by C(harles) G(erbier), 1651 (1650), and may have suggested something to R(obert, or Richard) B(urton), i.e. Nathaniel Crouch for his *Female Excellency*, 1688.   [2] Colophon; cf. To the reader.

[3] Cf. 462–3: 'One woman I had almost foꞇgotten . . . In this my worke shee hath risen earely with mee in the Morning, and againe sat up with me till past Midnight, shee will leave no man Waking, nor forsake him till shee see him fast sleeping. This woman's name is *Care*, the grand-mother of Feares and Doubts.'

[4] Heywood did not re-enter Worcester's service or patronage, as Mr. Murray (i. 256) supposed, for though a member of Queen Anne's company of players he never ceased to regard Worcester as his patron. His elegy on James I calls Worcester 'the unchanged Patron of all my weake and unperfect labours that have beene published, even from the first to the last'.

Heywood's first great compilation is a work the summary of which would be nearly as bulky as the thing summarized. Like *The Hierarchy*, Γυναικεῖον is divided and subdivided after an elaborate scheme which gives a deceptive appearance of order. Only a very imperfect attempt has been made in the nine books, each inscribed to one of the Muses after the manner of Herodotus, from whom a good deal of the matter comes, to arrange the narratives according as they pertain to goddesses, queens, 'Amazons', chaste women or unchaste, widows or wives, poetesses or pious daughters; besides, Heywood's taste was too catholic or rather too undiscriminating to reject anything that occurred to him and he consequently threw in pell-mell fabliaux, jests, commonplaces, scraps from chroniclers and Renaissance epigrammatists, poets and compilers, theologians and magicians, as well as more original miscellanea of varying dates, remarks on poetry, reflections on life and marriage, astrology and kissing, snatches of verse, and personal anecdotes. In his preface he anticipates objections to the hotch-potch and even justifies it: '*Some also may cavill,*' says he, '*that I have not introduced them in order, neither Alphabetically, nor according to custome or precedent; which I thus excuse: The most cunning and curious Musick, is that which is made out of Discords; and* Ovid *preferres a blunt Carriage and a neglected Habit above all spruceness and formalitie*', and later he maintains that it will be unfair to tax his 'too much intermixtion of historie, and . . . things inserted, not pertinent to my proiect in hand'.[1] He had the dramatist's sense of contrast and depends on it to 'avoid all prolixitie'[2] and tediousness, admitting stories of vicious women because they make more glorious the fame of the good and mingling *seria iocis* in imitation of '*our Historicall and Comicall Poets, that write to the Stage*'.[3]

Though Herodotus had suggested the division of the

---

[1] 213.   [2] 33; cf. 165.
[3] To the reader; cf. 253. Two of the *facetiae* appeared in *A Help to Discourse*, 1619, of W.B. and E.P., to which his friend Thomas Brewer contributed verses.

work into nine books, the models that he set before him were Aelian and Valerius Maximus, '*who epitomised great and memorable acts, reducing and contracting into a compendious Method wide and loose Histories, giving them notwithstanding their full weight, in few words*'.[1] But though Heywood reduces his authorities and condenses his stories to avoid tediousness, he too often achieves, like the unfortunate preacher, the distinction of being both short and tedious. One critic, who has spent more time on the book than it deserves, credits the dramatist with too direct a knowledge of the authorities mentioned.[2] But in days when the ability to clinch an argument with a tag from the classics was cultivated assiduously, the art of quoting and the hobby of culling quotations gave many writers a superficial erudition; and though the Jacobeans knew their classics better than do the moderns, they also appear to know them better than they did. Heywood himself was an insatiable miscellany-reader, and it is to the compilers, Athenaeus, Stobaeus, Aulus Gellius, Diogenes Laertius, Suidas, Vincent of Beauvais, Higden in Trevisa's translation, Alexander ab Alexandro, Fulgosus, Marullus, Sabellicus, Volaterranus, Rhodiginus, and the rest, classical and later, that we must go for the sources of his knowledge. Just as in *The Hierarchy* most of the citations from the Fathers and later ecclesiastical writers from Origen to Thomas à Kempis are from some such work as Jacques de Billy's *Anthologia Sacra*, 1575,[3] so a large part of Γυναικεῖον is simply translated in Heywood's usual erratic fashion from Ravisius Textor's *Theatrum Poeticum*, *Officina*, and *De Memorabilibus et Claris Mulieribus*.[4] Certain chapters from the last book along with Plutarch's *De Virtutibus Mulierum*, Philippus Bergomensis's *De Plurimis Claris Selectisque Mulieribus*, and other opuscula on famous women were printed at Paris in 1521;

---

[1] To the reader.
[2] R. G. Martin, *Critical Study of Thomas Heywood's Gunaikeion*, *S. in Ph.* xx.
[3] Referred to in *The Hierarchy*, 66.
[4] None of these was accessible to Mr. Martin.

Heywood, if he did not actually possess this compilation, was familiar with the separate treatises which make it up. Even the impressive array of early English chroniclers in Γυναικεῖον is merely transcribed from Bale's *Acts of English Votaries*. But, as we shall have occasion to remark again in discussing *The Hierarchy*, Heywood did know at first hand the literature of witchcraft and drew matter for both of his folios from many demonologists besides Bodin and Wier.[1] Naturally the more accessible and familiar classics, the more popular medieval and Renaissance writers,[2] and the later English chroniclers, he consulted directly.

There is something very appropriate in Heywood's setting up as the historian and champion of women. He was of all the dramatists the most tender to the other sex, almost the most feminine. But his Legend of Good, Bad, and Indifferent Women, was also a contribution to a bitter controversy. Acrimonious attacks on women and angry replies are never very scarce, though accidents seem to govern the phases of greater or less virulence. From 1615 onwards for ten or a dozen years the debate was more than usually violent. In that year appeared anonymously, though the author's name was probably an open secret from the first, a stupid pamphlet called *The Arraignment of Lewd, idle, froward, and unconstant women*. There is not a particle of wit in this misogynous production, but it enjoyed a scandalous celebrity and was reprinted in 1619, 1621, 1628, 1634, 1637, 1645, 1660, 1690, 1702, 1707, 1733, and 1738, in the last six editions with a spurious second part; it was even republished as late as 1807 along with *Esther hath hang'd Haman*, one of the early replies to it; and a Dutch divine, William Christaens,

---

[1] From whom Mr. Martin, *op. cit.* 175, would derive all Heywood's witch-lore.

[2] See 87 for the earliest citation in an English book of the Italian text of the *Divina Commedia* (Martin, *op. cit.* 176). Prof. C. H. Herford (*Literary Relations of England and Germany in the 16th century*, 170) notes that Heywood was one of the few Englishmen of his day acquainted with the German humanists Aventinus and Krantzius.

saw fit to translate it in 1641. Flattered by the notice taken of his book, the author abandoned the pseudonym of Thomas Telltroth and from 1619 stood forth as Joseph Swetnam. It is astonishing how seriously his coarse invective was received by his contemporaries. The champions of women rallied at once, the first to print being D(avid) T(uvil), a minor essayist, whose *Asylum Veneris* appeared in 1616 (S.R. May 7).[1] On November 14, 1616, was licensed *A Muzzle for Melastomus* by Rachel Speght, perhaps a daughter of Chaucer's editor; it was published in 1617. The 'Ester Sowerman', who learned after 'she' had begun her defence that 'a Minister's daughter' had a similar book ready but who found the *Muzzle* inadequate, published her *Ester hath hang'd Haman* the same year (S.R. January 4, 1616/17). Another advocate of women, who calls himself or herself 'Constantia Munda', a few weeks later published *The Worming of a Mad Dog* (S.R. April 29, 1617). Nor was this by any means the end of the wordy war. In 1618 Richard Brathwaite intervened with his *Description of a Good Wife*, reprinted next year as an appendix to Patrick Hannay's *Happy Husband*; in 1620 there came William Bladen's *Discourse of the married and the single Life*, and in 1622 Richard Fferrers's *Worth of Women*. Edition followed edition of Overbury's *Wife*, and numerous efforts, including *The Honour of Ladies* from the French, were put forth by anonymous pamphleteers. Moreover 'Our pulpits ring continually', writes Chamberlain in 1620 to Dudley Carleton, 'of the insolence and impudence of women, and to help the matter forward, the players have likewise taken them to task, and so to the ballads and ballad-singers ... And if all this will not serve, the King threatens to fall upon their husbands, parents, or friends, that have or should have power over them, and make them pay for it'.[2] It was Heywood's own company that

---

[1] Alex. Niccholes's *Discourse of Marriage and Wiving*, 1615, was opportune but not a reply.

[2] Nichols, *Progresses, etc. of James I*, iii. 588; cf. *C.S.P.D.*, 1619–23, 123.

brought the debate on the stage with *Swetnam, The Woman-hater Arraigned by Women,* 1620 (S.R. October 17, 1619), the phraseology of which occasionally reminds one of our dramatist. Other contributions in dramatic form were Fletcher's *Sea Voyage* in 1622 and probably Gunnel's *Way to content all Women,* Samuel Rowley's *Shift for Husbands,* and the anonymous *Woman's Plot* and *The Female Rebellion.*[1] The controversy had passed out of the acute stage before Heywood wrote his Γυναικεῖον. He displays in it a considerable knowledge of earlier literature in the perennial dispute, such as Riche's *Excellency of good Women* and Niccholes's *Discourse of Marriage and Wiving.* Indeed the design of his work may have been suggested by *A Woman's Worth,* 1599, translated from the French of the Chevalier de l'Escale. In any case he was quite aware of the satirists 'against the sex of women that call them fraile, inconstant, weake, and timerous' and bade them consider such and such instances to the contrary.[2] He had the satisfaction of converting 'one of these censorious fellowes' and wished that all who persisted in the same 'peevish obstinacie' would be as reasonable.[3]

It might have been thought that one edition of Heywood's folio would have sufficed for even the seventeenth century. But not so: in 1657 it was issued again as a stout octavo with the ambitious title *The General History of Women, Containing the Lives of the most Holy and Prophane, the most Famous and Infamous in all ages, exactly described not only from Poetical Fictions, but from the most Ancient, Modern and Admired Historians, to our Times. By T. H. Gent.* This venture was put forth by E. P., who initialled a new address to the reader, omitted the former address and the dedication, and was no other than Edward Phillips, Milton's nephew. The year before he edited Γυναικεῖον, he had published two novels, the first being dedicated in fustian phrases to the Marchioness of Dorchester, to whose husband, it will be remembered, *The Actors' Vindication,* as the 1658 issue of *An Apology for Actors* was called, was addressed. Heywood, had he been

---

[1] Cf. Schelling, *Elizabethan Drama,* ii. 238.   [2] 120.   [3] 160–1.

alive, might well have been indignant at the preface, so
unlike his own, with which Phillips recommended *The
General History of Women*, and to find his work considered
an encyclopaedia for the misogynist. But most of all
would he have been astonished at the skill with which
E. P. insinuated that he had had some sort of hand in its
composition without quite claiming to have had. This,
however, is not the only instance of his sharp practice.

Appropriate mention may be made here, in connexion
with Γυναικεῖον and with a side glance at Phillips, of a
literary project of Heywood's which never matured,
though begun apparently on an ambitious scale. It is
first noticed in *The Scholar's Medley*, 1614, of Richard
Brathwaite, who there alludes to '*Homer* an Excellent &
Heroicke Poet; shadowed onely at, because my Iudicious
friend Maister *Tho: Heywood*, hath taken in hand (by
his great industry) to make a Generall (though Summary)
description of all the Poets lives'.[1] In the 1638 edition,
which bore the title *A Medley of History*, Brathwaite adds
that Heywood's projected book, 'to which *He* wisheth
farre more felicity than accrued to his Mysterious Discourse of *Angels*', was to contain 'the Portracture of [the
poets'] Persons'.[2] When in Γυναικεῖον Heywood himself
alludes to 'a larger worke intituled The Lives of all the
Poets Moderne and Forraigne, to which worke (if it come
once again into my hands) I shall refer you',[3] it is still
curiously in connexion with Homer. By 1635 he had
apparently recovered his manuscript and made some progress with it; for once more in speaking of Homer he
stops short so as not to anticipate 'a Worke, which hereafter (I hope) by God's assistance to commit to the publicke view; namely, the Lives of all the Poets, Forreine and
Moderne, from the first before *Homer*, to the Novissimi
and last, of what Nation or Language soever; so farre as
any Historie or Chronologie will give me warrant'.[4] We

[1] 31; cf. index.
[2] Index; cf. 114. A third edition appeared in 1651.   [3] 174.
[4] *Hierarchy*, 245. Oldys (MS. note in Langbaine, 269: B.M.: C.28.g. 1)
thought 'it was too wide a plan: he would have found enough to have made

do not know how much of this grandiose plan Heywood ever completed, but the material which he would be likely to accumulate in his reading would pertain to poets of the most diverse dates, even though the total amount might have been comparatively small. One cannot argue that if several of the intended Lives had been compiled, Heywood, always needy and always fluent, would have hastened to get what he could from the stationers. However poor he was (and we have not only no reason to suppose him a pauper, but evidence to the contrary) and however fast his pen travelled, he did not by any means fulfil all his literary schemes; he promised several others which also fell through. Now it is just possible that Phillips, who speaks but scurvily of Heywood in his *Theatrum Poetarum*, 1675, and with only faint praise in his *Tractatus de Carmine Dramatico Poetarum, et compendiosa Enumeratio Poetarum a Tempore Dantis Aligerii usque ad hanc Aetatem,*[1] may have decided to carry out Heywood's plan.[2] Heywood was certainly one of Phillips's authorities, for the dictum on Lady Arabella Stuart who '*had a great facility in Poetry, and was elaborately conversant among the Muses*'[3] is from 'an English writer', namely the despised Heywood;[4] and not a few of the other paragraphs bear a very suspicious resemblance to passages in Heywood's published work, though Phillips makes no further acknowledgement of his indebtedness.[5] Not long after, Phillips was similarly 'consulted' by Winstanley, who was in turn pillaged by later compilers.

him weary, in giving an account of the poets of his own country, which no man has yet done. The scheme of William Brown, the pastoral poet, was more modest and practicable'. Langbaine, 269, supposed it was 'never completed, or at least published'. W. C. Hazlitt (*Collections and Notes,* i. 214) blunders badly over Heywood's intended compilation.

[1] In Buchlerus's *Thesaurus*, ed. 1669, 397–9.

[2] It is not uninteresting that when Phillips published *A New World of Words* in 1658 he included epistles to Sir Robert Bolles of Scampton, Lincs., a descendant of Richard Bolles who had presented the Rev. Robert Heywood to the living of Rothwell in 1575, and to Edward Hussy of Calthorpe, Lincs.   [3] 255.   [4] Γυναικεῖον, 398.

[5] Cf. *Theatrum Poetarum*, 235, &c., and Γυναικεῖον, 384, &c.

March 1624/5 opened ominously with 'windy and obstreperous rage' and on the 27th of the month, fatal also to his predecessor Elizabeth and his consort Anne, the King died; and with him Heywood mourns others, the Duke of Richmond and Lennox, his brother Lord Aubigny, the Earls of Dorset and Southampton, the latter's son, the Marquis of Hamilton, and Lord Belfast, who had all died about the same time. Heywood saw March go out 'In strange varietie of stormy weather' before finishing his lament, which was registered on April 4 and soon appeared, with a dedication to Worcester and a frontispiece of James's catafalque, as *A Funeral Elegy upon the much Lamented Death of the Trespuissant and unmatchable King, King James King of Great Britain, France and Ireland, Defender of the Faith.* Though in *Troia Britannica* Heywood had given James the credit of first inspiring him, he more truthfully asks us now to excuse him,

> *even the weakest, if I (tho*
> *Not knowne to him) that onely saw him grow*
> *To others profit, have my griefes displayed,*
> *Yet never tasted of his mast or shade.*

Nevertheless in this naïve specimen of laureate poetry Heywood pours forth his verbose sorrow for 'so gracious and so good a King, whose wisdome Christendome could not match, and his peaceable government the whole earth not equal'.[1]

[1] Cf. *Hierarchy*, 203-4:

> How comes it, that a Poet shall contrive
> A most elaborate Worke to make survive
> Forgotten Dust? when no King shall expire
> But he brings fuell to his funerall fire:
> No Optimate falls from the Noble throng,
> But he records his Elegeicke Song
> In mourning papers: and when all decayes,
> *Herse, Shewes,* and *Pompe*; yet That resounds his praise.
> Of every Match and Royall Combination;
> His Pen is ready to make publication:
> When all prove ag'd, forgotten, and blown o're,
> 'His *Verse* is still as youthful as before;
> 'And sounds as sweetly (though it now seeme dead)
> 'To after-Times it shall be ever read.'

The year did not pass without taking one nearer to him, his uncle, 'that good old gentleman Master *Edmund Heywood*',[1] who died in December or January 1625/6.[2] He was a person of some means and had been a civil servant. His will, dated October 7, 1624, describes him as 'of the parish of Christchurch London gentleman' and alludes to 'the Exchequer in which office I lived and spent moste of my daies', which infers that he was then retired.[3] By his will he left £6 to the poor of the parish and £3 'to the poore Children harboured in Christes Hospitall'. Sir Henry Appleton is mentioned as the recipient-to-be of a ring and in a familiar passage concerning certain sheep that Appleton had in charge for the behoof of Edmund's grandchild, Anne Wright. Other friends of some distinction were Sir William Birde [4] and his lady, both apparently dead before the will was drawn, the Lady Hamfert, Sir John Osborne, 'Treasurer, Remembrancer of the Exchequer', and the two brothers Daniel and Sampson Price and their wives.[5] Some of Edmund's many relatives we have not been able to trace: 'my cosen Hudson and his wife', apparently also Christopher Hudson and his wife, 'my cosen Henrye Pearson', 'my cosen Fairebrother his sister', 'my cosen Fawcett and his wief', and perhaps some of the godchildren mentioned but unnamed.[6] The legacies which are of most interest to

[1] Dedication of *English Traveller*.

[2] The Christ Church register for that period is lost. His will, printed by Miss Bates (ciii, &c.), was proved on Feb. 1 by his only child 'Anne Wright, widow' and William Screven.

[3] He perhaps was a scrivener as well; he mentions the 'money of my Client for businesse' and employed two clerks.

[4] Perhaps descended from the Cheshire family but born in Essex.

[5] See *D.N.B.*, article, *Daniel Price*. Sampson Price, rector of Edmund Heywood's parish, was chaplain to James I and Charles I. His sermon for staying the plague, 1626, was dedicated to Lord Keeper Coventry, who held the seals for a very few months in 1628, and on an anagram of whose name Heywood wrote an acrostic (*Pleasant Dialogues*, 263–4).

[6] The other beneficiaries were Susan Franklin, John Hooke and his wife, Edward Sanders and his wife, William Sutton and his wife, Anthony and his wife Alice Stoddard, Grace Revell, Sarah Houghton, Oliver Houghton, Walter Leigh, and David Buckle.

us are 'to Thomas Heywoode and his wief, William Heywoode and his wief each of them Twentie shillinges in goulde and to the said William Heywoode one of my ould Cloakes, a suite of ould apparell and a hatt such as my Executors shall thinke fittinge'. Thomas Heywood was not in destitution, then; but William, probably the dramatist's brother,[1] was decidedly a poor relation. All Edmund's grandchildren, Anne, Heywood, Henry, Mary, Elizabeth, and Martha Wright, were left, in addition to other legacies, various pieces of plate. To his only child, the widowed Anne Wright, Edmund left 'the rest of my plate and all my goodes and Chattells which I have (videl.) the Lease of my house wherein I dwell, And the lease of the George at Warwick-lane-ende, And the lease of the houses at Pye Corner which I boughte of the Executors of Mr. Kirke'. 'And whereas my intent and meaninge was to have given and left to Magdalen my well-beloved wief, with whom I have by the goodness of god lived a long time the greatest part of myne estate for her maintenance during her lief, and to have been disposed of by her after her death But consideringe howe it hath pleased god to vissit her longe with lamenes whereby and by reason of her other weaknes and imperfections which comonlie doth attende auld age she is nowe unfitt to take care of the thinges of this world I thought it better to dispose of these Temporall blessings with which god hath indued me; accordinge as it is declared in this my will And to leave my saide wief to the care of her naturall and onlie child, then to expose her and my substance to strangers that maie happen to regard it more then her.' But fifty pounds are to be paid to old Mrs. Heywood; she is to have all her apparel, including 'her hatt bande set with goulde buttons and her ringe', while her daughter is to see to all her needs and to engage a woman and a girl to wait on her; 'And this I charge her trulie and honestlie to performe accordynge to my will as she will answeare it before god at the dreadfull

---

[1] And the 'William Heywood householder' buried at Clerkenwell on Aug. 9, 1625; see 5 *supra*.

daie of Judgment when the secretts of all harts shalbe disclosed'.

When in the early summer of 1625 Queen Henrietta's theatrical company, the personnel of which was largely drawn from the Lady Elizabeth's, was assembled, Heywood seems to have transferred his services as a dramatist to it. He wrote for them, we believe, in the summer of 1626 his breezy *Dick of Devonshire*, soon after the eponymous hero had published his *Three to One: Being, An English-Spanish Combat, Performed by a Western Gentleman, of Tavistock in Devonshire with an English Quarter-Staff, against Three Spanish Rapiers and Poniards, at Sherries in Spain, the fifteenth day of November, 1625.*[1] The rather thin plot of Manuel and Eleonora may be older than the dramatizing of Pike's pamphlet, for signs of patching are not wanting. Could it possibly be the remains of *The Younger Brother*, played by Queen Anne's men at the Red Bull on October 3, 1617?[2] A reading in the light of recent analyses[3] of *A Cure for a Cuckold*, published by Kirkman in 1661 as by Webster and Rowley, strongly incline us to a belief that in some hasty and incomplete way Heywood was involved in its composition, perhaps also for the Queen's men in 1625.[4] It would not be difficult to supplement the parallels to his acknowledged plays, not to mention *Appius and Virginia*,[5] which have been collected; not the least striking is one hitherto unnoticed between the play[6] and *How a Man May Choose a Good Wife*.[7] Heywood's spirit is abroad in the main plot;

[1] S.R. July 18, 1626.
[2] Collier, *Memoirs of Edward Alleyn*, 107, and Fleay, ii. 336–7. For Bullen's ascription to Heywood and his half-hearted withdrawal see *Old Plays*, ii; for Fleay's ascriptions to Davenport and to Shirley see ii. 235, 236–7, 246, 380, 383, and *Stage*, 333, 341, 393; see also 276–86 *infra*.
[3] H.D. Gray, '*A Cure for a Cuckold*' by Heywood, Rowley and Webster, *M.L.R.* xxii. 389 &c., and F. L. Lucas's *Webster*, iii. 10, &c.
[4] Cf. Lucas, *op. cit.* iii. 3, &c.
[5] Cf. H. D. Sykes, *Sidelights on Elizabethan Drama*. [6] Ed. Lucas, iii. 31.
[7] Sig. C 2: 'Never was such a trewant in Loves schoole.' At least one edition of Heywood's translation of the *De Arte Amandi* was called *Love's School*: cf. 81 *supra*, note 4.

his are the sentiments, the ideas of good and evil, and, one is tempted to say, the characterization and motivation. But the vocabulary only occasionally recalls him, and we feel reluctant to concede him the actual writing of more than a very few scenes. The veteran presides over the tragicomic scenes and his coadjutors seem, as it were, to have aped his manner.

CHAPTER VI

1631–1634: PAGEANTS AND MASQUES: LAST PLAYS

AS a dramatist for the Queen's men, and perhaps still as an actor of minor parts, Heywood must have been sufficiently provided for. But in 1631 certainly, if not ten years earlier, he would be compelled by his age to leave the stage, and the increase of his non-dramatic work from that date proves him to have turned hack-writer in good earnest and, it would appear, with some financial success. His first venture under these new conditions was a reissue of a work by Sir Richard Barckley, 'brought to expresse it selfe after a long silence' and 'at the request of divers notable and well disposed Gentlemen', some of them probably those relatives of Barckley for whom the dedication of *The Exemplary Lives* was meant.[1] Sir Richard Barckley, or more correctly Berkeley, was an obscure Elizabethan, unknown to the *Dictionary of National Biography* or the literary historians, in spite of his recording his leisure meditations that all is vanity in which men put their trust and seek their felicity. This modernized Ecclesiastes, *A Discourse of the Felicity of Man: Or His Summum Bonum*, 1598, was dutifully addressed by Barckley to Queen Elizabeth. Into it he, like all men *unius libri*, has poured all his opinions, especially his fierce anti-papal sentiments and his no less bitter anti-puritanism. In 1603 the stout quarto reappeared 'newly corrected and augmented'; thereafter, though the copyright was frequently transferred, there was no other edition till Heywood's in 1631, from the first, somewhat shorter, version. The chief interest of the reprint is that Heywood omitted the discursive dedication to Queen Elizabeth and readdressed the book in very respectful and laudatory terms to the disgraced Robert Carre, Earl of Somerset,

[1] See 142 *infra*.

who in 1616 had stood his trial with his far more criminal wife for the murder of Sir Thomas Overbury. 'Right Honourable,' it begins, 'Most requisite it is, that all *bookes* should bee protected by such noble *Patrones*, whose Dispositions and Indowments have a Sympathy & Correspondence with the Arguments on which they intreate. The Title of this, is *Summum bonum*: to the attaining of which, those which best know you, can give assured testimony, that your *Matutini*, and *Lucubrationes*...are devoutly intended'; here the true felicity of man is 'learnedly and religiously discoursed, and therefore desirous to bee shadowed under your wing, who are as able to apprehend, as judicially to censure', Heywood has selected him 'the sole *Mecaenas* of so weighty and worthy a work; whose serious contemplations are aymed at Reality, not Forme, as studying to be actually that, which others strive to seeme in appearance'. In this very curious passage the phrases ring as true as, if not truer than, most dedications; and we cannot but take the address at its face value, not as a very subtle piece of irony. It is true that Heywood, having lost his old patron Worcester, was casting about for a new; but it is extraordinary that, even for the paltry reward of forty shillings, any one, especially an Elizabethan journalist, dependent for his livelihood on pleasing the greatest number, should choose as his Maecenas out of all the noble patrons the wretched Carre, exiled from court and in strict retirement, poor, shunned, and almost forgotten. Why, then, was Heywood concerned to flatter a hated but fallen favourite, who had figured in one of the most unpleasant cases in English law?[1] He was not so devoid of friends that he must court Somerset. Nor does it seem likely that the latter, who had not completely abandoned hope of a partial return to public life, suggested the dedication and offered a handsome fee for it. We may perhaps deduce from the following facts that Heywood was not altogether unknown to Somerset before the dedi-

---

[1] Somerset was again prominently before the statists of the time in 1629–30; see Gardiner, *Personal Government of Charles I*, i. 172, &c., and *C.S.P.D.* 1629, 31, 88, 95, 268; 1631, 3, 13.

cation was written. The very wording of it implies a previous acquaintance. Secondly, Sir Gervase Helwysse, Lieutenant of the Tower during Overbury's imprisonment, and executed in 1615 for his supposed part in the murder, was the father of Heywood's friend and countryman, Sir William Helwysse. Lastly, by a not very tactful juxtaposition, it is true, Heywood in *Pleasant Dialogues* sets cheek by jowl an acrostic on an anagram of Lady Anne Carre's name, and another on Sir Ranulph Crew,[1] who had been on the commission to try Weston for the murder of Overbury in 1615, and had part with Bacon and Montague in the prosecution of Carre and his Countess the following year. But beyond this we can say nothing. Barckley's commonplace-book fell into the right hands when it came to Heywood, with whom the accumulation of anecdotes, quotations, and *sententiae* was a disease; and into his own compilations, *The Hierarchy of the Blessed Angels*, *Philocothonista* and *A Curtain Lecture*, he decanted some of Barckley's overflowing measure.

From Elizabeth's official Heywood turned the same year to the great queen herself and retold in prose those passages of her 'tender and sappy age [of which] all our domesticke remembrancers have been sparing to speake' and from which he had already chosen the incidents for the first part of *If You Know Not Me*. The result, *England's Elizabeth: Her Life And Troubles, During Her Minority, from the Cradle to the Crown. Historically laid open and interwoven with such eminent Passages of State, as happened under the Reign of Henry the Eighth, Edward the Sixth, Q. Mary; all of them aptly introducing to the present Relation* (S.R. April 26), with its frontispiece of the queen as all but a martyr for religion, was a kind of Protestant manifesto and sufficiently popular to be reissued again in 1632 and in 1641. It gives the popular legend of Elizabeth's troubles from the cradle to the crown with such events in the three preceding reigns as concerned the main theme. But this popular account, which Heywood himself had helped to establish by *If You Know Not Me*,

---

[1] *Pleasant Dialogues*, 265-6.

part I,[1] was taken from the chroniclers, Fabyan, Holinshed, and Foxe. He returned to them for his prose narrative, and extracts practically the same facts as he had used
for his play, though the earlier part of *England's Elizabeth*,
the fall of Anne Boleyn, and the short reign of Lady Jane
Grey, were either not dramatized by Heywood or formed
part of the lost *Lady Jane*. Yet Heywood seems rather
to conceal his sources and refers to the Latin historians
of Elizabeth, meaning probably Camden and Francis
Godwin, to neither of whom was he indebted. Heywood
'could not apprehend unto whom the Patronage [of his
tract] might more iustly belong' than to Henry Carey,
Earl of Dover, grandson of Elizabeth's kinsman and Lord
Chamberlain, who had been the first to bring her news
of her accession, and was for his pains created Baron
Hunsdon on the spot.[2] But he had another inducement
so to address his work, for 'It hath pleased your Lordship
to censure favourably of some of my weak Labours not
long since presented before you'. This probably refers
to a play of which the only remains are the prologue and
the epilogue '*spoken at the right Honourable the Earle of
Dovers house in* Broadstreet, *at a Play in a most bountifull
Christmas hee kept there; the Speaker Hospitality a frollick
old fellow: A Coller of Brawne in one hand, and a deepe
Bowle of Muscadel in the other*'.[3] From the allusions to
the earl's and the countess's cognisances, a swan and a
cock respectively, it seems likely that the play was for
1630, the Christmas after the earl's second marriage. On
a certain Candlemas Day, probably in the following year,
another play was performed for Dover with prologue and

---

[1] Cf. Niccols's *England's Eliza*, in the 1610 *Mirror for Magistrates*.

[2] See *If You Know Not Me*, pt. I (Pearson, i. 241–2). The dedicatee
married (1) before 1608 Judith (d. Nov. 1, 1629), daughter of Sir Thomas
Pelham, and (2) on July 6, 1630, Mary (d. Jan. 1648/9), daughter of
Richard Morris, once Master of the Ironmongers, and widow of Sir
William Cockayne. The earl's sister, Blanch, married Sir Thomas Wood-
house of Kimberley, Norfolk; see 122 *infra*.

[3] *Pleasant Dialogues*, 242. Cf. *Christmas comes but once a year*, 34–5,
supra, and *Philocothonista*, 'a Noble house-keeper, who kept liberall hospi-
talitie (not common in these dayes)'.

epilogue by Heywood.[1] The masque at Hunsdon from which Heywood in *Pleasant Dialogues* printed only a preliminary speech and Truth's presentation of the nine lady-masquers [2] was for January 1, 1636/7. The same miscellany also contains an acrostic upon an anagram of Dover's name.[3] Some one, perhaps Shirley, to whose quarrel with our dramatist we shall refer later, had ruffled Heywood, and his address to the reader of *England's Elizabeth* shows more spleen than usual. *'Were I able'*, he says, *'to write this little Historicall Tractate with the Pen of* Tacitus, *the Inke of* Curtius, *and set down every line and letter by* Epictetus *his Candle, yet can I see no possibilitie to avoyd the Criticks of this age, who with their frivolous cavils and unnecessary exceptions, ambush the commendable labours of others, when they themselves will not or dare not either through idlenesse or ignorance, adventure the expence of one serious hower in any laborious worke intended for the benefit of either Church or Common-weale; and such* Polupragmatists *this age is full of*;—Sed meliora spero.'[4] The 'good friend Mr. H. H. Stationer', to whose 'industrious Collection, Intituled Herologia Anglicana' Heywood acknowledges himself indebted for some of the matter in his *England's Elizabeth*, was Henry Holland, son of Philemon, the 'translator general of the age'. The next year Heywood, who seems to have been on intimate terms with both the Hollands, praised the son's editing of the father's version

---

[1] *Pleasant Dialogues,* 243.

[2] *Pleasant Dialogues,* 245–7; 'the last New yeares night', however, since *Pleasant Dialogues,* though not published till 1637, was registered on Aug. 29, 1635, may have been Jan. 1, 1635/6, or even Jan. 1, 1634/5.

[3] 264.

[4] This preface, though it purports to be by the author and is in Heywood's style, is signed 'Thine N.R.' and describes the 'little historicall Tractate' in prose as a 'Poeme'. Collier (ed. of *If You Know Not Me,* x) thought the preface was not by Heywood and really belonged to a verse pamphlet on the same subject. Miss Bates, lxv, sees an allusion to some nickname of Heywood but makes no other suggestion. In commending *Philocothonista* John Ford addresses Heywood as 'Nephaliophilus', and in the same tract Heywood signs certain verses 'Tho: Foeni-lignum'. None of the other pamphlets bearing the initials N.R. is by Heywood.

of Xenophon's *Cyropaedia* and paid a notable tribute to the old man's commerce with the classics.

As soon as might be after his sketch of the youth of Elizabeth, Heywood offered the public *The Fair Maid of the West, Or a Girl Worth Gold. As it was lately acted before the King and Queen with approved liking. By the Queen's Majesty's Comedians* (S.R. June 16, 1631). The performance at Hampton Court before the King and Queen, for which occasion Heywood prepared a special prologue and epilogue, was almost certainly at Christmas 1630/1, but seems to have been only of part I.[1] Indeed, part II, which reflects the more sophisticated manner of Heywood's later period, may have been written as a sequel to the first in consequence of the court performance. Several years, perhaps as many as twenty, must have elapsed between the breezy simplicity of the one and the Fletcherian morality of the other. Our own reasons for dating part I in 1609 or 1610 against the rich variety of other suggestions are the phrase in *The Roaring Girl* of c. 1610, 'Oh, brave girls! worth gold',[2] and the appearance in 1609 of Robert Cotton's *Discourse of Muley Hamet's rising to the three Kingdoms of Moruecos, Fes, and Sus* (S.R. January 16, 1608/9), whence Heywood probably derived the extraordinary name of Muly-Sheck. The first part, then, may have followed at the decent interval of two years the success of *The Travels of the three English Brothers* which Heywood's company staged in 1607. That the play attracted attention, whether it was new or old, we gather from Stephen Brome's lines before his brother's *Northern Lass*, 1632:

> Not a Good woman[3], nor a Girle worth Gold,
> Nor twenty such (whose gaudy shewes take hold
> Of gazing eyes) shall in acceptance thrive
> With thee, whose quaintnesse is superlative:

[1] The prologue appears before pt. I, and the epilogue after pt. II; both appear with slight modifications in *Pleasant Dialogues*, 236–7. Pt. I is some ten pages shorter than pt. II, and shows many small cuts.

[2] Pearson's *Dekker*, iii. 206.

[3] Perhaps Rowley's *New Wonder, or A Woman Never Vext*, 1632.

and Cowley's *Guardian*, 1641, echoes Heywood's proverbial subtitle, 'a wench, a wench worth gold, i' faith'.[1]
The two parts were addressed in familiar and affectionate
terms to two lawyer friends, 'without the sordid expectation of reward, or servile imputation of flatterie', as the
dedication of part I assures 'the much worthy, and my
most respected, IOHN OTHOW, Esquire, Counsellour
at Law, in the noble Societie of *Graies Inne*'.[2] The dedicatee
of the second part was 'the true favourer of the Muses, and
all good Arts', Thomas Hammon(d), to whom, as we
have already seen[3], *The Iron Age*, part II, was addressed
in 1632, to whom also in 1633 Heywood presented *The
Jew of Malta* in a most cordial letter, and who along with
Richard Gething the calligraphist provided plate 9 for
The Hierarchy of the Blessed Angels.[4]

[1] Ed. Grosart, i. 219. The ballad of '*The married man's joy, or a loving
wife's worth gold*' was registered on June 28, 1636, and in 1656 appeared
*Now or Never: Or, A New Parliament of Women—Whereunto is annexed,
The fair Maid of the West's Love Sonnet, Very pleasant and delightful for
all Young-men and Maids, both in City and Country. A warning for married
women, by the example of Mrs. Jane Renalls, a west country woman, &c.*
which begins 'There dwelt a fair maid in the West'.

[2] Second son of Thomas Athow, as the name is more commonly spelt, a
lawyer of some note at Gray's Inn and the father of other sons all trained
to the bar. John Athow was admitted to Gray's Inn on Feb. 2, 1607/8,
called to be an 'utter barrister' on July 11, 1614, and to be of the 'grand
company', i.e., an ancient, on June 7, 1627.   [3] See 66 *supra*.

[4] Heywood also knew John Ford of Gray's Inn, cousin of the dramatist;
see 128 *infra*. *The Fair Maid of the West* was performed in 1662 at the
King's Arms, Norwich (MS. Sloane 1900; cf. W. C. Hazlitt, *Manual for
the Collector of Old Plays*, 79). About the same time appeared *The
English Lovers: Or, A Girl Worth Gold. Both Parts, So often Acted with
General Applause; now newly formed into a Romance. By the accurate Pen
of I. D. Gent.*, 1662; the title-page of pt. II is dated 1661. The author in
dedicating his work to Lady Elizabeth Bloundel calls himself John Dauncey.
See Ross Jewel (*Thomas Heywood's Fair Maid of the West* in *Studies in
English Drama*, First Series, ed. Allison Gaw, 72) for various mistakes
over Dauncey's name. In Aug. 1791 at the Haymarket was performed
The Northern Inn; or The good Times of Queen Bess, a farce altered by
S. Kemble from Heywood but never printed (*Biographia Dramatica*,
1812); according to Genest (viii. 41), who gives the alternative title as *The
Days of Good Queen Bess*, the occasion was Mrs. Stephen Kemble's benefit on
Aug. 16. Pt. I of Heywood's play was given at the Hyperion Theatre, New

With the change from the stage to the publisher's back-shop Heywood ventured to come forward in the new role of pageant-poet, which secured an annual ten pounds for him during seven of the years he had yet to live. It is Rowley who has been called the most loyal of Londoners,[1] but Heywood, who was neither a native of London nor connected with it, like Middleton and Webster, by any official or hereditary ties, ran him close in his devotion. His strong love, more artless than Dr. Johnson's, for the city of his adoption manifests itself again and again. Of all the dramatists he is the kindest to the citizen class and the most thoroughly bourgeois; he had celebrated the apprentices in *The Four Prentices of London*; he had brought on the stage its merchant princes, Sir Thomas Gresham, Sir Thomas Ramsey, and Sir John Crosby, together with other London worthies, Matthew and Jane Shore, Hobson and Dr. Alexander Nowell; he was an ardent admirer of the city's institutions and buildings, the trained bands and the Artillery Company, Saint Paul's and the Royal Exchange; and he was intimately acquainted with its customs, its traditions, and history. There could be no one, therefore, in 1631, by which time Dekker, who had designed the shows for 1627, 1628, and 1629, had probably retired from the competition, better fitted than Heywood in the eyes of the Haberdashers to write a pageant for the mayoralty of their fellow, George Whitmore; and in *London's Ius Honorarium. Exprest in sundry Triumphs, pageants and shows* he did not fail to rise to the height of the Londoners' expectations. Next year the Haberdashers provided another Lord Mayor, Nicholas Raynton, and Heywood another pageant, *Londini Artium & Scientiarum Scaturigo: Or, London's Fountain of Arts and Sciences*. And when Richard Fenn of the same corporation was Lord Mayor elect in 1637, Heywood prepared his *Londini Speculum: or, London's Mirror*. His first two pageants had pleased so well that the Clothworkers

Haven, Connecticut, on Apr. 23 and 24, 1901, by the Yale Dramatic Association; and by the Phoenix Society at the Lyric Theatre, Hammersmith, in Apr. 1920.   [1] Swinburne, *Age of Shakespeare*, 184.

entrusted him in 1633 with the design of a show for Ralph Freeman. In it, *Londini Emporia, Or London's Mercatura*,[1] Heywood takes the opportunity of thanking the wardens and the committee of the company 'for their affability and courtesie, especially unto myselfe, being at the time to them all a meere stranger, whom when I sent my then unperfect papers, were as able to judge of them as attentively to heare them; and rather judicially considering all things, than nicely carping at any thing'. In 1634 Heywood was busied with his *Love's Mistress* for the court and his friend John Taylor wrote the show for the mayoralty of R. Parkhurst of the Clothworkers. But in 1635 Heywood provided *Londini Sinus Salutis. Or, London's Harbour of Health, and Happiness*, for Lord Mayor Christopher Cletheroe of the Ironmongers, in whose records are some interesting details. Apparently the Ironmongers were in the habit of haggling over the bargain with the poet and with his artisan. Thus in 1629 the committee, after covenanting with Garret Christmas and Dekker for *London's Tempe or The Field of Happiness*, thought £200 too much and offered £180, stipulating moreover for '500 bookes of the declaراcon for the said shew' and demanding that the sea-lion, the two sea-horses and the 'Estridge' be set up after the procession in their hall, to all of which but the cession of the sea-horses Christmas and Dekker had to agree.[2] In 1635 first of all Robert Norman and John Taylor presented to the court on October 2

'their project of five pageants for the Lord Maior's shew, for which they demanded 190li, and under that price they would not undertake it—John Christmas and Thomas Heywood also presented their invencon of five pageants for the said shew, viz.—

One of the three celestiall goddesses, Juno, Pallas, and Venus.

---

[1] Fleay (i. 102) thought the whale in a pageant mentioned in Davenant's *Wits* (S.R. Jan. 19, 1633/4) referred to *Londini Emporia*, in which, however, there is no whale. Freeman died in office; see S.R. Apr. 8, 1634, for an elegy entered by Raworth, who printed *The English Traveller* in 1633 and Heywood's 1635 pageant.

[2] Nichols, *Some Account of the Worshipful Company of Ironmongers*, 203-4.

One of a Sagettary, because ye sun entreth y^t day into the signe of Sagettary: Both theise for the water and land.

One antique pageant for pleasure.

One of the castle of the god Mars.

One of the harbour of happines.

W^{ch} pageants they offered to make, furnish well and sufficiently to the Compa^s liking, for 180^{li}, w^t children and speakers, and their apparell and necessaryes thereunto belonging, land carriage by porters, water carriage by boats and watermen as is accustomed, the green men ^{1} w^t their fire-works, the musick for the pageants, w^t linkes and torches for the same, and to give the Company five hundred bookes of the declaracōn of the said shew, wch offer the courte accepted and agreed thereunto; and, for pformance thereof as abovesaid, the said Xp̄mas and Haywood have hereunto subscribed their names.

John Christmas
Mathias Christmas.' ^{2}

Among other arrangements it was:

'agreed w^h Tilbury Strange, waterman, for the furnishing and fitting of a galley foist w^h 10 pieces of ordinances, 16 musketeirs, 20 rowers, one m^r, one boatswaine, and 3 gunners, w^h powder and match, and all other necessaries; for wch he is to have 28^{li}, whereof he desireth the half in hand, w^h ribbon for the m^r, boatswaine, and 3 gunners, and ye Company are to provide 2 drums, 5 trumpets, 17 pendants, 4 flaggs, wch are to be redelivered after the service pformed.   It was also ordered, on the mocōn of John Xp̄mas, that if he doe pvide two horses w^h their furniture, and two men in white armour to ride thereon, for the gracing of the Shew, then the Company will allow him xl^s'.^{3}

Ten fencers, probably for the foist, were provided by Thomas Bradshaw and Thomas Jones for £5.^{4} The following are some of the detailed expenses:

	£	s.	d.
Paid more for the hier of two horses and the children's breakfast on the Lord Mayor's day	3	0	0
Paid Mr. John Wilson for Mocado to make the poor men's sleves and for white callico	8	9	10
Paid for 10 Broad clothes for the gowns and coats	74	0	0

---

^{1} Or woodman, a common figure in pageants (Nichols, *Some Account of the Worshipful Company of Ironmongers*, 223). ^{2} *Ibid.* 222–4.
^{3} *Ibid.* 224. ^{4} Herbert, *Twelve Great Livery Companies*, ii. 594.

Spent at the viewing of the pageant twice	0	12	1
Paid for 60 round and 50 long caps of Thomas Hinch-			
man	11	9	0
Paid 3 ensign-bearers on the Lord Mayor's day	3	0	0
Paid for the loan of 2 armours for 2 horsmen	0	10	0
Paid gratuities to the Cittie Trumpeters	0	10	0
Paid the keeper of Blackwell hall	1	0	0
Paid 2 Cittie Marshalls for their attendance	4	0	0
Paid John Fosse for the hire of his barge	4	0	0
Paid 7 drums for their service at 18s. p^r piece	6	6	0
Paid 4 fifes do do at 18s. p^r piece	3	12	0
Paid Rich^d. Alavit for his Scarfe	0	10	0
Paid the M^r of the Waye house for his attendance at			
Guildhall	1	0	0
Paid Wm Michell for his dinner on Lord Mayor's day	0	2	0
Paid for 34 doz. torches	22	14	0
Paid for 22 new streamers for the galley foist	4	0	0
Paid Edw. Ballard, beadle, for his gown	3	0	0
Paid Wm Michell, under beadle	2	0	0
Paid Robt Smith for 20¼ ells of watchett and white			
taffitie sarsnitt at 6s. 6d. pr. ell	6	11	6
Paid Robt Swain for providing the hangings at Guild-			
hall	6	13	4
Paid Danl Cartrie for ribbon	7	5	0
Paid Philip White, gunner, for chambers and powder	35	0	0
Paid Willm Winchell [?Michell] for painting the			
banners and streamers	32	10	0
Paid the Lord Mayor's butler for providing of plate			
and linen for Guildhall	10	0	0[1]

Nothing is known of the pageant for 1636 or whether, indeed, Lord Mayor Bromfield enjoyed that luxury at all. In 1637 Heywood produced his *Londini Speculum*, already noticed. Next year the Lord Mayor elect was Sir Maurice Abbott, brother of the Archbishop and of Robert Abbott, Bishop of Salisbury, both bitter enemies of the Romaniz-ing tendencies of the time. Sir Maurice himself, though by no means subservient to the crown, was zealous in collecting ship-money, and one of those entrusted by the Lords of the Admiralty with fitting out ships as London's

[1] Nichols, *op. cit.* 224–5.

quota. Just before the pageant was due Heywood, who had designed the carving for the magnificent Sovereign of the Seas, published his *True Description of His Majesty's Royal Ship*; and in his *Porta pietatis, Or, The Port or Harbour of Piety*, puritanically flavoured to take the taste of the new Lord Mayor, to whose piety and family history allusion is made, he introduces a ship fully rigged as the third show by land. But as he had delivered himself of all his opinions on shipping in his recent pamphlet, he refers the curious to it. In 1639 the Drapers again engaged him for a fitting celebration of Henry Garway's term of office. The outcome was the still more pronouncedly puritanical *Londini Status Pacatus: Or, London's Peaceable Estate*, a tragically ironic title for the last pageant before the Civil War.

For the perfecting of a mayoral pageant, as for the more aristocratic masque, an architect, or at least an artisan, was as requisite as a poet. The coadjutor of Heywood, as of most of the earlier city-poets, in the mounting of the pageants for 1631, 1632, and 1633—his office was completely subordinate to that of the inventor of the show— was old Garrett (Gerard or Gerald) Christmas, whom living and dead our poet most cordially praised. As Augustus found Rome brick and left it marble,

'So he who found these Pageants and showes of Wicker and Paper, rather appearing monstrous and prodigious Births then any Beast (presented in them) in the least kind imitating Nature: hath reduc't them to that sollidity and substance for the Materialls, that they are so farre from one dayes washing to deface them, that the weathering of many Winters can not impeach them: and for their excellent Figures and well-proportioned lineaments, (by none preceeding him) that could be sayd to bee paralleld: In regard therefore there bee so many strangers of all Countries, and such as can iudge of Workemanship, come to be spectators of these Annuall Triumphs, I could wish that the vndertaking thereof might be hereafter conferd (for the Honour of the Citty) vpon men like able and sufficient. For his owne particular I conclude: *Hunc aliquis vix imitando superare potest*'.[1]

[1] 1632, sig. C 2 verso.

The talent, however, was hereditary and Heywood was on as agreeable terms with the sons, John and Matthias Christmas, successors to their father 'as well in the Exquisite performance of his qualitie, as in his true sinceritie and honesty; . . . concerning whom I make no scruple, thus Ingeniously to conclude: *Ars patris, in filiis etiam, post fata viget*'.[1] The two sons of Garrett made the monsters and chariots for Heywood in 1635, 1637, 1638, and 1639, and were the carvers of his symbolism for the Sovereign of the Seas in 1637.[2]

Originality in Lord Mayors' pageants would have been misunderstood in Heywood's day, and he did not try the experiment. The companies expected in their peripatetic displays on Simon and Jude's Day, and Heywood gave them, the formless, half-chronicle, half-morality play with an abundance of exposition and no plot, which appears to have been the established style from the middle of the sixteenth century, when the inauguration of the Lord Mayor became a pageant. The trade symbolism, the heraldic creatures of the various companies endowed with life, the patron saints, the personified cities, the more famous Lord Mayors, the Palace of Honour, the Bower

---

[1] Pearson, iv. 300.

[2] Garrett Christmas about 1614 was appointed to the lucrative post of carver to the navy, and it is as such he styles himself in a petition to have the office conferred on his sons (*C.S.P.D.* 1633/4, 521). By his will of 1633 he left to his wife Rachel and to John, Matthias and other children various legacies, partly in lands in Kent, bought of his brother-in-law John Honywood, a member of a family with whom Heywood was acquainted (see 155 *infra*). His wife was probably daughter of Arthur Honywood and Elizabeth Spencere, and granddaughter of Robert Honywood of Charinge and Mary Atwater. John and Matthias were also creditable carvers and may have had some part in Heywood's appointment as designer of the carving of the Sovereign. Heywood the pageanter is perhaps glanced at in Glapthorne's *Wit in a Constable*, 1640, i. 1:

> you may arrive to be the City Poet,
> And send the little moysture of your braine
> To grace a Lord Maiors festivall with showes,
> Alluding to his trade, or to the company
> Of which he's free.

Cf. the allusion to shows in Jasper Mayne's *City Match*, 1639, i. 3.

of Bliss, Porta Pietatis, sea-monsters, ships and aquatic deities, Ulysses, Janus, and the celestial goddesses, Prudence and Honour and Death 'exprest to the life',[1] fireworks and anti-masques of 'Anticke gesticulations, dances and other Mimicke postures, devised onely for the vulgar',[2] ethical instruction, and complimentary speeches, Heywood has them all. If he seems to us a little more recondite and pedagogic than his fellow-pageanters and his speeches more turgid and clumsy than Dekker's, whose *London's Tempe*, 1629, was probably the best of the seventeenth-century shows, his own tastes in history, mythology, and the other invariable ingredients of a pageant, his civic patriotism, and his ethical bias at least pleased the authorities as much as did the efforts of any of his contemporaries.

Apart from his pageant for 1632, Heywood seems to have done little that year except to republish *The Four Prentices*, which, however, was not '*new revised*' as the title-page claimed, and to prepare for the press *The Famous Tragedy Of The Rich Jew Of Malta. As It Was Played Before The King And Queen. In His Majesty's Theatre at Whitehall by her Majesty's Servants at the Cockpit*, 1633 (S.R. November 30, 1632).[3] That Heywood in issuing Marlowe's old play was not falling back on the last resource of needy dramatists is clear from what we know of his own circumstances and from those of the publication. As he had 'usher'd it unto the Court and presented it to the Cock-pit, with these Prologues and Epilogues here inserted' he was loath to publish it 'without the ornament of an Epistle'[4] to mark his own share in the undertaking. The public revival, which was no doubt the earlier, may be safely dated rather in 1632 than in 1631;[5] the command performance must have been before the end of the year. Besides writing the two prologues and epilogues Heywood seems to have had his hand

---

[1] Pearson, v. 371.   [2] *Ibid.* iv. 312.
[3] Probably post-dated; the dedication calls it 'a New-yeares gift'.
[4] Dedication.
[5] W. C. Hazlitt (*Play-Collector's Manual*, 120) suggests *c.* 1625.

r his finger in the play itself; accordingly against our
ndebtedness to him for having given us the melodrama at
ll, we have to balance his vandalism at the last revision, in
oatching it with episodes already used by him in *The
Captives* or *How a Man may choose a Good Wife from a
Bad*, and thus so completely ruining the play that it is
mpossible now to discover its original plan.[1]

The same year came '*accidentally to the Presse*' *The
English Traveller. As It Hath Been Publicly acted at the
Cockpit in Drury Lane: By Her Majesty's Servants* (S.R.
uly 15, 1633),[2] for which Heywood, thinking '*it not fit
hat it should passe as* filius populi, *a Bastard without a
Father to acknowledge it*', supplied a hasty list of characters,
an often-quoted address to the reader and an interesting
dedication to Sir Henry Appleton, a beneficiary of the
will of 'that good old Gentleman, mine unkle (Master
Edmund Heywood) whom you pleased to grace by the
Title of Father', and whom he had known long and inti-
nately enough for 'that alternate Love, and those frequent
urtesies which interchangably past' between them to
develop.[3] *The English Traveller* was fairly certainly
vritten for the Lady Elizabeth's men in the early twen-
ies of the seventeenth century. For though there is no
ign that the play was very recent,[4] and none that it was
very old, it was old enough to have escaped from the
hands of the '*Actors, who thinke it against their peculiar
profit to have*' plays come in print, and to be numbered
by Heywood as '*one reserved amongst two hundred and
twenty, in which I have had either an entire hand, or at
least a maine finger*'. The play with which *The English
Traveller* has most in common is *The Captives*, and a date
or it in 1624 would agree admirably with such evidence
as there is and with the mawkish tone caught from

[1] See 287–94 *infra*.
[2] Certainly from the stage copy. See S.R. July 8, 1633, for two ballads,
The true experienced Traveller' and '*The Northern Traveller*'.
[3] Appleton's second wife was Alice, daughter of William Riplingham of
t. James's, Clerkenwell; see 58-9 *supra*.
[4] The last two lines of the prologue are quoted in *The Fair Maid of the
West*, pt. I, preface.

Fletcher.[1] The main plot of the former and the sub-plot of the latter are both told as true histories in Γυναικεῖον; and the sub-plot of the former and the main plot of the latter are both Plautine adaptations, the one of the *Mostellaria* and the other of the *Rudens*, englished with the same faithfulness and not a little of the same incompleteness of translation into modern conditions; in both plays without much reason the educative value of travel is insisted on; and, lastly, while in *The English Traveller* there is a famous description, imitated from Athenaeus, of young Lionel' and his friends' shipwreck by land,[4] in *The Captives* there occurs either a reminiscence or an anticipation of it:

> CLOWN. What danger? what extreames?
> SCRIBONIA. From the sea's fury, drowninge; for last night
>   Our shipp was splitt, wee cast upon these rocks.
> CLOWN. Sayd in a jest, indeede! Shipp-wrack by land! I perceive you tooke woodden waggen for a shipp, the violent rayne for the sea, and bycause some one of the wheeles broake and you cast into some water plash, you thought the shipp was splitt and you had bin in danger of drowninge.[5]

Probably the allusion to 'the picture of Dame Fortune Before the Fortune Play-house'[6] refers to the theatre rebuilt in 1622 after the fire on December 9, 1621, and reopened early in 1623.[7]

Though in 1633 Heywood had been totalling up his dramatic labours, he still continued to add to them. Next year he and Richard Brome produced a piece of dramatic journalism following hard on the events themselves. Brome had been writing for the King's men for some time before this, and it was probably he who approached the

---

[1] The use made of a passage in Athenaeus (Pearson, iv. 24, &c.) and the Plautine sub-plot furnished Cowley, who may also have known *The Captives*, with many hints for his Latin *Naufragium Joculare*, 1638. There are some resemblances to Heywood's play in Jasper Mayne's *City Match*, 1639, especially in iii. 2 and 3. Fielding did not, as Chetwood, 19, thought, take his *Intriguing Chambermaid* from *The English Traveller*, nor yet did he get it indirectly from Heywood through Regnard.   [2] 193, &c., 253, &c.
[3] Pearson, iv. 7–8, 10–11, &c., and *The Captives*, ed. Judson, 128.
[4] Pearson, iv. 24, &c.   [5] Ed. Judson, 67.   [6] Pearson, iv. 34.
[7] Cf. Chambers, ii. 443, and Murray, i. 214.

free-lance Heywood,[1] a famous witch-lorist, to assist him in a play on the topic of the moment, the Lancashire witch scare of 1634. There had been stagnation in the staple of news, as the prologue indicates:

> *Corrantoes failing, and no foot post late*
> *Possessing us with Newes of forraine State,*
> *No accident abroad worthy Relation*
> *Arriving here, we are forc'd from our own Nation*
> *To ground the Scene that's now in agitation;*

indeed than this sensational witch-trial nothing could have been more opportune.

The county of Lancaster had carried an evil reputation for witches since the supposed bedevilment of Henry VI by the Duchess of Gloucester and her Lancashire associates. The celebrated Dr. Dee, warden of the collegiate church at Manchester, nearly lost his life for dabbling in the occult; and his collaborator Edward Kelly did lose his necromantic ears. Then there were the cases of demoniacal possession in Nicholas Starkie's house and the exorcisms of John Darrel which provoked Samuel Harsnet, the author of *A Declaration of Popish Impostures*, 1603. In 1612 burst a sensation of the first magnitude. Two women of eighty or more had, partly by the assumption of preternatural wisdom but more by infirmity and dotage, conveyed the impression of being witches. Both had accomplices, and 'in the anxiety which each felt to outvie the other, and to secure the greater share of the general custom of a not very extended or very lucrative market, each wished to be represented as more death-dealing, destructive, and powerful than her neighbour'.[2] Their reputation sooner or later invited the attention of an officious magistrate, Roger Nowel of Read, who committed the two witches along with two others to Lancaster Castle on April 2, 1612. But according to the evidence of the chief witness at their trial, Jennet Device, a girl of

---

[1] Heywood was never a member of the Lady Elizabeth's, Queen Henrietta's, or King Charles's companies, as Fleay supposed (i. 281, and *Anglia*, viii. 410).

[2] Crossley, ed. of Potts's *Wonderful Discovery of Witches*, xliii.

nine and granddaughter of Mother Demdike, the friends and children of the imprisoned witches assembled within a week at Malkin Tower with the intention of killing the jailer and blowing up the Castle. The indefatigable Nowel, therefore, on the strength of this farrago, signed more warrants, and when the trial began on August 17 about a dozen men and women were convicted and sentenced to be executed the next day. All of these unfortunate persons were of a humble walk in life with the exception of Alice Nutter, a woman of property, well conducted and connected. It has been traditionally delated that her own nearest relatives instructed the impish Jennet Device and that Roger Nowel had his own private grudge against her over a disputed boundary.[1] It has, too, been asserted that Mrs. Nutter served Heywood as a model for his Mrs. Generous; but there is no resemblance in their diabolical practices or in their circumstances, except their rank above that of most supposed witches; and though this story of the condemnation and execution of a Lancashire gentlewoman for unlawful arts may have been known to Heywood, it is certain that in *The Late Lancashire Witches* he does not follow in the very slightest Potts's standard account of the 1612 sensation.

Some twenty years after this scare Pendle Forest was again much troubled by witches, and again part at least of the nation-wide interest in the affair was due to the rank of some of the accused. It seems that one day in February 1633/4, Edmund Robinson, son of Edmund Robinson, a mason of Newchurch in Pendle, had been sent to bring home the family cows but had instead idled his time with other children, and being of an imaginative turn of mind invented an elaborate story of diablerie which incriminated several persons in the neighbourhood. This deposition, corroborated by the father, was carefully followed by the play.[2] Then on March 2 a suspected

[1] *Ibid.* lv.

[2] Whittaker, *History of Whalley*, ed. 1872, i. 300, &c., a more reliable authority than Baines's *History of the County Palatine of Lancaster*, ed. 1836, i.604, &c., or Webster's *Displaying of Supposed Witchcraft*, 340, &c.

witch, Margaret Johnson, aged sixty,[1] and apparently of
feeble mind, confessed before the same justices as had
examined the boy Robinson,[2] and again the dramatists
used the confession or contemporary reports of it.[3] At
the trial the jury was convinced of the guilt of seventeen
of the accused, who were recommitted to Lancaster Castle.
But the judges appeared to have penetrated the imposture,
respited the execution, and reported the case to the King
in council.[4] The Privy Council's decision was to remit
seven of the accused to Dr. Bridgeman, Bishop of Chester,
for examination.[5]   On June 15 he dispatched his report
to Secretaries Windebank and Coke, certifying that of
the seven examinees three had died in prison and one was
sick beyond recovery; Margaret Johnson, who made
certain picturesque additions to her confession,[6] was
obviously not of sound mind, though the bishop only
hints that such was the case; and the other two, he
thought, would soon discover their guilt or their innocence. But the bishop was not empowered without further
orders to question certain persons who volunteered to
testify that Robinson senior in consideration of forty
shillings had proposed to Mrs. Dicconson, one of the
accused, to withhold any evidence against her. Both
Mary Spenser and Frances Dicconson made eminently
sensible statements, that of the former at least, or something like it, being known to Heywood and Brome; and
Dicconson confirmed what was alleged of Robinson.[7] As
the bishop's report indicated that there had been a mis-
carriage of justice, four of the witches who figure in *The
Late Lancashire Witches*, Margaret Robinson, Frances
Dicconson, Mary Spenser, and the wife of one Har-
greaves, Alice or Allison by name, were summoned to

---

[1] *C.S.P.D.* 1634–5, 77–8.

[2] Richard Shuttleworth and John Starkie, the latter one of the demoniacs
treated by Farrel in 1595.

[3] Baines, ed. 1836, i. 607–8; Whittaker, ed. 1801, i. 189, &c.; ed. 1872.
i. 303–4.

[4] The judges were in London before May 22; cf. *Hist. MSS. Com.*
XII, Ap. ii. 53.   [5] *C.S.P.D.* 1634–5, 77–8, 79.   [6] *Ibid.* 78–9.

[7] *C.S.P.D.* 1634–5, 78–9.

London and lodged in the Ship Tavern, Greenwich, where on their arrival towards the end of June they were medically examined for witch-marks by the King's physician, Harvey, and a committee of surgeons and midwives, who reported favourably.[1] After Charles had seen them, the royal pardon was extended to all the surviving condemned, there being strong presumptive evidence that the boy Robinson had been suborned. Indeed on July 10 the boy, who had persisted in his story till his confession to the King's coachman at Richmond, confessed on his further examination by order of Windebank that his original deposition was a fabrication to excuse his disobedience; and on July 16 with more detail, before George Long, he attributed the basis of his story to popular reports of the 1612 witch-scare.[2] Public opinion, however, must have veered round before this, for Edmund Robinson senior had been imprisoned as early as June 28. About July 16 he, being in great want and without friends, petitioned Windebank from the Gatehouse, affecting to be ignorant of the cause of his imprisonment; he understood that one of the jurymen had lodged a petition against him, denied having persecuted Mrs. Dicconson, and prayed for release.[3] Charles's pardon did not bring about any material change in the treatment of the witches; they were taken back to Lancaster Castle in December,[4] and were still there in the autumn of 1637 and probably till their deaths.[5]

The news of the scare does not seem to have burst on London till about May 16, 1634, when a wild report that nineteen witches had been condemned and at least sixty discovered, 'and yet daily there are more revealed' was the 'greatest news from the country'.[6] The judges arrived about the same time, and the Privy Council discussed the

---

[1] C.S.P.D. 1634–5, 98; cf. Webster, op. cit. 276–8, and Scott, Somers Tracts, iii. 98.

[2] C.S.P.D. 1634–5, 141, 152–3; cf. Webster, op. cit. 277.

[3] C.S.P.D. 1634–5, 152.   [4] Cf. Hist. MSS. Com. X, Ap. iv. 433.

[5] Cf. The Narrative of the Life of Mr. Henry Burton, 1643.

[6] C.S.P.D. 1634–5, 26: cf. Sir William Brereton's Travels, ed. Hawkins, i. 33.

matter before May 22.[1] The whole affair was the topic of the hour; the author of *The Displaying of Supposed Witchcraft* mentions the '*Alarm that the* Pendle-forest *Witches gave to all this Kingdom, that they were sent for to* London, *great sums gotten at the Fleet to show them, and publick Plays acted thereupon*'.[2] The last clause refers not only to Heywood and Brome's collaboration but to an old play, *Doctor Lambe and the Witches*, relicensed because of some new scenes for the Prince's men.[3] Our collaborators probably did not set about their tragicomedy till they had seen and perhaps conversed with '*Those Witches the fat Iaylor brought to Towne*',[4] towards the end of June. It was staged by the King's men at the Globe when the rumour of a pardon was abroad, for the epilogue says

> *Now while the Witches must expect their due*
> *By lawfull Iustice, we appeale to you*
> *For favourable censure; what their crime*
> *May bring upon 'em, ripeness yet of time*
> *Has not reveal'd. Perhaps great Mercy may*
> *After just condemnation give them day*
> *Of longer life.*

Now the medical report on the witches was not made till June 29, and the day before suspicions of the veracity of the chief witnesses for the prosecution had resulted in their arrest. The epilogue must have been written before Charles's pardon on June 30 or very early in July in consequence of the confession of Edmund Robinson, the younger of the above-mentioned crown witnesses. Fleay,

---

[1] *Hist. MSS. Com.* XII, Ap. ii. 53.

[2] Webster, *op. cit.* 346.

[3] Herbert, 36. In Nabbes's *Tottenham Court* (ed. Bullen, i. 104), acted in 1634, there is an allusion to the witches. See S.R. Aug. 22, 1634, for two ballads, '*Prophane pastime or the witches' mad humours*' and '*The Witches' Dance*', and for the latter see Chappell's *Popular Music*, i. 86, and Add. MS. 38, 539, f. 4. Cf. 'wee neede no further witnesse, then that of the *Lancashire* witches some few yeares since; of which I make no doubt, but this whole City hath taken especiall notice of': *A certain Relation of the Hog-faced Gentlewoman called Mistress Tannakin Skinker*, 1640 (S.R. Dec. 5, 1639), a pamphlet very much in Heywood's manner.

[4] Prologue.

who advances useless emendations, misquotes the play,
misnames the witches, and generally misrepresents the
facts, finds 'positive proof' that Brome in 1634 revised
a hypothetical witch-drama of 1613 based by Heywood
on Potts's *Discovery of Witchcraft*.[1] There is not a vestige
of evidence for such a theory and not a single detail is
traceable to the 1612 witch-hunt. Why Brome preserved
obsolete diablerie instead of bringing it up to date is a
question to be asked. And why did Fleay start such a
canard in view of the fact that the play must have been
written at the very time Heywood was busy on his
Hierarchy (S.R. November 7, 1634)? There is absolutely
no sign of patching; one scene involves directly or indirectly every other; the supposed remains of the older
play are anticipated in earlier passages; they have their
consequences in later; there are allusions to them throughout; they are, in short, woven into the purely invented
plots of Generous and his wife, and Whetstone and his
tormentors, which Heywood contributed, and of Seely,
Lawrence, and Parnell, which was Brome's share. The
Generous plot, too, may be dated by the soldier's declaration of his service 'With the Russian against the Polack,
a heavy war, and hath brought me to this hard fate. I was
tooke prisoner by the Pole, & after some weeks of durance,
got both my freedom and passe'.[2] Wladislaus IV of
Poland, after a series of heavy engagements with the
Tsar's general, forced him to surrender with his whole
army on March 1, 1634. When the Turks threatened
him from the south he concluded peace with Russia on
May 28, 1634. The Turkish attitude and ultimatum
were known in England early in June,[3] and news of the
treaty must soon have followed. Again, the Whetstone
episode is dated not only by its dramatizing an anecdote
in *The Hierarchy*,[4] but by an allusion[5] to Prynne's ear-
cropping on May 7 and 10, 1634, and by another to 'the
last Farthing's with the double rings and [the] late Coy'ned

---

[1] i. 301–2; cf. i. 38, *Stage*, 341, and Ward, ii. 28.
[2] Pearson, iv. 194.   [3] *C.S.P.D.* 1634, 5, 55.   [4] 512.
[5] Pearson, iv. 198.

peeces which they say are all counterfeit'.[1] As great
difficulty was encountered in getting the new coins into
circulation and in suppressing counterfeiting, a proclamation was issued on February 22, 1633/4, permitting the
patentees to depreciate the old farthings of 1613 in order
that 'double-ringed' coins, distinguishable from the others
by a double beading, might supersede them.[2] When the
excitement had died down the play was published without
introductory matter, though with Heywood's consent at
least as his motto on the title-page shows, as *The late
Lancaster Witches. A Well received Comedy, lately Acted at
the Globe on the Bankside, by the King's Majesty's Actors*
(S.R. October 28).[3]

It was not the only piece on which Heywood and
Brome had worked together. On April 8, 1654, were
registered two lost plays, *'The life and death of S* Martyn
Skink, wth the warres of the low countries*, by Rich: Brome
& Tho: Heywood, & *The Apprentices Prize*, &c', the
second of which is not certainly by the same authors as
the first. Fleay's statement that both were probably old
plays by Heywood altered by Brome about 1634 is a
guess from the titles, which look early.[4] The two collabora-

[1] *Ibid.* iv. 197; cf. 182.

[2] Cf. Martin, *Is The Late Lancashire Witches a Revision?* M.P. xiii.
82–3, and *C.S.P.D.* 1634–5, 18, 31–2, 85 for complaints in May and June.
The F. Adson, in a stage direction (Pearson, iv. 196), may be the second of
two players in a direction 'enter two servants Rowl : Ashton' in *Love's
Pilgrimage*, presented by the King's men in Sept. 1635 (cf. Murray, i. 172,
table, and Fleay, i. 195, who makes 'Rowl:Ashton' one person). There was
also a musician Adson; see B.M.: MSS. Addit. 10444.

[3] Chetwood, 32, mentions a mythical 1646 ed. Shadwell's *Lancashire
Witches and Teague a Divelly the Irish Priest*, 1681 (published 1682), is
based on the witch-scares of 1612 and 1634, and owes some hints to Heywood, as Chetwood had averred, 19. See Clarence, *'The Stage' Cyclopaedia*,
for other plays on the Lancashire witches.

[4] i. 41; see i. 303, where they are assigned to 1634, when Heywood and
Brome were working together. Collier's list of ballads (*New Particulars
regarding the Works of Shakespeare*, 46), including *The London 'Prentice's
Tragedy*, by Thomas Heywood, which he pronounced the foundation of a
lost play, is spurious. A genuine ballad, *The honour of an Apprentice of
London. Wherein is declared his matchless Manhood, and brave adventures
done by him in Turkey, and by what means he married the King's daughter*

tors had several common friends and were perhaps acquainted for a year or two before 1634. John Ford, the dramatist's cousin and a friend of Heywood, wrote verses for Brome's *Northern Lass*, 1632. Brome commended *Fancy's Theatre*, 1640, by John Tatham, who dedicated the volume to John Ford. Both Heywood and Brome praised Marmion's *Cupid and Psyche*, 1637, and Thomas Jordan's *Poetical Varieties*, 1637. Other members of the circle were F. T., probably Francis Tuckyr, J. B., perhaps a brother of Anthony Brewer, Thomas Nabbes, Dekker, and the Beestons.

In his *Pleasant Comedy called A Maidenhead Well Lost. As it hath been publicly Acted at the Cockpit in Drury Lane, with much Applause: By her Majesty's Servants*, somewhat but not much earlier than *The Late Lancaster Witches*,[1] and printed like it in 1634 (S.R. June 25), Heywood, though he did not think highly enough of it to dedicate it to any one, chose its preface for adverting again to Prynne, to whom in the dedication of *The English Traveller* he had already promised a reply. Yet, in spite of the public's good reception of this unhealthy Caroline plot, it was scarcely the best opportunity to denounce '*that most horrible* Histriomastix *whose uncharitable doome having damned all such to the flames of Hell, hath it selfe already suffered a most remarkeable fire here upon Earth*', and all such '*whose prepared palats disgusting all* Poems *of this nature, are poysoned with the bitter iuice of that* Coloquintida *and* Hemlocke, *which can neither relish the peace of the* Church *of that same Country*, was registered on Mar. 13, 1655/6, and Mar. 1, 1674/5 (*R.B.* vii. 589), and perhaps as early as Oct. 16, 1633; see S.R. May 15, 1588, Nov. 9, 1639, and Mar. 11, 1639/40, for other 'prentice ballads. There is as well a prose chap-book, *London's Glory or, The History of the Famous and Valiant London 'Prentice: Being an Account of his Parentage, Birth and Breeding, together with all the many brave and Heroic Exploits perform'd by him throughout the whole course of his Life; to the Honour of London, and the whole English Nation*. The other play recalls the 'liffe & death of martin swarte' mentioned by Henslowe in 1597, *H.D.* i. 53; cf. ii. 185, and Heywood's *Life of Merlin*, 292.

[1] See prologue and epilogue. Fleay (*Stage*, 341) thought it an old play revived or (*ibid.* 156 and i. 244-5, 299) *Joan as good as my Lady* (see 12-13 *supra*).

nor Common-weale'. He again returned, but with more
skill and wit, to attack Prynne in *Love's Mistress*. That
it was not an old piece resuscitated is clear from its agreement in style and plot with characteristic Caroline plays.
The words 'Madame, will you give me a License to sell
Wine',[1] may refer to the troubles of the Vintners' Company which began in 1632, and to an abuse to which
Heywood turned his attention in the early days of the
Long Parliament.[2] The year 1632 would also agree with
the production of the play by the Queen's men at the
Cockpit.

In some ways *Love's Mistress Or, The Queen's Masque.
As it was three times presented before their two Excellent
Majesties, within the space of eight days: In the presence of
sundry Foreign Ambassadors. Publicly Acted by the Queen's
Comedians, At the Phœnix in Drury Lane*, 1636 (S.R.
September 30, 1635) and 1640,[3] is the most important
of Heywood's plays for his biographer. Though written
for a court audience, the resulting mixture of the masque
is not very different from what he provided for the public
stage; but it is more poetical and more carefully written,
and the author lets us see in the allegory that his previous
submission to popular tastes was a condescension of which
he was not a little ashamed. In rejecting Fleay's theory
that the kernel of Heywood's masque dates from 1597,
that the clown scenes were added at 'the 1633 public
performance', and the Apuleius framework at the royal
view,[4] we need give only a few arguments of a general
character for dating the whole play in 1634 and no earlier.
In the first place, we know that there was no public or
private performance in 1633, and that the first performance was before the King and Queen, though in a public
theatre, and only a day or two before the King's birthday,

---

[1] Pearson, iv. 126.   [2] See 199–206 *infra*.
[3] Dr. Greg (review of Bang's ed. of *Pleasant Dialogues, Modern Language
Quarterly*, vii. 30) dates one of the 1640 issues not long before 1660, perhaps in 1651. On May 22, 1640, 'a Comedie called *Loues Masterpeece* by
Thomas Heywood' was registered; it cannot be the same as *Love's Mistress*,
as is suggested in *Old English Plays*, 1814–15, vi. 104, and Collier's
Dodsley, vii. 222.   [4] i. 286, 299; cf. *Stage*, 341, 393.

for which the masque was designed. Secondly, the Apuleius and clown scenes are not separate from, but coalesce with the rest. It is not possible that the nice balance which Heywood has struck between the contrasted motives of the masque and the anti-masques by the alternation of Apuleius, Midas, and the clowns, with the serious main plot, was achieved by the mere addition of lively scenes of farce to an old play. Thirdly, Heywood transcribed passages from 'The golden Ass & Cupid & Psiches', which Dekker, Day, and Chettle wrote in concert in 1600.[1] Fourthly, *Love's Mistress* not only bears no resemblance to what must have been Heywood's manner in 1597, but was obviously written after the complete development of the masque, after the beginning of the Platonic craze in court circles—it was probably the Platonic masque of which Howell had got wind by June 3, 1634[2]—and after the appearance of Lyly's *Six Court Comedies*, 1632, to which it owes not a little. Lastly, as we try to show, the masque was subsequent to Prynne's trial and punishment, and can be pretty certainly dated in the very weeks when Heywood would ordinarily have been preparing his Lord Mayor's pageant. On its publication, Heywood addressed his work to the handsome fourth Earl of Dorset, grandson of the poet Sackville; his influence at court had been firmly established by his appointment in 1628 as Lord Chamberlain to the Queen, in which capacity he would make the arrangements for the presentation of the masque. Heywood offered his play, then, rather to the official than to the patron; he perhaps hesitated to address again the Queen, who had shown such favour to the piece, so soon after he had dedicated to her *The Hierarchy*, 1635. The masque was first presented on the public stage, probably on Saturday, November 15, but at a private performance at the Phoenix, attended by both the King and the Queen, perhaps a full-dress rehearsal to which the actors had invited the royal

---

[1] *H.D.* i. 120–2; cf. *England's Parnassus*, ed. Crawford, xxxi–xxxii, 274–5, 349, 509–10, 529, and Chambers, iii. 346.

[2] *Epistolae Hoelianae*, ed. Jacobs, i. 317–18; cf. 407.

pair, and for which Heywood wrote a special prologue.
Therefore, as with all other masques, it had never been
clapperclawed with the palms of the vulgar when 'Her
Majestie Inviting the *King* to *Denmarke House*, in the
Strand, upon his Birth-day, being November the 19. This
Play (bearing from that time) the Title of the *Queenes
Masque*, was again presented before Him: *Cupid* speaking
the Prologue.' This was the occasion for which it
was designed and for which Inigo Jones's scenery and
machinery were prepared. As for *'the rare decorements
which new apparrell'd it'*, says the delighted Heywood,
*'when it came the second time to the Royall viewe, (Her
Gratious Majestie then entertaining His* Highnesse *at* Den-
marke-House, *upon his Birth-day) I cannot pretermit to give
a due Charracter to that admirable Artist, Mr.* Inego Iones,
Master surveyor of the Kings *worke, &c. Who to every Act,
nay almost to every Sceane, by his excellent Inventions gave
such an extraordinary Luster; upon every occasion changing
the stage to the admiration of all the Spectators: that, as I must
Ingeniously confesse, It was above my apprehension to conceive,
so to their sacred Majesties, and the rest of the Auditory; It
gave so generall a content, that I presume they never parted
from any object, presented in that kind, better pleased, or more
plenally satisfied.'*[1] Indeed a second *court* performance was
immediately ordered, and Heywood composed for it 'The
Prologue To the King and Queene, the Second time it was
Acted, the same Weeke'.[2] This was the apex of Heywood's career; for one dizzy week he was a court poet,
the writer of a masque three times performed before
royalty within twelve days. It is little wonder that in
commending it to the reader he is of the opinion that
his *'Dramatick Poem'* needs no apology, although he
follows custom in offering one. But when his young

---

[1] Probably some of the scenery and machinery was used later for the
public performances. Killigrew's *Conspiracy or Pallantus and Eudora,*
acted in 1634, and *Love's Mistress* were the first plays presented on a public
stage in England with scenery. Fleay (i. 41) sees allusions in the prologue
to Brome's *Court Beggar* to early scenery.

[2] Perhaps on Thurs., Nov. 27.

friend, Shakerley Marmion, published his long narrative of *Cupid and Psyche*,[1] no one applauded more sincerely than Heywood his 'worthy friend's' poem in these lines:

> Love and the soul are two things, both divine,
> Thy task, friend Marmion now, which once was mine.
> What I writ was dramatical; thy Muse
> Runs in an epic strain, which they still use,
> Who write heroic poems. Thine is such,
> Which when I read, I could not praise too much ...
> These had they issued from another's pen,
> A stranger, and unknown to me, I then
> Could not have been so pleased; but from a friend,
> Where I might envy, I must now commend.
> And glad I am this fair course thou hast run,
> Unvex'd to see myself so far outdone.
> 'Twixt intimates, who mutual love profess,
> More's not required, and mine could show no less.[2]

[1] Marmion's poem is dedicated to the young Elector, for whose welcome to England in 1635 Heywood wrote a prologue and epilogue (*Pleasant Dialogues*, 250–1).

[2] The lines of Francis Tuckyr read almost like a criticism of Heywood:

> Let those voluminous Authours, that affect
> Fame rather great, than good, thy work reject.
> Jewels are small: how 'nlike art thou to those,
> That tire out Rime, and Verse, till they trot Prose:
> And ride the Muses Pegasus, poor jade,
> Till he be foundred; and make that their trade:
> And to fill up the sufferings of the beast,
> Foot it themselves three hundred miles at least.
> These have no mercy on the Paper rheames,
> But produce *plaies*, as Schole-boys do write theams.
> Thou keepst thy Muse in breath, and if men wage
> Gold on her head, will better runne the stage:
> And 'tis more praise, than hadst thou labour'd in't,
> To brand the world with twenty such in print.

See S.R. June 24, 1637, for '*Cupid and Sica with a description of a ffeast without Meat. &c.*' of Heywood's friend, John Taylor. In *Now or Never: Or, A New Parliament of Women*, 1656/6, is '*Cupid's* Revenge, or Bad News for Poor Maids ... To the Tune of, Love's Mistress', apparently the tune of a ballad in S.R. Mar. 12, 1655/6, and Mar. 1, 1674/5, *Love's Mistress or nature's rarity*, by Samuel Smithson (Bodl. Wood E 25 (79) and R.B. viii. cxxiii). Pepys saw *Love's Mistress* no less than five times. On Mar. 2, 1660/1, at Salisbury Court he was specially pleased by the 'good jeer to the old story of the Siege of Troy' (cf. Pearson, v. 113). The play

Except *The Fair Maid of the Exchange*, for all of which we are by no means sure that Heywood was responsible, *Love's Mistress* is the only one of his plays that is undoubtedly satirical of actual persons. In view of this fact and in our attempt to interpret the topical allegory we ought to look first perhaps for any shafts aimed at Jonson, whose quarrel with Heywood's collaborator was still raging. Jones, whose position at court was more secure than Jonson's, had unscrupulously exerted his influence to oust his enemy completely from favour, a task made all the easier by the latter's violent abuse. Did Jonson's resentment extend to Jones's collaborators? did his indignation at seeing such a botcher of plays as Heywood engaged to produce a specimen of his own speciality provoke him to some sarcasm at which even Heywood retaliated? Certainly Heywood's admiration for Jones's

appears with the date Oct. 26, 1661, in Herbert's list of pieces performed by the King's men at the Red Bull and at a new house in Gibbon's Tennis court, Clare Market (Herbert, 118). Pepys saw *Love's Mistress* again on Mar. 11, 1660/1, at the Theatre, Vere Street, near Clare Market, and though not so well pleased as on the first occasion, he went to see it once more at Salisbury Court on Mar. 25. He found 'pretty things and good variety' but 'no or little fancy in it' when it was played at the King's Playhouse on May 15, 1665; and such was his opinion of it on Aug. 15, 1668, at another revival at the same theatre. Apparently it was acted also on June 3, 1669 at the court theatre, Whitehall, on the occasion of the visit of Cosmo III, Grand Duke of Tuscany; see Count Lorenzo Magalotti's *Travels of Cosmo III, Grand Duke of Tuscany*, English translation, 1821. Mr. W. J. Lawrence (*Foreign Singers and Musicians at the Court of Charles II, Musical Quarterly*, Apr. 1923) notes that despite Pepys's faint praise of the singing of eunuchs (Feb. 16, 1667/8) he went three times in Oct. 1668 to the King's house to hear 'the French Eunuch', but 'bred in Italy' (Oct. 12, 14), sing in *The Faithful Shepherdess*. Mr. Lawrence believes that the eunuch in question was Baldassare Ferri and that Pepys was mistaken in the nationality. On one occasion after Ferri had played Zephyr in an unspecified piece, he was presented by a masked lady with an emerald of great value. Now in *Love's Mistress*, revived in Aug. 1668, less than two months before Pepys heard the 'French Eunuch', there is a character Zephyrus who has nothing to say but could be very easily made to sing. When Shadwell presented his *Psyche*, adapted from Molière, at the Duke's Theatre, Dorset Gardens, in Feb. 1674 (Genest, i. 163), the age of Charles II found something nearer its own grosser taste and no longer needed Tom Heywood's beautiful *mélange*.

machines proves his sympathies to have been with '*that admirable Artist*'. There is, of course, no possibility that Midas, the contemner of poetry and the things of the mind in *Love's Mistress*, was meant for Jonson, but we are not sure that '*a Proud Asse with eares*' was a mere antimasquer:

> A selfe-will'd insolent foole,
> Who spights at those above him, and those beneath
> Despiseth, and his equalls jets upon;
> Riche in his owne conceit, in judgement poore,
> Still carping, tho' a coxcombe, and may passe,
> As these dayes goe, for a proud arrogant Asse.[1]

There is an even more curious phrase in a passage approved of Pepys:[2]

CLOWN. But heare mee, oh you misse of understanding; this *Troy* was a Village of some twenty houses; and *Priam*, as silly a fellow as I am, onely loving to play the good fellow, hee had a great many bowsing lads; whom hee called sonnes.

SWAIN. As we have heere in *Arcadia*.

CLOWN. Iust the same.[3]

Nevertheless we can deduce nothing from these obscurities, and in any case their *éclaircissement* would throw no light on the riddle of the allegory of Apuleius and Midas.

A very unconvincing interpretation of it was submitted by Fleay.[4] Apuleius, the presenter of the story of Psyche, is, according to Fleay, Heywood himself, an identification which is obviously right. Midas Fleay guesses to be Christopher Beeston, and Midas's clownish son to be William Beeston; 'Midas', he continues, 'prefers the song

---

[1] Pearson, v. 104–5.   [2] See 132 *supra*, note 2.   [3] Pearson, v. 113.

[4] i. 299; at ii. 244, however, Shirley is the clown, in revenge for his satire of Heywood's pageants in *The Contention of Honour and Riches* (S.R. Nov. 9, 1632), dated by Fleay (ii. 238) *c.* June 1631, before Heywood had written any pageants; see also Schipper (*James Shirley, sein Leben und seine Werke*, 299), who agrees with Fleay. *Love's Mistress*, according to Fleay (ii. 239), is 'filled with allusions' to Shirley's *Arcadia* (perhaps written for the King's birthday in 1632; cf. Fleay, ii. 239, and A. H. Nason, *James Shirley*, 44, 70, 90); but the resemblance between the two plays is quite fortuitous. In *Anglia*, viii. 414, Fleay declared Henry Shirley to be the father of James and the Midas of *Love's Mistress*.

to Pan, the Arcadian god (Shirley's *Arcadia*), to Heywood's song to Apollo (perhaps an intended revival of
Apollo and Daphne), (a song in which "*semel in anno redet*
[sic] *Apollo*" is alluded to in iii. 2)'. But even if the court
was interested in the petty squabbles of actors and dramatists, there is an almost complete refutation of Fleay's
theory in the fact that the masque was produced by the
Queen's company, of which Christopher Beeston was the
manager and his son William a member. The Beestons,
moreover, retained the play when they seceded from the
Queen's men, and the acting rights of it and a large
number of other pieces were confirmed to their company
of boy-actors on August 10, 1639. There is no evidence
whatever of the elder Beeston's having preferred Shirley
to Heywood; and, so far from our dramatist being on bad
terms with Christopher and his son, they paid for two of
the plates in *The Hierarchy of the Blessed Angels* (S.R.
November 7, 1634). Lastly, if *Love's Mistress* treated
Shirley so scurvily, it is strange that he showed no soreness
in *The Opportunity*, licensed to the Queen's men only ten
days after the first command performance at court of
Heywood's masque.[1]

It is undoubtedly true that about the time when Heywood was writing his masque he had good cause to be
uneasy at the popularity of his young rival. They had
been for some years the principal dramatists of the Queen's
men, and may well be the 'two poetical Drury Lane
writers, the Cobler and the Tapster' of *Covent Garden
Weeded*.[2] Perhaps it was Heywood's temporary success
in 1631 that drove Shirley with his *Changes* to the very
inferior Revels company at Salisbury Court.[3] This was
but a short retreat and he returned to the Queen's players
with his next play, *Hyde Park*.[4] In his next again, however, *The Ball*,[5] Shirley's satire 'both of lords and others

[1] Herbert, 36.   [2] iii. 1.
[3] Jan. 10, 1631/2 (Herbert, 33).   [4] Apr. 30, 1632 (Herbert, 34).
[5] Nov. 18, 1632 (Herbert, 19, 34); cf. A. H. Nason, *op. cit.* 91, 230, &c.;
T. H. Pranlin, *Study in Shirley's Comedies of London Life*, 39, &c.; and
Fleay, i. 67, ii. 238–9.

of the court' was too overt; even as revised the comedy was objectionable, and the author thought fit to justify himself in *The Lady of Pleasure*.[1] This adds significance to a remark in the preface to *The Iron Age*, part II: '*I know not*', says Heywood, '*how they* [i.e. the two parts] *may be received in this Age, where nothing but* Satirica Dictæria, *and* Comica Scommata *are now in request: For mine owne part, I never affected either, when they stretcht to the abuse of any person publicke, or private*.' But Shirley regained the ground lost and reformed his ways; *The Young Admiral*,[2] 'being free from oaths, prophaness or obsceanes', was thought by Herbert a model production; the King considered *The Gamester*, based on a plot supplied by himself, 'the best play he had seen for seven years';[3] and *The Beauties or The Bird in a Cage* and his revision of Fletcher's *Nightwalker*[4] were both very well received. Not only had Shirley become first favourite on the stage; but in his *Contention for Honour and Riches*, 1633,[5] he sneered provokingly at the city pageants. It is possible, too, that Confident Rapture in *The Example*[6] is a caricature of Heywood; '*a pretended wit*', given to classical allusions, 'well read in books', 'the elegant time wit', he is one who makes 'A noise i' the town'; to what purpose, he asks, should his

> wits be clogg'd
> With heavy acres, when the town's exchequer
> Is mine, and every mercer is my tenant
> If he pretend to wit, and hope to justify
> His shop-book, and orthography of his bills?[7]

There can be less or no doubt that in the play Shirley

---

[1] Oct. 15, 1635 (Herbert, 37). Cf. Nabbes's *Covent Garden*, prologue and sig. C 3 verso; and Fleay, ii. 119.

[2] July 3, 1633 (Herbert, 19–20, 35).

[3] At court Feb. 6, 1633/4 (Herbert, 35, 54–8).

[4] Jan. 21, 1632/3, and May 11, 1633 (Herbert, 34, 54). Cf. H. T. Pranlin (*op. cit.* 2) for Shirley's contemporary reputation.

[5] Ed. Dyce, vi. 296–7; cf. *Honoria and Mammon*, ed. Dyce, vi. 10, and Massinger's *City Madam*, iv. 1.

[6] June 24, 1634 (Herbert, 36).

[7] Ed. Dyce, iii. *dramatis personae*, 284, 301–2, 317–18, 332, 333–4, 363.

produced within a few days of *Love's Mistress*[1] he glanced
at one of the incidents and at the machinery of Heywood's
masque:

> If I
> Forget this opportunity, let Midas
> Transplant his goodly ears to this dull head,
> And let all women laugh at me. My stars!
> I bow to you, and kiss your influence;
> I am exalted to your sphere already,
> Where, with the duchess, I will sit and shine
> A constellation.[2]

We may perhaps guess from a phrase in the prologue to
The Coronation,[3]

> *although dull souls his pen despise*
> *Who think it yet too early to be wise,*

in conjunction with the mention of '*Poets that wrapt
divinity in tales*',[4] and '*give . . . copies forth of angels*',[5] that
the ageing Heywood had reflected on his rival's juniority.
Though Heywood may have let fall some such remark,
he published nothing that justified Shirley's long resentment; for we must except the quite general reproof already
quoted from *The Iron Age* and the equally general regret
expressed in the prologue to *A Challenge for Beauty* that
the Caroline dramatists dealt exclusively with '*puling
Lovers, craftie Bawdes or cheates*', a regret at once qualified
by the commendation of

> *their quick fancies, who can fit*
> *These queasie Times, with Humours flash't in wit.*

Shirley, on the other hand, not only rewrote his *Contention
of Honour and Riches*, probably after Heywood's death, as
Honoria and Mammon, but in *The Triumph of Beauty*[6] holds
up to scorn the poor old city-poet and his pageants.[7] But

---

[1] *The Opportunity*, Nov. 29, 1634 (Herbert, 36).
[2] Ed. Dyce, iii. 433; cf. Pearson, v. 88, 127.
[3] Feb. 6, 1634/5 (Herbert, 36).   [4] ?*Love's Mistress*; cf. preface.
[5] ?*The Hierarchy*.
[6] C. May, 1640.
[7] Ed. Dyce, vi. 320, &c. The judgement of Paris is the subject of one of
Heywood's *Pleasant Dialogues* as well as of Shirley's interlude; the three
goddesses also appear in *Londini Sinus Salutis*, 1635.

time has its revenges; in 1651 an enthusiastic admirer of
Cartwright was prepared to sacrifice for his favourite

> Don's *rich Gold, and* Johnson's *silver Mine;*
> *Then to the pile add all that* Fletcher *writ,*
> *Stamp'd by thy Character a currant Wit:*
> Suckling's *Ore, with* Sherley's *small money, by*
> Heywood's *old Iron, and* Shakespear's *Alchemy.*[1]

But Shirley's fame was to sink even lower still; Dryden's
MacFlecknoe associated the rivals in an inglorious quartet
with the contemptible Ogilby and the unspeakable
Shadwell:

> Much Heywood, Shirley, Ogilby there lay,
> But loads of Shadwell almost chok'd the way;

and Gildon charges Langbaine with lauding inferior poets
'so that shou'd a Stranger to our Poets read him, they
wou'd make an odd Collection of our English Writers,
for they would be sure to take Heywood, Shirley, etc.,
and leave Dryden'.[2]

But however much strained the relations of the two
dramatists were about 1634, Heywood was not replying
in *Love's Mistress* to the countercheck quarrelsome of
Shirley's *Contention of Honour and Riches.* There seems
to us little doubt that Heywood's Midas was not Shirley,
but William Prynne, and that the clown of the masque
was that strange and monstrous child, *Histrio-Mastix.*
About 1624 Prynne began collecting material for this
encyclopaedic attack on actors and acting. By October 16,
1630, he had proceeded far enough to have it licensed,

---

[1] William Bell, in the 1651 ed. of Cartwright. Cf. *An Elegy upon the
Death of Sir William Davenant,* 1668:
> Imagine him encircled in a Sphere,
> Of those Great Souls who once admired him here . . .
> *Shirley* and *Massinger* comes in for shares
> For that his language was refin'd as theirs:
> Laborious *Heywood,* witty *Brome,* and *Rowley,*
> The learned *Chapman,* and ingenious *Cowley.*

[2] 131.

and about Christmas the fat, squat, cubical volume of a thousand-odd pages appeared, an unreadable, chaotic, illogical, and repetitious book, made up for the most part of citations in the margin, at the foot of the page, or thrown into the belly of the paragraph. It would have excited little surprise, save by its bulk, had it appeared a few months earlier. But unluckily for Prynne, who had characterized the appearance in Michaelmas term 1629 of 'some French-women or Monsters rather' in a French play at the Blackfriars as 'an impudent, shamefull, un-womanish, gracelesse, if not more than whorish attempt', the Queen and her ladies on January 8, 1632/3, presented Walter Montague's pastoral, *The Shepherd's Paradise*, before the King at Denmark House. Laud and other prelates, hostile to Prynne for his ecclesiastical opinions, drew the King's attention to the book the day after the above performance 'and that place of it,[1] *Women actors notorious Whores*, and they informed the King and Queen that Prynne had purposely written this Book against the Queen and her pastoral, whereas it was published six weeks before the Pastoral was acted'.[2] Though the King and the Queen prudently declined to take any steps, Laud set Heylin, another of Prynne's enemies, to extract the quintessence of the venom; and on the receipt of the most offensive passages, probably with the approval of Secretary Coke who had also been given a copy, charged the At-torney-General Noy with the prosecution.[3] After an appearance in the Star Chamber, Prynne was committed to the Tower on February 1, 1632/3, where he remained for a year without liberation or bail or convenient access to his counsel; he even alleges that his counsel, who made no defence at the trial, had been tampered with. On February 17, 1633/4, after a most unfair trial, he was sentenced by the Star Chamber to imprisonment for life, a fine of £5,000 (reduced on his petitioning to £3,000), expulsion from Lincoln's Inn, loss of his degree at Oxford, disablement from his profession, and to stand in Palace

[1] Index.
[2] Whitelocke, *Memorials of English Affairs*, ed. 1682, 18.   [3] *Ibid.*

Yard and in Cheapside, to lose an ear at each stance, and
to have his offending work burned by the hangman.[1]

Before Prynne's trial and sentence, Shirley on three
occasions expressed his hatred for the puritanical lawyer.
Perhaps in consequence of his contemptuous apostrophe
to Prynne in commendatory verses for Ford's *Love's
Sacrifice*, and of the ironical dedication to the theatrophobe
himself of *The Bird in a Cage*, which comedy contains an
object lesson for the 'inimitable Mecenas' in the play
acted by Eugenia and her ladies, the Inns of Court commissioned him to provide the libretto of a masque, first
mooted about Allhallowtide 1633 in order to show the
lawyers' detestation of Prynne and all his works.   The
result was the magnificent *Triumph of Peace* presented at
Whitehall at a cost of £21,000 on February 3, 1633/4,
and, so much was it to the royal taste, with identical
splendour on February 11.[2]

Heywood himself, as a noted defender of the drama as
well as an actor and playwright, was specially obnoxious
to Prynne. 'As these Pagans of olde', he says in one
passage, 'so some [who] would be deemed Christians now,
(as namely one *Thomas Lodge*, a Play-poet, in his *Play of
Playes*, and one *Thomas Heywood*, a player in his *Apology
for Actors*,) have lately pleaded as hard for Stage-playes,
as ever *Demetrius did for his great Diana*.'[3] Elsewhere and
more offensively he declares the unanimity of writers
against players so complete 'that I never met with any
Christian or Heathen Authour (*Lodge* onely and *Heywood*,
two English Players, excepted) that durst publikely pleade
in any printed worke' for the stage.

'It is true that these two Players *Lodge* & *Heywood*, the first of
them in his *Play of Playes*, the latter in his *Apologie for Actors*,
thrust out in print by stealth,[4] perceiving Play-houses, Playes and
Actors to grow into disgrace by reason of sundry pious Bookes that
had beene written against them, by *Mr. Northbrooke*, *Mr. Gosson*,
Mr. Stubs, *Dr. Rainolds*, and others forecited; undertooke the

[1] See S. R. Gardiner's *Documents relating to the Proceedings against
Prynne*, and *State Trials*, i. 423, &c.
[2] See Carew's *Coelum Britannicum* for a parody of Prynne's style.
[3] 722.   [4] See 79 *supra*, note 2.

patronage of Playes and Players ... for their own private ends, it being *the craft by which they got their wealth and living*. But their ridiculous Player-like Pleas, savouring of nought but paganisme, ignorance and folly, were no sooner published by connivance, but they were presently so soledly refuted, (the first of them, by *Mr. Stephen Gosson*, a penitent Play-Poet, in his *Playes confuted in 5 Actions*; the latter by I:G: in his *Refutation of the Apologie for Actors*, London 1615. both published by authoritie:) that they durst not, yea they could not since replie unto them.'[1]

Heywood, roused by this, expressed the hope in dedicating *The English Traveller* that by the following term he would be able to vindicate satisfactorily 'many particulars ... maliciously exploded and condemned' by Prynne. This reply to the separistical humourist was fortunately abandoned, but in the preface to *A Maidenhead Well Lost* he has another fling at '*that most horrible* Histriomastix', and in one of his court prologues justifies the stage against 'a factious peevish malecontent'.[2] But it would seem that *Love's Mistress* is Heywood's real revenge.

The Apuleius-Midas framework of the masque and the clown scenes have both a topical and permanent function. But though the opposition of art and ignorance is an antithesis sufficiently real to make the play intelligible to a reader without any knowledge of the circumstances of its composition, it is the reading of the satirical intent that concerns us now. Apuleius, by general consent identified with Heywood himself, is hardly more than the presenter of Psyche's adventures; but it is not improbable that from time to time the author speaks in his own character. Indeed the very first speech of Apuleius may allegorize Heywood's story:

> How art thou *Apuleius* retransform'd?
> Or else how cam'st thou metamorphis'd first
> Into an Asse? Why to so dull a beast,
> Of slow, and so obtuse a memory?
> I had a braine aym'd at inscrutable things,
> Beyond the Moone; what was sublunarie,
> Me thought was for my study all too meane;
> Therefore, I therefore was I thus transform'd:

[1] 699–700.   [2] *Pleasant Dialogues*, 235.

That knowing man who keepes not in his bounds,
But pries into Heavens hidden mysteries
Further then leave; his dulnesse is increast,
Ceaseth to be a man, and so turnes beast:
And thus I fell, yet by the selfe same power
That calls all humane wisedome foolishnesse,
Am once more to my pristine shape restor'd;
Onely to shew how vaine my ambitions were,
This follies crest I still about me beare:
I fain would know the way to *Helicon*.[1]

Certainly whatever his ambitions may have been, he had been reduced to living with and pandering to the asinine vulgar, whose absurdities are exposed in the first anti-masque;[2] and the pilgrimage to the Muses' hill may indicate that Heywood, now restored to self-respect and the dignity of an artist by the royal approval, had resolved no longer to live for the rabble. As for Midas, he is the personification of ignorance to whose taste Apuleius occasionally condescends by presenting anti-masques. But he is also the avowed enemy of the arts—

I know no *Muses*,
No *Muses* hill, no *Aganippes* spring;
And what is more, I care for no such toyes;[3]

he is guilty of 'treason 'gainst the *Muses* majestie',[4] he is one 'By whom the *Muses* are dishonoured',[5] and the brother of the Ignorant Ass,

A piece of moving earth, illiterate, dull;
Who having in himselfe naught commendable,
Envies what's good in others; and yet dare
In his own impudence, with Arts compare:
A blocke, a stone, yet learning hee'le revile.[6]

Such an adversary of humane letters Prynne appeared to his age to be, and we have no hesitation in equating him with Midas or in identifying the overgrown child of his brain with Midas's clownish bastard.

---

[1] Pearson, v. 91; cf. 120, 124; *Hierarchy*, 203–9; and *Royal King*, prologue.
[2] Pearson, v. 104; cf. 93, 'those asses, With whom my lost soule wandred in a mist'.   [3] *Ibid.* 92.   [4] *Ibid.* 93.   [5] *Ibid.* 92.   [6] *Ibid.* 106.

CHAPTER VII

1634–1640: MISCELLANIES AND COMPILATIONS

IN *Love's Mistress* Heywood took his farewell of the stage he had served so long, and, except for the publication of a few earlier plays and the writing of odd prologues and epilogues, depended henceforward for his livelihood on the non-dramatic muses. He had already prepared a substantial earnest of the miscellaneous work to which he was about to devote himself, in *The Hierarchy of the blessed Angels. Their Names, orders and Offices. The fall of Lucifer with his Angels.* It was licensed for the press on November 7, 1634, by Dr. William Heywood,[1] less than three weeks before *Love's Mistress* was performed, and in gratitude for Henrietta Maria's approval of that masque was inappropriately dedicated to her. Whatever Heywood and those of his friends who paid for the engraving of the plates for it thought of the work,[2] others were less kind.

[1] Laud's domestic chaplain, whose imprimatur for '*A Divine Poem, intituled The Hierarchie of Angels*' is printed on the fly-leaf. See S.R. Aug. 12, 1635, Mar. 27, 1637, and May 21, 1639, for other similarly named works. From the entries in S.R. 'under the hands of Master Heywood' (Oct. 17, 1631–Apr. 13, 1637), Fleay (i. 282) thought that the dramatist may have been a master-stationer. These were, of course, licences to print, from Dr. William Heywood.

[2] Plate 1, engraved by John Paine, whose engraving of the Sovereign of the Seas Heywood highly commends (see 178 *infra*), for Thomas Mainwaring (see 5–6, 66 *supra*). Plates 2 and 3, by Paine, respectively for William Toomes, cashier of Sir Paul Pindar and a Clerkenwell neighbour of Heywood (see 59 *supra*), and John and Matthias Christmas (see 113–17 *supra*). Plate 4, by William Marshall who made the frontispiece of *The Phoenix of these Times* (see 173–5 *infra*), for John Witt of Clerkenwell (see 59 *supra*). Plate 5, by G. Glover who both made and presented plate 7, and plate 6 by John Droeshout, respectively for William and Christopher Beeston. Plate 8, by Droeshout for (Sir) Harbottle Grimstone, successor of Sir Edward Coke as recorder of Harwich and one of Laud's bitterest enemies. Plate 9, probably by Glover, for Thomas Hammon(d) (see 66, 111 *supra*)

The epigram in *Wit's Recreation*, 1640, seems to combine good nature and contempt:

> Thou hast writ much and art admir'd by those,
> Who love the easie ambling of thy prose;
> But yet thy pleasingst flight, was somewhat high
> When thou did'st touch the angels Hyerarchie:
> Fly that way still it will become thy age,
> And better please then groveling on the stage.

Richard Brathwaite, who was more candid, believed that his old friend had been at work on his *Lives of the Poets* 'to which He wisheth farre more felicity than accrued to his Mysterious Discourse of *Angels*'.[1] And though in 1657 '*Hewood of Angels*' and his *Pleasant Dialogues* were among the books consulted by the compiler of *The English Parnassus*, yet in 1656 Cowley was of the opinion that 'if any man design to compose a sacred poem, by only turning a story of the Scripture, like Mr. Quarle's, or some other godly matter, like Mr. Heywood of angels, into rhyme; he is so far from elevating poetry, that he only abuses divinity. In brief, he who can write a prophane poem well, may write a divine one better, but he who can do that but ill will do this much worse.'[2] It was indeed a serious, nay a laborious and unsuccessful attempt to be a divine and a poet, a theologian and a man of letters, to make a contribution to respectable literature and to turn an honest penny. As he approached his grand climacteric Heywood, like many of his contemporaries, was rethinking his philosophy of life amid the growing seriousness of affairs; and there is a curious presage of the mental change which he was to undergo and to which we shall refer later[3] in the rejection of his old motto for his title-pages, *Aut prodesse solent, aut delectare poetæ*, in favour of another more uncompromising, *Vita scelesta vale, cælica*

and Richard Gething the calligraphist. In the engraved title-page by T. Cecill some of the figures are imitated from Michael Angelo's Last Judgement; the figure of Jacob asleep in the left corner may be meant as a representation of Heywood. See George Estoutville's praise of the book in *Exemplary Lives*.

[1] *Medley of History*, 1638, table; see 98–9 *supra*.
[2] *Poems*, 1656, preface.   [3] See 153, 169–71, 183–5, 187–207 *infra*.

veni. More obviously than in *Love's Mistress* he laments lost opportunities and past failures:

> Meane time we spend our fruitlesse houres in vaine,
> And *Age*, of Want and Hunger doth complaine;
> It grieves us now, although too late, at last,
> Our Youth in idle Studies to have past;
> And what a folly 'tis, we now have found,
> To cast our Seed in an unfaithfull Ground:
> That in our Youth we have layd up no store,
> Which might maintaine us when our heads be hore;
> And that our shaken Vessell, torne and thin,
> Can finde no easie Port to harbor in.
> Then Barren *Muses*, seeke some other Friend,
> For I henceforth a Thriving Course intend.
>   None with fresh Violets my Ashes grace,
> Or strow sweet fragrant Roses in the place.
> If any loves me, and intends to give?
> I wish to taste his bounty whilest I live.
> What care I, when the Fates my Thread have spun,
> Though Briers and Thornes my Grave shall over-run.[1]

Nevertheless in the preface, though he bids us not expect 'new conceits from old heads', he confesses that write he must, for 'as *Time*, the producer of all things, though he be aged himselfe, is every houre begetting something new, so we, on whose heads he hath cast such a snow, as no radicall or naturall heate can melt, in imitation of him ... will never suffer our braines to leave working, till our pulses cease beating'. Therefore he puts away his *juvenilia* which were suited to his age and among which he probably numbered his too numerous plays, for 'Maturitie hath since better instructed me: remembering that excellent Sentence of *Sophocles, Si Iuvenis luxuriat, peccat; si senex, insanit*'.[2]

The Hierarchy of the Blessed Angels is the monument of a ruined philosophy. It summed up the medieval spirit-istic beliefs when the great fabric of superstition was crumbling to its fall. It was indeed a sign of the times that such books as this and John Dove's *Confutation of*

---

[1] 207-8   [2] Preface.

Atheism, to which Heywood refers, were being written in support of these beliefs and against the scepticism of Wier, Montaigne, and Scot. For centuries every country in Europe had been administering laws of terrible severity against those suspected of witchcraft; tens of thousands had perished at the stake and by still more cruel deaths; books by jurisconsults and ecclesiastics, and these the most enlightened of their age, appeared, not to prove for none doubted, but to expose the machinations of the devil; and the reality of witchcraft was an integral part of the teaching of the Church. The miraculous intervention of angels and saints, on the other hand, was no less readily believed. As Lecky says,

'there was no solution to which the mind of man turned more readily in every perplexity [than to the supernatural hypothesis]. A miraculous account was then universally accepted as perfectly credible, probable, and ordinary. There was scarcely a village or a church that had not, at some time, been the scene of supernatural interposition. The powers of light and the powers of darkness were regarded as visibly struggling for the mastery. Saintly miracles, supernatural cures, startling judgments, visions, prophecies, and prodigies of every order, attested the activity of the one; while witchcraft and magic, with all their attendant horrors, were the visible manifestations of the other'.[1]

In Γυναικεῖον and *The Late Lancashire Witches* Heywood had embodied without question traditional or contemporary witch-lore; in his *Hierarchy* he attempts to describe, with full documentation, the government of the world by God and His ministers, and the efforts to frustrate the divine plan by Satan, his fallen angels, and his witch-servants.

The division of the material, relevant or irrelevant to the proof of the existence of beings intermediate between God and man, and, as a corollary, of the fallen angels, into nine books gives an impression of order that is totally false. Rather is the volume a great jungle of fact and fiction, science and the reverse, superstition and shaky metaphysics. Each book is preceded by two arguments in octo-

[1] *History of the Rise of Rationalism in Europe*, i. 1-2.

syllables; the exposition in the book itself is in shambling decasyllabic couplets; this is followed by 'Theologicall, Philosophicall, Poeticall, Historicall, Apothegmaticall, Hierographicall and Emblematicall Observations' in prose plentifully sprinkled with verse; and lastly comes a verse 'Meditation'. The exposition proceeds chiefly by the citation of authorities: the Bible, the classics, the philosophers, the Fathers, the post-classical and Renaissance poets more or less in that order. But Heywood readily breaks this loose arrangement for a historical deduction *ab ovo*:

> Something I had forgot in my great speed:
> Of Musicke then, e're further I proceed;
> I must derive it from the first of dayes;[1]

or he excuses himself for a digression thus:

> We shall not deviate much, nor order breake,
> If something we of Stars and Planets speak;[2]

or he thrusts in eight hundred lines of narrative in the spirit of the Greek romances as an illustration 'out of the many' of how the devil imitates for man's deception the works of God:

> For in those great works which all wonder aske,
> He is still present with his Anti-Maske.[3]

The sources of the medieval conception of the celestial hierarchy and the spiritual government of the world are innumerable, but by far the most important are the works of the pseudo-Dionysius. The author, who by a pious fraud attributed his books to the Areopagite Dionysius, was not the originator of the beliefs expounded in his writings; rather he resumed and ordered in an organic system notions of very diverse origin. But it is little to be wondered that the four extant works, *Concerning the Celestial Hierarchy*, *Concerning the Ecclesiastical Hierarchy*, *Concerning Divine Names*, and *Concerning Mystical Theology*, were regarded almost as authoritative as Holy Writ. After the translation of his works into Latin by Erigena in the ninth century the authority of the pseudo-Dionysius

[1] 582.   [2] 123.   [3] 415.

among the schoolmen was unquestioned. Hugo of the Abbey of St. Victor, whom Heywood frequently cites, produced ten books of enthusiastic comment on the *Heavenly Hierarchy*, and St. Thomas Aquinas, still more frequently referred to by Heywood, was the author of *A Commentary on the Divine Names*. By the time of Dante the theology of the pseudo-Dionysius had become part of the common background and was accepted later without demur by Ariosto and Tasso, Spenser, Giles Fletcher, and Milton. It was from the pseudo-Dionysius, then, to whom Heywood probably went directly, that he took the main lines of his mystical theology. In the *Ecclesiastical Hierarchy* and in the *Divine Names* he would find the symbolism and mysticism which he carried over to *The Hierarchy of the Blessed Angels* and which is illustrated in the plates. To the *Mystical Theology* and still more to the *Celestial Hierarchy* he was largely indebted for the conception of God as the ultimate Source from Whom power and life streamed through all the gradations of creation, the idea that all being is in degrees, and the description of the beings intermediate between God and man.

The authorities for the infernal hierarchy, of which Heywood has as much to say, were far more numerous. The kinds of devils and witches were classified, their pranks and practices were codified, lists of devils and their names were drawn up, remedies and precautions were supplied, in short the whole system of the satanic was presented in innumerable volumes. Heywood refers, for example, again and again to *Malleus Maleficarum*. This collection of treatises by Sprenger (whose book supplied the general title), Institor, Nider, Basin, Molitor, Gerson, and others, is probably the most complete corpus of demonology; 'It laid down a conception of witchcraft which has become classical in literature . . . and it started the frenzy of witch persecution on the career in which for two hundred years it hardly relaxed'.[1] If there was any latent scepticism, it found little expression till John Wier,

[1] Herford, *Literary Relations of England and Germany in the 16th Century*, 223-4.

an excellent Protestant physician at Cleves, published his
De Praestigiis Daemonum, 1563. He wisely pretended to
believe in the frequent interference of the devil in human
affairs and in the devilries of sorcerers, and only attacked
the belief in the diabolical practices of old women whom
he held to be mere innocent victims of satanic delusion.
This humanitarian document was followed by his *De
Lamiis, Pseudomonarchia Daemonum*, and several other
works, most of which Heywood knew. Soon Bodin summoned all his vast learning and his judicial experiences of
witch-trials to confute Wier. Much of his *De la Démono-
manie des Sorciers*, 1580, was written before Wier's last
work appeared, but it is a direct reply to his general view.
Heywood accepted Bodin's work, which he probably read
in a Latin edition, as orthodox, though he also uses
many of Wier's stories. Only four years after Bodin's
treatise had appeared, Reginald Scot published his *Discovery of Witchcraft . . . whereunto is added a Treatise upon
the Nature and Substance of Spirits and Devils*, referring
with great respect to Wier, to whom he was much indebted. But the chief value of the book, apart from its
enlightenment, lies in the fact that Scot had studied the
superstitions at first hand in his own district. Only once
does Heywood refer to this encyclopaedia of demonology,

> Let them the bookes of *Scotus* well peruse;
> It is no subiect for my modest Muse.[1]

But he was familiar with it and with most of, if not all,
the answers to it, such as Henry Holland's *Treatise against
Witchcraft*, 1590, George Gifford's *Discourse of the Subtle
Practices of Devils*, 1587, and his *Dialogue concerning
Witches and Witchcraft*, 1593, King James's *Demonology*,
1597, John Dove's *Confutation of Atheism*, 1605, William
Perkins's *Discovery of the damned Art of Witchcraft*, 1608,
John Rainolds's *Censura Librorum Apocryphorum*, 1611,
John Cotta's *Trial of Witchcraft*, 1616, Richard Bernard's
Guide to Grand Jurymen, 1627, and the like. He was well
abreast, too, of the accounts of witch-trials; he refers, for

[1] 500.

example, to an attempt to bewitch Queen Elizabeth, the witches of Warboys of 1593, the two Lancashire sensations of 1613 and 1634, and other contemporary cases. In his unshaken faith in the reality of witchcraft Heywood was neither in advance of, nor behind his time; greater thinkers than he, Bodin, Melanchthon, and Calvin, Baxter, Sir Thomas Browne, and Sir Matthew Hale, Henry More and Glanvill, held fast to the orthodox views and would have agreed with Browne 'that there are witches: they that doubt these, do not onely deny them, but Spirits; and are obliquely and upon consequence a sort not of Infidels, but Atheists'.[1]

Our first sight of Heywood's next venture, *Philocothonista, Or, The Drunkard, Opened, Dissected, and Anatomized*, 1635 (S.R. May 26),[2] suggests the suspicion that the old Adam was only half regenerate. This pot-boiling mixture of puritanism, pedantry, and ribaldry was welcomed by the jesting verses of two of Heywood's friends, George Donne, the second son of the Dean, who testifies to Heywood's own temperance, and John Ford,[3] the dramatist's cousin. The vice of drunkenness was a stock theme of preachers, of ballad-mongers, and of pamphleteers in their more puritanical moments. It was castigated by the literary puritans from Stubbes in his *Anatomy of Abuses* to Prynne in his *Healths: Sickness. Or, A Compendious and brief Discourse; proving, the Drinking, and Pledging of Healths, to be Sinful, and utterly Unlawfull unto Christians*, 1628, and Richard Rawlidge in *A Monster late found out and discovered. Or the Scourging of Tipplers, the ruin of Bacchus, and the Bane of Tapsters*, Amsterdam, 1628. But puritanical as Heywood was, and serious as was his end in dissuading from intemperance, he saw the need of

---

[1] *Religio Medici*, ed. Keynes, i. 38.

[2] We have been unable to trace a new edition of June 1641, mentioned by Mr. H. E. Rollins (*T.L.S.*, Aug. 3, 1922).

[3] He was a member of Gray's Inn where Heywood had other friends. To him were dedicated Jordan's *Poetical Varieties*, 1637, and his cousin's *Lover's Melancholy*, 1629, and *Love's Sacrifice*, 1633; he may have been the author of verses for Barnes's *Four Books of Offices*, 1606. Heywood appears to have known the dramatist as well; cf. *Hierarchy*, 206.

'mixing *Democritus* with *Heraclitus*';[1] and his lack of Prynne's singleness of purpose and his own weakness for irrelevance led him off to more genial authorities and to a serio-comic treatment in which his original intention was forgotten. He undoubtedly knew Prynne's work, little as it accords, with his own, and Rawlidge's less erudite pamphlet. Throughout Prynne's book is matter more or less parallel to Heywood's, and some of Heywood's maxims and of his great Burtonian congregation of authorities may be derived from his old enemy. But as usual many more of his authors were cited only from such proxies as Stobaeus or Athenaeus. From Athenaeus, as translated into Latin by Natale de' Conti,[2] Heywood has borrowed roughly a third of his pamphlet; sometimes he will translate a whole chapter, sometimes he runs his finger down the pages, choosing a sentence here and there and jumbling them together without rhyme or reason; yet only once is Athenaeus mentioned.[3] For the first part of his book Heywood used a little book of macaronic prose and verse, *De Generibus Ebriosorum, et Ebrietate vitanda* one of the minor works of Ulrico de Hutten, more famous for his *Epistolae Obscurorum Virorum*. In the 1516 edition is a cut representing six drunkards with the heads of animals, from which Heywood's title-page was imitated, and Latin verses which Heywood printed on his fly-leaf with an English translation.[4] He knew and copied the hearty good-fellowship of Gaspard Dornavius's compilation of Latin *facetiae*, burlesque eulogies, and humorous composi-

---

[1] 6.

[2] Venice, 1556. See S.R. May 29, 1609 and May 18, 1636; and cf. Γυναικεῖον, 65.   [3] 11.

[4] Heywood's cut was copied in the 1663 edition of Mennes and Smith's *Recreations for Ingenious Head-pieces*; a more elegant engraving of the same kind appears in *Les Aventures de Docteur Faust*, Amsterdam, 1798. Cf. Nashe's *Pierce Penniless* (ed. McKerrow, i. 204, &c.); S.R. March 30, 1609, '*A discription of the most vile . . . sinnes of Drunckenness devided into ffive sortes of Drunkards*'; and Freeman's *Run and a Great Cast*, epigram 77:

> Ape-drunkards they are merry, Lion-drunkards mad,
> Fox-drunkards cheat, Swine-drunkards lie and spew,
> Goat-drunkards lust, etc.

tions in Greek, Latin, and German, *Amphitheatrum Sapientiae Socraticae Ioco-Seriae*, 1619, which contains such pieces as Andrea Arnaudius's *Bacchi Apologia,* Christopher Hegendorf's *Declamatio in laudem Ebrietatis,* Berard Bucholdianus's *Pro ebrietate oratio,* Robert Turner's similar *Oratio,* Frederick Taubmann's *Bacchanalia* and Beroaldus's *Orationes adversativae ebriosi scortaloris et aleatoris.* A similar compilation was Johannes Gulielmus Stukius's *Antiquitatum Convivialium Libri III in quibus Hebraeorum, Graecorum, Romanorum aliarumque nationum antiqua conviviorum genera, mores . . . explicantur,* 1597, which contained nearly all that Heywood needed. Pliny, in his *Historia Naturalis,*[1] book xiv, has much to say on wines and their effect and in condemnation of drunkenness; but all of this was available in various other compilations. Much of the second part of *Philocothonista* sets forth the 'new order of *drinking lately come up amongst us, call'd a drinking Schoole or Library*' with the canting terms of the eighth liberal science, probably from Richard Brathwaite's *Disputatio inauguralis theoretico-practica Jus potandi,* 1616,[2] which was so popular that in 1617 the author issued an English version and Dornavius included it in his *Amphitheatrum.* The Rabelaisian stories and the modern instances of Calverley, the protagonist of *A Yorkshire Tragedy,* and others were matters of common talk with which Heywood prepares the reader before his earnest admonition at the close. Our author makes no such protest as R. Junius (Richard Young) who, in the dedication of his eight hundred-odd pages, *The Drunkard's Character or A True Drunkard with such sins as reign in him . . . lively set forth in their colours,* 1638, perhaps like Taylor's *Drink and welcome: or the famous History of the most part of Drinks,* 1637, suggested by Heywood's essay, declares that '*to all this Frame, I have not much more then made the Pins, which fasten the joynts together*'. Yet we can leave Heywood little

---

[1] Translated by Holland, 1601, and reissued in 1634–5. Cf. William Turner's *New Book of the natures and properties of all Wines,* &c., 1568.

[2] Brathwaite only systematized the drinking cant. Cf. *I Henry IV,* ii. 4; *The Silent Woman,* ii. 6; *A Yorkshire Tragedy,* scene 1; and 326–7 *infra*

but the prefatory matter, one or two anecdotes, the verse translations and the rambling style with its occasional suggestions of Dekker.

For all its ribaldry *Philocothonista* is really more significant than *The Hierarchy* of a change in Heywood. The latter might have been written by many who were not Puritans, but in *Philocothonista* Heywood ranged himself with that party in the state which was willing to sacrifice even breadth and tolerance for a purer national life. Never riotous or adventurous in his morals, he had always been essentially bourgeois in his standards; but, whereas previously his profession had separated him from the Puritans with whom he had much in common, now on his retirement from the Caroline stage, the tendencies of which he deplored in the prologue to *A Challenge for Beauty* more than he praised, he set himself against the fashionableness of one of the national vices and associated himself in a jocose way with such views as his old enemy Prynne had expressed in his *Healths: Sickness*. But by contributing, probably late in 1635, to *Annalia Dubrensia. Upon the yearly celebration of Mr. Robert Dover's Olympic Games*, 1636 (S.R. January 11), he was uniting with many of the literary men of the period in honouring Dover's Cotswold games,[1] a wholesome protest against puritanical opposition to all sports and recreations. It was, therefore, the saner prohibitions and, as we shall see, the ecclesiastical policy of the Puritans that won Heywood's support, not their extreme asceticism and their more fanatical philistinism.

For he never forgot that he was university-bred and a servant of the Muses, however low circumstances had compelled him at times to stoop. Besides, as a royal masque-writer and the author of a learned work, dedicated to the Queen, he had now the character to maintain of a scholarly poet capable of pleasing more cultured ears than were usually pricked in the public theatres. In 1635, therefore, he set about collecting such further credentials

[1] See Grosart's reprint of *Annalia Dubrensia,* Gosse's *Seventeenth Century Studies,* and A. F. Sieveking's article in *Shakespeare's England,* ii. 452, &c.

as *Pleasant Dialogues and Dramas, selected out of Lucian, Erasmus, Textor, Ovid, &c. With sundry Emblems extracted from the most elegant Jacobus Catsius. As also certain Elegies, Epitaphs, and Epithalamions or Nuptial Songs; Anagrams and Acrostics—With divers Speeches (upon several occasions) spoken to their most Excellent Majesties, King Charles, and Queen Mary. With other Fancies translated from Beza, Buchanan, and sundry Italian Poets,* which, though registered on August 29, 1635, was not ready till 1637. This miscellany, intended for many a noble and right honourable eye, contained, therefore, besides the dialogues and the like and the court prologues, speeches for two plays at the town house in Broad Street of the dedicatee, Henry Carey, Earl of Dover,[1] and for a masque at his mansion at Hunsdon; an elegy on Sir George St. Paul;[2] an epitaph on Sir Philip Woodhouse;[3] epitaphs or more cheerful

---

[1] See 108–9 *supra*. [2] See 1, 4 *supra*.

[3] 255; for the tomb at Kimberley, Norfolk, erected by his son, Sir Thomas. They were representatives of a very ancient house, which by the marriage of John Woodhouse to Margaret, daughter of Sir Thomas Fastolff of Kimberley, acquired estates in Norfolk. The son of this marriage, another John, was an official of Henry IV and Henry V, and won great fame and 'that eternis'd Motto, *Frappe fort*' by an exploit at Agincourt. Sir Philip, the theme of Heywood's epitaph, was both a soldier and a sailor in Elizabeth's reign and for a time represented Castle Rising in parliament. He was knighted by the Earls of Essex and Nottingham at the taking of Cadiz in June 1596. His son, Sir Thomas, by his wife Grizel, daughter of William Yelverton of Rougham, Norfolk, was knighted by James I on June 13 (?27) 1603. Sir Philip was buried at Kimberley on Oct. 30, 1623. It was probably after the death of his wife on Aug. 4, 1635, that their son erected the memorial on which Heywood's lines appear. Heywood's other epitaph, 256, '*upon a worthy Gentlewoman whose name was* Patience', with the lines,

A losse indeed this *Grizels* losse implyes,
Since here with her all womens patience lyes,

was perhaps for Sir Thomas's daughter Grizel, buried at Clerkenwell (see 58 *supra*). Sir Thomas Woodhouse had several children by his wife Blanch, daughter of John Carey, Lord Hunsdon, and sister of the dedicatee of *Pleasant Dialogues*; he died in 1658. Several passages of a poetical history of the Woodhouses (Blomfield, *History of Norfolk*, ii. 541, &c.) which ends with the life of Sir Philip are so remarkably like Heywood's in style and so agreeable with his epitaph that we are inclined to assign this curious document to him. The verses on Sir Thomas, however, are clearly by another hand and of a date about 1648.

verses on other gentlefolk of Heywood's acquaintance;[1]
and acrostics on anagrams of Lord Keeper Sir Thomas

[1] Heywood seems to have become acquainted with the Kentish Hony-
woods through the Christmases (see 113–17 *supra*), for old Garrett
Christmas had married a niece of Robert Honywood and grand-daughter
of Mary Atwaters, on whom and her 'numerous Issue' Heywood wrote
an epitaph (*Pleasant Dialogues*, 255). Mary Atwaters, a lady famous for
her piety, age, and the multitude of her descendants, was born in 1527, the
daughter of Robert Atwaters or Waters of Royton in Lenham, Kent. Her
husband, Robert Honywood of Henewood, in Postling, Kent, whom she
married in 1543, died in 1576; she herself survived till 1620. Thomas and
Katharine Skip for whose tomb Heywood wrote two epitaphs (*ibid.*
256) appear to have had some connexion with Clerkenwell; see 59 *supra*.
The lines on Katharine Skip, who according to Heywood died in 1630
aged 29, are,

> Can foure weake lines comprise her vertues ? no,
> Not volumes can, here lyes beneath this stone,
> All that her sex since *Eve* could learne or know,
> (Alas) where shall they harbour now shee's gone ?

Thomas Skip was lord of the manor and patron of the living of North
Tudenham, Norfolk, from at least 1621. By his second wife, Susan,
daughter of Sir Edward Bleverhasset of Norwich, he had a son Thomas;
he died on May 19, 1632. Though Heywood does not print it, he obviously
wrote the epitaph for the tomb in North Tudenham Church to Thomas
Skip's first wife and her two daughters:

A Sacred of Love from THOMAS SKIPPE of *North Tudenham* in the
County of *Norfolk* Esq; one of the Gentlemen of his Majesties Privy
Chamber.
To the lasting Memory of KATHARINE his Wife by whom he had issue two
only Daughters FRANCES who lyeth buried at the West end of this Chancell
& MARY who sleeps by her mother. She expired Anno Dñi 1629. her age
31. her Wedlock 12.

> Whom God much lov'd, who merited mans praise,
> Whose virtuous Acts in number past her days,
> Lovely, Wise, Pious, Charitable, Chast,
> KATHARINE beneath these cold Stones sleeps her last,
> Loving & Lov'd of all, her Husband cheif,
> Lived to our great joy, dyed to all our greif.
> What's earth of her beneath this Marble lyes,
> What was in her Divine transcends the Skyes.

In *Pleasant Dialogues*, 257, Heywood has an *Epitaph upon a virtuous
young Gentlewoman, who after seven years' marriage expired* which looks like
a revision or a draft of the Tudenham inscription.

> Well borne, well bred, brought up with cost and care,
> Sweet Infant, hopefull child, and virgin chaste,

Coventry,[1] the Earl of Dover, Lord Chief Justice Sir
Ranulph Crew,[2] Lady Anne Carre,[3] and Sir Paul Pindar.[4]

> Marriage which makes up women, made her rare,
> Matron and maide, with all choise vertues grac't,
> Loving and lov'd of all (her husband chiefe)
> Liv'd to our great joy, dyde to all our griefe.

The first line is used again in the elegy on Mary Littleboys which also
employs the conceit in the first quoted epitaph on Mrs. Skip and repeats
the last line of it. This Mary Littleboys, daughter of George Littleboys
of Ashburham, died on Mar. 8, 1635/6, aged 20. Heywood wrote both
A Funeral Elegy on the occasion and an epitaph for her tomb in Clerkenwell Church (*Pleasant Dialogues*, 257–9). Her father, who was descended
from a family settled at High Wycombe, was servant 'to the Quenes
Maiesty'. He married (1) Anne, daughter of John Clarke of Battell, by
whom he had two sons and two daughters, and (2) Mary, daughter of
George Vane and sister of Sir Thomas Vane of Wadsell, Kent. See
C.S.P.D. 1637, 122–3 for his reply to a charge of being in possession of
money belonging to Benedictine monks. Frances Longe, for whom Heywood wrote an epithalamion on an acrostic of her name (*Pleasant Dialogues*,
260–1), may have been the daughter of George Long, who died on
Feb. 1, 1654/5, aged 73, and was buried in Clerkenwell near his first wife,
Frances Lollyman. A certain William Long of Clerkenwell and his wife
Frances had several children baptized in the parish in the fifties of the
seventeenth century. The poem which follows the epithalamion in
Pleasant Dialogues was probably also for Frances Longe '*at the parting
from her own Father's house, to live with her husband at her Father-in-
lawes*'.

We have been unable to discover anything about James and Anna Waade,
for whose marriage Heywood wrote another epithalamion on an acrostic and
the song 'Pack clouds away' (262–3), inserted also in the 1630 and 1638
editions of *The Rape of Lucrece* (Sir William Waad, Lieutenant of the
Tower, was dismissed for too great leniency to Overbury); or the worthy
citizen on whose tomb was '*ingraven a white hand pointing to a Starre*'
(257); or the '*vertuous Maide, who dyed the very day on which shee should
have beene married*' (254), and for whose untimely death Heywood adapted
his funeral ode on Queen Anne in Γυναικεῖον, 123–4.

[1] See 101, note 5, *supra*.

[2] See 6, 107 *supra*.

[3] See 107 *supra*.

[4] The acrostic on '*that worthy and most religious Knight*' (*Pleasant
Dialogues*, 266) was probably written at the suggestion of William
Toomes of Clerkenwell (see 59 *supra*), Pindar's cashier. Pindar, one of
the wealthiest men of his day, was born at Wellingborough, Northants,
but was perhaps connected with the Pindars of Lincolnshire. Heywood
specially referred to Pindar's munificent contributions for the repair of
St. Paul's; cf. Pearson, iv. 278, 316. Pindar was persuaded by Sir William

These occasional pieces were like so many dedications to win the notice of the great for Heywood's '*small Cabinet of many and choyse*' jewels, as he complacently calls it in the dedication, and to incline the generous private readers 'of what capacity or condition soever' to a more charitable censure of his 'Miscellane of sundry straines in Poetry'. He was daring to appear before the public, not as the Red Bull hack, but as a genuine poet, and even to suggest himself as the next laureate. That ambition did not seem ridiculous to the three friends, Marmion, D. E., and S. N.,[1] who welcomed this new effort opportunely published when Jonson was dying or just dead;

> Who will deny thee the best Palme and Bayes?

says the first;

> Therefore doe thou, ô *Heywood*, weare the Bayes
> As thy just merit many thousand wayes,

declares the second; while the third is sure that

> *Envies* selfe, in spight of all Assayes,
> Shall crowne thy Tombe-stone with eternall Bayes.

But even Heywood's most charitable critic will find in it nothing in the least memorable and even little that is passable. Heywood was a fluent, rather than an easy, translator, a dramatist rather than a lyrist or writer of occasional verses. He is better, therefore, in the 'Stage poetry' of the 'divers *Dramma's* never before published' [2] of *Jupiter and Io* and *Apollo and Daphne* after Ovid,[3] and in the short pastoral of *Amphrisa, or the Forsaken Shepherdess*. But in the dialogues from Erasmus, Ravisius Textor, and Lucian, 'Which though I met with in Prose onely, yet upon better acquaintance, I have taught to goe

Cockayne and Sir Arthur Ingram to become a farmer of customs. By this and by advances to Charles during the Civil War his estate was seriously embarrassed; indeed Toomes, one of the executors of the estate, was so discouraged by the entanglements that in 1655, four years after Pindar's death, he committed suicide.

[1] Of D. E. we can discover nothing. S. N. may have been Samuel Nicholson, a poet-puritan of St. Catharine's Hall, or Stephen Nettles, a controversialist against the Puritans.

[2] Preface.   [3] *Metamorphoses*, i. 568–747, 452–567.

upon even feet and number',[1] in the emblems from Jacob
Cats which Heywood translates without reprinting the
fine engravings that made the text intelligible, in the
various prologues and epilogues, acrostics upon anagrams,
translated epigrams from the humanists, and the sundry
other Fancies, he is pedantic, heavy, awkward, uninspired,
and dull.

For us to-day the chief interest of the miscellany is the
dating of the items in it. The earliest we can definitely
assign to any year is the elegy on Sir George St. Paul in
1613.[2] But it may be that *Jupiter and Io* and *Apollo and
Daphne* were originally written for inclusion in *The Ages*,
the one perhaps for *The Silver Age* and the second for *The
Brazen Age* after the episode of Mars and Venus. But it
is far more likely that both were prepared for the enriching
of that '*handsome Volume*', announced in the preface to
The Iron Age, part II, which was to contain the whole
cycle '*with an Explanation of all the difficulties, and an
Historicall Comment of every hard name, which may appeare
obscure or intricate to such as are not frequent in Poetry*'. For
this reason and others we have rejected Fleay's identification of 'v playes in one', acted at the Rose by the Admiral's
men from April 7, 1597,[3] with *Deorum Judicium*, *Jupiter
and Io*, *Apollo and Daphne*, *Amphrisa*, and either *Time's
Triumph* (as he calls Heywood's version of Lucian's
Misanthropos) or *Cupid and Psyche*, a hypothetical form of
Love's Mistress 'without the clown'.[4] The entry in Henslowe for April 13, 1597, which Fleay and Collier read as
Time's Triumph and *Faustus*, is really 'times triumpe and
fortus',[5] that is *The Triumphs of Time and Fortune*: and we
cannot infer from the fact that Fletcher's *Triumph of Time*
in *Four Plays in One* is based on Lucian's dialogue that
the Admiral piece was a playlet from the same source,
still less that it is identical with the 'unrelieved tedious-

---

[1] Preface; Textor's *Earth and Age* in the original is in verse.
[2] See 1 *supra*.   [3] *H.D.* i. 51–3.
[4] i. 286–7; he also suggests an identification with Heywood's 'bocke' of
1596; cf. ii. 302, and *Stage*, 100, 114.
[5] *H.D.* i. 52; cf. ii. 183–4.

ness'[1] of Heywood's dialogue. Dr. Greg, who dismisses Fleay's argument so far as *Misanthropos* is concerned and hesitates about *Deorum Judicium*, would like to accept it for *Amphrisa, Apollo and Daphne*, and especially for *Jupiter and Io* because of an Argus head in an Admiral inventory, and is inclined also to concur with Fleay's suggestion of an earlier form of *Love's Mistress*.[2] The certainty that *Love's Mistress* was written in 1634 and no earlier has already, we hope, been established.[3] *Amphrisa* is undoubtedly Caroline and may be the remnant of some masque or longer pastoral for private performance, as the style and the machinery seem to indicate.[4] And *Deorum Judicium* from Lucian is a translation as tedious as *Misanthropos*, and belongs to the 'Dialogues' which Heywood in his preface clearly treats as distinct from the dramas;[5] moreover in Γυναικεῖον[6] Heywood translates a considerable part of the same Lucianic dialogue into prose, as he would scarcely have done if he had already put it into verse. He had shown his love for Lucian as early as *The Ages*. But it is in Γυναικεῖον that his familiarity with the dialogues is first clear; besides the above-mentioned passage from *Deorum Judicium*, he has a prose translation of the dialogue of Juno and Latona[7] and an admirable verse paraphrase of the description of the house of Sleep.[8] In *The Hierarchy* Heywood versified all he took from Lucian, namely, part of a dialogue of Mars and Mercury,[9] three *Dialogues of the Dead*,[10] and a few fragments;[11] he gives, too, an epitaph on Lucian[12] and a sketch of his life and character.[13] In *Love's Mistress* he drew much from the *Dialogues of the Gods*, and in *Londini Sinus Salutis*, 1635, he introduced the three goddesses of *Deorum Judicium*. We do not hesitate, therefore, to date the fifteen

---

[1] *Ibid.* ii. 183.   [2] *Ibid.* ii. 183; cf. Fleay, i. 286, 299.
[3] See 129–31 *supra*.
[4] The name Pelopaea occurs in *The Hierarchy*, 35, 37, and Amphrisus is a river-god in *Apollo and Daphne*.
[5] The dialogues are in couplets, the dramas in blank verse. Cf. Chambers, iii. 346.   [6] 454.   [7] 20.   [8] 115.   [9] 218.
[10] 234, 348, 391.   [11] 34, 218.   [12] 14.   [13] 33; cf. 218.

dialogues from Lucian after, rather than before *The Hierarchy*. Heywood's introduction into his translation of Erasmus's *Procus et Puella* from the *Colloquies* of a detail from Apuleius which he used as well in *Love's Mistress*,[1] and his identification in a gloss to the same dialogue of Nemesis and Venus, for which he was again indebted to Apuleius,[2] date the version of *Procus et Puella*, and probably also that of *Naufragium* after 1634. The long dull interchange of arguments which Heywood calls 'An Emblematicall Dialogue' is a tedious rendering of Jacob Cats's moralized *Ars Amatoria* for the instruction of young women, *Maechden-Plicht ofte Ampt der Ionck-vrouwen, in eerbaer Liefde, aen-ghewesen door Sinne-Beeldon. Officium Puellarum in castis Amoribus, Emblemate Expressum.*[3] Cats was in England in 1610 and as ambassador of the States-General in 1625. But probably the first sign of Heywood's interest in him is the translation of a number of his emblems for *The Hierarchy*. Professor Bang, therefore, may be right in attributing the signs of haste he sees in *Anna and Phyllis* to the fact that it was not ready for the press in time; and Heywood, he suggests, certain by 1637 that his annotated edition of *The Ages* would never appear, stayed the printer's mouth with *Jupiter and Io, Apollo and Daphne*, and, less certainly, *Amphrisa* (which are not in couplets like the other dialogues) till the translation from Cats should be finished.[4]

The prologues and epilogues in *Pleasant Dialogues* have no artistic value whatever. His addresses to public audiences are merely deprecatory with nothing like the range of ideas and the weight that Jonson could command; and his prologues and epilogues for private performances, to which class most of those in *Pleasant Dialogues* belong, are verbose and pedantic compliments. Nevertheless their

---

[1] Cf. *Pleasant Dialogues*, 26 (see also ix, 361), Pearson, v. 98, 106, and Apuleius, iv. 85.
[2] Cf. *Pleasant Dialogues*, 27 (see also ix, 361) and Apuleius, iv. 28–31.
[3] Middelburg, 1618, apparently the first edition. There were other editions in 1622 and without date; in 1625 the dialogue was incorporated in Cats's *Houwelijck*.   [4] *Pleasant Dialogues*, viii.

dates have a certain importance in dramatic history. The
first when the Queen feasted the King at Somerset House,
'*upon his Birth-day, hers falling in the same weeke*', together
with the speech at parting,[1] was for November 19, 1630,
after the birth of 'a sweet and hopefull Prince . . . little
Charles' on May 29. The speech to Charles and his Queen
'*at the first Play play'd by the Queenes Servants, in the new
Theater at White Hall*'[2] is wrongly dated by Fleay[3] in
1630; the theatre in question was opened about 1632.[4]
The prologue and epilogue, spoken before the King and
Queen on '*a New-yeares day at night: the Two-fac't Ianus . . .
the Presenter*'[5] were for January 1, 1630/1, when an heir
had been born and a second child (Princess Mary, born
November 4, 1631) was expected. The next two speeches
before the King alone were delivered in the seventh year
after his marriage and apparently not long before the
birth of the princess.[6] We would date the next pair[7] soon
after the birth of Princess Mary, but Fleay puts them
after the Queen's birthday on November 17, 1633, when
she and the King saw the King's men act *Richard III* at
St. James's; the first performance at which the Queen was
present after the Duke of York's birth on October 13.[8]
The defence of the stage and the allusion to 'a factious
peevish male-content' and his 'bald unlicenc't papers'
determine the composition of the next prologue and epilogue before the King and Queen at Whitehall[9] as probably rather after Prynne's trial in February 1633/4 than
between the publication of *Histrio-Mastix* and the trial.
Heywood prints next the speeches for a play at Hampton
Court before the King and Queen,[10] which are the same
as those published with *The Fair Maid of the West*, 1631,
soon after its court performance; Fleay is probably right
in dating this at Christmas 1630.[11] The dates of the next
prologue and epilogue before the King and Queen at

---

[1] 231-2.   [2] 232.   [3] i. 303.
[4] Chambers, i. 217.   [5] 232-3.   [6] 234.
[7] 234-5; at Whitehall before the King and Queen.
[8] i. 304; cf. *Stage*, 315 and Herbert, 53.
[9] 235-6.   [10] 236-7.   [11] i. 295.

Whitehall and another pair *'upon the like occasion'*[1] are uncertain; they may have been for some of the nine plays given by the Queen's men at Hampton Court and White-hall during 1635,[2] though by that time he had begun to write for the King's men; but it is much more probable that they were for two of the '8 plays acted by the Queen's players at Court, in 1634, whereof one at Hampton Court'.[3] Cupid's prologue *'at the second time of the Authors Play cald* Cupids *Mistresse or* Cupid *and* Psiche' before the King and Queen and the next *'eight dayes before, being the King's birth-day: presented at* Somerset *house, by the Queenes appointment, she then feasting the King'* with the epilogue[4] were respectively for November 27 and 19, 1634. The New Year's Day performance for which the next prologue and epilogue[5] were written was probably on January 1, 1635/6; the Queen was not present after the birth of Princess Elizabeth on December 28. There is no clue for dating the prologue and epilogue *'at the Court to the like purpose'*;[6] the allusions to Apollo and Pan have no reference, as Fleay maintains,[7] to the rivalry of Shirley and Heywood. The occasion of them was perhaps in 1636 after the preceding pair. For some reason the speeches for the King's thirty-fifth birthday[8] were not printed with the other court addresses; the date was November 19, 1635. Elsewhere we have given our reasons for dating the prologue and epilogue at a Christmas performance in the Earl of Dover's house in Broad Street[9] and the speeches for a Candlemas play before the same patron[10] at Christmas and Candlemas 1630/1.[11] But the speech *'as a preparation to a Maske'* on *'the last New-yeares night'* at Dover's Hunsdon mansion,[12] was probably for January 1, 1636/7. The speeches for the young actor playing Richard III at the Red Bull, for the revival of *The Jew of Malta*, and for *The Play of Queen Elizabeth*,[13] have already been sufficiently

---

[1] 237–8.   [2] Fleay, i. 304; cf. Murray, i. 270.
[3] Murray, i. 270.   [4] 238–40.   [5] 240–1.   [6] 241–2.
[7] i. 304.   [8] 249–50.   [9] 242–3.   [10] 243–5.   [11] See 108–9 *supra*.
[12] With Truth's speech in presenting the masquers, 245–7; see 109 *supra*.
[13] 247–9; see 33, 88–9, 118 *supra*.

considered. Lastly, the prologue and epilogue spoken to the Palsgrave '*at his first comming over, in the presence of his Majesty, &c.*',[1] was for November 22, 1635.

There remains, therefore, for consideration only the epigrams from the humanists, a piece in praise of archery, another upon '*a Booke late published by one* Bird *a Coach-man, calld* Byrds *businesse*', a third '*Against a base and infamous Balladder, who disperst a scandalous riming Libell, in which hee malitiously traduced the noble exercises weekely practised in the Artillery Garden*', and a fourth 'concerning the worth of Physick, and Physitians, deriving my president from a worthy Gentleman called M. *Perisaulus Faustinus*'.[2] Of the Renaissance epigrams only two were apparently not available before 1609;[3] the only reasons for dating Heywood's paraphrases much later are the likelihood, if not certainty, that most of *Pleasant Dialogues* dates from the thirties of the seventeenth century and the signs, more evident in *The Hierarchy* than in Γυναικεῖον, of Heywood's reading among the humanists. Faustinus's verses, which occur in an undated volume,[4] may have been omitted by an oversight from *The Hierarchy*, and owe their strange position in *Pleasant Dialogues* to Heywood's clearing his desk of everything printable. The base and infamous ballader did not dare to register the verses which roused Heywood's generous scorn, but his answer to them was certainly a recent effusion.[5] The praise of archery seems to belong to the same period as his pageants. No copy of *Byrd's Business* has survived and the Stationers' register records it not; but a *jeu d'esprit* on its metrical irregularities must have followed it at no distant date.

Heywood apparently did not regard the publication of

[1] 250–1.

[2] *Pleasant Dialogues*, 267–79, 280–1, 281–2, 283–4, 302–4.

[3] *Ibid.* 277 from *Johannis Secundi Opera*, Leyden, 1631, 97 and *Delitiae Poetarum Gallorum*, ? Paris, 1609, pt. iii, 868: cf. Bang's edition of *Pleasant Dialogues*, 351.

[4] *Perisauli Faustini tradocii de honesto appetitu.*

[5] Cf. Pearson, iv. 294, and v. 263. See also *A brief historical Account of the Hon. Artillery Company*, ii. xxxii, and G. A. Raikes's *Royal Charter . . . granted to the Hon. Artillery Company*, 21.

these 'Dialogues borrowed from sundry Authors' and 'taught to goe upon even feet and number', or of the 'divers *Dramma's*, never before published: Which though some may condemne for their shortnesse, others againe will commend for their sweetnesse'[1] as inconsistent with his abjuring the unprofitable dramatic muses. Nor did his deepening puritanism inhibit his printing even his own or other people's plays. The publication of his last dramatic venture, *Love's Mistress*, followed hard on his renouncement of the stage in *The Hierarchy*.[2] What was probably the last but one of his plays to be composed, *A Challenge for Beauty. As it hath Been Sundry Times Acted, By the King's Majesty's Servants: At the Blackfriars, and at the Globe on the Bankside*, was issued in 1636 (S.R. June 17), in a very corrupt quarto with Heywood's name and motto but no prefatory apparatus; it seems to have been printed from a stage copy, shortened perhaps for court performance. The likelihood that Heywood derived some features of his tragicomedy from Massinger's *Picture*, licensed for the stage on June 8, 1629,[3] and published the year after, and the fact that *A Challenge for Beauty* contains a song first printed in the 1630 quarto of *The Rape of Lucrece*, though these details do not help to fix the date any more definitely within the last five years of Heywood's dramatic career, at least supply corroboration to the evidence from the style and economy of the play and from allusions in it to Prynne's punishment,[4] and the Platonizing fashion at court,[5] that it was not the 1597 'womon hard to please' of the Admiral's men.[6] The play itself proves that Heywood did not retire from the stage because he was written out as a dramatist; it is the most polite and fashionable of his dramas and shows him adapting himself with great success to the standard that the King's men demanded.

---

[1] Preface.   [2] See 145 *supra*.   [3] Herbert, 32.   [4] Pearson, v. 41.
[5] *Ibid.* v. 13; the allusion to the judgement of Paris, *ibid.* 17, probably synchronized with the translation of Lucian's dialogue for *Pleasant Dialogues*; the three 'Caelestiall Goddesses' were also introduced into Heywood's 1635 pageant.
[6] *H.D.* i. 45; cf. ii. 182.

for Blackfriars. The plays he published later were much more primitive. If *A Challenge for Beauty* was printed for the company in a season of plague, *The Royal King, And The Loyal Subject. As it hath been Acted with great Applause by the Queen's Majesty's Servants*, 1637 (S.R. March 25), though lacking preface or dedication, was certainly Heywood's own speculation, and for it he wrote an epilogue 'to the Reader'. The possibility that this tragicomedy was a revision of *Marshal Osric* has already been discussed.[1] Besides the reissues of *The Rape of Lucrece* in 1638 and of *Love's Mistress* in 1640, Heywood gave to his generation one more of his own plays, *The Wise Woman of Hogsdon. A Comedy. As it hath been sundry times Acted with great applause*, 1638 (S.R. March 12, 1637/8). The edition has been suspected of being surreptitious, but it is proved authentic by the uncritical verses of Samuel King, a Clerkenwell neighbour of Heywood,[2] 'To His Chosen Friend; the learned Author', printed at the end because

> *Thou wants no Herald to divulge thy fame;*
> *'t needes no Apologie.*

The commendatory poem was written when

> *some Criticke showes*
> *His Ignorance in seeking with new songs,*
> *To gaine the Honour; which to thee belongs,*

and when Atropos was hovering about the dramatist. Yet the farce itself is not new; for it manifestly dates from a much earlier period, perhaps from the flourishing of the patient wife plays when Heywood wrote his very similar *How a Man May Choose a Good Wife from a Bad*. It was probably one of the first pieces acted by Queen Anne's men after their removal to the Curtain, and may be identical with *How to Learn of a Woman to Woo*, performed before the King on December 30, 1604.[3]

Though Heywood was not, as Fleay plausibly con-

---

[1] See 29–30 *supra*.   [2] See 59 *supra*.

[3] See 42 *supra*. According to Genest, x. 590, Mrs. Cowley shows a familiarity with the play in her *Who's the Wife?*

jectured, a master stationer in the sixteen-thirties,[1] he does
seem to have acted as an agent for the Okes with whom he
had been on good terms since 1612 and who had printed
more of his work than any other printer. The evidence
lies in two plays published by John Okes in 1638. The
first of these, registered on November 27, 1637, appeared
the next year, perhaps in consequence of the death of its
author in 1636. This was *A Merry And Pleasant Comedy:
Never before Printed, called A Shoemaker a Gentleman. As
it hath been sundry Times Acted at the Red Bull and other
Theatres, with a general and good Applause*, on the face of
it a very early piece, first acted, it would seem, during
William Rowley's association with Queen Anne's men
before 1610. Its interest for us is the pretty clear proof
in the address of 'The Printer to the honest and High-
spirited Gentlemen of the never decaying Art, called the
Gentle Craft', that either Heywood wrote this preface or
John Okes adapted Heywood's preface to *The Four Prentices*. 'None but to you (as whom of right it doth con-
cerne)', it opens, 'I thought good to present this Play:
Which though written many yeares since, ought not
therefore to be slighted.' The address, 'To the Honest
and High-spirited Prentises, the Readers' of *The Four
Prentices of London* runs '*None but to you (as whom this Play
most especially concernes) I thought good to Dedicate this
Labour . . . written many yeares since in my Infancy of Iudgment in this kinde of Poetry*'. As for *A Shoemaker a Gentleman*, 'we have better for Language in these our exquisite
and refined Times . . . I know it may come short of that
accurateness both in plot and style that this witty age doth
with greater curiosity acquire, I may thus excuse; that as
Plaies were then, some twenty yeares agone, it was in
the fashion. Nor could it have found a fitter or more
seasonable publication than at this time; when the glory
of our Nation is so much admired.' But *The Four Prentices*
also '*comes short of that accuratenesse both in Plot and Stile,
that these more Censorious dayes with greater curiosity acquire*',
which Heywood thus excuses '*That as* Playes *were then*

---

[1] See 143 *supra*, note 1.

some fifteene or sixteene yeares agoe it was in the Fashion. Nor could it have found a more seasonable and fit publication than at this Time when to the glory of our Nation' ... and so on. *The Martyred Soldier: As it was sundry times Acted with a general applause at the Private house in Drury lane, and at other public Theatres. By the Queen's Majesty's servants,* 1638, Henry Shirley's only surviving play, was registered by John Okes on February 15, 1637/8, along with a pamphlet by Heywood.[1] It was probably originally a Queen Anne play that passed by the agency of Christopher Beeston to the Lady Elizabeth's company and later to Queen Henrietta's men. When the latter company re-signed the Cockpit, and a number of plays as well, to Beeston's Boys, some of the older items on the repertoire, *The Royal King and the Loyal Subject, The Wise Woman of Hogsdon,* Kirke's *Seven Champions of Christendom,* and the two dramas of Rowley and Henry Shirley, may have been released for the press. Fleay suspected that John Kirke, who dedicated *The Martyred Soldier* to Sir Kenelm Digby, was the means of several of these plays reaching Okes.[2] Be that as it may, Heywood's connexion with four of them is established; and there is a strong probability, not only that he wrote the address to the reader of *The Martyred Soldier,* though Kirke signed the dedication, but that he had a finger in the play itself.[3]

To the Courteous Reader (of *The Martyred Soldier*): *the worke it selfe being now an Orphant, and wanting him to protect that first begot it, it were an injury to his memory to passe him unspoken of. For the man his Muse was much courted but no common mistresse; and though but seldome seene abroad yet ever much* admired *at. This worke, not the meanest of his labours, has much adorned not only one but many stages, with such a generall applause as it hath drawne even the Rigid*	To the Reader (of *The Golden Age*): I was loath ... to see it thrust naked into the world ... without either Title for acknowledgement, or the formality of an Epistle for ornament. To the Reader (of *The English Traveller*): [I] *thought it not fit that it should passe as* filius populi, *a Bastard without a Father to acknowledge it.* To the Reader (of *A Maidenhead Well Lost*): *the Criticall censure of that most*

[1] See 179 *infra.*　　　[2] ii. 248.　　　[3] See 295–300 *infra.*

Stoickes of the Time, who, though not for pleasure yet for profit, have gathered something out of his plenti-full Vineyard.

horrible Histriomastix ... *This hath beene frequently, and publickly Acted without exception.*

To the Reader (of *The Iron Age,* part I):
the Playes often (and not with the least applause,) Publickely Acted by two Companies, uppon one Stage at once, and have at sundry times thronged three severall Theaters.

It is, in any case, a curious fact that the prologue of *The Royal King*, printed by the Okes the year before, was inserted by John Okes in *The Martyred Soldier* before Shirley's own epilogue.[1]

But those were the only plays Heywood managed to lay his hands on; his real resource after 1634 was miscellaneous journalism. He was even not above writing broadsides, as is proved by the survival of *The Three Wonders of this Age*, 1636 (S.R. April 8), with a cut of William Evans, the King's giant porter, the Queen's dwarf Jeffrey Hudson, and the centenarian Old Parr. Though no author's name is appended, the idiosyncracies of style and vocabulary, the ascent in time to the Titans and Goliath, the Pigmies and Noah, the other classical and Biblical instances, the references to '*Robert Wainman*, who served M. *Willoughby* in Lincoln-shire[2] of an exceeding low stature, and excellent Huntsman', to the Earl of Southampton's dwarf, and to a diminutive graduate of Cambridge, and the personal and intimate tone make certain the identification of the sheet with the item 'by master Haywood' registered by John Okes. It is likely, too, from *The Three Wonders* that Heywood was responsible for another similarly worded broadside of the year before, *The Wonder of this Age: or, The Picture of a Man living, who is One Hundred Fifty-two years old, and upward*, 1635 (S.R. November 12, three days before the ancient wonder died). It gives another portrait of Old Parr, and discourses in the same learned way as *The Three Wonders* on the patriarch. In the first of these

---

[1] See 295–300 *infra*.   [2] See I *supra*, note 1.

broadsides Heywood refers the inquirer for more informa-
tion about dwarfs to 'the Booke called *The New-yeares
Gift*, lately come out, (a learned though a little work)'.
This was a duodecimo entered by John Okes as 'by master
Slater' on the Stationers' Register only two days before
The Three Wonders and printed as *The New Year's Gift:
Presented at Court, from the Lady Parvula to the Lord
Minimus, (commonly called Little Jeffrey) Her Majesty's
Servant, with a Letter as it was penned in shorthand: wherein
it is proved Little Things are better than Great. Written by
Microphilus*, 1636 and 1638. The style of this erudite
production makes us suggest that Master Slater, other-
wise unknown,[1] is itself perhaps only one of the numerous
pseudonyms affixed to the papers of verses in it and that
Slater was perhaps no other than Heywood.

These pieces are of but little interest for the dramatist's
biography. But soon after their appearance he gave a
glimpse into his own mind in a short pamphlet with a long
title, *A True Discourse of the Two infamous upstart Prophets,
Richard Farnham, Weaver of Whitechapel, and John Bull,
Weaver of St. Butolph's Aldgate, now Prisoners, the one in
Newgate, and the other in Bridewell: with their Examinations
and Opinions taken from their own mouths April 16. Anno
1636. As also of Margaret Tennis now Prisoner in Old
Bridewell, with the Heretical Opinions held by her, at the
same time examined*, 1636 (S.R. June 7). This was a long
journey from *Troia Britannica* in which the *dulce* had far
outweighed the *utile*. In the Γυναικεῖον Heywood had
been serious without being didactic. His editing Barckley's *Felicity of Man*, a decidedly edifying work, was a
more definite step. Then had come *The Hierarchy* which
was perilously near doctrine. But *A True Discourse* is
frankly controversial. In it we see Heywood the conservative churchman, the supporter of uniformity, order,
and decency, and the enemy of innovators whom, for the
time being, he took to be all on the left wing of the church.
As later we find him an outspoken opponent of the novelties of Laud, we must class him as one of the moderates

[1] Unless he is to be identified with William Slatyer.

who had trusted their bishops to a point and then in a revulsion of outraged conservatism allied themselves more or less enthusiastically with the opposition. At present, however, Heywood still imagined himself an anti-Puritan, as he had tried to believe himself when he had introduced, after the manner of his fellow-dramatists, scandalous reflections on the separatists in *How a Man May Choose a Good Wife from a Bad*[1] and on the opinionated Puritan in *Troia Britannica*.[2] 'Let no man wonder', he says in opening *A True Discourse*, 'that such vaine triflers are now, who studie to bring in new Doctrines and Opinions into the Church, since it is apparent that even from the time of the Apostles, no Age hath beene without them.' Ranging himself with authority he forbears 'to speake for any foraigne Vipers, onely to shew you the Spiders bred under our owne roofes, & the Snakes bedded in our native Earth . . . many new and upstart schismaticall opinions have lately troubled the peace of the Church; all different in themselves, onely agreeing in this, that they unanimously conspire to disturbe the common quiet. . . . Onely this I faine would know, were there no Ecclesiasticall government, what rubricke should stand? or how, after what manner would they have *God* served? One sect beleeves wee have a Saviour, but counts it superstition to have his name reverenc't, and bow'd unto: Some approve of no Sacraments at all, others allow of Sacraments, but hold, that to kneele before the Table or Altar when the Blessed Supper of the Lord is to be received, is meerely Idolatrous.' Some would sit to receive the Holy Communion; some claim all licence; others allow 'no commendable exercises or lawfull recreations'. But all of them he finds 'as they altogether impugne the Churches authority, so cunningly and cautelously, they would trench upon the high Supremacy'. Without authority in ecclesiastical matters there will be nothing but confusion and disorder, and there can be no greater malice than when a Protestant Church which has severed itself from Popish superstitions 'shall . . . fall into these sottish and ridiculous Chimeraes,

[1] Sig. G 2ᵛ–3.   [2] Sig. I 2 &c.

to betray weaknesse in themselves, and beget distraction in others'.[1] Heywood may have visited Farnham in Newgate for, with strict fairness, he tacked on to the end of his own pamphlet Farnham's apologia 'After divers visitations, by sundry *Divines* and men of quality . . . for the better clearing of that Aspersion laid on him, and some others in that kinde'.[2] There need be no hesitation in ascribing the pamphlet which was *Written by T. H.* to Heywood; the evidence of the style alone is overwhelming.

Another very different publication of 1636 (S.R. November 18) has failed to survive, 'Master Haywood's' collection of '*Mistakes Clinches Tales &c.*'[3] This was not his only contribution to the doubtfully respectable jestbook literature; his Γυναικεῖον, his *Philocothonista* and *A Curtain Lecture* devote a good deal of space to ribald jests to make you merry.

The just-mentioned *Curtain Lecture: as it is read By a Country Farmer's wife to her Good Man. By a Country Gentlewoman or Lady to her Esquire or Knight. By a*

[1] 1–2, 5 &c.

[2] Of Margaret Tennis we can discover no more than the little Heywood says about her. Farnham, who with his wife and children had lived near the sign of Whittington's Cat in Long Acre, Whitechapel, and his fellow Bull were weavers, 'simple Tradesmen, who never look't upon any University, or scarcely have been acquainted with a Grammar Schoole; who onely can read English, though yet know not how to speake it truely'. But Farnham was something of a penman both before and after he came to Newgate, as he himself says in one of his three vigorous petitions (*C.S.P.D.* 1636/7, 459, 487, 507). After his examination in Apr. 1636 he was detained in Newgate without trial; a year later two of his children were being maintained by the parish and the other by a poor widow. Probably the Council whom he addressed after the failure of his previous petitions discharged him.

[3] Miss Bates, lxxix–lxxx, on inadequate grounds supposed that *A New Book of Mistakes, Or, Bulls with Tales, and Bulls without Tales, But no lies by any means*, printed by Nicholas Okes in 1637 and surviving in a unique copy not now accessible, was Heywood's collection. But the latter, the name of which in S.R. was almost certainly copied and condensed from the title-page, was probably issued in 1636. *A New Book of Mistakes* is attributed in W. C. Hazlitt's *Handbook*, 81, to Robert Chamberlain, the probable author of two other jest-books.

Soldier's wife to her Captain or Lieutenant. By a Citizen's or Tradesman's wife to her husband. By a Court Lady to her Lord. Concluding with an imitable Lecture read by a Queen to her Sovereign Lord and King, 1637 (S.R. July 6, 1636),[1] was a return by Heywood to his championship of women and his praise of marriage. He had already reverted to his favourite subject in *The Hierarchy,* but his *Curtain Lecture,* a smaller and more popularly priced Γυναικεῖον with a larger proportion of Rabelaisian stories, was forestalled by two other pamphlets which gave a new liveliness to the old dispute, '*Haec Homo wherein ye excellencie of the Creation of woman is discribed by way of an Essay &c.*' (S.R. April 26)[2] and *The Curtain Drawer* (S.R. May 18). It would almost seem that Heywood had opened his folio at the contents, glanced at random over them and begun to write; indeed, though there is a considerable amount of new matter, he at times repeats verbatim passages from the larger work.[3] Probably *A Juniper Lecture with a description of all sorts of Women* appeared soon after Heywood's pamphlet; it was reprinted in 1639 and again in 1652. The author followed it up in 1639 with *Divers Crab-tree Lectures* and in 1639 or 1640 with his *Wormwood Lecture*; in *The Women's Sharp revenge,* which seems to have been by the same author and was registered with the *Crab-tree Lectures* (S.R. April 24, 1639), the three former pieces were assigned to Taylor. Then on November 25, 1639, was licensed Brathwaite's *Art Asleep, Husband? A Bolster Lecture,* a stout, well-printed quarto. In this renewal of the war there were as before editions of Overbury, sermons, translations, and the like. But the controversy now progressed on more genial lines, Swetnam was remembered only as a type, and the tone was never more than gently satirical. Heywood only initials the preface to *A Curtain Lecture,* but this fact, along with the garrulous style, proves beyond a doubt the authorship of this brief collection of commonplaces from

---

[1] With a frontispiece by ? Marshall, perhaps meant for Heywood.
[2] *Haec Vir* and *Hic Mulier* appeared in 1620.
[3] Cf. 19, 244–6, and Γυναικεῖον, 302, 233.

his favoured Athenaeus, Stobaeus, and other compilers.[1] Though he concluded that his age afforded 'more Poets than Patrons (for nine Muses may travell long ere they can find one *Mecaenas*)', he had at least found that marriage was not a failure.

The same year Heywood reverted to the kind of popular biography that had occupied him in 1636. Of the five brochures smuggled past the Stationers' registrar by John Okes for the one fee on January 25, 1636/7, two at least were by Heywood—'*the Life and death of Sir Richard Whittington*',[2] and a history of a London eccentric whom death had just made famous, *The Phoenix of these late times: Or the life of Mr. Henry Welby, Esq; who lived at his house in Grub street forty-four years, and in that space, was never seen by any. Aged 84. Shewing the first occasion, and the reasons thereof. Whose Portraiture, you may behold, as it was taken at his death. With Epitaphs and Elegies of the late deceased Gentleman, who lieth buried in S. Giles's Church near Cripplegate, London.* To his aid in celebrating this worthy, Heywood summoned William Marshall to engrave Welby's 'portraiture', which shows the venerable Phoenix meditating on the text of the Preacher; Thomas Brewer the miscellanist and J. B., perhaps his kinsman; [3]

[1] Despite the signature to the address W. C. Hazlitt (*Handbook*, 675) tentatively ascribed it to Richard Brathwaite, probably because of his similar *Art Asleep, Husband? A Bolster Lecture*, 1640, which refers several times to Heywood's book (13, 14, 74, 80, 107, 150, 152). For other replies to *A Curtain Lecture* see S.R., Aug. 2, 4, 1638, Apr. 24, 1639.

[2] A chap-book which is probably a reprint or revision of Heywood's appeared in 1656 and 1678 as *The Famous and Remarkable History of Sir Richard Whittington. Three times Lord Mayor of London Who lived in the time of King Henry the Fifth, in the year 1419. With all the remarkable Passages, and things of Note, which happened in his time: with his Life and Death. Written by T. H.* Bodley: Wood 254 is a fragmentary Whittington chap-book of *c.* 1680. Cf. *If you know not me*, II (Pearson, i. 276–7) and *R. B.* vii. 585 for a ballad of Whittington (S.R. July 16, 1605) and S.R. Feb. 8, 1604/5, for a play on the subject.

[3] See 128 *supra*; Brewer also wrote commendatory lines for *The Exemplary Lives*, 1640; and the dedication of *The Life of Merlin* to James Mettam mentions 'Your Kinsman and friend Mr. T. B.' (see 182, 186 *infra*).

the epicurean Shakerley Marmion; and lastly, the ever-
obliging John Taylor who probably wrote both the fully
signed and the initialled verses. As the first edition was
soon exhausted, a second, corrected and enlarged, appeared
before the year was out, the additions including lines by
Thomas Nabbes and an anonymous remembrance of
Welby, possibly by Heywood. Though Heywood had
signed only an epitaph on Welby, his mark as general
editor is everywhere, and in this second edition we see why
he had written the tract: 'In his former yeares', he says,
'and also when he returned from his travaile, hee kept the
best company, and had good language in him for the
expression of himselfe, as I can testifie which knew him of a
youth, and being my Country-man, and familiar acquaintance, can remember some of his witty sayings.'[1]

---

[1] Sig. E 3ᵛ. According to the title-page and *N. & Q.*, 1863, 197, Welby
was eighty-four at his death in 1636; but as he matriculated as a pensioner
at St. John's, Cambridge, on May 24, 1558, he must have been over ninety
when he died. He was the eldest son of Adlard Welby, a scion of a very
ancient family, by his first wife Ellen Hall of Hull. Adlard Welby early in
Elizabeth's reign purchased an estate at Gedney in S. Lincolnshire, where
he died on Aug. 11, 1570. After completing his education at Cambridge
and the Inner Temple which he entered in Nov. 1562, the Phoenix 'being
accommodated with all the parts of a Gentleman . . . retyred himselfe into
the Countrey, and matched nobly unto his good liking' (*The Phoenix*, &c.
sig. C 2) with Alice, daughter of Thomas White of Woodhead, Rutland
and Tuxford, Notts. and niece of the first Lord Burghley. The only child
of the marriage, Elizabeth, married Sir Christopher Hildyard on July 13,
1598. From Lord Wentworth Welby purchased the estate of Coxhill in
north Lincolnshire, probably after his father's death, from whom he
inherited 'a faire revenue, amounting to a thousand pounds by the yeare,
and upward' (*ibid.*). But 'he . . . had a great minde to travell, as well to
profit him in experience, as benefit himselfe in Language, and to that purpose spent some few yeares in the *Low Countries, Germany, France*, and
Italy, making the best use of his time' (*ibid.*). The occasion of his abandon-
ing society 'was the unkindnesse, or (which I may rather tearme it) the
unnaturalness and inhumanity of a younger brother [really his half-brother
John], who upon some discontent . . . rashly and resolutely threatened his
life: Some report it was, because hee was overthrowne in a suite of Law;
others said, that it was some discontent about the losse of money which he
was cozened of' (*ibid.* 2nd ed. sig. D 2). When the two brothers met
John presented a loaded pistol which fortunately misfired. The Phœnix,
deeply affected by this attempted fratricide, withdrew to a house in Grub

It must have been Heywood's display of allegory and symbolism in his pageants that secured for him this year, perhaps through the agency of his friends the Christmases, an unexpected commission to design the carving for the Sovereign of the Seas, the largest ship in the navy. The great vessel appears to have been Charles's own idea. Though, like his father, he was too apt to regard the navy as an imposing appurtenance of his royal dignity, he took a keen interest in all naval affairs, and was alive to the dangers of Richelieu's policy to unite France and Holland in a maritime league to the prejudice of Britain. He appears to have talked over the construction of 'a great new ship', first with Phineas Pett[1] on June 26, 1634,[2] and from time to time we hear of the proposal soon after tabled at the Admiralty.[3] On April 7, 1635, a committee

Street for the rest of his life, spending his time in three rooms, reading every book that was published, preserving the best of them, meditating, praying, and helping his needy neighbours. He died on Oct. 29, 1623, and was buried in St. Giles's, Cripplegate.

[1] The general supervisor in the building of the Sovereign and the principal representative in his own day of a family that had been shipwrights for the navy for generations. The eldest son of Peter Pett by his second wife, Elizabeth, daughter of George Thornton, he was born at Deptford on Nov. 1, 1570; from his school at Rochester he was sent at Shrovetide 1586 to the puritan stronghold at Cambridge, Emmanuel. His *Autobiography* 1600–37, is the chief document for the details of his life. The actual builder of the Sovereign was his third son, Peter, by his first wife, Anne, daughter of Richard Nicholls of Highwood Hill, Hendon; 'before he was full five and twenty yeares of age [he] made the *Model*, and since hath perfected the *worke*' (*True Description*, 47).

[2] Pett's *Autobiography*, ed. W. G. Perrin, 156–7.

[3] *C.S.P.D.* 1634–5, 153, and Hist. MSS. Com. XII. ii. 62. Though the greatest secrecy was observed, rumours of the design reached Trinity House, and the Master and some of the brethren on Aug. 9, 1634, addressed an unsolicited and adverse memorial to Secretary Coke (Pett, 214–15 and *C.S.P.D.* 1634–5, 184, 232). Their objections, puerile in themselves, seem to have been dictated by jealousy of Phineas Pett who did little to placate his enemies. In Oct. 1634 Pett had prepared a model which was thoroughly inspected by the King (Pett, 157). But it would seem that the protest had some effect, for on Mar. 7, 1634/5, Pett was instructed to build a 'new great ship' and to prepare a model (*C.S.P.D.* 1634–5, 565); perhaps, however, only a tabular statement, not a new model, was meant (Pett, xci). For the collecting of materials see *C.S.P.D.* 1634–5, 1635,

consisting of Sir John Pennington, Sir Robert Mansell, John Wells, store-keeper at Deptford, and Pett examined the plan and agreed on certain proportions, some of which were to be imparted only to the King, who on April 7 endorsed the specifications.[1] But Pennington seems to have advised certain modifications which the King approved on April 17,[2] and according to which with minor adjustments the vessel was built. By September 1635 the timber began to arrive at Woolwich and, though work did not start at once, Pett was sanguine of finishing the building in eighteen months.[3] The keel was laid on December 21, and on January 16 Charles paid the yard his first visit of inspection.[4] He came back again on March 28 with his nephews, the Palsgrave and Prince Rupert;[5] and a year later, on February 3, 1636/7, with his eldest nephew he thoroughly inspected the work, 'being very well satisfied in all points'.[6] According to Heywood the King and Queen both visited the great ship on June 17, 1637:

> *What a conspicuous Ray did it dart then?*
> *What more than a* Titanian Luster, *when*
> *Our* Phoebus, *and bright* Cinthia *joyntly sphear'd*
> *In that one* Orbe, *together both appear'd:*
> *With whom seven other* Stars *had then their station,*
> *All luminous, but lower* Constellation.[7]

At the end of August 1637 preparation had been made for launching, and on September 25, in the presence of the King and Queen, an effort was made to float the hull but without success.[8] Mansell, however, after consultation with some of the Trinity House authorities, decided to

---

and 1635–6; Pett, xcvii. 157–8, 160; and Hist. MSS. Com. XII, ii. 123, 130. The enemies of the great ship were not silenced by the progress made; in Sept. 1635 Pett appealed to the King for protection from the interference and malice of the officers antagonistic to the scheme (*C.S.P.D.* 1635, 20, 388: cf. *ibid.* 374).

[1] *C.S.P.D.* 1635, 13, 31, and Pett, xci–xciii.

[2] *C.S.P.D.* 1635, 31. [3] *C.S.P.D.* 1635, 388.

[4] Pett, 162; cf. Heywood's 'Epigrammatical rapture' on the unfinished ship, 26 &c. [5] *C.S.P.D.* 1635–6, 299. [6] Pett, 163. [7] 28.

[8] Pett, 163, and *True Description*, 2nd ed., 49–50.

make another attempt to launch the vessel on Sunday October 14. But on the Saturday evening Pett, despite advice to the contrary, triumphantly succeeded.[1]

'Shee so freely offered her selfe to the River', says Heywood, 'as if weary of being so long imprisoned in the Docke, she voluntarily exposed her selfe to the Channell, of which (next under God,) she . . . is the sole Soveraign and Commander, of which there is the greater hope, in regard that no great ship or smaller Barke which ever floated upon the river of Thames hath, or can with more dexterity or pleasure play with the Tide. She, though of that vast burden, yet dancing upon the River as nimbly as a small Catch or Hoy, which indeede hath proved somewhat above expectation, bearing the weight of one thousand six hundred thirty and seven Tun, besides other Tackling.'[2]

Immediately after the launch, on receipt of word from Pett, Mansell arrived and named her the Sovereign of the Seas.[3] Within three weeks the masts were planted and the ship finished. After two more visits by the King on June 6 and July 12, 1638, the Sovereign made her maiden voyage, on which subject old Phineas is strangely reticent.[4] Pett's original estimate for the cost of the ship, £13,860 which the officials increased to £16,000,[5] proved far too small, partly through the extravagant method adopted for collecting material, still more from the lavish expenditure on painting and carving which consumed £6,691 alone, and perhaps by the inclusion, as Pett had feared, of extraordinary expenses by officials inimical to the whole business. The total cost, exclusive of ordnance, was finally returned at £40,833 8s. 1½d., the wage bill amounting to £20,948; the armament, increased by the King from ninety to a hundred and two, cost £24,753 8s. 8d. more.[6]

Heywood's pamphlet, *A True Description of His Majesty's Royal Ship, Built this Year 1637, at Woolwich in Kent. To the great glory of our English Nation, and not paralleled in the whole Christian World*, 1637, which the title-page

[1] *Autobiography*, 165–6; the difficulty of launching was a fresh opportunity for Pett's enemies (*ibid*. 165–6).
[2] *True Description*, 2nd ed. 49–50; cf. Pearson, iv. 309.
[3] Pett, 166–7.　　　　　　　　　　　　　[4] *Ibid*. 166, &c.
[5] *C.S.P.D.* 1635, 50, 61, 64.　　　　　　[6] Pett, xcviii.

declares to have been published by authority,[1] was licensed on September 15, 1637, probably for the first attempt at launching on September 29. We gather from Marmion's lines on this occasion—

> To thee, friend *Haywood*, who hast Royall leave
> To publish it unto the worlds broad eyes,
> And art well skil'd in all her properties—

that Heywood, as the only literary man concerned in the matter, had received some sort of commission from Charles to whom Heywood consecrated 'these his humble endevours'. A second edition, dated 1638, was printed with the names of the newly appointed officers after the launching. Both impressions have a somewhat sophisticated frontispiece of the Sovereign, probably by William Marshall; but Heywood recommends the engraving, made at Peter Pett's request, by John Paine.[2] Heywood of course was of Pett's faction in the bickering over the Sovereign, and he suffered some of the criticisms directed against the vessel, in his case in respect of 'those Decorements which *beautifie* and *adorne her*', the purport of his allegorical and other devices, and the grammatical construction of his Latin legends.[3] Besides his conversance with emblems and symbols, Heywood had a superficial knowledge of shipping which he displays here and elsewhere. It would, therefore, be some satisfaction to us to prove him, despite his age at the time, the Thomas Haywood recommended by Captain William Cooke on November 1, 1636, to Lord Treasurer Juxon as a suitable boatswain for the Lion or the Saint Andrew.[4]

[1] The authority was Peter Pett; see imprimatur and S.R. Sept. 15.

[2] See *C.S.P.D.* 1635, 15, for Peter Pett's request for the King's permission to publish the plate.   [3] *True Description*, 29.

[4] *C.S.P.D.* 1636–7, 327. In 1653 Matthew Simmons published with plates for Thomas Jenner, an engraver and etcher of the Sovereign, a considerable part of Heywood's pamphlet in *The Commonwealth great ship commonly called the Sovereign of the Seas built in the year 1637*, &c. Mr. H. B. Culver, who executed a scale model of the Sovereign, expressed the opinion in *The Mariner's Mirror*, viii. 368, that certain draft designs in oils on four wooden panels, obviously for the Sovereign and of Dutch workmanship, and probably by Van Dyck, were Van Dyck's working out

In 1639 appeared two pieces of anonymous hack-work, one of which was certainly Heywood's, while the other was, if not his, a plagiarism of his chap-history of Elizabeth in her minority. Both of them were copyrights of Heywood's friend John Okes, the first having been slipped through the Stationers' Register on February 15, 1637/8 in the licence for 'a Playe called *the Martyred Soldiour with the life and Death of Purser CLINTON* by H: SHIRLEY'. The second title, however, refers not to a play but to a black-letter pamphlet, *A True Relation, of the Lives and Deaths of the two most Famous English Pirates, Purser, and Clinton; who lived in the Reign of Queen Elizabeth. Together with the particular actions of their Takings, and undertakings. With other pleasant Passages which happened before their surprisal worth the observing,* 1639. There can be no doubt that the narrative, of which a part is borrowed almost verbatim from Stowe through Holinshed, was from the tireless hand of Heywood. For not only does it display his characteristic Latinisms, his stylistic pedantries, and his pretentious generalizations, 'Of the power of Justice', 'Wherefore Lawes were made', and the like, but it contains a passage verbally parallel to his *True Description* of the Sovereign of the Seas.[1]

A True Description, &c., 34:	*A True Relation*, &c., sig. A 6 :
being at *Chester*, he provided himselfe of a most Princely Barge, which was to be rowed with Oares, which were silvered all over, with which hee entered into the *River Dee*, and sitting at the Sterne, tooke the charge of the *Helme* and caused eight of the before-named *Contributary Kings* to rowe him up and downe the *River*, unto the Church of *Saint Johns*, from, and unto his Pallas distant three miles, to let the World know that Hee was *Lord* and *King* of so many provinces.	It is also reported of this King *Edgar*, by divers approved and Authentick Cronologers, that upon a time being at *Chester*, hee entred the river of *Dee*, and sitting in a new barge for that purpose, hee himselfe tooke the charge of the helme, and was the stearesman; and was rowed by eight Contributary Kings which hee commanded to row him up and down the Ri = (*sic*) unto y^e Church of St. *Thomas,* and from thence backe againe to his owne Pallace; to shew that he

of Heywood's scheme. But while it is unlikely that Heywood drew anything himself, it is still more unlikely that Van Dyck acted as his draughtsman.

[1] Cf. also *A True Description*, sig. A 6, and *A True Relation*, 34.

Ibid., 34 (margin):
Maxentius *made the eighth, who was after Emperor of* Rome.
Ibid., 32:
He ... surprised by Sea a Prince of the *Romans*, whose name was *Maxentius*, who had done many out-rages upon the Ocean, and was the greatest Arch-pirate that those times afforded.

was sole Soveraigne of so many provinces: amongst them was numbered a Roman Arch pirate, whom hee surprised; who was called *Maxentius*, and after was Elected Emperour, and woure the Imperiall purple.

And what is more interesting, we get practically word for word the scene in *Fortune by Land and Sea* between the pursuivant and the provoking rustic who parodies his reading of the proclamation of a reward for the apprehension of Purser and Clinton, as well as a number of other parallels.

Fortune by Land and Sea, Pearson, vi. 409, &c.:
Enter a Pursevant meeting the Clown.
    Pursev. Whither away so fast sirrah in the Queens name, I command you stay.
    Clown. What are you that look so big?
    Pursev. A Pursevant.
    Clown. If you be so pursey, can you lend 's any money, I assure you it was the last business we were about; or else tell me the reason why you stay my passage.
    Pursev. Sirrah I have a Proclamation to publish, and because my self am somewhat hoarse, and thou hast a wide large mouth, and a laudible voice I charge thee for the better understanding of the multitude to speak after me word by word.
    Clown. If it be nothing else, do but advance (*sic*) me and Ile speak high enough, come now, and teach me my new lesson.
    Pursev. Whereas two famous Rovers on the Sea.
    Clown. Whereas two famous Rogues upon the Sea.
    Pursev. Puser (*sic*) and *Clinton*.

A True Relation, &c., sig. B 8 ᵛ, &c.:
    And heere a pleasant accident I am loath to overpass, in the executing of these publications: a Pursevant by reason of riding in the wet, and thereby catching so great a cold, that hee had such a horsenesse that hee could bee scarcely heard to speake twice his lengthes distant from him, agreed with a plaine and crafty Country fellow, who had a cleare audable voyce to speake from his mouth, as hee should dictate unto him, who comming into one of these maritime Townes upon a market day, and in the market place set upon an empty Cart, and he standing close behind him with the Proclamation in his hand, prompts him as followeth.
Whereas the two famous Rovers of the sea, (who thus answered him)
Whereas the two famous Rogues of the sea,
He proceeds, *Purser* and *Clinton*:
who ecchoeth to him againe,
Who hath lost their Purses at the Clinke:
Notwithstanding her Maiesties Proclamation:

Clown. That lost their purses at the Clink.

Pursev. Long since proclaimed Pirates.   [spirats.

Clown. Long since proclaimed

Pursev. Notwithstanding her Majesties commission.

Clown. Notwithstanding her Majesties condition.

Pursev. Stil keep out.

Clown. And will not come in . . . &c.

Answer, *Notwithstanding her Majesties Declaration:*

Still keepe out: sayth the pursevant. Answer. *And they will not come in* . . . &c.

Fortune by Land and Sea, Pearson, vi. 427, 429–30:

Enter the Sheriffs, the silver Oaere, Purser *and* Clinton *going to Execution.* . . .

Purser. . . . how many gallant spirits, equal with us in fame, shall this gulf swallow, and make this silver oare to blush in blood ? . . .

Purser. And set sail from the fatal Marshal seas, and *Wapping* is our harbour, a quick sand that shall swallow may a brave marine souldier. . . .

Purser. Yes, that way points the Needle, that way we steer a sad course, plague of the Pilot: hear you Mr. Sherif, you see we wear good clothes, they are payd for, and our own, then give us leave our own amongst our friends to distribute: There's, Sir, for you.

Clinton. And you.

Purser. The work man made them took never measure on a Hangmans back; wear them for our sakes, and remember us; there's some content for him too.

Hangman. Thank your worship.

Cf. also *Fortune by Land and Sea,* Pearson, vi. 416–17, 411–12, 414, 427, 429–30 and *A True Relation,* B 2ᵛ–33ᵛ, 8ᵛ, C 5–5ᵛ.

A True Relation, &c., sig. C 5–C 5ᵛ: and two dayes after brought by the Officers out of the Marshalsees, (with a silver Oare borne before them) and conducted through South-warke over the Bridge, through *London,* and so to *Wapping,* and to the place of execution there, where they appeared as brave in habit, as bold in spirit: some of their garments they then wore, they distributed amongst their private friends who came to see them dye, that they might remember them after their deaths. Many questions were asked them concerning their Piracies, which they punctually resolved: desiring first, pardon of all men whom they had wronged, and then remission of their sinnes from God, whom they had most heinously offended: when imbracing one the other in their armes, it seemed they no more ioyfully lived together than they were willing to dye together: and so being at once turned off from the Ladder, it appeared to all the multitude that were then present, that they could not live more irregularly, than they dyed resolutely and so there they hanging . . . &c.

The pamphlet, therefore, is important as practically settling Heywood's authorship of the pirate scenes and the comic passages, which were in doubt, and as depriving Rowley of the very fragments which an a priori judgement would, in consequence of the double ascription on the title-page of the first edition, plausibly have postulated as his contribution. The second of the above-mentioned booklets is *The life and death Of Queen Elizabeth, From the womb to the Tomb, from her Birth to her Burial. The Many and mighty dangers, and miraculous deliverances of the All-beloved, admired, and renowned Queen Elizabeth, of England, &c. Written in Heroical Verse* (S.R. March 28, 1639). It throws into shambling rhymed couplets with as little change as might be episodes from *England's Elizabeth*, and *If you know not me*.

About the same time Heywood had been employed on a rather more ambitious sketch of the great Queen's history for his *Exemplary Lives And Memorable Acts Of Nine The Most Worthy Women Of The World: Three Jews. Three Gentiles. Three Christians. Written by the Author of the History of Women*, 1640 (S.R. September 19, 1639). The feminist had come round again to his recurring theme and the 'duty in all that have had mothers, as far as they can to dignifie the Sex'.[1] Though less comprehensive than Γυναικεῖον, that 'meare miscellaine of all ages, sexes, qualities, complexions, conditions, disposition',[1] *Exemplary Lives* astonished the old man's enthusiastic friends.

> Will neither rugged time nor vast expence
> Of thy unfathom'd fancy and cleare sence,

asks George Estoutville, the actor,

> Perswade thee to leave off, but thou wilt still
> Make all 'twixt heaven & hell flow from thy Quill? ...
>> I doe not flatter but I may admire
>> To see fire turn'd t' Ashes returne to fire;
>> Thy age goes backward, and thy *Phoenix* bràine
>> From the old Ashes growne younge Againe;

while Thomas Brewer is sure of the eternal renown of 'This Golden issue of thy Silver head'. No less generous

[1] To the reader.

are 'William Ball (*alias* Bennet) Esquire' and Heywood's
Clerkenwell neighbour Stephen Bradwell [1] whose main
end in writing was to boast that he knew the author.
Heywood's handsome quarto, embellished with plates,
must have been begun not long before or after the sign-
ing of the treaty of Berwick when Charles's popularity
had sunk very low indeed. We are the less surprised,
therefore, to find Heywood, recently a devoted Caroline,
neither dedicating his new work on women to the Queen,
before whom, when peace was still piping, he had set that
strange dish *The Hierarchy of the Blessed Angels* in gratitude
for her reception of *Love's Mistress*, nor including her
among his nine worthy women or even making the most
distant allusion to her virtues. Nay, he went so far as to
dedicate his work in the first place to Theophila, Lady
Coke, wife of Sir Robert Coke and daughter-in-law of the
terrible Sir Edward, attributing to her all the virtues,
graces, and accomplishments.[2] The excellences of this

[1] Except Brewer these persons are very obscure. Ball, who writes very
metaphysical lines, is probably not the eldest son of Sir Peter Ball, recorder
of Exeter and attorney-general to the Queen in the reigns of Charles I
and II. A Master William Bennet, *alias* Ball, of Cambridge is a character
in *The Fair Maid of the Exchange*. For Bradwell see 6, 58 *supra*. Estoutville or Stutfield was an actor, first heard of as a leading member of the
King's Revels on Mar. 10, 1635, along with Wilbraham, the Cartwrights,
Christopher Goad, Thomas Jordan, and John Robinson; he acted later
with Queen Henrietta's company, and from 1637, or thereabouts, with
Beeston's Boys. His name appears several times in stage directions in
B.M.: MS. Egerton 1994 (cf. F. S. Boas, *Shakespeare and the Universities*,
103-4, 106, 109, 141-2).

[2] She was the daughter, born on Dec. 11, 1596, of Sir Thomas Berkeley,
son of the seventh Lord Berkeley and Elizabeth, daughter of George, Lord
Hunsdon. 'The education of ... Theophila was both in Court and Countrey
under the sole direction of her mother' (Smyth, *Lives of the Berkeleys*, ii.
400), and, as became the sister of George, Lord Berkeley, 'the traveller,
or ... the linguist' (*ibid.* ii. 423) she had, according to Heywood's dedication,

> The severall tongues, in which you so excell,
> *Greek, Roman, French, Castilian,* and with those,
> *Tuscan, Teutonick,* in all which you pose
> The forreigne Linguist: in the most select
> Both native *Ideom,* and choice dialect.

On Aug. 12, 1613, she married Sir Robert Coke, the undistinguished

'rare, (*Scarce patternd*) Patroness',[1] which were as axio-
matic as the lily's whiteness, the chastity of the turtle dove
or the beauty of the nightingale's song, were celebrated
in some of his most flowing couplets. But Heywood had
another patroness to be approached more formally in
prose. What 'dutie and service' he owed to this lady,
'Mistris Elizabeth The Vertuous Consort of *Clovill Tanfield* of *Copt-Fold* Hall, in *Essex* (Esquire)', we do not
know, but a certain primness in the phrasing suggests
that she was a Puritan and known to Heywood only
through her husband.[2] A very slight connexion between
the two dedicatees may be traced through the fact that
Sir Laurence Tanfield, Lord Chief Baron of the Exchequer, one of Sir Edward Coke's steadiest supporters,
was the first cousin of Cloville Tanfield's father.

Heywood had remarked that, provided his readers
judged favourably of his *Exemplary Lives*, 'the Nine worthy
Women going before, it may bee presumed that the Nine worthy
Men may at some small distance follow'. But this was one
of his unfulfilled pledges: and instead he turned to '*The
lives of king Henry the Eight, Cardinall Woolsey & Queene
Mary*' (S.R. March 29, 1641) which has not survived, and
to the prophecies of Merlin,[3] which were to him authentic,
amply verified and in an altogether different category from
those of Farnham and Bull. Heywood's interest in Merlin's prophecies was partly temperamental, for he was as
credulous as a child of the strange and wonderful, partly
in the way of business. In 1636 he had rejected the hetero-

second son of Sir Edward Coke. She died on Apr. 22, 1643, ten years
before her husband. Sir Robert's sister, Elizabeth, married Sir Maurice
Berkeley, great-grandson of Sir Richard Barckley whose *Felicity of Man*
Heywood edited in 1631 (see 105–6 *supra*).

[1] Lines before the life of Deborah.

[2] The representative of an old Northamptonshire family, and son of John
Tanfield and Catherine, daughter of George Combe of Chichester. His
wife was daughter of Sir Edward Engham or Ingram of Goodnestone in
Kent. A kinsman of Sir Edward married a daughter of Robert Honywood
(see 155 *supra*). The 'E Tanfeld' whose letter to Sir John Hobard is in
Bodley: MS. Tanner, cclxxxii, 105, was more probably the daughter of
Sir Laurence Tanfield to whom Drayton dedicated his epistle of William
de la Pole. [3] Cf. *Hierarchy*, 540.

dox utterances of the simple weavers with the more decisive vigour because of his real interest in probing the future. In 1640–1, when the first meetings of the Long Parliament were filling the nation at large with vague enthusiasm and only a few with apprehension, when it seemed that a new age was dawning and men were searching the skies for signs and wonders and the bookstalls for predictions, warnings, and allegories, his neat quarto with its frontispiece of the prophet and the types of his prophecies was excellently printed, apparently in a large edition, as *The Life of Merlin, Surnamed Ambrosius. His Prophecies, and Predictions Interpreted; and their truth made good by our English Annals. Being a Chronographical History of all the Kings, and memorable passages of this Kingdom, from Brute to the Reign of our Royal Sovereign King Charles. A Subject never published in this kind before, and deserves to be known and observed by all men* (S.R. July 13, 1640). And thereafter for twenty years the prophets flourished, and pamphlets, often with Merlin's name as a guarantee on the title-page, poured from the press. It had been a good opportunity for Heywood to turn an honest penny and to utilize the historical notes he had already made; and it was an easily made dish, neither long in preparation nor slow in cooking. Few of Heywood's compilations have much originality, but in none is he so unashamedly and continuously plagiarizing. In vouching for the truth of the predictions Heywood refers to Alanus de Insulis's 'explanation or Comment upon *Merlins* Prophesies, the original being extracted out of *Jeffrey* of *Monmouth*', quotes about a page, and adds 'so much Doctor *Alanus* concerning the truth of his prophesies, with whom I conclude the first Chapter'. But Heywood was very much more indebted than he admits to Alanus's *Prophetia Anglicana Merlini Ambrosii Britanni . . . a Galfredo Monumetensi Latine conversa una cum septem libris explanationum in eandem prophetiam.*[1] For the historical matter his chief source was Fabyan, whom he quotes for pages at a time with as much assurance as if he had himself written *The Concordance of*

[1] Frankfort, 1603 and 1608; Heywood used the earlier edition.

Histories. In the later reigns he supplements Fabyan with
levies from the other chroniclers, 'so that thou mayst say,
that in this small compendium or abstract, thou hast
Holinshed, Polychronicon, Fabian, Speed, or any of the rest,
of more Giantlike bulke or binding'.[1] The reissue of 1651,
to suit the new times, ends with the funeral of James I and
omits the praise of Charles and his Queen in the last
chapter.[2] This, the last of Heywood's volumes with a
dedication, was addressed in terms of equality to an en-
courager '*of all good Arts, and Sciences, but especially the
professions of Literature and Learning*', James Mettam, who
had admired some of his '*weake Labors*' and with whom
at last he had become acquainted through Mettam's kinsman Mr. T. B., probably Thomas Brewer.[3]

Two more of Heywood's friends were obliged to him
this same year for papers of commendatory verses. The
first of these, James Yorke, the blacksmith-author of *The
Union of Honour*, has already been noticed.[4] The other
was Heywood's 'adopted sonne Mr. Humphrey Mill', a
puritanical castigator of vice, whose second literary venture,
*A Night's Search Discovering the Nature, and condition of
Night-Walkers with their associates*, dedicated to the Earl
of Essex, Heywood warmly welcomed.[5] The young
aspirant had been admitted to the circle about Heywood
and managed to extract other verses for his *Night's Search*
from Stephen Bradwell, Nabbes, Thomas Brewer, and
Richard Brome.

[1] To the reader.

[2] E(dmund) C(urll) in 1736 plagiarized *The Life of Merlin* in *The
Rarities of Richmond: Being an Exact Description of the Royal Hermitage
And Merlin's Cave. With his Life and Prophecies.* An extract from
Heywood's book was reprinted in *Seven Several Strange Prophecies*, 1642,
Nine Notable Prophecies, 1644, and *Twelve Strange Prophecies*, n.d.

[3] See 173 *supra*, note 4. There were Methams, or Mettams, at Barnehill,
Metham, and Cadeby, Yorkshire. James Mettam was probably the son
and heir of George Metham of Cadeby and his second wife, Anne, daughter
of John White of Harwode. He married Janet, daughter of — Cartwright,
alias Vykers.   [4] See 1 *supra*, notes 1 and 2.

[5] Humphrey was the (? younger) brother of Thomas Mill(e) (1604–50),
who matriculated at Queen's College, Oxford, on Dec. 8, 1620. Their
father was William Mill(e) of Grattam, Sussex.

CHAPTER VIII

1640–1641: POLITICS AND PURITANISM: HEYWOOD'S DEATH

THE prophecies of Merlin, fulfilled and vindicated to Heywood's satisfaction, may have recalled to him the predictions of Thomas Brightman,[1] a Puritan divine of Elizabeth's reign, which were, according to two pamphlets we are about to claim for Heywood, in process of coming to pass. These anonymous ventures, without printer's or publisher's name, were *Brightman's Predictions And Prophecies: Written 46. years since; Concerning the three Churches of Germany, England and Scotland. Foretelling the misery of Germany, the fall of the pride of Bishops in England by the assistance of the Scottish Kirk. All which should happen (as he foretold) between the years of 36 and 41 &c.,* 1641, and *A Revelation of Mr. Brightman's Revelation, Wherein Is shewed, how all that which Mr. Brightman on the Revelation, hath foretold concerning Germany, Scotland, and England, hath been fulfilled, and is yet afulfilling, comparing his writings, and our Times together. In A Dialogue between A Minister of the Gospel, and a Citizen of London, whereby it is manifest, that Mr. Brightman was a true Prophet,* 1641. That both were by the same author is indubitable, and that that author was Heywood is, we suggest, no less clear.

Brightman's Predictions, 2:	*Life of Merlin*, 1:
Divers and sundry Predictions and Prophesies have bin made by our ancient Prophets, Bards, and fatidicall Vaticinators, which in their due time have futurely, both punctually and exactly come to passe, as of the *Sybills* (so often and frequently alledged by the Fathers) who many	To Prophets there be severall attributes given, some are called *prophetae*, some *vates*, others *videntes*: that is Prophets, Predicters, and Seers: and these have been from all antiquity. The name of prophets was, and ought to be peculiar, to those that dealt onely in divine

---

[1] Brightman (1562–1607), a voluminous expositor, was celebrated as a preacher and noted for his extreme puritanism. His chief works were his *Revelation of Revelations* (1st English ed. 1615; cf. S.R. Dec. 10, 1640, and Feb. 24, 1640/1) and the *Exposition of Daniel* (1st English ed. ? 1635).

years before predicted of the Incarnation of our blessed Saviour. The like did *Merlin Ambrosiu.*, that famous *Cambrian* Prophet, who flourished in the time of *Vortiger* King of *Britaine*, whose South-saies (for so they called them in old time) have proved true even to these latter dayes, which is made plenally apparent in a Book not long since published by the Title of *Merlins life and Prophesies*, which whosoever shall read may be amply satisfied what prevalence his prenotions had, all of them in the processe of time, being seasonably and maturely accomplished.[1]

Mysteries. But *vates* was a title promiscuously conferd on prophets and poets, as belonging to them both: of the first were, *Moses, Samuel, David, Isaiah, Jeremiah, Daniel*, and the rest.

5:
Neither was this any wonder in blessed *Job*, . . . when even all the *Sibils* (who were Prophetesses and Virgins, and Gentiles of severall Nations (for so *Varro* affirmes) predicted not onely of the Incarnation, passion, and death of our blessed Saviour, but of his second comming to judgement, of the consummation and dissolution of the World.

To the Reader:
I have here exposed to thy especiall perusall, the life and prophesies of our famous predictor, *Merlinus*, sirnamed *Ambrosius*, who though he lived in the time of profane paganisme, was a professed Christian, and therefore his Auguries the better to be approved, and allowed: thou hast withall their exposition and explanation, expressly and punctually making plain and evident, how genuinely and properly they comply with the truth of our Chronologie.

---

[1] Cf. Γυναικεῖον, 77:
Amongst these are counted some of the Sibells, though not all, as hirelings of the divell, for the conservation and confirmation of his Kingdome: for out of their bookes the Romans were drawn into many lunacies and frenzies, as (besides many others) it is manifest in *Zozimus*, who recites many of their verses full of tradition, and superstitions meerelie unlawfull, though the two Sibells *Erythraea* and *Cumana* in heroicke poems prophesied of Christ and sung and declared his prayses: . . . There were also a kind of sorcerists, which some call *Lemures*; the word importing the spirits and ghosts of such as perish before their times, or abortivelie, for from such they fathered their predictions and prophecies.
83: Without this Laurell . . . the Tripos in *Boetia* (plac't neere the vaticcinating cave) cannot be erected.

8:

We of thee *Laodicea* further find
The Text saith, thou art naked,
poore, and blind:
Not poore in Spirit, that were a
blessed thing;
For some have dar'd to write, *I and
my King*:
Yet beggers too, but not of pence,
but pounds,
And besides Clergie Tithes of temporall grounds.

Reader here, &c., 1:

Is it because . . .
they had ingrost into their
hands
Such ample purchase of the temporall lands?
That not with their due *Decimates*
content,
Both Tythes and Totall must en-
crease their rent?
Or as *Prelati*, steering the Church
helme,
They thought t'out-brave the *Pares*
of the Realme?
Nay more than that, an higher
straine had runne,
As divers proud priests had before
them done?
As *Wolfstan*, *Becket*, *Wolsey*, who
durst write,
I and my King, even in his Soveraigne's sight.

3:

His Predictions were out of the 3.
and 4. Chapters of the *Revelations*:
in which there is mention made of
7. Epistles sent to the 7. Churches
of *Asia*, which were types of 7.
other succeeding Churches to come.
The 7. *Asian* Churches as you shall
finde there mentioned, were *Ephe-
sus*, *Smyrna*, *Pergamus*, *Thyatira*,
Sardis, *Philadelphia*, and *Laodicea*;
. . . The Church of *Germanie* had
its initiation or beginning in *Martin
Luther* of *Wittenburg* a Towne in
Saxonie: in the yeare of grace 1517.

*A Revelation of Mr. Brightman's
Revelation*, 3:

in the 3d and 4. Chapters of the
Revelation, there is mention made
of seven Epistles, which our Lord,
Iesus Christ sent to the seven
Churches in *Asia*, which seven
Churches were tyypes of seven
other succeeding Churches, which
were to be counterpaines of them,
and the Counterpaine of the Church
of *Sardis*, as Mr. *Brightman* saith, is
the Church of *Germany*, the first
reformed Church begun by the
speciall providence of godly *Martin
Luther* at *Wittenberg* which is a
towne in *Saxony*, by the River
Altis in the yeare 1517.

77: she brought certaine bookes . . . which spake . . . what should futurelie
betide them.

297: She is only conversant . . . punctually to discover the causes of all
things.

687: Of Truth the Scriptures plenally report.

5:

To which may be added . . . what happened to a learned and godly Preacher of especiall note and remark, at the taking in of *Magdeburg*, who was dragged from the Church unto his owne house, where having seen his wife and daughter ravished before his face, and his young infants torne from their Mothers armes, and pitcht upon the tops of Pikes: when his eyes were blood-shot with these savage and bruitish objects, they led him bound to the Market-place, and having tied him to a stake, pill'd all his books about him, of which setting fire, they burnt them with his bodie to ashes.

8:

What art thou then? some medley stuff compos'd
Of hodge podge temper, (fit to be disclos'd)
Thou art not cold . . .
'Tis equal with thee to be Romish all,
Or one of those which we reformed call. . . .
Geneva standing on a ticklish ground,
As by the forraigne foe incompast round;
For many yeares attempted, but in vaine,
By the three potent powers, Rome, France, and Spaine,
Shall flourish still: the Hollander opprest
By Spanish tyrant, shall still keep his crest
Levell with theirs, &c.

3:

notwithstanding which, she still retained many errors, as Consub-

11:

At the taking of *Magdenburge*, a Preacher of great esteeme was dragged out of the Church to his owne house, that he might see his Wife and children ravished, his tender infants snatcht from the mothers breast, and stuck upon the top of a Lance, and when his eyes and heart were glutted with so cruell a spectacle, they brought him forth bound into the street, and laid him in the midst of his owne Bookes, and setting fire thereto miserably burnt him, and thus have I given you a text of the Lamentations of *Germany*.

25:

the *Romish* and Reformed Churches, of both which we make a medley, as Martin Bucer, complaineth . . . preferreth *a wicked Religion*, yea, none at all before this hotch-potch luke-warmnes.

17:

What mischiefe saith he is it, that the *Frenchman*, *Spaniard*, and *Pope*, have not plotted, and indevoure to worke, for the rooting out of the men of *Geneva*, a small people, environed from all with Enemies, and barred out from all aid of neighbours, Cities, and Churches, yet saith he, it flourisheth to this day, blessed be *God* for it, and shall flourish hereafter *Maugur* the envy and malice of all adversaries, though they burst for anger.

4:

That consubstantiating of the body of *Christ* in the Sacrament of the stantiation of the Lords Supper, and about free-will, good works, &c. by which he foreseeing the miserie since come upon them, admonished the *Germans* to consider of it before hand, and to prevent these impending judgements by reformation and timely repentance.

Supper, upon the which many other absurdities doe follow, which creepe like a Leprosie, and doe utterly take away the life of those members, that in themselves were alive, and this death did not come upon particular men. But also upon many whole Cities and Provinces, for to this errour about the Supper of the Lord, and person of *Christ*, other errours also were added as about originall sinne, *free-will, Iustification, Good Workes*, the *Law* and the *Gospell, &c.* . . . that joined with Christs threatning in the Text, was the cause that moved him so to conjecture, and therefore he foreseeing it, did admonish the *Germans* to consider of it afore hand, and prevent it by true and timely repentance.

Heywood had been interested in prophets, false and true, as was the author of *Brightman's Predictions*, who refers in one of the parallels cited above—Heywood frequently refers to his own works—with the Latinisms and phraseology of Heywood to '*Merlin Ambrosius*, that famous *Cambrian* Prophet, who flourished in the time of *Vortiger*, King of *Britaine*, whose South-saies . . . have proved true even to these latter dayes, which is made plenally apparent in a Book not long since published by the Title of *Merlin's Life and Prophesies*, which whosoever shall read may be amply satisfied what prevalence his prenotions had, all of them in the processe of time, being seasonably and maturely accomplished'. As we shall see, Heywood, like the author of this pamphlet, was a royalist presbyterian, furious at Laud and his innovations. The same grievances against the prelates are recounted in his *Reader, here you'll plainly see*, the same criticisms levelled at the establishment. As for *A Revelation of Mr. Brightman's Revelation*, it is for the most part a prose repetition, practically verbatim, of the prose and verse of the other, with the same object of proving the churches of Germany,

Scotland, and England the modern parallels to Sardis, Philadelphia, and Laodicea.[1]

From time to time we have noted signs of a gradual change in Heywood and have indicated whither it would eventually lead him. Until the ascription to him of certain pamphlets already discussed and of others still to be mentioned be accepted, it would seem incredible that an actor, a dramatist, an apologist of the stage, an Ovidian translator, and a hack-writer with a penchant for broad stories should ally himself with the Puritans, with whom, we may too easily have concluded, his opinions must necessarily have conflicted. Among the actors and the dramatists no doubt a secession to the puritan pamphleteers was the exception, but Heywood himself was an exception within his own circle. Except Dekker, who did not live long enough to make a decision for or against militant Puritanism, none of the other dramatists had displayed so much interest in religion and edification as Heywood; he seems to us now like a man destined for the Church whom the accidents of the time rushed into dramatic journalism. Like Dekker, too, he was essentially bourgeois, intensely loyal to King and Church, but with no love for courts and courtiers, and with an enthusiasm for London, its citizens and their standards, its wealth, splendour, and institutions; a devotion which no doubt was instrumental in securing for him the commissions for all but one of the civic pageants in those very years before the Short Parliament, when the city companies were most jealous of their privileges and liberties. Far from showing an anti-puritan bias, Heywood was a Puritan himself in all but name, and too much of a moralist to object to puritan strictures on immorality and irreligion. As it was the circumstances of his youth which drove him into a dramatic career, so it

---

[1] *Reverend Mr. Brightman's Judgement, or Prophecies what shall befall,* &c., n.d., and, with additions, 1643, though on the same theme, is not in Heywood's manner nor in the style of the other two pamphlets. In *Seven Several Strange Prophecies,* 1642, *Nine Notable Prophecies,* 1644, and *Twelve Strange Prophecies,* n.d., is reprinted the versifying of Brightman in *Brightman's Predictions.*

was his reputation among his persuasive fellows as a man
of unblemished character and a worthy representative of the
quality that forced on him the defence of the stage against
probable attacks.   But it is characteristic of Heywood
that his *Apology* is to a great extent a puritan document;
Love's Mistress, his reply to *Histrio-Mastix*, was more personal and secular merely to suit the occasion.   When he
pokes fun at the stricter sort in his other works he is far
from the merciless satire of Middleton or Jonson.   One
anecdote at the expense of women Puritans is told in *How
a Man may choose a Good Wife from a Bad*, itself a glorification of the domestic virtues in a middle class household.[1]
Timothy Thinbeard in *If you know not me*, part II, is a
dishonest Puritan, but most of the other characters are
as puritanic as he but honest; and it is the dishonourable
Wendol in *A Woman Killed with Kindness* who thinks
Mrs. Frankford talks 'too like a Puritan'.[2]   Heywood's
most outspoken pronouncement is the verse character of
the false professor in *Troia Britannica*,[3] repeated years
after in the prose character of the hypocrite in *A True
Discourse*.[4]   His progress from the secular to the edifying
and from the edifying to the doctrinal and the controversial has already been traced as far as his castigation in
A True Discourse of such disturbers of the peace of the
church as he considered Farnham and Bull to be.   As the
revolution in church and state draws near, Heywood begins
to show signs of nervousness.   In *Porta Pietatis*, his penulti-
mate pageant, he is whistling to keep his courage up:

> *This structure is a citadell, or tower,*
> *Where piety, plac't in her heavenly bower,*
> *Poynts out the way to blisse, guirt with a ring*
> *Of all those graces that may glory bring.*
> *Here sits* Religion *firme (though elsewhere torne*
> *By schismaticks, and made the atheists scorne).*
> *Shining in her pure truth, nor need she quake,*
> *Affrighted with the faggot and the stake;*
> *Shee's to you deare, you unto her are tender,*
> *Under the sceptre of the Faith's defender.*[5]

[1] Sig. G 2ᵛ–3.   [2] Pearson, ii. 135.   [3] Sig. I 2, &c.
[4] See 170–1 *supra*.   [5] Pearson, v. 272–3.

His next pageant optimistically introduces Janus with a golden key to 'shut up the yeare past, as never more to come; and open to the yeare future: it may also be an Embleme of noble policy to unbosome and bring to light their trecherous devices and stratagems, who seeke to undermine and supplant the prosperity of a faire and flourishing Common-weale'.[1] But the incidents of 1639 had deeply alarmed him; and though in the last paragraph of his *Exemplary Lives*, written immediately after Charles's humiliation at the hands of the Scots, Heywood gives the King, his 'Royall, chast and beautifull Consort' and their 'most hopefull and numerous Issue' the conventional praise, he declines, as well he might, to say anything of his reign 'concerning whose sacred person my rude pen dare not be so bold, nor with any of his just and royal proceedings'. That Heywood in the autumn of 1639 should have expressed even the most guarded doubt of Charles's government is significant. For until the stormy Short Parliament of April and May 1640 a public opinion with direction and force did not exist. There was widespread discontent in every class, but the lack of regular newspapers and the strict press-censorship had completely concealed from the public how general the irritation was. Heywood was really one with every thinking man in ranging himself against Laud, Lord Keeper Finch, and the monopolists. He was a conservative driven into opposition by the flouting of his most cherished traditions. Had he lived longer, there is no doubt that that very conservatism would have seen more to fear in puritan supremacy than in the restoration of the *status quo ante*, with such desirable modifications as the removal of Laud and his kind. His was no isolated case; George Wither had passed through almost the same phases, and Heywood's own friends, Richard Brathwaite, Henry Peacham, John Taylor, and Henry Holland, were equally inimical to schismatics, innovators, and governmental abuses. It is not, then, the change in the politics of the kindly old man who had so long wielded a blunt pen that need surprise

[1] Pearson, v. 364.

us, but the unexpected vigour he displays in the few months before his death.

For the sake of clearness we shall begin with the ultra-protestant pamphlets, and first of all with *The Rat Trap: Or The Jesuits taken in their owne Net &c. Discovered in this year of Jubilee, or Deliverance from the Romish faction,* 1641 (S.R. February 9, 1640/1 as 'by master Heywood').

The Rat-Trap, 20:

Troubles also were raised in her Kingdom of Ireland by one *Nicolas Saunders*, a pestilent Traytour, and one of that seditious Order, whose pen and tongue spared not only maliciously to calumniate the Queene her selfe, but the Lady *Anne Bulleine* her mother, who having purchased a consecrated Banner with power Legantine, landed amongst the Rebels, whither was sent also *S. Josephus* with an army of Italians and Spanyards, to joyne with the revolted Earle of Desmond, his brother *Fitz Morris,* and others: but their army was soone distrest, the Earle dyed wretchedly, and Saunders fell mad, and dyed starved in the cliffes of an almost unaccessible mountaine.

Exemplary Lives, 206:

Notwithstanding the death of *Stukeley*, new troubles were raysed in Ireland by one *Nicolas Saunders*, a pestilent Traytor; whose pen and tongue were most maliciously saucie against her sacred Majestie, who in his contumelious Libells neyther spared the Queenes mother dead, nor the daughter living; hee having purchased a consecrated Banner landed among the Rebells, with power *Legantine*, whether also was sent one *Sam. Iosephus* with seven hundred *Italians* and *Spaniards* to joyne with the revolted Earle of *Desmond* his brother Fitsmoris and others, but in small processe after much effusion of blood on both sides the Earle dyed miserably, and *Saunders* mad.

The Rat-Trap, 22–3:

I will conclude all the Iesuittical Treasons against her (and those by her own Subjects,) which (*sic*) that as (*sic*) *Edward Squire* are (*sic*) belonging to the Queenes stable, who being in *Spaine* was perswaded and seduced from his allegeance by one Walpoole a revolted runnagate and entred into the Iesuiticall order (one of these before named *Invats,*) who gave a mortiferous confection in a bladder, to poyson the pummell of her saddle, who after his return into *England* attending his opportunity, one day when her Majesty was to

Exemplary Lives, 211–12:

I conclude all her miraculous preservations with that of *Edward Squire*, one belonging to the Queenes stable; who being in *Spaine* received from one *Walpoole* a *Iesuite*, a strong and mortiferous confection in a bladder, to poyson the Pummell of her Saddle, who after his returne wayting his opportunitie, and by reason of his place and former acquaintance not being suspected, when her Majestie was to take horse, he came openly with a smiling countenance in the presence of many, and having prickt take horse, came openly with a smiling countenance in the presence of many, and having prickt the bladder, and wearing a thick tand glove for his owne security, clapt his hand vpon the pummell of the saddle, and with a lowd and cheerefull voyce sayd God save the Queene: but it pleased God out of his mercifull providence, to take his word not his meaning; for neither mounting, nor alighting, nor all the way shee roade, (wearing a thinne glove) shee once layd her hand vpon the pummell: but the Treason beeing after discovered, he by his owne conviction was convicted and condemned.

the bladder wearing a thicke tan'd glove clapt his hand upon the Pummell of the Saddle, and with a chearefull voyce sayd, *God save the Queene*, wherein it pleased God (as mine author saith) to take his word not his meaning; for by Gods great providence neither in mounting nor alighting, nor all the way she rode shee once touched the Pummell. For which attempt he by his voluntary confession was convicted and condemned.

This piece of propaganda starts as a moderate attack, according to the ideas of the time, on the Jesuits, but soon becomes more violent towards those whose 'study is onely for blood, their Religion is Rebellion, their treaties are only treacheries, their plots are only powderplots, their matches onely to out-match us',[1] and so on. The author reviews some of the political crimes attributed to Jesuit agency, such as the murder of Henry III of France, the attempt on the life of Henry IV by Chastell and Ravaillac, and the assassination of William of Orange. He is more imaginative in his description of a synod of Jesuits at Salamanca in 1629 on the anniversary of Loyola's birth, at which 'one grave Seignior, who was the Prolocutor',[2] proposed to extend the power of the order by setting England and Scotland, 'Nations that have too long lived in fraternall love and amity', at odds. It would be easy, he argues, to sow trouble by securing responsible posts for Jesuits in these kingdoms and in Ireland, or to incense Papist against Puritan and both against the Church of England, and 'to bring in new Innovations into the Churches of England and Scotland, such as wee know the most distaste, and can worse digest; to alter their ancient

[1] 26.   [2] 13.

Liturgy, by inserting new additions into their books of Common prayer, and by admitting into Church livings, none but such as can conforme themselves to all such Tenents as shake hands with the Romish Traditions and Doctrines; and to thrust out of their Benefices, all such as stand stiffe for the Reformed Religion, but especially to thrust in Ceremonies (such as they call Superstitious) Altars, and the like, into the Scottish Kirk, which Nation we know to be perverse, obstinate, and impatient of any Innovation or change, especially in their Religion'.[1] The assembly thereupon 'dissolved, with a determinate resolution to put all the former projects in speedy practice with an *Et caetera*'.[2] Verily Heywood was now involved in one of the most hotly disputed questions of the day. After the dissolution of the Short Parliament, Convocation had continued to meet at the command of the King, who required the clerical supplies and who, to reassure the more timid that their meeting was legal though the other estates had been prorogued, obtained the opinions of Finch and a committee of lawyers. When the subsidies were voted, Convocation proceeded to pass seventeen new canons; the most offensive of them was the oath to be imposed on the clergy that they approved the doctrine and discipline of the Church of England and would never bring in Popish doctrines contrary to what was by law established or consent 'to alter the government of this Church by archbishops, bishops, deans, and archdeacons, &c.' This unlucky phrase was the Puritans' opportunity; all manner of innovations might be introduced under so indefinite a rule. When on December 16 the Long Parliament declared the obnoxious canons illegal, Sir John Hotham, with whom Pym agreed, saw in them good grounds for accusing Laud of treason. Two days later Harbottle Grimstone, who had subscribed for a plate for Heywood's *Hierarchy*, expressed the general opinion with ponderous oratory and unpleasant figures. Laud was 'the stye of all Pestilent filth, that hath infected the State and Government' of this commonwealth, and 'a viper' who should no

[1] 17.   [2] 19; cf. 27.

longer be allowed to 'distil his poison [into the] sacred
ears' of the King; moreover he was the friend of Windebank, and Strafford was his agent.[1] Though Heywood
rejoiced at 'the beginning of this now hopefull Parliament,[2] he, like Grimstone, was very respectful of the King
whose 'great and unbounded clemency & mercy' [3] in
reprieving one John Goodman, a Catholic priest, is mentioned.[4] He was no doubt as indignant at the Roman
Catholics as his pamphlet shows him to have been, but
the immediate reason for writing was an incident which
brought their machinations home to him through one
of his own name.   For 'but yesterday [i. e. Saturday,
November 21, 1640],[5] one *Iohn James* [6] a *Kentish* man a
Iesuiticall Romist, thinking now by a pretended madness
to colour his notorious mischiefe, in *Westminsterhall*, in
the very face of the Iudiciall Courts, with a rusty dagger,
stabbed Iustice *Heywood*, as he was going to the parliament house to deliver up a catalog of divers papists and
Iesuits names which inhabited in or about *Westminster*, . . .
thinking to have deprived him of his life, which God be
thanked, proved otherwise'.[7]

[1] Grimstone's *Speech . . . upon the Accusation and Impeachment of
William Laud.*
[2] *The Rat Trap*, 25.   [3] 30.
[4] Goodman, once an Anglican clergyman, and Henry Mosse, priests,
were committed by the High Commission to Newgate on June 18, 1640,
but were released by Windebank's order on July 3. Goodman was re-
arrested and sentenced to death. On Jan. 23, 1640/1 the King reprieved
him, thus provoking the Lords and Commons to a remonstrance on Jan. 29
at the general slackness of the administration of the law against recusants.
The King on Feb. 3 replied that he had no intention of relaxing the penal
laws, and announced his intention of ordering all Jesuits and priests to
leave England within a month; Goodman's case he referred wholly to
Parliament, but urged them to consider what other nations would think of
their severity. Goodman was still in prison in Oct. 1641.
[5] Heywood's pamphlet, registered on Feb. 9, alludes to the case of Goodman being remitted to Parliament and could not, therefore, have been
finished before Feb. 3. See S.R. Nov. 24 for a ballad on the attack on
Justice Heywood.
[6] See *C.S.P.D.* 1601-3, 136 for Henry James, a Clerkenwell recusant.
[7] 25-6. On Nov. 23 Charles expressed his indignation to the Commons
and recommended them to take action. The committee of investigation

The logical, if not the chronological, sequence of Heywood's later pamphlets brings us now to his more outspoken attacks on the monopolists. The parliament of 1621 had taken strong measures, almost with royal approval, against patentees. But the provisions of the Monopoly Act of 1624 were scarcely stringent enough; for it left with the King the power to institute as many monopolies as he liked, provided that the right was vested in a corporation, not in an individual. The first serious attempt at evasion of the act was the soap monopoly of 1631, which roused great opposition, and drew satires from the dramatists of the whole system of jobbery. After the soap-boilers came the salt-makers, then the coal-brokers, the brick-makers, the hackney-coachmen, the post office, the starch-makers, and lastly the vintners. The first to be considered of Heywood's satires on monopolists, *Machiavel. As He lately appeared to his dear Sons, the Modern Projectors.*

submitted a report on Nov. 27. But nothing further was done till January when the whole question of the expulsion of priests and Jesuits was canvassed. A proclamation of Mar. 8, 1640/1 warned all Romish priests to leave the country within a month. On April 27 a bill for the severe punishment of James and for the forfeiture of his goods was read for the first and second times. From time to time the bill was reconsidered and passed but it never received the King's signature. On Oct. 7, 1643, however, the Commons ordered the profits of two parts of the land of James to be sequestered into Sir Robert Pye's hands for the benefit of Mrs. Elizabeth Heywood, until an ordinance could be passed instead of the bill. Peter Heywood belonged to the Lancashire Heywoods, of Heywood Hall; he was the second son of Peter Heywood and his wife, Margaret, daughter of Robert Gartsyde. By his first wife, whose name is not known, he had no children, but by his second wife, Elizabeth Thirrall of Leeds, he left a large family. He was in prosperous circumstances and proved himself an efficient and busy justice. He died in Jan. 1641/2, his will being proved by his wife on the 24th. See Corsor's ed. of James's *Iter Lancastrense*, introduction and notes, and *Civil War Tracts*, 345; *Victoria County History of Lancashire*, v. 138 &c.; *Memorials of St. Margaret's, Westminster*; J. E. Smith's *Catalogue of Westminster Records*; *C.S.P.D.* Baines's *History of the County Palatine of Lancaster*, i. 586, ii. 676, and its revisions by Harland and Whatton, and Croston propagated the absurd story that Peter Heywood arrested Guy Fawkes. Thomas Heywood, one of the choristers in the Chapel Royal after the Restoration, was a grandson of Peter's, and not related, as Cunningham imagined (*Extracts from the Accounts of the Revels at Court*, xx), to the dramatist.

Divulged for the pretended good of the Kingdomes of England, Scotland, and Ireland. Printed by authority: In the yeare of Grace 1641, (S.R. January 25, 1640/1),[1] is an appeal with all the zest of a reformer to the members of Parliament. The high and honourable court of Parliament is the Hercules that has destroyed the projecting '*vipers*' and the '*bright English sunne*' that has scattered '*the mists of errour*'.[2] After Machiavelli's verse address to his dear sons, the monopolists, come the author's preface, a longish character-sketch of the genus projector, and a series on the species thereof, the wine, tobacco, salt, rag, card, butter, soap, coal, and corporation criminals. Twice the author refers familiarly to the stage.[3] In the same good set terms he assails the same abuses as Heywood in *Reader, here you'll plainly see*.

Machiavel as he lately appeared, sig. A 3:	*Reader, here you'll plainly see,* 5:
You were indeed the onely Men of men,	Yet we may finde them in our bread, our meat,
That did with cautious industrie supplie	In every draught or bit wee drinke or eat.
Natures defects; and to Monopolie	Our Bevers, and the Bootes wee plucke on, whether
Reduce all Trades, and Sciences within	We have them made of Calve-skin, or Neats Leather,
The Kingdome, from the Bever to the Pin.	Our Salt and Oatmeal, Porridge are not free,
With what a care of sobernesse did you	But they from their ingredience must have fee;
Enhance the price of Wine, and make men brew	Our cloath, stuffe, lace, points, tagges, even to a pinne,
By License onely: not the Coals, or Salt,	Nay even the linen next unto our skinne,
But was excis'd, not Butter, no not Malt;	Our needle it is sow'd with: they make Boote,
Nay, even the Rags themselves did tribute pay,	Of everything we wear, from head to foote.
Tobacco too, and every thing that lay Open to your Inventions: Cards and Dice,	Nay I may speake it to them (with a pox) I find them even in my Tobacco box.
Laying an imposition on mens vice.	

As Heywood in *The Rat Trap* [4] and *Reader, here you'll*

---

[1] Some copies have *Machiavel's Ghost*, &c.
[2] To the reader.　　　　[3] Sig. B 4ᵛ–C, D 2.　　　　[4] 14.

plainly see [1] accused the Jesuits and the Romanizing bishops of setting England and Scotland at feud, so in *Machiavel as he lately appeared* the projector is one who 'hath wrought under hand with Seminaries and Jesuits like a Mole, to set dissention betweene the two Kingdomes'.[2] The theme of *The Rat Trap* is the trickery of the 'Jesuiticall Machiavells'.[3] In *Reader, here you'll plainly see* the monopolists are a 'swarme of Locusts'; a 'crew of moaths and cankers' in a flourishing orchard,

> those Drones, that fly about in mists,
> Divelish *Projectors*, damn'd Monopolists,
> Who now are hid in holes and keepe a loofe,
> Being indeed not Parliamentall proofe.[4]

The address to the reader of *Machiavel as he lately appeared* refers to the '*mists of errour*' the sun of parliament has dispelled and to the patentees as '*more pestilent Vermine . . . than Foxes; not onely content to devoure for satisfaction of their hungers, but making mischiefe their sport*'. There are, too, many of the rare words Heywood affected, 'Jovelike', 'characterd', 'participate of', 'gymnosophists', 'architecture' (= architect), 'vendable', and the like. But it is unnecessary to extend the list of parallels in phrase, word, and idea which are far more than sufficient to establish identity of the authorship of *Reader, here you'll plainly see*, *The Rat Trap*, and *Machiavel as he lately appeared*.

There are the same abundant signs of Heywood in *A Dialogue or accidental discourse Betwixt Mr. Alderman Abel, and Richard Kilvert, the two main Projectors for Wine, and also Alderman Abel's wife, &c. Containing their first manner of their acquaintance, how they began the Patent itself, how they obtained it, and who drew the patent. Also in what state they now stand in, and how they accuse and rail at each other*

---

[1] 12. [2] Sig. O 3.
[3] 5. *The Atheistical Politician: or a brief Discourse concerning Nicholas Machiavel* is not by Heywood. The verse in *Machiavel as he lately appeared* was added to *A New Political Catechism For The Present Times*, 1740 and stated to be a second edition. The character of a projector in general was reprinted with slight changes in *Hog's Character of a Projector*, 1642. [4] 5.

*with invective speeches, &c. With the manner and fashion
how Projectors and Patentees have rode a-Tilting in a Parliament time, &c.* 1641.

A Dialogue or accidental Discourse,
8:
  Abel. If I do ? it is of thy driving.
I tell thee *Kilvert* thou art worse
then *Caine.*
  Kilvert. Indeed, we read that in
old time *Caine* kild *Abel*, but now
Abell kils *Caine*; and I am afraid
there is a young *Gregory* born to
make an end of us both.
Machiavel as he lately appeared,
sig. A 4:
Nor shall *Tiburnian Gregorie* with
  stroak
Of paltry penny bard have power
  to choak
Wesands so meritorious.

Reader, here you'll plainly see, 6:
  Abel and *Cain* were shepheards
  (the Text saies)
But which is strange, turnd Vintners in these days.
The wicked *Caine* his brother *Abel*
  slew:
Which in these brother Vintners
  proves not true.
For unto this day, *Caine* keepes up
  his signe,
But *Abel* lyes drownd in his *Medium*
  wine.
Projecting *Kilvert* (some say) was
  the cause,
Who making new Lords, had devisd
  new lawes.
But those that would the ancient
  custome vary,
Shall now ('tis thought) be made
  exemplary.

A Dialogue or Accidental Discourse,
6:
Kilvert. I know you Mr. Alderman
to be a man every way *Abel*, ioyne
but your purse with my policy, and
if I procure you not a Patent, thinke
me to be a meere paltry fellow, and
not worth the name of a Proiector:
I am none of those fellowes which
were borne in a *Dul-age*, nor do I
dwell at *Dul-age*; I am accounted
wiser than ever my father was.
6:
And that the Merchants shall pay
to the King forty shillings upon
every Tun ere hee shall vent it to
the Vintner: in lieu of which, that
the Vintner may be no loser, he
shall rayse the price also of his
Wines, upon all French Wines a
peny a quart, upon all Spanish

*Machiavel as he lately appeared,*sig.C:
if you seeme to doubt any of these
Projects, hee hugges himselfe with
conceit of your ignorance, and his
owne wit: if you question him, his
answer is; 'This age is a cherisher
of Arts, and new Inventions, the
former dull and heavie, that these
times are active, as may appear by
the draining of the Fens.'
Reader, here you'll plainly see, 6:
And then thinkes one, where sope
  hath fayl'd without,
Balderdash wines within, will worke
  no doubt.
And then comes in (that project
  once begun)
New imposts upon every Pipe and
  Tun.
The price of French and Spanish
  wines are raisd,

Wines two pence a quart: it is no matter how the Subiect suffer, so we get and gaine by it.

6:
I am a man Parliament proofe.
8:
You are Parliament proofe with a pox.

4:
and by that meanes [I] have admittance into all the Courts of iustice, where I have subordinate intelligencers, which I allow a groat a day throughout the yeare, that skrew themselves into other mens causes, and affoord me materiall sufficient to worke upon: now, when I have cast in my conceits to picke an hole in another mans Coate, or to find the least flaw by which I may overthrow him or his fortunes, then is my Spirits animated, my peticranion is imployed to purpose, for my braine upon such an occasion is in the most able agitation.

How ever in their worth deboyst and craisd.
The subject suffers in each draught he swallows,
For which may they be doomb'd unto the gallows.

5:
Divilish *Projectors*, damn'd *Monopolists*,
Who now are hid in holes and keepe a loofe,
Being indeed not Parliamentall proofe.
The Rat-Trap; 2:
Of whom to make a more generall discovery: They first skrew themselves into the hearts and thoughts of Princes.
3:
[They] by the meanes of their correspondents, who disperse themselves into the principall Cities of that Province, first informe themselves of the state, condition and quality of that Kingdome, and informe the assistants of all passages and occurants, of which they give notice to the Father generall at Rome.
4:
they are Confessors to the greatest part of the Nobility...by which they penetrate into every designe and purpose, of which they give intelligence to their further (*sic*) generall.

It is full of Heywood's uncouth neologisms, 'peccant', 'arch-solicitor', 'agitation', 'fatuate', 'effascinate', and the like; it affords parallels every few lines to Heywood's other political pamphlets, to say nothing of his earlier work. The scandal of the wine monopoly was one of the most recent and flagrant examples of Caroline misgovernment, and had aroused as much disaffection as, or more than, any of the other similar abuses. Till the opening of the Long Parliament, which took action in the matter within a fortnight of its assembling on November 3, squib and satire had been kept under. But immediately thereafter, 'instead of *Encomiums* on the excellence of virtuall *Canary*', all the poet-victims of the tax on wines 'write nipping Satyres against the base extortion of this ravenous Citie-member who makes himselfe merry with other mens misery'. Alderman Abel, who with his accomplice Richard Kilvert had managed the job to their own advantage and the public detriment, 'is (it seems) a man generally belov'd still: for every man limnes his Picture, and scarce any Stationer in Towne, but has some Pamphlet, Sonnet or Ballet in his praise'.[1] After the arrest of Abel and Kilvert in November 1640, the Commons let the matter rest till May 26, 1641, when they declared the impositions on wines illegal and resolved on a bill against the aforesaid projectors. It must have been some time after this that *A Dialogue or Accidental Discourse* was written.[2]

[1] *An Exact Legendary compendiously containing the whole life of Alderman Abel*, 1641. William Abel, from being the humble host of a tavern, had blossomed into a member of the Vintners' Company, an alderman in which capacity he arrested Prynne in 1637, sheriff, and master of the Vintners. According to *An Exact Legendary* he was a cousin of Richard Kilvert. The latter had risen from a subordinate position in the Canterbury Prerogative Court to be a proctor. He first became notorious as an informer in the impeachment of Sir John Bennet, judge of the Canterbury Prerogative Court, and was a damaging crown agent in the proceedings against Bishop Williams. Abel had come to office in his company during a crisis in their affairs. In 1632 the Vintners had refused to pay a premium of £4 per tun of wine. But next year they were found to have been dressing meat for sale in contravention of their charter. In 1635 they bought condonation for some months from the Star Chamber at the cost of £6,000. The promised exemption, however, was not thereby secured. They rejected the Attorney-General's offer of a pardon in consideration of their paying a penny per quart of wine sold; but in 1637 they were wearied into surrender by Abel, the terms of their agreement being to pay 40*s.* per tun of wine (or as later arranged £30,000 a year in all) in return for permission to charge a penny extra per quart of French wine and twopence per quart of Spanish. Kilvert's reward was £1,000, paid by the Vintners' Company, but without the knowledge of all the members; while Abel was appointed a farmer of the new tax, and in 1639 a licenser of taverns.

[2] *The last Discourse Betwixt Master Abel and Master Richard Kilvert*, 1641, is an imitation by another hand of Heywood's *A Dialogue or Accidental Discourse*.

Heywood had maintained his anonymity in these squibs, an evasion of criticism of which Martin Parker in his *Poet's Blind Man's Bough*, 1641, pronounced him innocent:

> Whatever yet was published by mee,
> Was known by *Martin Parker*, or M.P. . . .
> *Sydney* and *Shakespire*, *Drayton*, *Withers* and
> Renowned *Ionson* glory of our Land:
> *Deker*, Learn'd *Chapman*, *Haywood* all thought good,
> To have their names in publike understood.[1]

As for the nameless ones, almanac-makers and originators of impossible scares, revealers of incredible plots and inventors of absurd libels, Parker has nothing but contempt. In any case Heywood on the title-page of his triple attack on Laud and the Romanizing clergy, Lord Keeper Finch and the pliant bench of judges, and the monopolists, *Reader, Here you'll plainly see Judgment perverted By these three: A Priest, A Judge, A Patentee*, 1641, which summarizes his other political pamphlets, boldly manifests himself on the title-page. An allusion in the text to the Commons' proclamation of the illegality of the wine impost fixes the date of this tripartite lampoon also after May 26, 1641. Heywood in it rakes up all his charges against the bench of bishops, their pride and pretensions, their

> inclining to the *Arminian* Sect,
> And preaching in the Romish Dialect . . .
> New Cannons, Oathes, and Altars, bending low,
> To where, in time the images must grow,
> Reviving antient and forgot Traditions,
> Grounded upon old Popish superstitions,

and their fatal alteration of the Scottish service-book. He almost takes sides with Prynne, Bastwick, and Burton, whose anti-prelatical sentiments are here practically re-

---

[1] Taylor, who is also mentioned by Parker, did *not* sign all his pamphlets.

peated. Yet like Hyde, Falkland, and most of all Digby, he wanted the retention of a reformed episcopate:

> Th' offendors once being punisht and remov'd,
> The function might remaine, to their disgraces,
> To try who better might supply their places;

indeed the whole passage reads like a versification of Digby's speech of February 8, 1640/1 on the London petition for the abolition of episcopacy. The less comprehensive satire on the judges is directed rather at an individual than at the whole judicature. This person was John, Lord Keeper Finch, notorious for his iniquity and brutality in his earlier office of Chief Justice of the Common Pleas; he appeared once before the House of Commons on December 21, 1640 in consequence of the motion of the moderate Falkland, supported by Hyde, for his impeachment, but fled to Holland the same night. In the section on the patentees Heywood adds little to what he had asserted in *Machiavel as he lately appeared* and *A Dialogue or Accidental Discourse*; as he seemed to echo Digby on the bishops, so now he might be paraphrasing Sir John Culpepper's speech on monopolies on November 9, 1640.

We have come at last to the end of these dull tracts, illuminated by few flashes of wit and unredeemed by any distinction from the poor level of contemporary journalism. The more ambitious non-dramatic work which preceded this final rubbish of Heywood's career is not much more stimulating; and indeed the long sequence of his plays, his modest claim to renown, presents his biographer with only the most unsuggestive facts concerning him. His migrations from company to company, the shadowy procession of his friends and patrons, the other certainties from which so many more probabilities have had to be deduced, have been recorded as the life-story of a typical journeyman-playwright, not for their intrinsic interest. It is, therefore, with profound thankfulness that we report the last fact of this long and uneventful history. On

August 16, 1641 was 'Tho. Heywood, Poet b^d in ye Church' of St. James's, Clerkenwell.[1]

[1] The first posthumous allusion to Heywood (*The Actor's Remonstrance*, 1643) leaves in doubt whether the writer was aware of the dramatist's death. Nor is it clear that the author of *The Great Assizes holden in Parnassus by Apollo*, 1645, who classes Heywood with the 'Poets good and free' and puts him in the jury of writers living and departed, was better informed. Samuel Sheppard in *The times Displayed in Six Sestiads*, 1646, might still be writing in ignorance of Heywood's death:

> Nor thine O *Heywood* worthy to be read
> By Kings, whose bookes of eloquence are such
> Enough in praise of thee, can nere be sed
> Nor can my Verse, ere extoll too much
> Thy reall worth, whose lines unparaled
> Although some envious criticks seem to grutch
> Shall live on earth to thy eternall Fame
> When theirs in grave shall rot, without a name.

F. Palmer in 1647 (Beaumont and Fletcher folio) probably implies knowledge of the fact that Heywood was by then dead. But in *A Satire against Separatists*, 1648, Heywood is spoken of as still alive:

> Go on brave *Heroes*, and perform the rest,
> Increase your fame each day a yard at least,
> Till your high names are growne as glorious full
> As the foure *London* Prentices at the Red Bull . . .
> So may your goodly Ears still prickant grow,
> And no bold Hair increase to mar the show,
> So may your *Morefield's* pastimes never fail,
> And all the Rooms about keep mighty Ale . . .
> And so rare Pageants grace the Lord Mayor's show,
> And none find out that these are Idols too.
> So may you come to sleep in Fur at last,
> And some *Smectimnuan*, when your days are past,
> Your funerall Sermon of six hours rehearse,
> And *Heywood* sing your praise in lofty verse.

The *Smectymnuus* allusion points perhaps to composition, if not to an earlier edition, in 1641. In the 1675 edition Taylor's name takes the place of Heywood's as a bourgeois poet. For other posthumous allusions to Heywood see 6–7, 14, 67, note 1, 99, 138, 144 *supra*, and for a list, Bates, 281, &c., to which should be added Oldham's *Works*, ed. 1686, 169:

> Quarles, *Chapman*, *Heywood*, *Withers* had Applause,
> And *Wild*, and *Ogilby* in former days;
> But now are damn'd to Wrapping Drugs, and Wares,
> And curst by all their broken Stationers;

and *Visits from the Shades: Part II*, 1705, 73 &c. for a dialogue between Heywood and Durfey.

CHAPTER IX

HEYWOOD THE DRAMATIST

HEYWOOD is decidedly a poet 'of the second Magnitude';[1] and he has rightly been called 'the model of a light and rapid talent',[2] for talent, rather than genius, is the appropriate word. He was the journeyman-playwright *par excellence*, with a facility, not unlike the knack of a skilled artisan, with a dramatic insight which never altogether failed him, and without the vagaries and transcendencies of a conscious artist. He was not like Webster torn 'between the immediate demands of the theatre and high literary ambitions';[3] for though in his later years he followed the examples of Massinger and Ford in dedicating his plays to friends, he never considered them great literature; they were professional, rather than artistic. Yet Heywood was a scholar with a familiar knowledge of the critics; and it would be possible to extract from his compilations an Apology for Poetry with formal disquisitions on the dignity and antiquity of the poet's calling. In Γυναικεῖον we can hear again, though a little less clear and confident, the voice of Sidney justifying the ways of Plato to poets. Literature was to Heywood a teacher of morals, eloquence, and patriotism, and in *An Apology for Actors* he defends the contemporary stage on the same utilitarian grounds. But he was one of the most modest of men and had few delusions about his own plays. On occasions, it is true, he displays an amiable complacency at his own success, as, for example, when *If You Know Not Me* so filled the theatre that the printers thought it worth while to print an edition from shorthand notes, or when *The Ages* were acted with applause by two companies together on three different stages; he was proud, too, of his two hundred and twenty plays. But he never makes

---

[1] Langbaine, *sub* William Rowley.
[2] Tieck, *Shakespeare's Vorschule*, i, Vorrede xl, as cited by Ward, ii. 585.
[3] A. H. Thorndike, *Webster and Tourneur*, 2.

extravagant claims for his dramas as poetry; he is content
if the reader find

> *Some Mirth, some Matter, and perhaps some Wit.*[1]

Not without a sly glance at Ben Jonson, he explains that
*'my Playes are not exposed unto the world in Volumes, to beare
the title of* Workes, *(as others.)'*[2] Beaumont and Fletcher
opposed the vulgar taste of the day and Jonson the un-
lettered, but of all the dramatists Heywood was the most
compliant with the public and yielded with an easy
acquiescence and whole-hearted surrender. What the
public demanded, that would it get, whether incredible
romances or lachrymose tragicomedies of the home,
chronicle-histories, showy mythology or classical tragedies, adventures on the high seas, intrigue comedies or
courtly romances. In words which apply better to his
own than to the work of any of his contemporaries, he
says of the dramatic plenitude of the time:

> To give content to this most curious Age,
> The gods themselves we' have brought downe to the Stage
> And figur'd them in Planets; made even Hell
> Deliver up the Furies, by no spell,
> (Saving the *Muses* rapture) further, we
> Have traffickt by their helpe; no History
> We have left unrifled, our Pens have been dipt
> As well in opening each hid Manuscript,
> As Tracts more vulgar, whether read, or sung
> In our domesticke, or more forraigne tongue:
> Of Fairy Elves, Nymphs of the Sea, and Land;
> The Lawns and Groves, no number can be scan'd
> Which we' have not given feet to, nay 'tis knowne
> That when our Chronicles have barren growne
> Of Story, we have all *Invention* stretcht,
> Div'd low as to the Center, and then reacht
> Unto the *Primum Mobile* above:
> (Nor scapt things intermediate).[3]

He tried all styles without any valuation of changing

---

[1] *The English Traveller*, prologue; quoted in the preface of *If You
Know Not Me*, part I.   [2] *The English Traveller*, preface.
[3] *The Royal King and the Loyal Subject*, prologue.

fashions; in the epilogue to the reader of *The Royal King and the Loyal Subject* he asks

> And what's now out of date, who is't can tell,
> But it may come in fashion and sute well?

His cognizance of classical and Renaissance canons never entered into conflict with his tradesmanlike energy, not even in *Love's Mistress*, where for once he affected to despise popular tastes. He was one of those who dared to 'serve the ill customs of the stage' which Jonson so sternly rejected in the prologue to *Every Man in his Humour*.

Heywood's first surviving play, the boyish *Four Prentices of London*, was an essay in the ranting Ercles vein of Greene. In 'this Quixotic romance of the City, with its serio-comic ideal of crusading counter-jumpers,' [1] Heywood was translating into drama, as they were never again to be so completely understood, the romantic notions of a civic audience. Verily it was

> something notably
> In honor of the Commons of this City; [2]

not, as Warton supposed, 'a mixture of the droll and serious . . . evidently written to ridicule the reigning fashion of reading romance', [3] but a perfectly sincere appeal, which Heywood in his more sophisticated days half-excused and half-defended from the ridicule of *The Knight of the Burning Pestle* as an effort which, though coming '*short of that accuratenesse both in Plot and Stile, that these more Censorious dayes with greater curiosity [re]quire*', was to be regarded as of the fashion '*some fifteene or sixteene yeares agoe*'. [4] If it was perhaps Jonson who did most to create a demand for a stronger probability than the absurd operatic plays of this class provided, the classical attack, so kindly and genial for all its acuteness, was of course *The Knight of the Burning Pestle*, in which Beaumont about

[1] Swinburne, *Age of Shakespeare*, 222–3.
[2] *The Knight of the Burning Pestle*, induction.
[3] Quoted in *Old English Drama*, 1825, ii, preface to *Love's Mistress*, viii.
[4] Address to the Apprentices.

1607 [1] rightly took Heywood, rather than Munday, as the leader of the plebeians. No doubt Beaumont had the whole school in view from Peele's *Edward I* and

> the storie of Queen *Elenor*,
> With the rearing of *London Bridge* upon Woolsacks, [2]

Mucedorus, and *The Spanish Tragedy* to *The Travels of Three English Brothers*, and 'the Legend of Whittington'; nay even the rant in *Henry IV* does not escape. But it was above all Heywood's *Four Prentices* that was held up to ridicule. Beaumont's citizen is a grocer; and Ralph the hero of the impromptu drama is bound, like Eustace the youngest of Heywood's brethren, to the same trade. He has, too, a proper respect for it: 'Why should [not I] then pursue this course both for the credit of my self and our company, for amongst all the worthy Bookes of Atchievements, I do not call to mind that I yet read of a Grocer Errant, I will be the said Knight ... hence my blew apron, yet in remembrance of my former Trade, upon my shield shall be purtraid a *Burning Pestle*, and I will be call'd the *Knight of the Burning Pestle*.' [3] Probably, too, the genial satire of 'the youths together in battle-ray, with Drums, and Guns, and flags', and the 'very notable matter ... to the eternal honour and glory of all Grocers' [4] refer as much to the battles in 'the play of the *Foure Prentices of London* where they tosse their pikes so' [5] as to the citizens' militia. But Heywood's other plays are as merrily satirized. It is the story of his '*Ralph and Lucrece*' [6] that is painted on the arras, and Master Merrythought not only sings one of the songs of the merry Lord Valerius in that strange tragedy, but was probably meant to be taken as a parody of him. There are sly allusions to *Jane Shore* and *The Bold Beauchamps*; [7] and 'the life and death of Sir *Thomas Gresham* With the building of the Royal Exchange' [8] is taken by the citizen as a piece in eminently

---

[1] Cf. Chambers, iii. 221.   [2] Induction.
[3] i. 3: cf. Pearson, ii. 174, 224.   [4] v. I, iv. 5.   [5] iv. I.
[6] ii. 8.   [7] Induction.   [8] Induction.

good taste without any abuse in it. It is curious that in thus laughing off the stage the simple heroics, the prodigies of valour, the attempts at pomp, even the simple earnestness of these plays Beaumont was only preparing the way for another kind of romance, much more sophisticated, ethically much more unsound, fundamentally as improbable though more plausibly and skilfully carried off, which was to degenerate into the heroic play of the Restoration, as childish as Heywood's but with the absurdity of the drama's second childhood, not its first. In *The Four Prentices* Heywood transformed the Crusades from an account of epical struggles and an allegory, as Tasso meant it to be, of the life of man, into a painted arras, a background with a picture of Jerusalem on it, for an amateur's dramatization of the symmetrical material of folk-literature. With his four thrasonical brothers, two subsidiary heroes, Tancred and Robert, two lifeless heroines, four villains, and the old Earl of Boulogne as the centre of repose, he has carried the parellelism inherent in popular tales to absurd lengths and has made his play as absolutely and impartially symmetrical as a child's design. Everything has to be done in twos and fours to keep all the characters equally prominent and because the youthful dramatist has no other plan. So character, episode, and speech are balanced against character, episode, and speech throughout the play.

This was the limit of Heywood's unreality; and as the breath of fashion soon changed he veered with it. His first play is so unlike anything else he wrote that it may never have been much to his taste; a certain manner of realism was afterwards characteristic of him; and whatever he touched—kings and queens in the chronicle, deities and heroes in the mythological pieces, the court of Fez and Italian novellas—he reduced to the bourgeois actualities. Certainly the play of adventure, the more realistic successor of Greene's heroics, adumbrated perhaps in such pieces as '*The Black Smiths Daughter*' which *The School of Abuse* says contained 'the trechery of Turks, the honourable bountye of a noble mind, and the shining of vertue in distresse',[1] was more to Heywood's taste, and in this vein he produced the very promising *Fortune by Land and Sea*, half adventure-play, half domestic tragicomedy, then his breezy masterpiece *The Fair Maid of the West*, with its second part in the Fletcherian manner, and *Dick of Devonshire*, half courtly romance and half penny-dreadful. In Henslowe are mentioned earlier attempts of the same sort, Day, Haughton and Smith's 'conqueste of the weste enges'[2] and Massey's 'sedge of doncerke wth alleyn the pyrete';[3] there still survive the anonymous *Captain Thomas Stukeley*, Daborne's *Christian turned Turk*, and Day, Wilkins, and Rowley's *Travels of three English Brothers*. But *Fortune by Land and Sea* far surpasses them dramatically, though they are all, as it were, only dramatized novels. Heywood's is a play with adequate shadow-characters, a dramatic plot, and a fairly effective *dénouement*. It was, however, in *The Fair Maid of the West*, part I (which, it is only fair to say, must be judged more than any of Heywood's as a play for acting, not for reading), that he shows himself without a rival in the breezy manner. With all the heartiness of the sea ballads, with the Islands Expedition and Essex in the background, privateering and the Spanish Main, every device for winning a tear or a smile or complacent applause, scenes in English inns pleasing by their familiarity and others in oriental palaces as pleasing by their unfamiliarity, broad humour, braggarts exposed, death averted, the very soul of honour, fervent patriotism, a credible hero and a robustious heroine, *The Fair Maid* is the quintessence of popular literature. In the second part, though he preserves the racy manner, Heywood is deriving his standards from the slippery ethics of Fletcher and Massinger, his plot from situations which are constantly recurring in their world, and his characters from their favourite types. Whereas Mullisheg in part I is drawn after the pattern set in *Tamburlaine* and *Alphonsus, King of Arragon*, in part II he is the typical tyrant of the later romantic stage. The very first lines of the sequel are spoken by a new character,

[1] Ed. Collier, 30.   [2] *H.D.* i. 135.
[3] *Ibid.* i. 174.

the jealous Queen Tota, who begins in the true Massinger-
Fletcher vein:

> It must not, may not, shall not be indur'd:
> Left we for this our Countrey? to be made
> A meere neglected Lady here in *Fesse*,
> A slave to others, but a scorne to all? . . .
> I have a thousand projects in my braine,
> But can bring none to purpose;

a very romantic perplexity, the escape from which is as
ingenious and questionable as any in Heywood's models,
for at the end Tota can declare, 'Howe're my minde, then
yet my bodies chast'.[1]　Bess Bridges, introduced into the
courts of princes, the innocent temptress of Mullisheg
and the admired mistress of the Duke of Florence, bursts
from her buxom homeliness into romantic splendour.
Still chaste, true, and likable, she is no longer the hearty
barmaid of Plymouth and Foy, and the undaunted virago
of the seas; she who in part I was a virtuous Long Meg,
a more amiable Mary Ambree, has become a noble lady
on whom signs and omens attend:

> BESS. Sir, I bleed.
> FLORENCE. Ha, bleed?
>   I would not have a sad and ominous fate
>   Hang o're thee for a million:
>   Perhaps 'tis custome with you.
> BESS. I have observed,
>   Even from my childhood, never fell from hence
>   One crimson drop but either my greatest enemy
>   Or my dearest friend was near.[2]

She is the heroine of an exalted morality which Heywood
copied from the romantic dramatists, though a little
dazed by the showy sentiments of his masters.　She is
thrown into the most compromising situations and almost
reft of her husband by a false point of honour.　She is
engaged innocently in a midnight intrigue, and generally
conducts herself with all the dignity and romantic *abandon*
expected of a Fletcherian heroine.　But as becomes a lady
of such sensibility, she resigns her place in the second part

---

[1] Pearson, ii. 384.　　　　[2] *Ibid.* 402.

of the play to her husband who steps out from behind the
skirts of his Amazonian wife. After performing prodigies
of valour in Morocco and in Italy, he finally engages himself in the romantic court of Florence to woo a lady on
behalf of the Duke:

> FLORENCE. . . .
>> Swear by thy faith and thy religion:
>> Not to taste the least small favour for thy self,
>> Touch or come near her bosome; for, fair stranger,
>> I love her above measure, and that love
>> Makes me thus jealous.
> SPENCER. By my honesty,
>> Faith, and religion, without free release
>> From your lips, all this will I perform.[1]

It needs but a slight acquaintance with the romantic
drama to know from this passage that Spencer must be
false to his marriage-vow—made, it is true, in Morocco
and in part I—to keep inviolate a more recent promise.

> Oh heavens, it is my *Besse*; Oh, sudden rapture![2]

he cries when he understands what he has bound himself
to; though, to be sure, in accordance with the obtuseness
of romantic heroes, he has no excuse for supposing Bess
dead, nay, has heard of her escape from the wreck, has
seen her in the Duke's company, has even received a jewel
from her as she rode through the streets.

> Let me retire to more considerate thoughts.
> What should I think, but presently to wake her?
> And being mine, to seize her when I finde her.
> Oh, but mine oath, that I should never, never
> Lie with her being my wife, nor kisse her, touch her,
> Speake to her one familiar syllable.
> Can oaths binde thus? My honesty, faith, and
> Religion are all ingag'd, ther's no dispense for them.[3]

Was ever man thus served outside the drama of Fletcher
and his school? Bess herself swoons at Spencer's cruelty,
very rightly spurns him when next they meet, and drives
him to distraction by flirting with the Duke. She goes
even farther; some cheating fellow, she declares, snatched

[1] *Ibid.* 409–10.   [2] *Ibid.* 411.   [3] *Ibid.* 411.

the jewel from her arm that she threw earlier in the play
to Spencer, and she demands that

> With whomsoe're the jewell may be found,
> The slave may die.[1]

Spencer is of course immediately discovered; Bess descends
to taunt him, claims Florence's oath to do with him what
she will, and then pronounces the romantic doom:

> I give thee back thy life,
> And in thy arms throw a most constant wife;
> If Thou hast rashly sworn, thy oaths are free,
> Th'art mine by gift. I give my self to thee.[2]

When Heywood came to write the second part some twenty
years after the first he had to cater for a new taste, and
to the detriment of the play added to the old ingredients
Italian courts and intrigues, banditti and other properties
of the transpontine picturesque. But both parts move with
a swiftness, which the Elizabethan stage made possible,
from the admirable tavern scenes of part I to the happy
conversion of Bashaw Joffer in part II and the final un-
stinted good fortune of the hero and the heroine.

The chronicle-history was really in its decline when
Heywood turned his hand to it. The least interesting
scenes of *Edward IV*, the siege of London in the first part
and the inconsequent and almost fictitious war in France
in the second, with the few irrelevant scenes towards the
end of part II imitated from *Richard III*, are true enough
to type and, except for flashes in the siege scenes, among
the dullest and least effective of the species; they are in
no sense epical, and the two parts together are by no means
'the dramatic presentation in a single action of the leading
events of a reign . . . the scenic exposition of our annals'.[3]
The play in fact, after the manner of the modern historical
romance, lives by the racy and unhistorical fable of the
king and the miller and by the domestic tragedy, largely
apocryphal, of Mistress Shore, on which Heywood lavished
his homely pathos and in which he established his charac-

---

[1] Pearson, ii. 420.   [2] *Ibid*. ii. 421.
[3] J. A. Symonds, *Shakspere's Predecessors*, 364.

teristic manner. The matter of the ballad, the chap-book, and the folk-tale has crowded the historical off more than half the stage. *Lady Jane*, however, to judge from the remains in *Sir Thomas Wyatt* and *If You Know Not Me*, was a real chronicle-history centring in Lady Jane, Wyatt, and Princess Elizabeth. The two plays which remain are of course even scrappier and more deficient in such unity as the average chronicle-history possessed than the original must have been. The events in which Elizabeth is the central figure seem more unified because they derive from a source which aimed at presenting Elizabeth as a martyr; but they are feeble and tedious. Only in the bustling Armada scenes, with which part II of *If You Know Not Me* ends and which we believe belonged to *Lady Jane*, part II, is Heywood's contribution more than commonplace; there is an epic quality in the clap-trap, the verse is ringing, and the characters of Elizabeth and her supporters have a histrionic heroism. But we cannot say that Heywood did much to revive a species of the drama that was no longer fashionable. As for *If You Know Not Me*, part II, more than three-quarters of it belong to a not very successful variety which was an off-shoot from the chronicle-history, the dramatic biography. It was, we have little doubt, *The Life and Death of Sir Thomas Gresham with the building of the Royal Exchange*, which was classed with the other appeals to civic prejudice in *The Knight of the Burning Pestle*.[1] It was an attempt to flatter local, rather than national, pride with details from the lives of London worthies, Gresham, Hobson, and the rest. But Heywood constructed his biography rather from fiction than from fact, with an abundance of farce and realistic scenes of city-life and the thinnest thread of narrative running through them. His model seems to have been *The Shoemaker's Holiday*, the hero of which is unblushingly imitated in Hobson. But Heywood lacked the vitality of Dekker, and his glorification of the civic virtues of Gresham falls rather flat.

Yet all of his historical plays are interesting when com-

[1] Induction.

pared with the two pseudo-chronicle-histories, *The Royal King and the Loyal Subject*, and *Nobody and Somebody*. The first was a dramatization of an abstract situation, suited only for narration as an apologue, and both it and *Nobody and Somebody*, which is based on one of the least dramatic, not to say least credible, reigns in the fictitious history of ancient Britain, move in 'the debatable border-land' [1] between the older morality and the mature drama. Heywood has done as little to infuse life into the wildly improbable tale of the persecuted Marshal as into his revision of the childish plot of the thrice-crowned King Elidure. But, it should be added, the main plot of Elidure three times crowned king, as told by Holinshed and trace-able to that veracious historian Geoffrey of Monmouth, is carried on by persons so shadowy and unreal that no mere revision could have made them interesting. They are not even types, though in some respects they anticipate later types: Cornwall the faithful, blunt soldier who appeared garnished again and again in Beaumont, Fletcher, and Massinger, and survived at least till Dryden's Ven-tidius; Archigallo the prototype of the vacillating tyrant on the later stage; Elidure the weak but amiable monarch; Sycophant the flattering and corrupt courtier; and Peri-dure and Vigenius the aspiring young princes. Probably the stiff awkwardness of these figures is the strongest argument against attributing more than a slight revisal to any one between 1600 and 1606. The Nobody and Somebody scenes constitute a belated morality, an elabora-tion of 'the grim old jest of Οὖτις', [2] together with a satiric exposure of such abuses as were attacked in the archaic dramas of Robert Wilson and the anonymous *Knack to know a Knave*. But so abstract are all the characters that one can pass from the mythical history to the didactic satire without a shock. Heywood has taken his material for *The Royal King and the Loyal Subject* just as he found it, without considering whether the narrative as it stood had any dramatic value, and hastily fitted it to the stage. But as he himself seemed to have no interest in the pro-

[1] Swinburne, *Age of Shakespeare*, 153.   [2] Ward, *C.H.E.L.* vi. 92.

cess, it is not astonishing that he never interests us. His plot has been left in its naked simplicity without variation or shadow of turning; the characters are feebly drawn, deficient in variety, and, when they are not obscure by reason of Heywood's own haziness about their motives, rigid and wooden; the humour of the sub-plot is primitive, and the comic satire which dismally fails to relieve the tedium is trite and toothless; and the style is as pedestrian, as any hack-writer might achieve, with occasional hints of better things. Really the only excuse for dramatizing so undramatic a story is success. Perhaps Fletcher has shown his skill most in so altering the story that it is doubtful whether his source was the same as Heywood's, and by completely remotivating it; under his hands it gains a kind of stagey *vraisemblance*. But Heywood's own level was so matter of fact, his own diction so undistinguished, that he was successful only when he was dealing with comparatively normal actions and reactions.

In some ways the dramas of classical or contemporary foreign history succeeded to the popularity of the dramatized English chronicles. Heywood has left us two examples, the very tragical-comical *Rape of Lucrece* and the comparatively restrained *Appius and Virginia*. It has been said with some truth that the former is 'a sort of dramatic monster, in the construction of which every rule of propriety is violated, and all grace and symmetry are set at defiance'.[1] Critics have wholeheartedly condemned his debasing some of the noblest legends of Livy by the most shocking ribaldry and farce. One can only shudder at the disgusting catch sung by Valerius, Brutus, and the clown who has brought Lucrece's message to the camp; and even the best of the songs—'*Packe cloudes away, and welcome day*', or '*Now what is love I will thee tell*'[2]—beautiful in themselves, are inexcusable in their settings, while the humorous ditties of Valerius, sung by an actor who was not innocent in the matter, are for the most part rubbish. A different model for dramas of classical history

---

[1] *Old English Drama*, 1825, i, preface to *The Rape of Lucrece*, iii.
[2] Pearson, v. 227, 180.

had been provided by Jonson in his *Sejanus*. To the scholars of his own day the careful and conscientious fidelity to his authorities, whose names bristled in notes, no doubt appealed; but to the dramatists writing for the popular stage it seemed a pedantic affectation. Marston bids the readers of his *Sophonisba*, 'Know, that I have not labored in this poeme, to tie my selfe to relate any thing as an historian but to inlarge every thing as a Poet. To transcribe Authors, quote authorities, & transcribe Latin prose orations into English blank-verse, hath in this subiect beene the least aime of my studies.' There is little to choose between *The Wounds of Civil War*, long before Jonson's tragedy, and Heywood's *Rape of Lucrece* or his *Appius and Virginia*, some years after, for archaeological accuracy. Yet Heywood was perhaps a little old-fashioned. If Jonson stood alone in his pedantry, others could give classical gravity and dignity, if not the paraphernalia. For Heywood, with whom to the end play-writing was a trade, the readiest and most familiar background and a contemporary *milieu* were good enough as they had been for his elders. *The Rape of Lucrece* was definitely a popular presentation of a classical plot for the Red Bull audience, to whom symmetry, restraint, form, and congruity were less intelligible than sentiment, tragical speeches, ribaldry, and the rest of the *olla podrida* of the plebeian theatres. It grafts on a plot of classical tragedy the rude, incongruous, and unashamed stock of the native interlude. And yet for all its bewildering confusion *The Rape of Lucrece* is not ineffective. 'The author,' to quote again the editor of *The Old English Drama*, 'one would suppose, must have produced it when in a state of inebriety; in which a man of genius may frequently, amidst strange and foolish things, give birth to poetical and impassioned conceptions. The dignified characters of Roman story are, in the play, really infected with the madness which Brutus only assumes. But, with an exuberance of buffoonery and conceits, are mingled a considerable portion of poetry and some powerful scenes.'[1] The impugning of Heywood's

[1] i, preface to *The Rape of Lucrece*, iii.

temperance apart, this dictum is true. There are strong, dramatic scenes, the most moving interview of Sextus and Lucrece being but one of them; the poetry is frequently manly and vigorous; and the play as a Roman chronicle-history presents the story from the usurpation of Tarquin to the peace of Rome with Porsena lucidly and not altogether inadequately. Professor Schelling, who seems to consider the story of Lucrece (really rather less than half of the play) as the entire drama, pronounces it 'a ready but commonplace refashioning of an immortal story, inexplicably destroyed in its tragic and pathetic possibilities by the intrusion of the songs'.[1] Commonplace is not a very happy epithet. Ready it is, fluent, perhaps too easy; but there is, as in the rest of Heywood's work, a humanity all his own which is far removed from the commonplace. Nor is the criticism of it as a tragedy justified; it is in fact as much a chronicle-history as any play drawn from Holinshed. The apparent irrelevancies to the central incident, such as Mutius Scaevola's attempt to kill Porsena at the end and the usurpation of Tarquin at the beginning, are explicable as episodes in the section of Livy Heywood had marked out. In *Appius and Virginia* Heywood has really attempted a classical tragedy; he has forsworn, with only occasional lapses, the concupiscence of jigs and dances. The characters are more fully drawn and complex than he thought requisite for his Roman chronicle-history, and there is a fairly well-sustained harmony of the emotions such as is more in keeping with tragedy than the medley of discordant moods tolerable in a chronicle. But there is a certain dryness, insipidity, or frigidity unusual in Heywood. The dialogue has a rhetorical clangour in it, even in the final scene in which Virginius the outraged father stirs up his friends and fellow-soldiers to revenge his wrong, an episode that Swinburne thought Lamb might have selected as a counterpart to the camp scene in Rowley's *All 's Lost by Lust*.[2] Heywood almost certainly was chastened and overawed by *Coriolanus* in which Shakespeare miraculously catches the stoical and heroic

[1] *Elizabethan Drama*, ii. 27.   [2] *Age of Shakespeare*, 195.

spirit of ancient Rome. But he himself, except in intensely human phrases here and there, has failed to give his characters life. The love of Icilius and Virginia, which might have been so fervidly presented, is coolly passed over, and the other characters, except Virginius and Appius, the one a rather heavy father and the other a somewhat stagey villain, are almost insignificant. Structurally, however, the play is undeniably clever and, allowing for the cuts, lucid and straightforward. It has a simple dignity, and towards the end a kind of elemental pathos that is not far from true tragedy.

But probably the brilliant variety of *The Ages* was more to Heywood's taste than the comparatively austere monotony of his tragedy of ancient Rome. They were written with evident gusto and unflagging energy. The matter of Caxton and Ovid, Plautus, Virgil and Lucian—his delight through all his life—he fashioned with amazing vigour and skill into gay comedies, rollicking farces, beautiful pastorals and masques, and blood-and-thunder tragedies, with a superabundance of dumb-shows, spectacles, and machines. These popular parallels to the graceful court-dramas of Lyly and Peele are the best specimens of Heywood's versatility, and contain, though most critics but Langbaine and Lamb have failed to recognize it, some of his truest poetry. Even though the gracious old myths are vulgarized by their adaptation for the bourgeois theatre, these five dramas have no lack of the glow and colour of the Renaissance.

Heywood was, therefore, not without some experience in masque-writing when he was commissioned to provide one for the court. The first three *Ages*, with their descents from heaven and ascents from hell, metamorphoses, dumb-shows, battles and revels and hunting-scenes, elaborate and spectacular properties, fireworks and pageantry, illustrate well the influence of the masque on the drama. But in addition there are episodes in these plays which approximate still more closely to the masque. In *The Golden Age* in the entry '*with musicke (before* Diana) [*of*] *sixe Satires, after them all their Nimphs, garlands on their heads, and*

iavelings in their hands, their Bowes and Quivers',[1] and the
song of the Satyrs, accompanied almost certainly by either
a stately dance of the Nymphs or a grotesque gambol by
the Satyrs themselves, we have just such a tableau as the
masques presented. In *The Silver Age* there is a similar
episode; Ceres enters with Proserpine *'attired like the
Moone, with a company of Swaines, and Country Wenches'*,[2]
who sing twice in praise of Ceres; the rape of Prosperine,
and the consultations of Ceres (with Mercury who descends from the heavens, Triton *'with his Trumpe, as from
the Sea'*,[3] the Earth from beneath the stage, and the river
Arethusa), with the final judgement of all the gods who
'take their place as they are in height' [4] belong to the same
spectacular category. So in *The Brazen Age* in the presentation of the loves of Mars and Venus we have Aurora,
'attended with Seasons, Daies, and Howers',[5] the metamor-
phosis of Gallus, the Cyclops' forge, the Nymphs, and
another assembly of the gods in a kind of masque finale.
The short plays in *Pleasant Dialogues* were later anticipa-
tions by Heywood of the narrative masque with a complete plot which he was to write in *Love's Mistress*. The
Jupiter and Io, with its dramatic entries, singing, metamorphoses and the like, is not very different from incidents in
The Ages; nor is the *Apollo and Daphne*, at the end of
which is presented the joining of the Seasons, Aurora, the
Hours and Day in a song at Apollo's bidding, and perhaps
in a dance, in which the essential of the masque consists.
Amphrisa, or the forsaken Shepherdess is a veritable pastoral
masque. It professes to set forth

> *The innocence, truth, and simplicitie*
> *Of countrey Damsels: What felicitie*
> *They arrive to in their low estate ;*
> *What freedoms they participate,*
> *What ioy, what solace, what content*
> *To their innocuous life is lent.*

The audience Heywood must have had in mind for this
very polite pastoral, in which courtly shepherdesses discuss

---

[1] Pearson, iii. 27.   [2] *Ibid*. iii. 133.   [3] *Ibid*. iii. 138.
      [4] *Ibid*. iii. 161.   [5] *Ibid*. iii. 228.

with Caroline Euphuism the sorrows of Amphrisa, could
only have been such as the masque generally addressed.
The plotless dialogue with its interspersed lyrics concludes
with the command of the queen, who has overheard the
shepherdesses, to join her and her attendants in a dance,
and with her presentation of jewels, a common but not
invariable feature of the masques.[1] Lastly, Heywood
printed the introductory speech for a complimentary and
eulogistic masque, (written, unlike those just mentioned,
after *Love's Mistress*), '*which consisted of nine Ladyes.
Presented the last New-yeares night*',[2] before the Earl of
Dover at Hunsdon House, and the speech of '*Truth presenting the Maskers*':

> Appeare then O thou treble Trine
> Of number, with the *Muses* nine.
> (*Appolloes* sacred daughters) still
> Frequent about *Pernassus* hill.
> Or if you number them by Threes,
> The first are the three *Charitees*,
> Handmaides to *Venus*, *Graces* stil'd,
> On whom their Father *Iove* still smil'd.
> The second *Chorus* doth containe
> Those beauties, by the *Trojan* swaine
> On *Ida* judg'd: The third we call
> The *Vertues* Theologicall,
> *Faith*, *Hope*, and *Love*, haply meet here,
> To crowne the parting of the yeare.[3]

Love's Mistress itself is a borderline piece between the
masque and the drama. At one time Heywood called it
The Queen's Masque;[4] then in his dedication it is 'this
(though unworthy) Poem'; soon it is compared with
'Dramma's of this nature',[5] and is reckoned a 'Dramatick
Poem',[6] or 'the Author's play'.[7] It is nevertheless a
genuine masque, with as many as four changes of scene
in one act, four antimasques, compliments, allegorical

---

[1] Cf. Chambers, i. 150, 196–7.
[2] i.e. Jan. 1, 1636/7.   [3] *Pleasant Dialogues*, 245–7.
[4] Title-page and heading of first court prologue.
[5] Dedication.   [6] To the reader.
[7] Prologue headings.

significance, elaborate machinery, music, songs, and the final masque proper, '*A Dance of* Cupid, Psiche, *the gods and goddesses*',[1] in which Cupid invites the spectators to join. But it is also a five-act play with a double plot, or at least a framework and an inset piece, and a series of comic episodes. Indeed *Love's Mistress* is probably the best example of the reciprocal influences of the drama and the masque, for in it the two genera have coalesced in a most successful union. *Comus* is more a poem than a masque; *The Sun's Darling* by Dekker and Ford, and Middleton and Rowley's *World lost at Tennis* have no plots to speak of and are more than a trifle tedious; and *The Triumph of Time* in *Four Plays in One* is a plot-less masque in the old style. From the time of Lyly's mythological allegories, and Peele's *Arraignment of Paris*, a masque in all but the masquers, the public theatre had adopted one or other of the characteristics of the masque in plays difficult to class: fairy-pieces like *A Midsummer Night's Dream* with its exquisite contrasts that no opposition of masque and antimasque could equal, mythological plays like those of Heywood himself, and belated moralities like Nashe's *Summer's Last Will and Testament* and Dekker's *Old Fortunatus*. On the other hand the masque had become, most definitely in the hands of Jonson the masque-genius, more and more dramatic, especially by the elaboration of the antimasques which, evolved by Jonson from earlier features, appeared for the first time in his *Masque of Queens* in 1608 and developed in *Love Restored* in 1612 into a scene of excellent comedy. Jonson continued to improve his antimasques, which in his later entertainments became little revues, touching more lightly than his comedies on foibles and abuses of the time. In the masques of Townshend, *Albion's Triumph*, on January 8, 1631/2, and *Tempe Restored*, on February 13, 1631/2, and in Shirley's *Triumphs of Peace*, on January 24, 1633/4, there was a return to the older, simpler antimasque. But if, as is reasonable, we consider the dialogues of Apuleius and Midas in *Love's Mistress*, the farcical interludes of the

[1] Pearson, v. 159.

clowns, and perhaps even the singing-match between the proxies of Apollo and Pan as antimasques (with the dances of the asses, of Pan and the rustics, of the king and the beggar, of the young man and the old woman, and the lean man and the fat woman, and lastly of Vulcan and the Cyclops thrown in), then Heywood followed rather Jonson's later examples. This adaptation of the framework for a play, a device which was old-fashioned by 1634 and which was not used after *Love's Mistress*, to the requirements of the masque is one of Heywood's happiest strokes, even though we admit that a presenter commonly introduced a masque and explained its purpose. But he has achieved as well a combination of the classical and the native, or more properly of the courtly and the popular, which made his masque-play, as doubtless its author intended, equally suitable for private or for public performance. For though in *Love's Mistress* Heywood, more under the influence of Jonson than at any other time, affects to despise the vulgar whom Midas represents, and only occasionally and deliberately condescends to what he supposes to be their tastes, his opposition to the popular is much more apparent than real. The play, for all its Platonism and its Jonsonian criticism and satire of fools, is really a rather plebeian but wholly delightful entertainment in practically the same style as Heywood's other mythological plays. Perhaps his work here has more maturity, but it has no less spontaneity and vivacity than usual; and he has lavished on it that simple Elizabethan poetry of his which he often neglected for a more pedestrian manner.

We can hardly agree with Courthope that in *A Woman Killed with Kindness* are two 'abstract situations', the one dealing with domestic virtue, the other with the idea of honour,[1] as if this were all that was to be said for it. Perhaps the Mountford plot may be an abstract situation like those in the moralities, and it may share with *The Honest Whore* the distinction 'of furnishing the earliest example of those abstract and paradoxical moral situations which

[1] iv. 215.

were afterwards more highly developed by Massinger and Ford'.[1] But this seems to us not in the least to apply to the main plot and indeed to class the play quite wrongly. *A Woman Killed with Kindness* belongs primarily to the domestic drama and is perhaps the type of that class. It is a tribute to Heywood's success that Ward, who did not know the source of the main plot, thought it not improbably the dramatization of an actual occurrence,[2] as are *Arden of Feversham* and *A Yorkshire Tragedy*, the only competitors with it for the primacy among domestic plays. It was a kind of drama in which Heywood had had considerable experience before writing his masterpiece, as for example in the two parts of *Edward IV*, in *How a Man May Choose a Good Wife from a Bad*, and perhaps in some of his lost plays,[3] and to which he returned from time to time later in *The Wise Woman of Hogsdon*, *Fortune by Land and Sea*, *The English Traveller*, and indeed in others, romantic or classical in setting but domestic in sentiment. Though Heywood was not the father of the English domestic drama, he made the style his own and in it achieved his greatest success. It is not too far to hark back to the moralities for the first appearance in English of attempts to recommend the meaning of the plays by 'the aid of familiar associations of time and place, while at the same time the emotions which they sought to stir and the sentiments on which they insisted were in the main those called into play by incidents which gain rather than lose force from the frequence of their occurrence in the familiar sphere of daily life'.[4] Indeed the love of realism was often catered for in the mystery plays themselves, both in the homely humour of the secular interludes and in the as homely representations of sacred history. When the morality was secularized and a more strictly dramatic fable took the place of the allegorical, we find plays still with a strong moral interest, almost completely domestic in tone. The drama was not long in dividing into the

[1] *Ibid*. iv. 224.   [2] Edition of the play, xvii.
[3] E.g. *Joan as good as my lady*, *The Blind eats many a Fly*, and *The London Florentine*.   [4] Ward, edition of the play, xiii.

domestic and, what we may call for want of a better word, the bourgeois classes, the latter being an ambiguous term since the domestic pieces are also essentially bourgeois. But it will serve to distinguish the two varieties which evolved, the first giving us that body of plays which centres in the home and the institution of the family, and the second producing in time the comedy of manners and humours. In the latter group we should class such an early piece as John Heywood's homely *Merry Play between Johan Johan the husband, Tyb his wife and sir Johan the priest*, which dramatizes a type of incident made familiar by medieval satirists and from which the descent to the bourgeois drama of Middleton is plain. On the other hand, in such plays or interludes as *Misogonus*, the domestic sentiment which is an essential element of the domestic drama of Heywood appears. So far was the flourishing of the romantic drama from affecting the appeal of the domestic drama that we may say the triumph of realism coincided in time with the greatest of the romantic plays; the first quarto of *Hamlet* appeared in the year in which *A Woman Killed with Kindness* was produced. Yet the domestic dramatists were quite conscious of the differentia of their appeal; says the curious Induction to *A Warning for Fair Women*,

> My Sceane is London, native and your owne,
> I sigh to thinke, my subiect too well knowne,
> I am not faind.

The dramatization of actual domestic happenings, more or less recent, was stimulated by the very considerable body of pamphlets purporting to narrate them, which were the Elizabethan prototypes of the lurid domestic histories in the modern Sunday newspapers. And if real incidents were not plentiful enough, dramatists, like Heywood himself, told with the required realism and simplicity stories originally of a very different character. The stream of domestic plays never completely dried up. The very *bizarrerie* of the later romantic drama, its vaguely localized and anachronistic setting, its excursions into legend, its pomp and pageantry, still left a place for the homelier kind of play, which indeed came as a kindly relief from the strident passions and incredible motives of the other. It was pleasant after the unfamiliarities of the sea-coast of Bohemia and the fustian kingdom of Gargaphy to recognize, even in such horror pieces as *A Yorkshire Tragedy*, English types and sentiment. We may leave to others the cataloguing of all the plays belonging to the genus, into a species or sub-species of which *A Woman Killed with Kindness* falls. The domestic as opposed to the bourgeois species of the genus was in two main divisions, the domestic comedies and the domestic tragedies; and it was to the more sombre department that Heywood's play belonged and to the fictitious, not to the historical, variety thereof. The comedies of domestic incident shade from such doubtfully comic plays as *The Miseries of Enforced Marriage*, which is made to end happily only by the violent rending from it of its proper and historical conclusion, *A Yorkshire Tragedy*, and the clapping of an incongruous reconciliation of the chief characters in its place, through the tragicomic *How a Man May Choose a Good Wife from a Bad*, to such hearty plays as *The Merry Devil of Edmonton*, or *The Wise Woman of Hogsdon*, which approximate to the satirical comedy of manners and humours. The domestic tragedy is, however, a more uniform and self-contained class. Except perhaps for the lost pieces, 'An history of the creweltie of A Stepmother', and 'The history of murderous mychaell', presented at court by the Lord Chamberlain's men on Innocents' Day, December 28, 1578, and March 3, 1578/9 respectively,[1] the domestic tragedy passed at one bound in *Arden of Feversham*, some years earlier than its first quarto in 1592, to a power comparable with the best of the romantic stage. It used its source, Holinshed's *Chronicles*, with the same particularity but to very different ends as did the chronicle-histories. The much inferior *Warning for Fair Women*, 1599, and Yarington's *Two Tragedies in One*, which has a romantic sub-plot, present similar crimes.

[1] Chambers, iv. 95–6, 154–5.

It is, we must frankly admit, regrettable that in *A Woman Killed with Kindness* of all his dramas Heywood should have used two plots, for both have suffered. From the unsatisfactory management of the secondary plot, we might almost conclude that Heywood had tired of it. As an abstract situation it has as much plausibility as, if not more than, the stories of Dorigen or Griselda; and just as they have a real power in the exquisite prose of Boccaccio or in the fresh verse of Chaucer, each of them set in a world created by the poet to hold them and as delicate as the ideal courtesy or the personal devotion with which they are concerned, so the tale of Angela in the graceful narrative of Illicini is not less acceptable. Painter has not been altogether unsuccessful in retaining the unreal atmosphere in which alone the frail legend can survive. But it is questionable whether in any drama its doubtful ethics are not too crudely forced on us, and certainly in 'Heywood's brief, blunt telling'[1] we find no compensation for the lost effusiveness and delicacy of the prose. The necessity, too, resulting from its union with a realistic plot, of alternating it with Nicholas and Jenkin and Cicely Milk-pail and of translating it to a world certainly English and bourgeois, local and peculiar, made it impossible for the dramatist to be convincing in it. No doubt there are plots in the Elizabethan drama yoked with others much more incongruous than this novella is with respect to the history of Frankford; and perhaps even this essentially undramatic story, alternating with a similarly romantic incident or with one frankly farcical (just as in *A Midsummer Night's Dream* different worlds with entirely diverse conventions succeed each other as the scenes change), might have adequately filled five acts. But Heywood retains the same atmosphere, conventions, kinds of character, manner of speech, and general accessories in the romantic tragicomic plot as in the realistic domestic drama; his evident pains, as in the scene of the quarrel of Mountford and Acton, to make the sub-plot true to the manners of the day and to bestow on it most of the local colour only

---

[1] Bates, cxvi.

accentuates the unreality of it. Nor is the plot, skilful as are some of the scenes, as carefully worked out as it required. It remains a little unintelligible, partly by the interruptions from the other plot, partly as has just been said from its unsuitability for a realistic setting. The main plot overshadows it in importance and interest; its function is simply to dilute the Frankford plot, to pad the play out to the orthodox length. We endure it, but its details escape the memory. Had Heywood related it more closely to the main action—and we cannot see the 'more than ordinary skill' with which Ward says it is fitted into the scheme of the play as a whole [1]—it might have been made to contrast with the Frankford plot and to throw a certain light on it. But a merely superficial connexion between the two is established. The triangular main plot was ample for one play; and no dramatist to-day, who might essay such a plot, would waste any of the five acts on a subsidiary story, but would concentrate on making credible the perversion and conversion which make the tragedy so poignant.

According to modern standards of stage credibility Heywood has failed to convince us in one essential. Whether from inability to show the play of motives, the gradual change in Wendoll from one who can win the affection of a man so genuine as Frankford to a domestic traitor, the temptation with all the necessary stages of resistance, vacillation, anguish, and fall, or whether from lack of time to develop credibly the central episode, Heywood has bungled this the crucial scene of the play, we will not express an opinion now. But usually he has been denied the requisite skill. Undoubtedly that scene was the most difficult to manage, and would tax most heavily the dramatist's powers. A man of tender charity like Heywood, ever kindly to the fallen and with a gift of homely pathos and simple poetry, could at least have conceived the other more moving scene outside Mrs. Frankford's chamber when Frankford pauses before entering, or that wonderfully restrained short scene when Frankford finds

[1] Edition of the play, xxi.

his wife's lute, or lastly the reconciliation of husband and wife. But only a master of psychological subtleties, which Heywood was not, could have successfully dramatized the fall of such a woman as Mrs. Frankford, not represented as almost hypnotized by Wendoll, nor in any way in his power, not infatuated, but a mother of children and a devoted wife.

We must remember, however, that to judge the Elizabethan, or for that matter any drama written for the stage —and the plays of Heywood and most of his contemporaries were written to no other end—by standards formed in the study and by the reading of leisurely novels where there is no time-limit for the working out of reversals of character, is uncritical. In one sense the drama is a crude medium compared with the novel, and it demands more impressionistic methods and the packing of much in little. In abstracting so much of life it abstracts also the more subtle motives and intangible causations. It is necessarily an exaggeration of life; being is more strenuous, dialogue more sparkling or poetical, motives more lofty, baser, in a sense simpler than in the novel. Dramatic technique is not without its subtleties, subtleties no less delicate than the methods of the novel; but they are rather in the nature of making the best of a bad job, in circumventing circumstances, in what we may lump under the word impressionism. This is particularly true of the Elizabethan drama which the very shape of the theatre, as well as less material circumstances, conditioned. A stage which projects into the auditorium and has members of the audience seated on it; which has comparatively few properties, no scenery, and the crudest machinery and lighting; on which the actors perform plays of all periods of history, themselves dressed in the contemporary fashions; and on which there is practically no dramatic illusion; such a stage forced on the dramatists a degree of artificiality and exaggeration and heightening, declamation and eloquence and peculiarities of style; which the modern window-stage, with its proscenium arch shutting out all the distracting incongruities of real life, with its abundance of scenery, its more or less complete realization of historical accuracy and local colour, its clever lighting, its elaborate machinery, renders unnecessary. The Elizabethan dramatist had to devise ways and means of seizing and holding the attention of an intractable audience; he could not rely to any extent on the standard features and scenic resources of the theatre or on the energies of managers and producers who now attend to the atmospherics of the drama. Moreover the taste of the time was for the romantic, the extreme, the paradoxical, the sensational,

> the dangerous edge of things,
> The honest thief, the tender murderer,
> The superstitious atheist, demireps
> That love and save their souls;

and had the Elizabethan audience not been as generous in accepting conventions as they were exacting in their demands, the task of supplying them with plays would have been almost impossible. But in proportion as the setting of a play lacks realism an audience, educated in the methods and traditions of the time, will make the greater allowances; and by mutual and tacit consent dramatist and auditor will establish certain conventions, which are the price we pay by the abrogation of our senses of truth and the ludicrous for our enjoyment of artistic creation, and which bridge the gap between aspiration and achievement. For the most part the agreement is so complete between the dramatist and his audience that he makes no excuse for his conventions. Yet occasionally the Elizabethan playwrights alluded to their difficulties, as when Shakespeare in the chorus of *Henry V* apologized for the stage, for

> this unworthy scaffold to bring forth
> So great an object: can this cockpit hold
> The vasty fields of France? or may we cram
> Within this wooden O the very casques
> That did affright the air at Agincourt?
> O, pardon! since a crooked figure may
> Attest in little place a million;
> And let us, ciphers in this great accompt,
> On your imaginary forces work;

and in the prologue to this very play of *A Woman Killed with Kindness* Heywood, while chiefly concerned to excuse the literary poverty and realism of his play, is conscious too of the inadequacy of his theatre.

Now one of the conventions of the Elizabethan stage was the suddenness of perversion and conversion; we can see how Shakespeare managed it twice in *Richard III*, in which the Lady Anne and Queen Elizabeth are separately won by Richard from disgust and loathing to agreement. Such revolutions on the stage, even on the French classical stage, must be condensed in time; and so though it would have required a Meredith to have made the fact of Mrs. Frankford's fall convincing, yet it is not quite fair to blame Heywood as if he had shirked the task. The scene that he has given was, no doubt, all that his audience required, and to have given more would have been a work of supererogation, a piece of lavish extravagance for a journeyman-playwright. Indeed it is by no means certain that even on the modern stage the fall of Mrs. Frankford would not seem adequately explained, though in the study it may not be. Again Heywood's management of the brief time which the exigences of presentation allowed him is very skilful. He has restricted himself in his main plot, which in its psychological revolutions is as rapid as anything in the drama, to little more than half the time his play would take to act. But he might almost have seen that the time demanded for the adequate presentation of a psychological change is in inverse ratio to the time supposed to elapse; that is to say, it is much less easy to make convincing the reversals of a night than of a month or a year, and the dramatist is forced to be the more explicit and detailed in sudden conversions, not because the change is impossible in the time, but because the mere suggestion of a lapse of time makes the alteration easier to follow and the points of fresh departure are, as it were, less crowded. So Heywood has made the main plot cover several years in which two children are born; [1] Mrs. Frankford does not fall immediately after Wendoll's

[1] The secondary plot, however, covers only a few months.

becoming an inmate of the house but after years in his company.[1] Heywood has thus 'allowed himself the utmost freedom in dealing with considerations of time, his one purpose being to bring before the spectator each successive step (so to speak) leading to the brink of the abyss where a higher hand arrests the vengeance that is in accord with the law. By means of a few but perfectly sufficient touches, he depicts the happiness of the husband, the weakness of the wife, his growing suspicions of her frailty, and the awful certainty of the discovery.'[2] He has chosen certain typical and representative scenes from a much longer series and made them samples of the rest.

In *An Apology for Actors* Heywood remembered the powerful effect of domestic tragedies upon 'guilty creatures sitting at' them. There is, however, something repulsive about most of the tragedies of domestic crimes. Their power is undeniable and their vigour saves them from the vulgarity and morbidity of popular accounts of the crimes. But such poetry as *Arden of Feversham* and *A Yorkshire Tragedy* have is only that of naked fitness. 'The imagination [of the authors] exercised itself [rather] in giving life to character, in analysing passion, laying bare the springs of hateful impulses, and yielding the most faithful picture of bare fact upon the stage.'[3] *A Woman Killed with Kindness*, on the other hand, is domestic drama with the difference that it does not present an historical crime. Yet not even the dramatists of veritable histories have so ably invested their plays with the savour and atmosphere of real life. The fact that Heywood was handling a story which had passed from the sensationalism of recent events —the novella was probably founded on fact—into that more logical world which the things of art compose, freed him from many of the temptations to which the dramatists of actual occurrences are liable. It breathes a different air from that of the police court; it has an inevitability and universality which even *A Yorkshire Tragedy* lacks. The

---

[1] Yet Jenkin calls Wendoll 'my new master' (Pearson, ii. 109).
[2] Ward, edition of the play, xviii.
[3] J. A. Symonds, *Shakspere's Predecessors*, 414.

motives of the characters could be more fully explained, the plot could be worked out to a more artistic and satisfying conclusion, and there was a greater opportunity for poetry that arose naturally from the theme than in the hastily co-ordinated incidents of historical crimes as represented on the stage. Moreover, by Heywood's modification of his plot, his play, like his earlier chronicle of Jane Shore, is distinguished from the other domestic tragedies which are based on reality, and indeed from all the tragedies of his day, by being 'Eine Ehebruchs-Tragödie, die sich im Gegensatz zu zahllosen ähnlichen Konflickten unblutig löst'.[1] It moves in a different world from that of the brutal Mosbie and the bourgeois Clytemnestra his accomplice. Heywood was not altogether unaware of the difference, and his prologue even suggests a little anxiety regarding the effect his bloodless catastrophe would have on an audience that had supped deep on horrors. He was attempting to reach their tears by new means; for no domestic tragedy so far as we know had made the erring wife lovable and the deceived husband dignified. Shakespeare himself is more conservative in tragedy and, infinitely subtler though his treatment of motives may be, he does not essay new problems of conduct or paradoxical situations.[2] Except that it is uninformed by any message, is not illustrative of any sociological criticism, and is more humane, *A Woman Killed with Kindness*, a tragedy of a middle-class household, anticipates the bloodless tragedies of Ibsen. In another way Heywood may be regarded as the forerunner of Richardson, the school of sensibility, and the *comédie larmoyante* of the eighteenth century.

A Yorkshire Tragedy is more conservative than *A Woman Killed with Kindness*, in that it is a grim and unswerving dramatization of a lurid crime. But it too has that spicing of humanity, that sense of the pity of it, which was characteristic of Heywood.

[1] Koeppel, *Quellen-Studien zu den Dramen Ben Jonson's, John Marston's, und Beaumont's und Fletcher's*, 135.

[2] Cf. L. L. Shücking, *Character Problems in Shakespeare's Plays*, 197.

Minor playwrights have ever been apt to repeat a successful device and attempt to recapture an old success by variations on a once lucky theme. *The English Traveller*, true though the tale may be, is just such an attempt, for in many essentials and in not a few details it is *A Woman Killed with Kindness* over again. Both are domestic trage-dies in prosperous middle-class English homes, and both hinge on the same sort of infidelity in a weak, rather than bad woman, with respect to a hero of uncommon character, forbearing in his punishment, but by his own forbearance producing in the women, vacillating in sin as in virtue, the same result of overwhelming and extinguishing peni-tence. A slight difference in the relations of the chief characters is obtained by making the party chiefly injured the lover, not the husband of the frail heroine, and by shifting the wronged one into the place of the household friend, doted on by the woman's husband. In *A Woman Killed with Kindness* Wendoll had filled the double role of paramour of the wife and friend of the husband; but *The English Traveller* is a quadrilateral, not a triangular drama. It is the story of January and May with a differ-ence.[1] The friendship of Frankford and Wendoll is repeated, and Old Wincot, a little more paternal than Frankford, presses on Geraldine the same intimate privi-leges as are bestowed on Wendoll:

> I would have you
> Thinke this your home, free as your Fathers house,
> And to command it, as the Master on't;
> Call bouldly heere, and entertaine your friends,
> As in your owne possessions, when I see't,
> Ile say you love me truely, not till then.[2]

The unsuspecting dupes have their suspicions first roused, in very similar scenes, by a servant Nicholas in the earlier play, by Bess, Mrs. Wincot's maid, in the later. The rest of the plot, Geraldine's visit at midnight to his mistress's chamber, his listening at the door, the discovery, his first

[1] Cf. Pearson, iv. 8.   [2] *Ibid.* iv. 10.

impulse to kill the lovers, and his finding that he has no
sword to wreak his vengeance—

> I'le act a noble execution,
> On two unmatcht for sordid villanie:—
> I left it in my Chamber, and thankes Heaven
> That I did so; It hath prevented me
> From playing a base Hang-man [1]—

the wife's shame, her renouncing the partner of her guilt,
her death and pardon, all these incidents are in the earlier
play. But we cannot endorse without qualification the
generally accepted view of this play and place it beside
A Woman Killed with Kindness as 'a domestic tragedy
scarcely inferior to it in pathos and in the elevation of its
moral tone'; [2] nor can we regard it as one of Heywood's
best dramas. The excellence of the play is much more
mechanical than is usual with him, and if he is superficially
more skilful in it, it has been a technical gain at a price.
He has acquired for his domestic variety of the Fletcherian
tragicomedy the knack which made his contemporaries'
plays so competent and so undistinguished. Young
Geraldine is the Fletcherian prig, sickled o'er with the
unhealthy complexion of the age of decadence. There
had been a certain unreality about the ethics of *A Woman
Killed with Kindness*, because all the Elizabethan drama
moved in an exaggeration and exaltation of life. But
Frankford's motives are not unintelligible, and the difficulty in which he finds himself is presumably a real
one. But on the Fletcherian stage the situations are themselves unreal; something more piquant was required and
the ethical standards were strained, perverted, loosened,
stretched to suit. Many of the situations in *The English
Traveller* are normal and presented with considerable
skill. It is the core of the play that is rotten; it is not the
husband of the woman who is wronged, not even the
lover of a widow, but the lover of another's wife; and this
hero has exchanged with the woman oaths of constancy
to be effective after her aged husband's death. The story

[1] Pearson, ii. 70.
[2] *Encyclopaedia Britannica*, 12th edition, article *Thomas Heywood*.

may be true, but even that cannot reconcile us to it. Perhaps Fletcher himself could not have realized 'a difficult scene with greater ease and delicacy than are displayed in the interview between young Geraldine and Wincot's wife'.[1] But why must this Paolo and his Francesca choose the bedroom of the woman to exchange their vows?

> Mid-night hath beene as Mid-day, and my Bed chamber,
> As free to you, as your owne Fathers house,
> And you as welcome to 't,[2]

says Mrs. Wincot. This is not merely unpleasant, it is absurd;[3] and the absurdity has vitiated the climax of the play. Geraldine's speech outside his mistress's chamber——

> Tush, bow to Heaven,
> Which thou hast most offended; I alas,
> Save in such (Scarce unheard [*sic*] of) Treacherie,
> Most sinfull like thy selfe; Wherein, Oh wherein,
> Hath my unspotted and unbounded Love
> Deserv'd the least of these? Sworne to be made a stale
> For terme of life; And all this for my goodnesse;
> Die, and die soone, acquit me of my Oath,
> But prethee die repentant; Farewell ever,
> 'Tis thou, and onely thou hast Banisht mee,
> Both from my Friends and Countrey [4]——

is sufficient to condemn him. This rigidly moral and virtuous young man, who in his relations skates on the thinnest of ice, is much less sympathetic than Frankford because he has been sophisticated according to fashion. Mrs. Wincot is equally a falling-off from Mrs. Frankford, who, however weak and even inconsistent she may have been, was one of the few entirely lovable women on the Elizabethan stage. Mrs. Wincot is a deceiver ever and is not made attractive; she attempts to blind her husband to her guilty intimacy with Dalavill as early as the beginning of act ii. She encourages Geraldine's suit in order to con-

---

[1] J. A. Symonds, introduction to *The Best Plays of Thomas Heywood*, xiv.
[2] Pearson, iv. 30.
[3] Cf. *Old English Plays*, 1814–15, vi, preface to *The English Traveller*.
[4] Pearson, iv. 91.

ceal the truth, and attempts in the end to brazen out her innocence. If her fall is more understandable than Mrs. Frankford's, her abrupt penitence and death are really far more incredible. Heywood has kept the temptation and seduction off the stage, and though our only preparation for the discovery is Bess's interview with Geraldine, at least we are left to suppose what we please led up to Mrs. Wincot's guilt. By making Dalavill less prominent than Wendoll and Mrs. Wincot less amiable than Mrs. Frankford, at the same time as he has diminished the tragic potentialities, Heywood has made more plausible one essential fact. But the freshness of Heywood has vanished in the process. As for the sub-plot, it is so different from the main interest that it hardly enters into competition with it at all, as did the secondary plot of *A Woman Killed with Kindness* with the story of Mrs. Frankford. It is a rollicking, neo-classic farce, nothing more than Plautus Anglicus, and the result when the conventions of Plautine comedy are accepted is rather like a comedy in the Jonsonian manner but without any very pronounced 'humours'. In the condensation from Plautus's somewhat wordy original, as in the adaptation of the *Amphitruo* in act i of *The Silver Age*, the plot has lost none of its vigour; and from start to finish it moves with that lightheartedness which Heywood sustained elsewhere only in *The Wise Woman of Hogsdon*. It presents the same cross purposes and mistakes, the same picture of the surface of life, the same easy forgiveness and gay confusion. Young Chartley in *The Wise Woman of Hogsdon*, still more of a scamp than young Lionel in this play, is only different from him in degree, and both are surrounded by the same varieties of dupes, bawds, clowns, and rioters.

Some attempt has been made elsewhere to relate Heywood's excursions into witch-lore to the vast literature on the subject in the sixteenth and seventeenth centuries,[1] but his use of the supernatural as a dramatic motive must be discussed here. So completely had the belief in the occult and the diabolical seized the popular mind that it is

[1] See 120–7, 143–50 *supra*.

not to be wondered if the poets and writers of pure literature, as distinguished from those whose study of witchcraft was professional or pseudo-scientific, should adopt the conservative point of view. Even if scepticism as to the reality of witchcraft had ever occurred to any of the dramatists, the strength of the popular prejudice gave a sanction and potency to the supernatural note, which they as caterers to the popular taste would be unlikely to ignore. But in truth probably none of the English dramatists, not even Shakespeare himself, suggested for an instant that they did not share to the full the popular beliefs, though the treatment might vary from the sublime in *Macbeth* to the realistic and jocular in *The Late Lancashire Witches*, or the satiric in Jonson's *Devil is an Ass*. 'Rationalism in this as in other subjects lay beyond the province of the playwright',[1] and the audiences in the public theatres, no less before than after James's accession, were easily caught by dramatic appeals to their superstitions. *Macbeth* is without question the finest adaptation in English of the supernatural to the purposes of the drama. From first to last the whole atmosphere is charged with terror; it is apocalyptic and foreboding and dark, shot by lightning flashes more terrible than the gloom they dissever; and it is by the witches, to whom Shakespeare has given some of the attributes of village hags, the grotesque witches of popular tradition, that the effect is chiefly produced. But these strange bubbles of the earth in *Macbeth* are far more awful than the vulgar victims of popular prejudice; they are, as Lamb says,[2] beings parentless, friendless, childless, independent ministers of evil and foreknowers of fate, sublime like the Eumenides of Aeschylus. Apparently Shakespeare's midnight hags were so impressive that Marston tried to rival them in his Erichto, but his *Wonder of Women*, 1606, piled up the horrible till it became ludicrous. The completest presentation of the received opinions on witchcraft is Jonson's *Masque of Queens*, 1609,

---

[1] Herford, *Literary Relations of England and Germany in the Sixteenth Century*, 232.

[2] *Specimens*, ed. Lucas, iv. 144.

in which every detail is fully documented and substantiated by citations from the witch-lorists. Middleton's *Witch*, *c.* 1621, which combines a story taken from Lombardic history and a witch story through Scot from Nider, is less erudite than Jonson's *Masque*, but it has occasional flashes of the wilder imagination of Shakespeare; his witches 'stand in dim middle air'[1] between the weird sisters and the humbler diabolists in the two plays which most realistically presented current beliefs on the popular stage, Dekker, Ford and Rowley's *Witch of Edmonton*, and Heywood and Brome's *Late Lancashire Witches*.

Both of these are based on actual witch-trials, the first on that of Mother Sawyer, of which an account was licensed for publication on April 27, 1621, and the second on the more sensational affair of 1634. They are both examples of dramatic journalism, hastily put together in collaboration to make capital out of a recent occurrence; *The Late Lancashire Witches* was even produced, as the epilogue indicates, between the examination of the accused by Bishop Bridgeman after the trial, and their pardon by the king.[2] It is not, however, the fact that Heywood and Brome 'had, *pendente lite*, done their utmost to intensify public feeling against "witches"'.[3] No doubt they did nothing to decrease the popular fury against witches in general, but in this particular case there were rumours of a royal pardon when the play was being written, and more than a suspicion of the *bona fides* of the two chief witnesses for the prosecution. Like the play of Dekker, Ford and Rowley, *The Late Lancashire Witches* belongs to the category of the domestic drama. It repeats with appropriate variations the plot of *A Woman Killed with Kindness* or *The English Traveller*, with an admixture of the occult art of which Heywood had been a diligent reader for years and which by the very frequency of its supposed manifestations in ordinary settings was particularly suitable for the domestic play. But as witchcraft

---

[1] A. Symons, *Middleton and Rowley*, *C.E.L.* vi. 76.
[2] See 122–5 *supra*.
[3] Ward, *Thomas Heywood*, *C.H.E.L.* vi. 104.

occupies a field debatable in a way unparalleled between tragedy and comedy, the witch play encourages the introduction of incongruous grotesque episodes which weaken the pathos that the essentially tragic situations might produce. The old theme of the unfaithful wife, which Heywood had already made his own and on which in his haste to produce a drama in the least possible time he had fallen back, makes a good enough plot for a play of witchcraft. But the powers of darkness which have tempted Mrs. Generous to sin are tricksy and fantastic, and she has to manifest her fall by taking part in ludicrous, if unhallowed, revels, by comic displays of her powers to revenge an insult to her nephew, by metamorphosing herself to a cat or being herself changed to a grey mare, and by presiding over assemblies of vulgar harridans. It was impossible to treat Mrs. Generous as tenderly as Mrs. Frankford, and when the *dénouement* comes there is no pathetic reconciliation of magnanimous husband and erring wife; she is handed over to justice by Mr. Generous 'without a qualm of conscience as to the rectitude of his act'.[1] Perhaps, too, Heywood had at last tired of his favourite plot; certainly when read alongside the vigorous farcical scenes of Brome's contribution it seems slight and lacking in interest.

The three plays *How a Man May Choose a Good Wife*, *The Fair Maid of the Exchange*, and *The Wise Woman of Hogsdon* all belong to the period before 1605 and represent three degrees of comedy. The first, with its statement of marital discord in which the Griselda-like wife ultimately triumphs and wins back to the paths of virtue an erring spouse of the type of the Husband in *A Yorkshire Tragedy*, is a tragicomedy; in some ways it is the most pleasing of Heywood's domestic plays, fresh and wholesome, and not meant to be taken too seriously on its tragic side, presenting a very attractive heroine, some lovable 'humours' and others more lively than amiable, but not, as the story goes, beyond redemption, and a delicately

---

[1] Schelling, *Some Features of the Supernatural as represented in Plays of the Reigns of Elizabeth and James*, M.P. i. 31.

sentimental plot with a touch of romance in its domesticity. *The Fair Maid of the Exchange*, of which only a small part at the most is Heywood's, is a comedy of manners, midway between the style of Dekker and that of Middleton. It is sprightly enough and goes to a good tune; but it is a little sharper than we expect from Heywood, as if he had allowed his clever young partner the biggest say. Whether or not the genius of the author limps on and off with the Cripple, as some have supposed, is a matter of taste; personally we find him an original humour but not very likable. Heywood's own part was to supply the foolish old Berry and the clown, and little else. They are amusing enough, but indistinguishable from their kinsmen in Heywood's other comedies. Heywood cannot be said to have excelled in humorous characters; such as he drew were diverting, but they conform to five or six types, the clown, the foolish old father of Plautine descent, the youthful prodigal, the shrewd citizen, the pedant, the bawd. Nor, except in *The Wise Woman of Hogsdon*, can he be said to have devised humorous situations unless his source supplied the hint; he depended rather on puns, well-known quips, and the simple merriment of traditional clowning. The wonder of *The Wise Woman of Hogsdon* is not that the versatile Heywood should have attempted a comedy in this style—though Ward and Gayley have found this so surprising as to question Heywood's authorship [1]—but that with little or no previous experience he should have rivalled Middleton, the admitted master of the *genre*. The farce is quite as masculine as any of the latter's irresponsible early works; the picture it presents of the trickeries, debaucheries, and humours of a way of life, which for all its improbable conditions is made thoroughly convincing, is as consistent and amusing; the very style is Middletonian, pungent and fluid, racy and coarse, running easily from prose to verse and back again. From the lively opening scene in the tavern, not surpassed by even the similar transcripts from life in *Fortune by Land*

[1] *Thomas Heywood*, C.H.E.L. vi. 99, and *Representative English Comedies*, III. xxix.

and Sea and *The Fair Maid of the West*, to the *dénouement* in the house of the Wise Woman, the speed of the action never slackens; nor does the machinery of the plot creak. In the comedy of intrigue it is, as Swinburne says,[1] the special temptation of the author to sacrifice propriety and consistency of character to situation, to effect sudden and incredible revolutions and especially to round off the farce with impossible reconciliations and pardons. But this convention of the unstable character 'that alters as it alteration finds and bends' to the requirements of an effective situation is but one of many which we must agree to accept if this kind of comedy is to exist at all; for just as melodrama is an all-round exaggeration of the more tragic side of life, so the comedy of farcical intrigue is, despite its realism in details of style, setting, and episode, a parody of the comic. Yet this inconsistency of character often extends no farther than the heroes and heroines, the forgiven and the forgiving, whose relations have been reversed by the revolution of the plot. Heywood has but two such in *The Wise Woman of Hogsdon*, young Chartley himself, a gay rascal whose repentance and promises of reform are as glib as his villainies are thoughtless, and the London Luce who accepts the fact of marriage to Boyster without demur, though Chartley had been her first choice. But the other Luce who pursues her erring lover and receives him penitent in the end is Heywood's lovable heroine, variously called Mrs. Frankford, Jane Shore, Mrs. Arthur, and Lucrece, whose amiability is consistent with all that we know of her; while Gratiana had never committed herself to such love for Chartley that she could not at the conclusion transfer her affections quite credibly to him who rescued her from the would-be bigamist. Sencer, the '*conceited Gentleman*', Boyster, '*a blunt fellow*', and Haringfield, '*a Civill Gentleman*,' whose differences are deftly suggested, maintain their characters intact. The other characters, Sir Harry, the WiseWoman, Sir Boniface, and Taber, are stable, because they are 'humours' or grotesques on whose invariability and in-

[1] *Age of Shakespeare,* 241.

tegrity their effect depends. The pedant Sir Boniface is like Sir Aminadab in *How a Man May Choose a Good Wife*, a refreshing example of the favourite Renaissance type, and Taber is Heywood's own peculiar clown. Sir Harry, a kind of Jacobean Sir Roger de Coverley, is a more original humour and wholly delightful. But it was on the exposure of the Wise Woman, in whom Heywood admirably hit off the whole class of fortune-tellers, baby-farmers, bawds, and impostors of all kinds, that he has concentrated. It was not, as has been supposed, that he was any less credulous of witches and magic than he was in later life. But here with a blunt common sense like Jonson's in *The Alchemist* he lays bare the tricks of all manner of pretenders to wisdom above the reach of their fellows. The genuine professors of 'that Art should be deepe Schollers'.[1]

After the long period 1613–22, in which none of Heywood's surviving plays can be definitely dated, he fell under the influence of the school of which he himself had been once the laughing-stock. All the pieces written later, except *The Late Lancashire Witches*, were designed to suit the new fashion. Heywood had now to please, in rivalry with his clever young rivals Massinger and Shirley, a different, more sophisticated audience; and it says much for the flexibility of his powers that he could produce such fresh examples of a not very healthy kind as *The Captives*, *Dick of Devonshire*, *The Fair Maid of the West*, part II, and *A Challenge for Beauty*. On the other hand, Heywood's romantic realism, though perhaps more tolerable to modern tastes than the tedious eroticism and intrigues of his rivals, was really only a passable imitation of the Fletcherian model. He had served too long an apprenticeship to the popular stage, and had had too little experience of the fashionable world to furnish the Caroline theatregoers with the caricature of life which they were pleased to imagine a reflection of their own. He was too plebeian and home-loving to provide them with the heroic inanities and slippery ethics of tragicomedy, too simple-minded

[1] Pearson, v. 293.

and sedate to give 'the more chivalric and erotic thrills, the idyllic and palatial passions'.[1] He set his scenes in unfamiliar lands, an unhistorical Spain, a Florence of an indeterminate duke, a sixteenth-century Provence where women slaves were bought and sold. But in all, save the unsuccessful *Maidenhead Well Lost*, the plots are linked to England by English men and women, who are patterns of valour and mirrors of beauty. He has taken over the Fletcherian *dramatis personae*, a uxorious king, a dictatorial queen, Italian dukes, scheming courtiers, an outspoken noble, conventional heroes and heroines, a wronged but not squeamish princess, unpaid soldiers, and the rest. But they are rather like Heywood's earlier characters masquerading than genuine creations of the Fletcherians. There are the usual villainies exposed, honour tested, chastity vindicated, moral paradoxes, questionable situations, bold solutions, and the end justifying the means. But however well Heywood managed these surprise plots, he never could force the note to the required shrill pitch, for he had little command over passion.

There were occasions when Heywood's construction was straightforward and capable, as in *How a Man May Choose a Good Wife* and *Appius and Virginia*, where the plot was enough with a little padding to fill the five acts. But Heywood worked for an audience that demanded variety and which he himself was only too ready to satisfy with double or even triple plots, and with dumb-shows and their expositors, and other pageantry. The effect of these interwoven plots on the interest of the plays has been already noticed; but it is doubtful whether Heywood had sufficient skill in characterization or in motivation to maintain the interest of one plot through an entire play. It has been said that Heywood was rather a novelist than a dramatist. '*The Woman Killed with Kindness*,' says Stevenson, 'is one of the most striking novels—not plays, though it's more of a play than anything else of his—I ever read'.[2] But this is scarcely true; for all his defects

---

[1] Gayley, *Representative English Comedies*, III. xxviii.
[2] To W. E. Henley, Apr. 1882.

in constructions Heywood had an instinct for the drama. Even if his separate scenes are but loosely strung together, these scenes are managed rather with a sense of their dramatic than of their narrative value; the emphasis is on the dramatic essential. Only in *The Wise Woman of Hogsdon* did he invent a good humorous situation; but in his serious plays effective situations, such as the murdering of the friar in *The Captives*, the climax of the sub-plot in *A Challenge for Beauty*, are frequent. He is especially good in his opening scenes on which much of the admirably suggested atmosphere of his plays depends. But his lack of invention—it can be seen in his self-plagiarisms in his non-dramatic work—is very marked. There are few of the dramatists who so frquently echo themselves as Heywood does; he has a trick too of echoing others, especially Shakespeare. He repeats chiefly in his domestic plays the same situations again and again. We have commented on the exact conformity of his humorous characters to five or six types. His serious types are more numerous; but their representatives are differentiated from the others only by their taking part in different plots.

We are scarcely justified in expecting a dramatist of Heywood's training and voluminousness to be a stylist; we might rather excuse such a one for adopting the *clichés*, mannerisms, and fustian of his day. But Heywood was for the most part saved from this by his own sincerity and directness, and by a not infallible but serviceable sense of style. Like his own versification, which is one of the easiest and most pliable of the minor Elizabethans, his style, after the bombast of *The Four Prentices*, was fluent, idiomatic, and manly. The perfect simplicity and reserve which Heywood used at times with thrilling effect, a middle style 'which neither seeks nor avoids occasional vehemence or occasional humility of expression',[1] is perhaps seen at its best in the domestic plays. The matter of them was suited to his genius, and in them by an economy

[1] Ward, edition of *A Woman Killed with Kindness*, xxi. Cf. E. T. Whipple, *The Literature of the Age of Elizabeth*, 1869, 122, and *Essays and Reviews*, 1856, ii. 48.

of means he achieves a homely pathos, not equalled by any of his contemporaries. Few of the Elizabethans ever earned the virtues of silence in dramatic dialogue; their characters' emotions, whatever they might be, the vocal and articulate passions or the mute and inexpressible, are to modern ideas all equally voluble and glib. We hesitate to ascribe all Heywood's effects in reserve to an art which conceals itself; yet, though we suspect his restraint at times to be from inability to reach the *abandon* which his contemporaries loved, it worked sometimes to such great ends that he may well enjoy the benefit of the doubt. There are other occasions when he can find words for the more vocal emotions, as for example in Wendoll's speech to Mrs. Frankford where a guilty love makes an impassioned declaration with none of the pauses of a more innocent affection:

> O speake no more,
> For more than this I know, and have recorded
> Within the red-leav'd Table of my heart;
> Faire, and of all belov'd, I was not fearefull
> Bluntly to give my life into your hand;
> And at one hazard all my earthly meanes.
> Go, tell your husband; he will turne me off,
> And I am then undone: I care not I,
> 'Twas for your sake. Perchance in rage hee'l kill me:
> I care not, 'twas for your sake. Say I incurre
> The generall name of Villaine through the world;
> Of Traitor to my friend; I care not I,
> Beggery, shame, death, scandall, and reproach,
> For you Ile hazard all, why what care I:
> For you Ile live, and in your love Ile dye.[1]

The sinking in the last line cannot affect the realism of the short, telling sentences with the reiterated 'I care not I'. The stabbing sentences of *A Yorkshire Tragedy* are even more thrilling; they are the perfection of realistic speech in prose drama and give magnificently the impression of unpremeditated utterance. Heywood was not strong at set speeches because his forte

---

[1] Pearson, ii. 112.

was rather the exchange of the commonplaces of a dialogue in comparatively short speeches, which were tied firmly to the action, than the pouring forth of general sentiments and reflections on the nature of things. Perhaps the most poetic of his plays are *The Ages*, *The Captives*, and *Love's Mistress*; in them is an abundance of pure but not exhilarating poetry. But even in these and in the later plays generally on which he seems to have lavished more care, there is little that lingers in the mind by reason of its music or felicity of phrasing. This undistinguished, adaptable style, which never seems too high or too low, was not the least valuable asset of Heywood the journalist.

Lamb's famous dictum has for ever linked Heywood's name with Shakespeare:

'Heywood', he says, 'is a sort of *prose* Shakspeare. His scenes are to the full as natural and affecting. But we miss *the Poet*, that which in Shakspeare always appears out and above the surface of *the nature*. Heywood's characters . . . are exactly what we see (but of the best kind of what we see) in life. Shakspeare makes us believe, while we are among his lovely creations, that they are nothing but what we are familiar with, as in dreams new things seem old: but we awake, and sigh·for the difference.' [1]

If we compare the treatment of parallel incidents in Shakespeare and Heywood—the plots of *Pericles* and of *The Captives*, the princes in the Tower in *Richard III* and in *Edward IV*, part II, the interview of Claudius and Isabella in *Measure for Measure*, and that of Mountford and Susan in *A Woman Killed with Kindness*—we can appreciate the justice of Lamb's dictum. Heywood, for all his magnanimity and warmness of sympathy and dramatic insight, has but a stammering utterance; the poetry he could command was of a lowly, pedestrian order, not lyrical and soaring; the waters of Hippocrene were troubled and muddy when he drank of them, and his inspiration was but an intermittent glimpse of a brighter world, too brief for him to see the proportions of it. But Shakespeare had a poetic view of that world and of human character, uninterrupted and unblurred; he lived

[1] *Specimens*, ed. Lucas, iv. 95.

continually in that ampler ether and diviner air; and he saw the life of man, his motives, actions, and destiny against a cosmic background. Heywood the journeyman, on the other hand, expressed no philosophy of life in his plays; his was a plebeian, homely intellect beside Shakespeare's imperial wisdom.

In all English literature perhaps Dekker is Heywood's nearest parallel. They were both dramatic journalists, though Heywood was the more staid, both pamphleteers, both good-humoured, patriotic, devout, charitable, and sentimental. They both loved London and its worthies, civic virtues, and domesticity. In both were the same impulsive sympathies and unflagging interest in their fellows without cynicism or weariness. Perhaps we may call Heywood a middle-aged Dekker. He is slower in movement, heavier of hand, more stable, less often inspired, more commonplace in his sentiments and outlook. Dekker is more boisterous, light-hearted, irresponsible, more naïve, fanciful, extravagant, and delicate like an Elizabethan Barrie; he is more imaginative and less provident of his imagination with something of the wildness of Aristophanes. Dekker is sentimental with a perky, bird-like pathos, Heywood with a warm, feminine tenderness. The most striking difference is Dekker's lyrical gift, a sweet bird-music, uncontrolled and untutored, which is constantly trying to find expression even in dialogue. Heywood rarely sings, and when he does so is not at his best. Yet the virtues are not all on Dekker's side; artistically Heywood is more secure and careful; his plays leave a deeper impression; he is gentler and perhaps sounded depths that Dekker never dreamed of; he was less freakish, and if he surprises us less often he more rarely disappoints us, and, to judge from his work and his history, he was a more clubbable man. But he and Dekker should be for ever placed together in the company of the other lovable writers of English, with Chaucer and Goldsmith, Lamb and Scott and Stevenson.

APPIUS AND VIRGINIA

THE attributions of plays in the second half of the seventeenth century, when the theatrical traditions had been broken, are thoroughly unreliable; publishers frequently appear to have assigned orphaned dramas by guess-work or on the authority of gossip. There seems, too, to have been a fashion in Webster after the Civil Wars; in addition to at least one revival about 1669 and the four issues of *Appius and Virginia* (two in 1654, and again in 1659 and in 1679)[1] and Phillips's absurd assignation to him of *The Weakest goeth to the Wall*,[2] there were quartos of *A Cure for a Cuckold* and *The Thracian Wonder* in 1661, both ascribed to Webster and William Rowley, editions of *The White Devil* in 1665, and again after its revival in 1672, and of *The Duchess of Malfi*, which was revived more than once, in 1678. Apparently, then, the most shadowy of the Elizabethan dramatists was an interesting figure whose name on a title-page was itself a recommendation.

Not a few critics[3] have commented, without going further, on the difference of one of these ascriptions, *Appius and Virginia*, from Webster's usual manner. At last in 1905 Mr. E. E. Stoll traced a dependence on the comic style of Heywood,[4] and in 1913 Mr. H. D. Sykes concluded from certain words first used by Heywood after Webster's death that Heywood may have revised the play.[5] Rupert Brooke, however, was a more thorough-going dissenter: 'general, critical, and aesthetic impressions, more particular examination of various aspects, and the difficulty of fitting it in chronologically, make it impossible to believe that *Appius and Virginia* is by Webster, while the evidence in favour of his authorship is very slight. All these considerations, and also remarkable features of vocabulary and characterization, make it highly probable that it is by Heywood. The slight similarities between *The Duchess of Malfi* and *Appius and Virginia* may be due to Webster's borrowing in *The Duchess of Malfi* from Heywood, or revising *Appius and*

---

[1] These are typographically identical but for the title-pages.

[2] *Theatrum Poetarum*, 116; rejected by Langbaine, 1691.

[3] E.g. Gosse, *Seventeenth Century Studies*, 64; William Archer, *Webster, Lamb, and Swinburne, New Review*, viii. 105, and A. H. Thorndike, *Webster and Tourneur*, 23.

[4] 34.

[5] *An Attempt to Determine the Date of Webster's Appius and Virginia, N. & Q.*, 1913, vii. 401, 422, 466; viii. 63.

Virginia, or having, not for the first time, collaborated with Heywood, but very subordinately. In any case, *Appius and Virginia* must be counted among Heywood's plays; not the best of them, but among the better ones; a typical example of him in his finer moments, written more carefully than is usual with that happy man.' Webster, he thought, only 'shortened and made more dramatic the very beginning of the play, and heightened, or even re-wrote the trial scene (iv. 1)'.[1] The present writer in 1921 attempted to supplement the evidence in favour of Heywood's authorship, and at the same time traced Webster's hand 'more frequently but not more integrally' than Brooke had done.[2]

The initial difficulty of dating *Appius and Virginia* convincingly in Webster's career, and the ease with which it fits into Heywood's, is an argument on our side of no little weight. Here is a play of bald simplicity of outline, a plot undeviating and complete, a style chastened but not striking, mature but not impressive. In structure and the more obvious virtues of dramatic technique it is far in advance of anything Webster ever wrote. In thoughtfulness and criticism of life, in characterization and dramatic sense, it is infinitely weaker than his typical plays. If *The Duchess of Malfi* and *The White Devil* are later works of the same author, why did not Webster carry over to their composition the mastery of technique which he had already achieved? If *Appius and Virginia* is a work of his maturest period, why is the play the least atmospheric of Webster's, why has he neglected every opportunity for the exercise of his peculiar powers, why in dramatic insight is it not to be compared with his masterpieces, and lastly, why does a play written in the third decade of the seventeenth century exhibit all the signs of composition in the first?[3] The tragedy was evidently profoundly influenced by Shakespeare's classical plays, especially the stern but arid nobility of *Coriolanus*, and was an attempt to conform to the fashion for dramas on Greek and Roman subjects. The metrical

---

[1] *John Webster and the Elizabethan Drama*, 204–5.

[2] *The Authorship of Appius and Virginia*, M.L.R. xvi. 1.

[3] *The Retrospective Review*, 1823, pt. i, 116; Ward, iii. 62; and Mr. M. W. Sampson (ed. of *The White Devil*, ix) put it at the end of Webster's career. Mr. Thorndike (*op. cit.* 6, 23, 253) dates it about 1624. From reminiscences of *Julius Caesar*, not printed till the 1623 folio, J. Lauschke (*John Websters Tragödie Appius and Virginia, eine Quellenstudie*, 10–11) assigns it to the years 1623–39; with which Mr. Stoll (*John Webster*, 33) agrees. Both he, 37, and C. Vopel (*John Webster*, 14) conclude that as *Appius and Virginia* is not mentioned in the preface to *The Devil's Law-case*, 1623, it must be of later date. We are unable to see with Mr. Stoll, *op. cit.* 38, the influence of Massinger and Fletcher, modified by Marlowe, Heywood, and Shakespeare, 43–4.

characteristics 'suit, and some rather demand, a date between 1600 and 1610. So does the influence of Marlowe and Machiavellism, and the character of the clown [and surely also the general characterization]. . . . Finally, the general and specific dissimilarity in style of *Appius and Virginia* and Webster's other plays forbids a middle date, and requires an early rather than a late one, if the play be his. Only a young hand could have disguised its individuality so completely'. But when one would fit it into Webster's first period, he meets insuperable obstacles. As it is 'strongly influenced by Shakespeare's Roman plays, and especially by *Coriolanus*. . . . So [it] must be at least as late as 1609. But that is definitely in Webster's middle, most individual, period. *The White Devil* appeared in 1611, and he was confessedly a long time in writing it. If the author of *The White Devil* wrote *Appius and Virginia*, it cannot have been only a year or eighteen months before. Then again you cannot slip the Roman play amazingly between *The White Devil* and *The Duchess of Malfi* (*c.* 1613). . . . And you must have a decent interval after *The Duchess of Malfi*.' The progress of style from that play to *The Devil's Law-case* is 'so clear and gradual that it is nearly as difficult to squeeze it in there as between the tragedies. Besides, if you get as late as 1617 or 1618, you may as well . . . take refuge in [Mr. Stoll's] spacious "1623–1639"; a date which is in direct opposition to all your first conclusions'.[1] Fleay, who was almost indifferent to aesthetic considerations, dates the tragedy about 1609 'from its allusion at the end to *Lucrece*', which play of Heywood he for the moment assigns to 1608.[2] The allusion might show unity of authorship but it proves nothing about the date. If, however, we agree that *Appius and Virginia* is Heywood's, we can at once date it after *The Rape of Lucrece*, and explain the difference from it by the fact that *Coriolanus* had intervened.[3] From Queen Anne's men it passed, like the companion *Rape of Lucrece*, probably by way of the Lady Elizabeth's and Queen Henrietta's companies, to Beeston's Boys in whose 1639 list of plays it is included.

Were it not that *Appius and Virginia* is still assigned to Webster, it would be unnecessary to labour the point of its unlikeness to the rest of his work. But that dissimilarity and its coincidence with Heywood's style must be illustrated in support of the plea for its transference in the main to the latter's credit.[4] Webster preferred

---

[1] Brooke, *op. cit.* 171–2.
[2] ii. 272; at i. 61, he gives *c.* 1607, and in *Stage*, 357, 1608–11.
[3] Cf. Brooke, *op. cit.* 192. For other suggested dates see ed. Lucas, iii. 121–3.
[4] Mr. Lucas's attempt to depreciate Heywood (ed. iii. 136) is uncritical. He doubts if Heywood 'could have produced unaided so well-planned and reason-

sensational centemporary plots and a setting in the stuffy anterooms of Italian palaces. But almost a third of Heywood's extant plays have a classical background, and one of them, *The Rape of Lucrece*, when we allow for the greater dignity and restraint that in the later play came to Heywood from imitating *Coriolanus*, is as like *Appius and Virginia* as one twin is to another. Heywood was avowedly voluminous, and to fit in another play of his of the type of his *Lucrece* into the decade to which, whoever may have been its author, *Appius and Virginia* obviously belongs, is easy; whereas no one has satisfactorily dated it in Webster's career at all. In just such a colourless way we should expect Heywood, classical scholar though he was, to handle a classical plot, without any feeling for atmosphere or local colour. But Webster, with all his scorn for the mere scholar, was something of a pedant, acutely sensitive to the atmospherics of his plays, and incapable of such a condescension to popular capacity, such a cavalier treatment of the classics as *Appius and Virginia* exhibits.

That tragedy has been pronounced ethically the ripest of Webster's plays. But the conventional distribution in it of rewards and punishments is puerile, and as like Heywood as it is different from the other. Swinburne may have been right in declaring that there was 'no poet morally nobler than Webster';[1] for it is true that his burning hatred of injustice, his remorseless exposure of traitors, liars, and all manner of villains, and his bitter anguish at the sorrows and crimes of life reflect the man. But his mind dwelt morbidly, gloatingly on corruption; there is an unhealthiness in him that is fundamental. The morality, however, of *Appius and Virginia* is very wholesome, very English, very simple, and utterly alien from the diseased and febrile morality of Webster's Italian courts, for it is identical with that of the conventional, middle-class Heywood. Again, the tragic conception implicit in *Appius and Virginia* is medieval; that is to say, the play is no more than the dramatization of a pathetic story. But such is the usual conception of tragedy in Heywood in whose plays we are never conscious of the triumph of the inner self, the emergence of the protagonist triumphant even in death, which is the essence of the Websterian as it is of the

able a play. For there is a peculiar oafish simplicity about him which made him unable ever to create a single piece, except perhaps *Edward IV* (*sic*), which is not deformed by pages of utter drivel'. Heywood, however, is pronounced *argumenti causa* 'a respectable scholar', as became 'the translator of Sallust' (ed. Lucas, iii. 138–9); as a matter of fact he was very inaccurate and had no compunction in translating Sallust from a French version; cf. 44 *supra*.

[1] *Age of Shakespeare*, 36.

Shakespearian drama. The story, it is true, is inherently unsuited for great tragedy; Virginia, a suffering and passive figure, is deeply pathetic but not tragic, Virginius is not central enough in the action to be a tragic hero, and Appius is merely the agent of an accident that produces the catastrophe. But the tragic dramatist is revealed as much by his choice of plot as by his development of it; we therefore cannot think that this unpromising and essentially untragic legend would have appealed to the sombre and exotic imagination of Webster.

The characters of *Appius and Virginia* are the merest shadows beside Bosola or Vittoria. We look in vain for the murky heat, the mysterious solemnity, and the unexplained but terribly natural motives of Webster's men and women. We do not feel that the characters are 'fey', doomed from the beginning as in Webster's undoubted plays; they do not partake of the stains of the tragedy, though for Webster's characters only implication in crime gives them complete entrance into tragic significance. With the exception of the Advocate none of Webster's recurring types is represented. Though Webster never drew a hero and has no weaklings among his women and no mere ciphers among his men,[1] yet in *Appius and Virginia* we have types Webster nowhere else attempts. Virginia, the limp heroine, is an unmarried Lucrece, not a Websterian creation, not even faintly suggestive of his hand. Her father and Icilius, the conventional heroes, Numitorius, Marcus, Minutius, and the other minors possess only that degree of individuality which their roles give them. Appius is the childish ogre of a man like Heywood, who never painted a convincing villain in his life. The clown is as certainly Heywood's as any other who appears in his certified dramas, besides being as un-Websterian as one could well imagine. He belongs to an early type of clown retained by Heywood till the end of his career; his only fellow in a Roman play of the adult Elizabethan theatre is Lucrece's servant in *The Rape of Lucrece*.[2] Heywood's clowns hardly ever fail to scatter a few Latin tags about their patter of old puns; and in *Appius and Virginia* we find amid the poor puns Latin phrases which are not to be explained as an attempt to give local colour.[3] This type of clown with his fluent conceit, his licentiousness of thought and allusion, his goodness of heart, his attachment to the heroine, his constant interruptions, his impudence, especially to a female attendant on the lady

---

[1] Cf. Brooke, *op. cit.* 104.

[2] Cf. *ibid.* 189–91; and Stoll, *John Webster*, 197–200.

[3] Mr. D. L. Thomas (*On the Play Pericles, Englische Studien*, xxxix, 232) says twenty-one of twenty-four plays by Heywood contain a few Latin words.

and even in the crises of the plot, his acquaintance with the town,
particularly its disreputable side, his frequent mention of meat and
drink, his pretence of stupidity, his assumption of dignity, his trick
of starting to say something and thinking better of it, his pro-
crastination, and his function rather of a licensed fool than of a
rustic, appearing as he does in practically every play of Heywood,
is sufficient to prove that Heywood had a hand in the play.[1] Webster
liked—perhaps he learned the device from Jonson—to make a
minor character describe the others in pithy sentences like the style
of the character-writers. But he does not always make good these
descriptions; he gives his characters a more detailed personality
than the play brings out. That is to say, he is lavish in characterizing
his people, and, it should be added, is inclined to over-elaborate the
minors. But there is not a trace of this in *Appius and Virginia*,
where the fault is that all the characters are colourless and cold.

Webster is startlingly 'romantic' in construction; he impresses us
by detached scenes and by studied effects in gesture and grouping,
never by a whole play; his plots are embarrassed and obscure and his
plays are completely lacking in unity, in the development of a single
interest to its conclusion. *Appius and Virginia*, however, is told
in full, not by a series of impressionistic scenes which make up by
their vigour for what they lack in continuity, but in a direct, naïve,
and unsuggestive way. And that is exactly Heywood's way; 'he
cannot keep counsel, he tells all', but as in this Roman tragedy with
the skill of an experienced playwright and actor. Webster, on the
other hand, can be distressingly *gauche* in the parts of the plot that
do not interest him; but it is inconceivable that he could ever make
Virginia soliloquize thus:

> My father's wondrous pensive, and withall
> with a supprest rage left his house displeas'd,
> and so in post is hurried to the camp:
> it sads me much; to expel which melancholy,
> I have sent for company.[2]

This is the 'shallow, easy' *gaucherie*[3] of the voluminous hack Heywood. Though Webster could descend in the intervals between his
crises to such antiquated and clumsy devices as the dumb-show, he

[1] Mr. Sykes (*Sidelights on Elizabethan Drama*, 137–9) tries most unsuccessfully
to minimize this piece of evidence. He seems unaware that Rowley's *A New
Wonder, A Woman never Vexed* has been attributed (wrongly, we believe) in
part to Heywood; see 332–3 *infra*.
[2] Ed. Lucas, iii. 167; the quotations from the play, however, follow the
1654 text.
[3] Brooke, *op. cit.* 168.

was at his best a master of dramatic legerdemain, a fertile inventor of effects; as Brooke says, he 'thought dramatically'.[1] But except in certain suspected passages there are no examples in *Appius and Virginia* of Webster's deliberate and calculated art in the constant stimulation of the spectator's attention, his realization of the effect of a pause, of silence, a dramatic entrance, a thrilling gesture, his careful weighing of the dramatic value of simple words, and the inevitability of his dialogue; in fact the dramatic method of the tragedy under discussion is thoroughly unenterprising and, what is more to the point, absolutely identical with that of Heywood.

The versification of *Appius and Virginia* which puzzled Mr. Stoll and upset his metrical tables[2] would alone brand the play as apocryphal in the Websterian canon. *The White Devil* and *The Duchess of Malfi* 'are among the most irregular productions, prosodically speaking, of all the great age; the others are much less so, and *Appius and Virginia* . . . is almost regular. . . . *The Devil's Law Case* stands nearer to the great plays than to *Appius and Virginia*. The last, when it is not prose, is fairly regular blank verse of the middle kind, neither as wooden as the earlier, nor as limber and sometimes limp, as the latter'.[3] We do not find in it 'Webster's loose, impressionistic iambics, with their vague equivalence and generous handling', his lines beginning with an anapaest, 'the continual use of substitution and equivalence in the feet, or, better, the thinking more in lines and less in feet'.[4] In Webster's best known plays, prose, verse, and versified prose are inextricably jumbled; one might even say that 'it was pain and grief' to him to write verse and that he 'shirked it as much as possible'.[5] But Heywood dropped naturally into a 'sehr gewandt und harmonisch gebaut',[6] and used it where prose was preferable. Unlike Webster he worked on a strictly iambic basis, admitting only the simplest metrical licenses, and even these rarely, and observing the decasyllabic length of lines divided between two speakers. Heywood does not break up his verse into short phrases but runs on from line to line; even in his most intense moments he never sacrifices the flow as does Webster, who throws all harmony to the winds to secure the desired dramatic effect. Such as we have described

---

[1] Brooke, *op. cit.* 93.

[2] *Op. cit.* 190, 193; cf. Martin Meiners, *Metrische Untersuchungen über den Dramatiker John Webster*; Sykes, *op. cit.* 134; and H. D. Gray, *Appius and Virginia: By Webster and Heywood, S. in Ph.* xxiv. 285–7.

[3] Saintsbury, *History of English Prosody*, ii. 76–7.

[4] Brooke, *op. cit.* 164–5; cf. 170–1, and Stoll, *op. cit.* 190.

[5] Saintsbury, *op. cit.* ii. 76–7; cf. Sykes, *op. cit.* 134.

[6] Schipper, *Englische Metrik*, ii. 335.

Heywood's easy, undistinguished verse, which has an individuality of its own by its very regularity and simplicity, is in every respect the medium generally employed in *Appius and Virginia*.

Webster's style is marked by a 'quick analogical instinct which loads' his plays 'with wide-ranging imagery, metaphor, and simile'.[1] Yet such is the acuteness of this instinct and such the keenness of his dramatic sense 'that scarcely ever do they seem forced or out of keeping. Language here seems to reach the extreme of ruthless and biting intensity. There is scarcely any faded imagery, and there are very few conventional tags: everything stands out in sharp lines, as if etched. The characteristic fault of Webster's imagery ... is that he errs if anything on the side of the bizarre, or even of the gro tesque.'[2] But the style of *Appius and Virginia* is conventional and declamatory 'with a slight permanent artificiality';[3] it is fluent and facile, but a trifle dull. It is impossible to attribute this extra-ordinary difference from Webster's style to his attempting here another vein to suit the classical subject.[4] So conscientious and laborious an artist as Webster, with one of the most individual and literary styles among the dramatists, could not have forsworn, even if he had desired, the mannerisms and accomplishments to which his study and efforts had been directed. On the other hand, all Heywood's authenticated plays and *Appius and Virginia* lack distinction, pregnancy, and picturesqueness of style, and display the same easy, rapid verbosity, competence, and conventionality, the acquired characteristics of the experienced journeyman-playwright.

Despite Mr. Sykes's dogmatic assertions to the contrary,[5] it should be added that Heywood was a great lover of *sententiae* and threw them readily into rhyme; that he could be and was as high-flown and bombastic when he pleased as any of his fellows; and that he constantly and blatantly, very deliberately or quite unconsciously echoes Shakespeare.[6] Heywood's indebtedness to Shakespeare for scenes, motifs, characters, and phrases, is no mere fancy; and it differs from the borrowing by Webster, who prefers the aphoristic. One often wonders, on the other hand, why particular Shakespearian phrases have fixed themselves in Heywood's memory.

In the actual words used Webster's choice was determined by

---

[1] J. C. Collins, *The Plays and Poems of Cyril Tourneur*, i. xlii.
[2] F. J. Carpenter, *Metaphor and Simile in the Minor Elizabethan Drama*, 75.
[3] Brooke, *op. cit.* 167. Cf. Sykes, *op. cit.* 134, 136.
[4] Cf. Carpenter, *op. cit.* 80.   [5] *Op. cit.* 134–6.
[6] For reminiscences in *Appius and Virginia* see the present writer's *Authorship of Appius and Virginia*, M.L.R. xvi. 9–10; Gray, *op. cit.* 278–9; and ed. Lucas, iii. 225, &c.

their significance and their suitability for his dramatic end, never for their preciosity or rarity. The vocabulary of *Appius and Virginia*, however, is impersonal, colourless, abstract, and full of strange words, often of Latin origin, and unfamiliar applications of more ordinary words. These neologisms are 'a mark of certain writers, especially of the period at the end of the sixteenth and beginning of the seventeenth centuries. . . . Of the major dramatists, Ben Jonson had a touch of it; Marston, Heywood, Chapman, and Shakespeare show it chiefly.' [1] Such peculiarly Websterian words as we find appear only in passages which we hope to prove suspect for other reasons. Practically all the uncommon words and usages are to be found, most of them again and again, in Heywood; the rest are strictly analogous to his formations and may be added to his otherwise long list of ἅπαξ λεγόμενα; several are peculiar to Heywood and *Appius and Virginia*; and the only really rare word found in Webster, 'mediate' (= beg on behalf of another), is used by him in quite a different sense (= take up a moderate position).[2] In the following list, which, long as it is, could be considerably extended by the incorporation of Brooke's parallels and many more examples of our own,[3] the weight of the evidence is diminished by the omission for the most part of the contexts in Heywood's accepted works; our parallels from the plays are fairly full, though not exhaustive; but from the non-dramatic canon we have cited not more than three from any one book or pamphlet.

Ed. Lucas, iii. 156:

> I was be-agued, fearing lest the Senate
> should have accepted.

>   arraign'd . . .
> for some suspect of treason.

> so great men should, that aspire eminent place.

Be-agued: cf. Pearson, v. 48, 49; and 'ague-shooke', *Hierarchy*, 504.
Suspect: see ed. Lucas, iii. 170, 'suspect of mutiny', and 196 'some suspect of Treason'; cf. Pearson, iii. 331, iv. 68;[4] *Hierarchy*, 526; and 'suspectlesse' (= unsuspected), Pearson, iv. 129; (= unsuspicious) *Pleasant Dialogues*, 170.
Aspire: cf. Pearson, iv. 273, v. 273; *Troia Britannica*, 82; Γυναικεῖον, 12.

Ed. Lucas, iii. 159:

> your suite to my faire Neece doth parallell
> her kindreds wishes.

[1] Brooke, *op. cit.* 166.   [2] *The White Devil*, ed. Lucas, i. 112.
[3] For other parallels to Heywood cf. Sykes, *op. cit.* 111–15; Gray, *op. cit.* 278, 282–3, note, 284; and ed. Lucas, iii. 140–4 and notes on the play.
[4] From *The English Traveller*, which both Mr. Sykes, *op. cit.* 111, and Mr. Lucas, ed. iii. 124, wrongly date *c.* 1627; see 119–20 *supra*.

You give me (noble Lord) that character
which I cood never yet read in my selfe:
but from your censure, &c.

Parallell: cf. Pearson, v. 11, 23; Γυναικεῖον, 245, 248, 260.

Censure: see ed. Lucas, iii. 193, 'referring my particular wrong to a particular
censure'; cf. Pearson, iv. 11, v. 7; *Hierarchy*, 141, 211, 586; 'censure'
(= think, comment on, sentence) very common.

Ed. Lucas, iii. 161:

why should my Lord droop, or deject his eye?
can you command Rome, and not countermand
a womans weaknesse? Let your Grace bestow
your purse and power on me. I'le prostrate you.

Deject: see ed. Lucas, iii. 220; 'Which of us two in our dejection is basest?';
cf. Pearson, ii. 167, 168, 405, iii. 91, vi. 24, 25, 43, 71; *Nobody and Somebody*,
sig. d$_1$, e$_2$, h$_1$; *Sallust (Jugurthine War)*, 61; *Troia Britannica*, 62, 125, 432;
Funeral Elegy, sig. B 3; 'dejection', Pearson, ii. 392, iii. 39; *Troia Britannica*,
392; and 'dejectedness', Pearson, vi. 15.

Prostrate: see ed. Lucas, iii. 165:

Your daughter . . .
                    most humbly
prostrates her filial duty;

cf. Pearson, i. 196:
Your humble subiects prostrate in my mouth
A general suit;

ii. 403:
                    [we] prostrate you
Our lives and services;

v. 74, vi. 64 ('prostrate duty'), 76 ('prostrate love'); *Troia Britannica*,
preface, 203; Γυναικεῖον, 127; *Curtain Lecture*, 54.

Ed. Lucas, iii. 163:

are you the high State of *Decemviri*,
that have those things in mannage

State: see 'Statists', *infra*; cf. Pearson, v. 166.

Mannage: see ed. Lucas, iii. 182, 'I'l leave it to thy manage'; cf. Pearson, ii. 316
('The manage of the fight'), iii. 95, v. 210; *Hierarchy*, 394.

Ed. Lucas, iii. 164:

the Statists of long flourishing Rome.

                    an infinite
of fair Rome's sons.

                    the iron wall
that rings this pomp in from invasive steel.

Let *Janus* Temple be devolv'd

Statists: see ed. Lucas, iii. 185, 'against that Statist, spare to use your spleen';
cf. *Sallust*, preface 8, *England's Elizabeth*, ed. *Harleian Miscellany*, x. 314,

330; *Life of Merlin*, 330; 'states' (= nobles), *Pleasant Dialogues*, 152; 'state affairs', Γυναικεῖον, 318; 'state business', 318; 'state-house' (= senate-house), Pearson, v. 193; 'state-quaking', Pearson, iii. 358; 'state' (= enthrone, fill high position), iii. 173, 189, vi. 30; *Hierarchy*, 397; 'instated' (= enthroned), Pearson, iii. 213; see 263, 282 *infra*.

Long flourishing: cf. 'long-neglected', Pearson, i. 384; 'long-divorced', *Troia Britannica*, 228; 'long-shut', Γυναικεῖον, 91; 'long-breath'd', 231.

Infinite: cf. Pearson, iii. 284, iv. 310, v. 8, 28; *Troia Britannica*, 247; Γυναικεῖον, 102, 133, 232; *Hierarchy*, 438, 466, 479; *Phoenix of these Times*, sig. E 4; *Philocothonista*, 24, 45, 81; see 281 *infra*.

Rings: see ed. Lucas, iii. 210; 'within a ring of steele'; (= surround) cf. Pearson, v. 242; ('thou art ring'd With million swords'), *Troia Britannica*, 350.

Invasive: cf. Pearson, iii. 40; *Troia Britannica*, 184, 246, 306.

Devolv'd: cf. Pearson, v. 244; *Troia Britannica*, 400.

Ed. Lucas, iii. 167:

>   It sads me much.
>   a politician,
>   when he would compasse ought to fame his industry.

Sad: cf. Pearson, iii. 218.

Fame: cf. Pearson, ii. 178, iii. 131; *Troia Britannica*, 132, 423; 'famous' (= make famous), *Sallust*, 8, 46, (*Jugurthine War*) 13; 'bed', 'tawny', 'captive', 'slave', 'glad', 'pale', 'raw', 'naked', &c., as verbs, Pearson, iii. 229, 236, 242, 246, 248, 250, 251, &c.

Ed. Lucas, iii. 168:

>   You mediate excuse for courtesies.

Mediate: cf. Pearson, iv. 296, vi. 374; Γυναικεῖον, 447; *Pleasant Dialogues*, 277; ('to mediate a peace betwixt them') *Exemplary Lives*, 166; *Jew of Malta*, ed. Tucker Brooke, 306 and *Cure for a Cuckold*, ed. Lucas, iii. 66 (see 287–94 *infra*, 103–4, 118–19 *supra*).

Ed. Lucas, iii. 169:

>   'Tis a motion
>   which nature and necessity commands.

Motion: see ed. Lucas, iii. 194, 'I think the motion's honest'; cf. Pearson, i. 252, 261, 263, ii. 308, 320, iii. 307, 393, 399, iv. 45, 177, 309, v. 289; Γυναικεῖον, 120, 121, 130; *England's Elizabeth*, ed. Harleian Miscellany, x. 310, 322; *Hierarchy*, 550; *Philocothonista*, sig. ¶ 2, *Curtain Lecture*, 58; (= propose) *Sallust*, 50; Γυναικεῖον, 138, 254.

Ed. Lucas, iii. 178:

>   grant me a treble Dowry, yet interpose me
>   a poor third from the common Treasury ?

Interpose: cf. Pearson, iii. 425; *Troia Britannica*, 320; Γυναικεῖον, 19; *Hierarchy*, 275, 428; *Life of Merlin*, 330; (= mediation) *Hierarchy*, 274; 'interposer' Pearson, v. 271, *England's Elizabeth*, ed. Harleian Miscellany, x. 303 'iuterponents', Pearson, v. 171.

Ed. Lucas, iii. 179:

> Now by my vow, insculpt in heaven, I'l send thee—
> APPIUS. You see I am patient.
> ICILIUS. But withal revengeless.

Insculpt: cf. Pearson, iii. 248, iv. 286, v. 265; *Hierarchy*, 485.
Revengeless: see ed. Lucas, iii. 212, 'this cause is to be pityed, and should not dy revengelesse'; cf. Pearson, iii. 427; 'ransomelesse', Γυναικεῖον, 439; 'remorse-lesse', Pearson, ii. 67; 'dangerlesse', iii. 18.

Ed. Lucas, iii. 180:

> All you Panthean Gods,
> confound me, if my soul be accessory
> to your distractions.

> first, to brave my Greatness . . .

> after all these deep disparagements,
> threat me with steel.

Panthean: cf. 'Promethean', Pearson, iii. 201; 'Hymenean', Γυναικεῖον, 337, 338, 456; 'enthean', *Hierarchy*, 25.
Distractions: see ed. Lucas, iii. 211, 'what means this ugly face of blood you put on your distractions'; cf. Γυναικεῖον, 31, 74, 195; *Hierarchy*, 434; 'dis-traction', *Hierarchy*, 434, 543; 'distract' (= drive mad), 248, 379; (= distracted), 543; see '*Disparagements*', *infra*.
Brave: cf. Pearson, ii. 200, iii. 315; *Troia Britannica*, 63, 313; *Pleasant Dialogues*, 184; (noun = boast) Pearson, ii. 233, iii. 175, 407, v. 244; *Troia Britannica*, 23, ('menac't Hostile braves 'Gainst Tyrants'); 'Bravado' (= bold exploit), *Sallust* (*Jugurthine War*), 19; 'out-brave', *Reader, here*, sig. A 2; see 300 *infra*.
Disparagements; cf. 'disparage' (= disgrace), Pearson, ii. 171, iii. 163; plural abstracts are a marked feature of Heywood's style; see 282–3, 297, 300.
Threat: cf. Pearson, iii. 17, 222; *Troia Britannica*, 121.

Ed. Lucas, iii. 181:

> upon my infallid evidence.

> the Cause is mine; you but the Sentencer
> upon that evidence.

Infallid: cf. *Captives*, ed. Judson, 115 ('infallid signes'); *Hierarchy*, 285 ('in-fallid testimonie . . . Of the most sacred Scriptures'), 308, 311 ('infallid testimonie of their faith').
Sentencer: see ed. Lucas, iii. 212, 'To you I appeal, you are my Sentencers'; cf. Pearson, v. 158; 'sentence' (= declare), *Hierarchy*, 357.

Ed. Lucas, iii. 183:

> If you will needs wage eminence and state,
> chuse out a weaker opposite.

> know you . . . what it is to scandal
> one of his place and sway?

> his smooth crest hath cast a palped film
> over *Romes* eyes.

State: see 261–2 *supra*.

Opposite: cf. Pearson, i. 195, 197, ii. 130, iii. 299, 320, 341, 362, v. 14, 23, 35, 192; *Troia Britannica*, 256; *Apology*, 44; *England's Elizabeth*, ed. *Harleian Miscellany*, x. 315, 330; *Hierarchy*, 12, 202; (= hostile) Pearson, iii. 74, 370, &c.; (= different) *England's Elizabeth*, ed. *Harleian Miscellany*, x. 306; (= unfavourable) *Hierarchy*, 180; 'opposure', *Life of Merlin*, 63; see 298 *infra*.

Scandal: cf. Pearson, i. 177, ii. 378, iv. 105, 119, 151; *Nobody and Somebody*, sig. E 2, *Sallust* (*Jugurthine War*), 63 ('he would scandall the warre').

Palped: see ed. Lucas, iii. 215, 'I will gull them all most palpably'; cf. *Troia Britannica*, 123 ('the Murke and Palped darknesse'), 395 ('palped darkness'); *Hierarchy*, 27; 'palpable', *Philocothonista*, 14, 76; 'palpably', Pearson, ii. 26, v. 23.

Ed. Lucas, iii. 185:

> one was before me with regreets from him.

Regreets: cf. Pearson, ii. 419, iii. 329; *Troia Britannica*, 123.

Ed. Lucas, iii. 190:

> I shall be proud to pleasure you.

Pleasure: cf. Pearson, ii. 67, v. 300, vi. 405.

Ed. Lucas, iii. 191:

> if you be found to double.

Double: cf. Pearson, i. 105.

Ed. Lucas, iii. 202:

> all *Rome* held this for no imposterous stuff.

Imposterous: cf. Pearson, iii. 112; Γυναικεῖον ('all their imposturous lies'); *Hierarchy*, 289 ('his impostr'ous lies'), 308, 468; see 300 *infra*.

Ed. Lucas, iii. 208:

> Comrague, I fear *Appius* will doom us to *Actaeons* death.

Comrague: cf. Pearson, iv. 244 ('my comrague and bed-fellow'); *Philocothonista*, 44 ('a merry comrague').

Ed. Lucas, iii. 210–11:

> entertain this novel
> within a ring of steele.

> Let him come thrill his partisan
> against this brest, that through a large wide wound
> my mighty soule might rush out of this prison
> to flie more freely to yon christal pallace,
> where honour sits inthronis'd.

> Or if the Generals heart be so obdure
> to an old begging souldier.

Novel: cf. Pearson, iii. 210, 373; *Troia Britannica*, 155, 250, 389; Γυναικεῖον, 134, 356, 408; *Hierarchy*, argument bk. viii, 28, 508, 611; 'novelties', Γυναικεῖον, 406; 'novelists' (= innovators), *True Discourse*, 16.

Thrill: cf. Pearson, iii. 299, 316; *Troia Britannica*, 347 ('He thrild a Iavelin'), Γυναικεῖον, 223, *Pleasant Dialogues*, 301.

Inthronis'd: cf. 'enthrone', Pearson, v. 170; 'eternize', Pearson, ii. 327; 'etimologise', Γυναικεῖον, 68; 'monarchise', *Hierarchy*, 25; 'panderize', Pearson, v. 18, &c.

Obdure: cf. Pearson, iii. 144, 171, v. 13; Γυναικεῖον, 46, 362, 393; *Hierarchy*, 312, 365, 498; *Pleasant Dialogues*, 114; (= harden) *Troia Britannica*, 116; Γυναικεῖον, 55, 365; *Hierarchy*, 82; 'obdurate', *Pleasant Dialogues*, 17; 'obdure-hearted', Γυναικεῖον, 353; 'obdureness', 55.

Ed. Lucas, iii. 214:

> a most eloquent Oration,
> that shall applaud their fortune, and distaste
> the cruelty of *Appius*.

Distaste: cf. Pearson, iii. 397, v. 46, 179, vi. 42, &c.; *Hierarchy*, 201, 259, 352; (noun) Pearson, ii. 359, 363, iv. 55, 66, 99, 137; 'distaster', *Hierarchy*, 436; 'distastive', *Sallust*, preface 6; 'taste' (= please), *Philocothonista*, 14.

Ed. Lucas, iii. 219:

> one rear'd on a popular suffrage,
> whose station's built on Avees and Applause.

> the same hands
> that yesterday to hear me conscionate
> and Oratorize, rung shril Plaudits forth.

> Grieves it thee
> to impart my sad disaster?

Suffrage: cf. Pearson, iii. 8, 95 ('With like applause and suffrage shall be seene the faire *Andromeda* crown'd *Argos* queen'); *Sallust*, preface 16.

Avees: cf. Pearson, iii. 8 ('all the people, with lowd suffrages, Have shrild their Avees'); *Troia Britannica*, 71 ('They signe his *Ave* with a shrill applause'); *Sir Thomas Wyatt*, ed. W. C. Hazlitt, i. 9 ('To whom . . . bends this your ave').

Conscionate (= moralize): cf. 'conscionable' (= reconcilable with conscience), Γυναικεῖον, 108.

Oratorize: see '*Inthronis'd*', *supra*; cf. Pearson, iii. 68 ('This your absence . . . Orators In your behalfe); 'oratorlike', *Sallust*, preface 3.

Impart (= share): cf. Pearson, ii. 194, iii. 95, iv. 63, 68, vi. 398 ('I am likely to impart his loss'), 404; *Pleasant Dialogues*, 174.

Ed. Lucas, iii. 220:

> before the Law convince him.

> but yesterday his breath
> aw'd *Rome*, and his least torved frown was death.

Convince: cf. *Hierarchy*, 216, 261, 294; *Exemplary Lives*, 92 ('the bones . . . convince it to have beene sepulcrall').

Torved: cf. Pearson, iii. 307 ('the torvity and strange alteration of his countenance').

Ed. Lucas, iii. 222:

This sight hath stiffned all my operant powers.

redeem a base life with a noble death
and through your lust-burnt veins confine your breath.

Virginius is a noble Justicer.

I have not dreaded famine, fire, nor strage.

Operant: cf. Pearson, vi. 6 ('may my operant parts Each one forget their office');
'operative' (= helpful, conducive) Γυναικεῖον, 19.
Lust-burnt: cf. Pearson, iii. 143 ('The lust-burn'd and wine-heated monsters');
'lust-burning', Pearson, iii. 180, iv. 58, v. 222, 236, 241; 'rage-burnt',
Troia Britannica, 321.
Confine: cf. Pearson, iii. 41, 211; *Troia Britannica*, 2, 437; Γυναικεῖον, 74,
98, 136; *Hierarchy*, 74, 438, 607; *Curtain Lecture*, 243; 'confinement'
(= limit), Γυναικεῖον, 85, 137, 363, *Life of Merlin*, 197.
Justicer: cf. Pearson, ii. 282; Γυναικεῖον, 179; *Curtain Lecture*, 177; *Life of Merlin*,
sig. B 4.
Strage: cf. Pearson, iv. 271, v. 371, 373; Γυναικεῖον, 441; *Hierarchy*, 54, 89, 163;
Pleasant Dialogues, 111, 143, 343.

Many other usages which are characteristic of Heywood's
vocabulary but also fairly common elsewhere might be cited.
Practically all the compounds—Heywood was an inveterate
compounder, and far more partial to them than Webster—are
identical or analogous with phrases in the Heywood canon:

Ed. Lucas, iii. 160: *Orespent*: cf. 'ore-swell'd', Pearson, v. 118; 'o'er-
sway'd', vi. 420.
161: *Virgin Tower*: cf. 'virgin fedde', Pearson, iii. 266; 'Virgin-saint',
v. 273.
169: *New-reapt*: cf. Pearson, iii. 137.
181: *Broad-waking*: cf. 'broad-eyed', *Troia Britannica*, 235; 'broad-
breasted', *Pleasant Dialogues*, 46.
188: *Sweet-tooth'd*: cf. 'sweet-fac'd', Pearson, iii. 367; 'sweet-tun'd',
v. 186; see 297 *infra*.
198: *Short-liv'd*: cf. Pearson, ii. 42, v. 227.
205: *Bondslave-like*: cf. 'Pater-noster-like', Pearson, ii. 47; 'madman-
like', *Troia Britannica*, 122; 'matron-like', 124.
219: *Hydra-headed*: 'three-headed', Pearson, iii. 215; 'many-headed',
Hierarchy, 126.
223: *True-bred*: cf. 'true-stampt', Pearson, i. 134; 'true-hearted', iv.
228.
Sword-proof: cf. *Troia Britannica*, 37, 263.

The little that can be deduced from the syntax supports Heywood's claim, especially the use of an imperative clause for a

protasis, the omission of 'neither' before a following 'nor', and the use of the reflexive instead of the personal pronoun. But even more convincing than single words, phrases, or grammatical peculiarities are the following, which will not be denied our client by any one who has once savoured his idiosyncrasies:

> Where should a poor man's cause be heard but here?
> To you the Statists of long flourishing *Rome*,
> to you I call, If you have charity,
> if you be humane, and not quite giv'n ore
> To Furs and Metall, if you be *Romans*,
> if you have any souldiers bloud at all
> flow in your veins, help with your able arms
> to prop a sinking camp, an infinite
> of fair *Rome's* sons, cold, weak, hungry, and clotheless,
> would feed upon your surfet.[1]

> Or if the general's heart be so obdure,
> to an old begging souldier, Have I here
> no honest Legionary of mine own Troop,
> at whose bold hand and sword, if not entreat
> I may command a death?[2]

Both of these extracts refer to the results of a plot suggested to Appius by Marcus Claudius; Virginia's father, he says, is

> busied in our foreign wars,
> and there hath chief employment: all their pay
> must your discretion scantle; keep it back;
> restrain it in the common treasury;
> thus may a statesman 'gainst a soldier stand,
> to keep his purse weak, whilst you arm his hand.
> Her father thus kept low, gifts and rewards
> will tempt the maid the sooner; nay, haply draw
> The father in to plead in your behalf.[3]

A very remarkable parallel to this departure from Livy and the other sources occurs in *A Maidenhead Well Lost*, in which Stroza lays practically the same plot against the general and his daughter.[4]

---

[1] Ed. Lucas, iii. 163–4.   [2] *Ibid.* iii. 211.   [3] *Ibid.* iii. 161–2.
[4] Cf. Pearson, iv. 105, 108–9, 111–17; and Brooke, *op. cit.* 187–8; cf. also *Appius and Virginia*, ed. Lucas, iii. 165:

> O my souldiers,
> before you want, I'll sell my small possessions
> even to my skin to help you, Plate and Jewels
> all shall be yours. Men that are men indeed,
> the earth shall find, the Sun and air must feed;

And in *The Rape of Lucrece* the sentry grumbles that

> thus must poore Souldiers do,
> Whil'st their commanders are with dainties fed,
> They sleepe on Downe, the earth must be our bed,[1]

which is expanded into the motif of the mutiny scene in *Appius and Virginia*.[2]

But though our endeavour thus far has been to transfer *Appius and Virginia* to Heywood's credit, we admit that there are traces in it, not of a collaborator, but of a reviser who seems to have been Webster. The first signs of his hand are in i. 1, half of which, that is from the beginning to the re-entry of the senators, we pronounce Webster's, or at least more his than Heywood's, whose humdrum manner is clear in the remainder of the scene. In this suspected passage the motivation is like that of Webster; the metrical regularity is sacrificed to the dramatic effect; prose crops out more than once; lines of verse divided between two speakers are not invariably decasyllabic as in Heywood; there occurs a characteristically Websterian apologue—

> I have heard of running footmen that have worne
> shoes made of lead some ten days 'fore a race
> to give them nimble and more active feet—

and a sentence

> I have seene children oft eat sweet meats thus,
> as fearfull to devour them,[3]

found almost verbatim in *The Duchess of Malfi*;[4] a fact of the utmost significance, for Webster had a habit of hoarding up phrases

and *A Maidenhead Well Lost*, Pearson, iv. 109, 113, 115:

> He has beene put to much extremity
> Of Dearth and Famine, many a stormy night
> Beene forc'd to roofe himselfe i' th' open field,
> Nay more then this, much of his owne revenue
> He hath expended, all to pay his Souldiers;
>   even for griefe,
> That he could neither furnish us with pay
> Which was kept back, nor guerdon us with spoile,
> What was about him he distributed,
> Even to the best deservers, as his garments,
> His armes, and Tent;
>   All his Gold and Iewels
> I have already added, yet are we still
> To score to souldiery.

[1] Pearson, v. 205.   [2] Ed. Lucas, iii. 169–75.   [3] *Ibid*. iii. 155–6.
[4] *Ibid*. ii. 50; Mr. Lucas, *ibid*. ii. 140, notes a similar passage in one of Webster's favourite quarries, Sidney's *Arcadia*, ed. Feuillerat, i. 96.

he liked and repeating them, sometimes in less happy contexts.[1]
The reviser, too, has seen fit to depart from the original conception
of the aristocratic Appius by making him at first decline to accept
office as one of the Decemviri for the unhistorical reason that he
was of humble birth:

> My lords, far be it from the thoughts of so poor a Plebeian, as your
> unworthy servant *Appius*, to soar so high: the dignity of so eminent a
> place would require a person of the best parts and blood in *Rome*;[2]

it should be added that in iv. 1, which is also suspect, Appius is one
known but eight months to the heralds.[3] But in v. 3,[4] he declares
before killing himself

> this black stain laid on my family
> then which a nobler hath not place in *Rome*,
> Wash [I] with my blood away,

and Claudius calls him 'one of noble blood', while Icilius allows
him to be of 'a noble strain' and to have died as became 'a Roman
Gentleman'.[5] A curious discrepancy in i. 2 probably disguises a cut
of some length. Numitorius, *à propos* of what has just been said,
remarks sententiously

> Thus ladies still foretell the funeral
> of their lord's kindness;

at which point

> (*Enter[s] a servant, whispers* Icilius *in the ear*);
> But, my lord, what news?

continues Numitorius, to whom Icilius is able to give a detailed
description of Virginius's arrival such as only an eyewitness could
provide:

> for his horse,
> Bloody with spurring, shows as if he came
> From forth a battle: never did you see
> 'Mongst quails and cocks in fight a bloodier heel,
> Than that your brother strikes with.[6]

In the unrevised play Icilius must have seen what he here reports
on hearsay. The next scene[7] begins a motif which leads nowhere;

---

[1] Eight other parallels to Webster's authenticated plays are found in *Appius
and Virginia*; all but the one quoted above and two others noticed later were
properly rejected by Brooke, *op. cit.* 175–8, as common catch-phrases.
[2] Ed. Lucas, iii. 155; Mr. Lucas, *ibid.* 137, 238, dismisses discrepancies much
too conveniently and airily.
[3] *Ibid.* iii. 206.   [4] v. 2 in ed. Lucas, iii. 219–24.
[5] *Ibid.* iii. 222–3.   [6] *Ibid.* iii. 159–60.
[7] In ed. Lucas, iii. 162, a new scene, i. 4, begins after Claudius's exit.

that is to say the already mentioned plot of Marcus and Appius to impoverish Virginius by withholding the soldiers' pay in order that Appius might seduce Virginia with his presents and even secure her father's help in his suit. Although Appius does withhold the money, he takes no steps, as the play now stands, to further his scheme in the way proposed. The scene, however, with its powerful, epideictic eloquence, absolutely the reverse of Webster's Tacitean style, shows no sign of tampering, except the appearance of a 'ghost', Spurius, who figures nowhere else in the play. A more important excision, which may have included Heywood's imitation of Valeria's visit to Volumnia and Virgilia in *Coriolanus*, is indicated by the fact that though Virginia in ii. 1 sends Corbulo to

> tell *Calphurnia*, I am walking
> to take the air: intreat her company.
> Say I attend her coming,[1]

Calphurnia[2] and the equally shadowy Julia appear only in the *dramatis personae* and in the suspected iv. 1, where they have nothing to say. In the third scene of ii Brooke has noted the strange collapse of Icilius's hostility to Appius after he has accused him of sinister intentions, and in iii. 1 the different version of the incident Icilius gives to Virginia.[3] Dyce also draws attention to the fact that though the interview takes place in an outer department of Appius's house he reproves Marcus for sending 'a ruffian Even to my closet'.[4] We would add that there is a good deal of parrying and obscure allusions to events outside the play as it now stands, and again mention is made of the retention of the soldiers' pay. The actual interview in ii. 3 ends thus:

> ICILIUS. I crave your pardon.
> APPIUS. Granted ere crav'd, my good *Icilius*.
> ICILIUS. —Morrow.
> APPIUS. It is no more indeed. Morrow *Icilius*.
>   If any of our servants wait without,
>   command them in.
> ICILIUS. I shall.
> APPIUS. Our secretary;
>   We have use for him; *Icilius*, send him hither:
>   Again, good-morrow.   (*Exit* ICILIUS.)[5]

Brooke, who comments on the meaningless 'It is no more indeed' and the tameness of this ending to the wordy combat, suspects a cut

---

[1] Ed. Lucas, iii. 167.

[2] As Mr. Lucas, ed. iii. 225, notes, there are several signs of indebtedness to *Julius Caesar*.   [3] *Op. cit.* 200–1.

[4] Ed. Lucas, iii. 180; cf. ed. Dyce, 160.   [5] Ed. Lucas, iii. 180.

or a hasty revision at this point.[1] Now in the old texts there is a suspicious dash before Icilius's 'Morrow'; the complication of motive during the interview is more in Webster's manner than in Heywood's, although one or two of Heywood's characteristic expressions survive; at the very outset of the discussion Icilius breaks into a very Websterian criticism of lawyers; and finally the roughness of the verse in the interview episode remind us strongly of Webster. But as soon as Icilius has gone Heywood words are much more numerous, 'Panthean', 'distractions', 'brave' and 'threat' as verb, 'disparagements', 'infallid', 'manage' (= management), &c.; the motivation of the rest of the scene is much less subtle; the verse runs smoothly; and not only does Icilius's account in iii. 1 of this interview differ from the facts as they now stand,[2] but Appius's own version to Marcus in this very scene after Icilius has withdrawn also differs from the facts and agrees with Icilius's narrative in iii. 1. Again, iii. 2 seems also to have been mutilated in some obscure way. In it Icilius sends the nurse for Sertorius, who except in the list of characters is unknown, and in his place comes Valerius. It is possible, too, that Appius's satiric character of Marcus in this scene is a Websterian touch. In revising the scene, however, he carelessly let slip Marcus's excuse:

> My purse is too scant to wage Law with them,
> I am inforc't be mine own advocate,
> not one will pleade for me;[3]

for in iv. 1, the most Websterian passage in the play, Marcus is represented by an advocate, introduced apparently by Webster for satiric reasons. Lastly, at the end of iii. 2, when Appius withdraws, seemingly enraged at Marcus whom he has committed prisoner to his own house to ensure his appearance, Icilius and Virginia are left alone; their dialogue is as follows:

> Icilius. Sure all this is damn'd cunning.
> Virginia. O my Lord,
>   seamen in tempests shun the flattering shore,
>   to bear full sails upon't were danger more.
>   So men o're born with greatness still hold dread,
>   false seeming friends that on their bosomes spread:
>   for this is a safe truth which never varies,
>   He that strikes all his sailes seldom miscarries.
> Icilius. Must we be slaves both to a tyrants will,
>   and confounding ignorance at once?
>   What are we, in this mist, or is this hell?
>   I have seen as great as the proud Judge have fell:

---

[1] *Op. cit.* 200–1.   [2] Ed. Lucas, iii. 184–5.   [3] *Ibid.* iii. 191.

The bending Willow yeilding to each wind,
shall keep his rooting firme, when the proud Oak
braving the storme, presuming on his root,
shall have his body rent from head to foote;
Let us expect the worst that may befal,
and with a noble confidence bear all.[1]

In style, verse, and grammar these lines are quite unlike the rest of
the scene, and they have no obvious connexion with what has gone
before.[2] We suggest, therefore, that this passage is a cento made by
the reviser from a much longer interview of Icilius and Virginia,
but without much care to assign the fragments to their respective
owners. That it was a dialogue in which Virginia advised and
Icilius opposed a policy of apparent submission is borne out by
Virginia's exclamation earlier in the scene:

O my *Icilius* Your incredulity
hath quite undone me.[3]

But in the extant play this is meaningless; we have heard nothing of
Icilius's credulousness to Appius or incredulity to Virginia. In the
third scene of the same act, which has some very rugged verse or
prose in the midst of verse and a typically Websterian figure—

make as much speed
As if thy father were deceas'd i' th' camp,
And that thou went'st to take th' administration
Of what he left thee—[4]

occurs another irrelevance; Appius has asserted his confidence in
the success of his schemes and Marcus agrees that Mercury could
not have managed matters better, to which Appius replies:

O my *Clodius*,
Observe this rule, one ill must cure another;
as *Aconitum* a strong poison, brings
a present cure against all Serpents stings.
In high attempts, the soul hath infinite eyes,
And 'tis necessity makes men most wise.
Should I miscarry in this desperate plot,
this of my fate in aftertimes be spoken,
I'l break that with my weight on which I am broken.[5]

But Appius's plans have as yet received no set-back. It may, therefore, be that we have here Webster's not very successful attempt to
heighten what seemed to him too tame. The medical and zoological

---

[1] Ed. Lucas, iii. 195–6.
[2] Cf. Brooke, *op. cit.* 201–2.
[3] Ed. Lucas, iii. 189.
[4] *Ibid.* iii. 196.
[5] *Ibid.* iii. 197.

lore, the somewhat cryptic style, and the close resemblance to a passage in Ben Jonson, one of Webster's favourite authors,[1] are noteworthy. In the trial scene, iv. 1, little of the original remains. Julia, Calphurnia, and Oppius appear but are mute, and the advocate, a common butt in Webster, though he has an important part to play, is not mentioned in the stage directions. The dialogue, too, includes the following striking parallels to Webster:

Ed. Lucas, iii. 201:

> ADVOCATE. Then have at you Sir.
> May it please your Lordships, here is such a lease
> so full of subtility, and as it were,
> so far benighted in an ignorant mist,
> that though my reading be sufficient,
> my practice more, I never was intangled
> in the like pursenet;

cf. *The White Devil*, ed. Lucas, i. 137:

> LAWYER. Well then have at you!

and *The Devil's Law Case*, ed. Lucas, ii. 292, 286:

> CONTILUPO (a lawyer). May it please your Lordsh[ip]
> & the reverend Court,
> To give me leave to open you a Case
> So rare, so altogether voyd of Pre[ce]dent,
> That I do challenge all the spacious Volumes,
> Of the whole Civill Law to shew the like;
> ARIOSTO (a lawyer). . . .
> you must find new stratagems, new pursenets.

———

Ed. Lucas, iii. 203:

> I vow this is a practis'd Dialogue:
> comes it not rarely off?

cf. *The Duchess of Malfi*, ed. Lucas, ii. 46, where the remark is much more appropriate:

> I thinke this speech betweene you both was studied,
> It came so roundly off?

———

Ed. Lucas, iii. 205:

> Think you, my Lord, our Lawes are writ in snow,
> and that your breath can melt them?

cf. *The Duchess of Malfi*, ed. Lucas, ii. 124:

> These wretched eminent things
> Leave no more frame behind 'em, then should one
> Fall in a frost, and leave his print in snow.

[1] Cf. *Sejanus*, iii. 3 (from Pliny, xxvii. 2) and *The White Devil*, ed. Lucas, i. 147.

Ed. Lucas, iii. 206:

> we wot
> the Office of a Justice is perverted quite
> when one thief hangs another;

cf. *The Duchess of Malfi*, ed. Lucas, ii. 102:

> The Office of Justice is perverted quite
> When one Thiefe hangs another.

The lawyer reappears in v. 1 in an unnecessary scene of satire on his profession. The second scene of the same act,[1] in which Horatio and Valerius appear but in which neither speaks, has been badly handled. Perhaps in the original first scene of the act the spectator was prepared for the hostility of Icilius and Virginius and their supporters in the second scene. But as it is, Virginius refers to something we now can only guess at:

> It seems, my Lord,
> now you have caught the sword within your hand,
> like a madman you'le draw it to offend
> those that best love you; and perhaps the counsel
> of some loose unthrifts, and vile male contents
> hearten you to't: goe to, take your course,
> my faction shal not give the least advantage
> to murtherers, to banquerouts, or theeves,
> to fleece the common Wealth.[2]

The hasty reconciliation of the bereaved father and Icilius and especially the last two speeches of the scene are much more in the manner of Webster than of Heywood. It should be remarked that the insignificance of the parts assigned to several of the characters, Horatio, Valerius, and others, as well as the survival of names in the *dramatis personae* and stage directions without corresponding roles in the play, indicates other cuts of uncertain length and importance.

Our conclusion of the whole matter, then, is that at an unknown date Webster revised the play somewhat carelessly. The obscurity of several scenes seems to preclude the possibility of his having collaborated at the outset;[3] but some years later, we suppose, he attempted to infuse some life into the frigid plot, excised a few of the

---

[1] In ed. Lucas, iii. 215–19, this is reckoned as v. 1, 62–191.

[2] Ed. Lucas, iii. 217.

[3] Mr. H. D. Gray, however, makes out a good case for pronouncing '*Appius and Virginia*': *By Webster and Heywood*, *S. in Ph.* xxiv. 275, &c., and not such a good case for an unknown reviser of their work; and Mr. Lucas, ed. iii. 134–46, arrived independently at a theory of collaboration, though he does not altogether reject Mr. H. D. Sykes's unconvincing thesis (*Sidelights on Elizabethan Drama*, 108–39) that in the play we have only Webster in disguise.

duller passages, wrote a scene or two and some odd speeches, generally made considerable minor alterations throughout—a good deal more than Brooke suspected—and roughly cobbled the play, half-heartedly, for the task was not much to his liking.

As for the source, Heywood was familiar with several versions, and frequently refers to the story of Virginia and 'that great Arch-champion of virginitie',[1] her father. In the main the play is based primarily on the *Roman Antiquities* of Dionysius of Halicarnassus,[2] and on Livy,[3] probably through the medium of Holland's translation, 1600. A conflation of these two authorities was included in Fiorentino's *Il Pecorone*,[4] and was thence translated by Painter,[5] to whom Lauschke[6] would trace a slight debt.

---

[1] *A Curtain Lecture*, 69–70; cf. *Troia Britannica*, sig. A 6; *Apology*, 57; Γυναικεῖον, 442; *The Felicity of Man*, 1631, 43; and *Exemplary Lives*, 134.

[2] xi. 28, &c.; possibly as Mr. Lucas suggests (ed. iii. 131, 226–7) in the Greek-Latin text of Sylburg, 1586.

[3] iii. 44, &c.   [4] xx. 2.

[5] Ed. Jacobs, i. 35, &c.

[6] *John Websters Tragödie Appius and Virginia, eine Quellenstudie*, 32. Cf. also C. Vopel, *John Webster*; Otho Rumbaur, *Die Geschichte von Appius und Virginia in der englischen Litteratur*; Adèle Ott, *Die italienische Novelle im englischen Drama*; E. E. Stoll, *John Webster*; Brooke, *op. cit.* 193–5; and Lucas, ed. iii. 131–3.

APPENDIX II
DICK OF DEVONSHIRE

THE date of that part of the plot which gives the tragicomedy its name is established by the licensing on July 18, 1626 of *Three to One: Being, An English-Spanish Combat, Performed by a Western Gentleman, of Tavistock in Devonshire with an English Quarter-Staff, against Three Spanish Rapiers and Poniards, at Xeres in Spain, The fifteenth day of November, 1625. In the Presence of Dukes, Condes, Marquesses, and other Great Dons of Spain, being the Council of War* by Richard Pike or Peake, the eponymous hero of the play.[1] Pike, born, it would seem, in the fifteen-nineties at Tavistock, had served as a common soldier at an attack on Algiers under Sir Robert Mansell in the winter of 1620–1. In the autumn of 1625 he enlisted as a volunteer for the expedition against Cadiz which set out exceptionally late in the season. After his adventures in Spain Pike arrived at Foy on April 26, 1626, and on May 18 delivered in London a challenge to Buckingham from the brother-in-law of the Conde d'Olivares.[2] An exploit of such a kind as his pamphlet describes would have to be staged at once if it were to catch the public notice at all, and was probably staged not later than the middle of August. The dramatist has followed Pike's narrative with singular fidelity, though he may have supplemented it with certain ballads on similar themes.[3]

The romantic sub-plot, though thin, is of considerable interest, and, strange as it may seem, is strengthened and buttressed by the breezy realism of Dick Pike. Without his support the story of the two brothers Manuel and Henrico, the one all nobility and loyalty, the other weak and selfish, would be too frail to stand alone;

[1] Reprinted in Arber's *English Garner*, i. 621, and *Stuart Tracts*, 275.

[2] *Court and Times of Charles I*, i. 104. Pike's story, dedicated to Charles I, is told with simple effectiveness and reads like the raw material of an epic. Pike besides becoming a hero of the theatre was celebrated in verses by J. D., printed at the end of *Three to One*, and late in Charles II's reign in a broadside ballad, *A Panegyric Poem: or Tavistock's Encomium*, by one Long, schoolmaster of Tavistock, reprinted in Mrs. Bray's *Borders of the Tamar and the Tavy*, i. 241.

[3] E.g. *The Attempt on the Town of Cales*, 1625 (W. Crosse's continuation of Ed. Grimestone's *General History of the Netherlands*, 1627, 1580–1); *The Famous Fight at Malaga* (S.R. July 1600; *Douce Ballads*, i. 72); and *The Spanish Lady's Love* by Deloney (S.R. June 11, 1603, Dec. 14, 1624, Aug. 4, 1626, and Mar. 1 1675; cf. Aug. 1, 1586; ed. F. O. Mann, 584). Cf. the title of the play with the titles of the ballads 'the Devill of Devonshire and Wilkins of the West his sonne' (S.R. Oct. 16, 1594) and *Philip surnamed the Devil in the West* (S.R. June 13, 1631; *Sherburn Ballads*, 130).

the masculine Dick gives to its tenuousness body and depth. There is not enough in it to have made a novella; rather would it seem to have been devised by the dramatist from his reminiscences of many romantic situations. It is typical of all the romantic stories of the later Elizabethan theatre, though it is not itself an analogue to any of them.

But, and this in no wise contradicts what has just been said, the romantic plot may be a fragment of an older play torn from its context to pad out Pike's adventures to five acts. The manner in which the plots are yoked suggests that here and there very rough cuts have been made in the older matter to get in all the new; the two plots do not seem to have grown together. A phrase at the very end of the play which like the opening episode belongs to the romantic plot—

> Letters shall forthwith fly into *Madrid*
> To tell the King the storyes of Two Brothers,
> Worthy the Courtiers reading. Lovers, take hands:
> *Hymen* & gentle faeryes strew your way:
> Our Sessions turnes into a Bridall day—[1]

may indicate that the Manuel-Henrico plot derives from the lost *Younger Brother*, played by Queen Anne's men at the Red Bull on October 3, 1617.[2] After this very natural couplet termination the text runs on:

> ALQUENEZES. Fare thee well, *Englishman*.
> PIKE. I will ring peales of prayers of you all,
>   My Lords & noble Dons.
> MACADA. Doe soe, if thou hast iust cause: howsoever,
>   When thy swift ship cutts through the curled mayne,
>   Dance to see *England*, yet speake well of *Spayne*.
> PIKE. I shall.—Where must I leave my pistoletts ?
> GENTLEMAN. Follow mee.[3]

This fumbling conclusion seems to have been dragged in after the real finish of Pike's story in order to leave with the audience the thought of the heroic Englishman. But this disconcerting note should have come before the romantic *dénouement* and not as now after:

> MACADA. Well said: in *England* thou wilt drinke her health ?
> PIKE. Were it a glasse as deepe to the bottome as a *Spanish* pike is long,
>   an *Englishman* shall doe't. Her health, & *Don John's* wives too.[4]

[1] Ed. Bullen, ii. 99.
[2] According to Collier's *Memoirs of Edward Alleyn*, 107—the record is doubtful—Alleyn received for this performance 'but £3 6s. 4d.' as his share. Cf. Fleay, ii. 336–7.   [3] Ed. Bullen, ii. 99.   [4] *Ibid.* ii. 97.

Dick of Devonshire is a remarkably competent play, well worth Bullen's care, and deserving more attention than the very limited edition of his *Collection of Old English Plays* has given it. In spite of the dichotomy of the plot it reads well and must certainly have acted effectively. There are many fine scenes and dramatic moments skilfully prepared and subtly worked out. It is a better play than Massinger could have written, fresher in poetry, more masculine in conception, more natural in execution, more convincing in dramatic plausibility, more adequate and consistent in characterization. It has not the sweating and unhealthy pallor of Ford, for it is played out in the open air and has a tang of the sea in it. Nor is it in the least like Dekker's buoyant light-hearted style, or Middleton's essentially non-moral cynicism. As Bullen says, 'There is nothing amateurish in the workmanship; the reader is not doomed to soar into extravagances at one moment and sink into flatnesses at another. Ample opportunities were offered for displays of boisterous riot, but the playwright's even-balanced mind was not to be disturbed. Everywhere there are traces of studious care; and we may be sure that a style at once so equable and strong was not attained without a long apprenticeship.'[1] Shirley, therefore, who had just entered on his dramatic career, could not by any stretch of the imagination be credited under the date 1626 with a play so generally workmanlike, so resourceful, and exhibiting so complete and easy an acquaintance with the possibilities and needs of the theatre; nor would a fresh convert to Roman Catholicism have written the scene (ii. 2) of Pike's interview with the friars. Yet when Bullen put forward Heywood's name in his introduction to the play, Fleay actually suggested Shirley. The tragicomedy was really, said he, *The Brothers*, licensed by Herbert on November 4, 1626, apparently for Queen Henrietta's men at the Cockpit.[2] But as a play of Shirley's called *The Brothers* was printed in 1652 Fleay had to identify the latter with *The Politic Father*, licensed for the King's men on May 26, 1641,[3] which he declared had wrongly been equated to *The Politician*.[4] Fleay, however, originally made the even more astonishing suggestion that *Dick of Devonshire* was by Robert Davenport, the obscure author of the reworking of Munday and Chettle's *Death of Robert, Earl of Huntingdon* into *King John and Matilda* and of two capable comedies, *A New Trick to cheat the Devil* and *The City Night-Cap*, in which play it was that Fleay saw resemblances in 'the conduct of the plot, the characterisation,

---

[1] Ed. ii. 1. [2] Herbert, 31, 39, 118; cf. *Stage*, 333, 341, 393; ii. 235-7.
[3] Herbert, 39. [4] ii. 236-7, 246.

the metre, the language' to *Dick of Devonshire*[1] and in which we can see certain characteristics of Heywood that may explain Fleay's opinion. If Davenport could have sustained the pitch as the anonymous author of *Dick of Devonshire* does through five acts, he would scarcely be so obscure as he is; but indeed there is no resemblance at all between his lifeless and pedestrian work and that of our anonymous author. For some reason Bullen was not so sure of his attribution of *Dick of Devonshire* when he came to the appendix of his *Collection*, but he has no other name to offer.[2] Swinburne thought Heywood had a main finger in it,[3] a more satisfactory faith than Ward's, who first of all could see little reason for Bullen's 'not very confident' conjecture, added that signs of Heywood's authorship in the Pike scenes are discernible but none at all where Bullen discovered even clearer evidence, namely in the Manuel-Henrico story, and finishes with the unhappy theory that William Rowley may have contributed the 'realistic' picture of Henrico's lust.[4] But 'Rough Rowley, handling song with Esau's hand', though he has some emotional power at times, had no knowledge either of the subtlety of i. 3 (Henrico's assault on Eleanora), or of the large control shown in v.

The fact is that no dramatist save Heywood has any real pretensions to the play. No other dramatist besides Heywood wrote more heartily the play of adventure, especially adventure by sea. The very characters of the two plots, which are as usually in Heywood almost independent of each other, are indications of his authorship, the one a romantic and conventional tragicomedy, the other a piece of veritable dramatic journalism. In the latter the author has extracted from Pike's unadorned narrative every essential; not a significant or picturesque touch is omitted; and the manner of doing this is exactly analogous to Heywood's use of his sources in, for example, *The Captives*. From about 1620 he had fallen under the influence of the Fletcherian romance and for the rest of his career as a dramatist, though he occasionally returned to his earlier manner, he was an imitator of the fashion. In *The English Traveller*, it is true, he repeated the theme of *A Woman killed with Kindness*; and in *The Late Lancashire Witches* he fell back on mere journalism again. But in all his other plays after 1620 the Fletcherian is noticeable in plot, setting, characterization, ethics, and style. In *A Challenge for Beauty*, and *A Maidenhead well Lost*, for example, the attempt is unmistakable; and in *The Captives* he has most

[1] Quoted by Bullen, ed. ii. 4.
[2] *Collection of Old English Plays*, iv. Miss Bates, xiii, sets aside Bullen's tentative attribution.   [3] *Letters*, ii. 223.   [4] ii. 583, iii. 104.

successfully added to his own natural gifts some of the graces which he imitated. Not one of his plays, however, is wholly Fletcherian; his bourgeois intelligence saved him from the falsetto of the more polite followers of the fashion. Heywood seemed afraid, except in *A Maidenhead well Lost*, of losing touch with England and English virtues; he felt insecure without a few English characters. Now *Dick of Devonshire*, too, is a Fletcherian play by one whose good sense and very incapacity for flights saved him from the extravagance of his model; it is the play of one who would fain be in the fashion but has too bourgeois an outlook. Though the style is more uniformly poetical than in Heywood's earlier plays, it is not more sustained than in *The Captives* or *A Challenge for Beauty*, the likest of all his plays to *Dick of Devonshire*. The sentiments, the phrasing of them, and the verse in which they are cast have all the indubitable Heywood quality. The play is not allowed to float away on romantic seas, for the author has made his hero a daring English adventurer who, like Mont Ferrars and Manhurst in *A Challenge for Beauty*, and Spencer in *The Fair Maid of the West*, wins the esteem of foreigners and their women-folk. Heywood, too, combines the homely patriotism with a chivalrous justice to other nations and especially to Spaniards; in *If you know not me*, part i, Philip's sentencing to death a cowardly follower of his who had basely killed an Englishman[1] is an exact parallel to the Teniente's and Don Ferdinand's reprimand to Don John in *Dick of Devonshire* for his unmanly treatment of Dick.[2] The characterization is in every respect consistent with Heywood's methods. The Spanish grandees are sketched from the same models as the princes and nobles in *A Challenge for Beauty* and *A Maidenhead well Lost*. Stroza in the last-named play is a villain of the same components as the vicious Henrico and with something of the same history. Manuel, his great-souled brother, has kinsmen in many of Heywood's plays. Old Don Pedro belongs to the less farcical type of father in Heywood, such as old Geraldine in *The English Traveller* or John Ashburne in *The Captives*. Buzzano, not a professional clown but as so often in Heywood a comic household servant, requires no comment; his humour is of a unique brand. Lastly, the heroine, the gracious and unaffected Eleanora, is as only Heywood drew a gentlewoman.

When we descend to details of vocabulary the proofs of Heywood's hands are no less striking:[3]

[1] Pearson, i. 225. [2] Ed. Bullen, ii. 44.

[3] Fleay, ii. 237, saw 'not the slightest resemblance' to Heywood's style; he does not appear to have been very anxious to discover it.

Ed. Bullen, ii. 8:
> No he *Spanyard*
> Is not a true reioycer at the newes.

He Spanyard: cf. 'Hee Gallants', Pearson, v. 25; 'he-bawde', Γυναικεῖον, 343; 'he-
devils', 470; 'Shee-Gallants', Pearson, v. 25; 'Shee-devill', 'Shee-Catter-
waullers', 'She-mastiffe', 295; 'she-minstrel', Γυναικεῖον, 302; 'she-dancer',
303; 'she-Centaure', 386; 'he' (= man) Pearson, iii. 326; 'she' (= woman),
v. 146; see 299 *infra*.

Ed. Bullen, ii. 9:
> How long hath it bene a voyce they were at sea?

Voyce: cf. Pearson, iii. 195, iv. 289 ('lift . . . up on voyces' (= acclamations));
'voyce' (= elect), Pearson, iv. 285 and Γυναικεῖον, 186.

Ed. Bullen, ii. 13:
> *Drake*
> And his brave Gings.

Gings: cf. Pearson, ii. 306 ('a ginge of lusty lads, Such as will bravely man her'),
310, 314, vi. 414.

Ed. Bullen, ii. 15:
> all the warlike furniture . . .
> For such a mayne designe.

> a royall fleete
> Infinite for the bravery of Admiralls.

Mayne: see ed. Bullen, ii. 42, 'Our mayne offensive strength, was quite defeated';
cf. Pearson, i. 32 ('Affaires . . . of so maine consequence'), 93 ('maine
France'), ii. 180, 214, iii. 317; (noun) *Sallust (Jugurthine War)*, 4; *Troia
Britannica*, 69; see 297, 299 *infra*.
Infinite: see 261–2 *supra*.

Ed. Bullen, ii. 17:
> I did prejudicate
> Too rashly of the *English*.

Prejudicate: cf. *Sallust (Jugurthine War)*, 3 ('a prejudicate and factious humour').

Ed. Bullen, ii. 21:
> Were't not defenced, there could nothing come
> To make this cheeke looke pale.

Defenced: cf. Pearson, iv. 313 ('defenc'd with men'), Γυναικεῖον, 183, 290, 447;
'defencible' (= defended), 298.

Ed. Bullen, ii. 29:
> not a Laborinth
> Is so full of Meanders.

Laborinth: cf. Pearson, ii. 51, 113, 378 ('You wrap me in a Labyrinth of doubts');
'labyrinthean', *Troia Britannica*, 332.

Meanders: cf. Pearson, iv. 226 ('The more I strive to unwinde My selfe from this
   Meander, I the more therein am intricated'); *Life of Merlin*, 122 ('intricate
   with . . . turning *Meanders*').

Ed. Bullen, ii. 30:
   Have I a life, a soule that in thy service
   I would not wish expird ?
Expird: cf. Γυναικεῖον, 365, 460; *Hierarchy*, 381; 'expiration', Pearson, v. 360;
   Γυναικεῖον, 189; *Hierarchy*, 243, 464; *Exemplary Lives*, 143.

Ed. Bullen, ii. 45:
   'Twere a weake state-body that could not spare such members.
State-body: see 261–2, 263 *supra*.

Ed. Bullen, ii. 46:
   we all can but condole the losse of him.

   rather than heare the misse of him at home complayned.
Condole: cf. Pearson, vi. 383; *Sallust*, 36.
Misse: cf. Pearson, ii. 62.

Ed. Bullen, ii. 47:
   If the Jaylors be so pregnant what is the hangman, troe ?
Pregnant: cf. *Hierarchy*, 441, 448.

Ed. Bullen, ii. 48:
   his wifes uniust reioycings.
Reioycings: as noted on 263 *supra*, plural abstracts are very characteristic of Heywood; see 282–3, 297, 300 *infra*.

Ed. Bullen, ii. 49:
Gratulations: cf. Γυναικεῖον, 450; *Hierarchy*, 448 (sing.); 'gratulate' (= praise,
   compliment), *Apology*, 62; Γυναικεῖον, 303; *Life of Merlin*, 33 ('to gratulate with him his former victories'), 342 ('to gratulate the nuptialls'); see
   297 *infra*.

Ed. Bullen, ii. 50:
   You shall goe to see your frend there totter.
Totter (= hang): cf. Pearson, i. 72.

Ed. Bullen, ii. 52:
      when your warlike lookes
   Have outfac'd horrour.

               you have outworne
   Dangers of Battaile.
Outfac'd: cf. *Hierarchy*, 259, 577, 586 see 300 *infra*.

Ed. Bullen, ii. 53:

> she would not
> Text up his name in proclamations.

> I would wave
> My weapon ore my head to waft you forth
> To single combatt.

Text: cf. Pearson, iii. 321 ('That shall my Launce In bloody letters text upon thy breast'); Γυναικεῖον, 315; *Pleasant Dialogues*, 248; see 297 *infra*.

Waft: cf. Pearson, iv. 417 ('wafting us With their bright swords'), v. 100; *Troia Britannica*, 250 ('his hand *Ulisses* wafts for silence'), 313, 318; *Life of Merlin*, 260; 'waftage', Pearson, iii. 145, 179, 209, vi. 403; *Troia Britannica*, 115, 119, 143; *Marriage Triumph*, ed. Collier, 19; *Hierarchy*, 355.

Ed. Bullen, ii. 65:

> have not you defac'd
> That sweet & matchles goodnes, *Eleonora*?

Deface: cf. Pearson, iii. 225; Γυναικεῖον, 16.

Ed. Bullen, ii. 69:

> For we are come
> To cure your old Corruptions.

> What Leprosies
> Have run ore all your Conscience.

Corruptions, Leprosies: see 263, 282 *supra*; cf. 'leprously', *Hierarchy*, 286.

Ed. Bullen, ii. 74:

> These braves cannot save you.

Braves: see 263 *supra*.

Ed. Bullen, ii. 79:

> without mayme to's army he might loose
> A thousand men.

Mayme: cf. *Hierarchy*, 430; *Life of Merlin*, sig. B 4.

Ed. Bullen, ii. 99:

> When thy swift ship cutts through the curled mayne.

Curled: cf. Pearson, iii. 5 ('curled waves'), 180 ('curled streames'), 209 ('curled Ocean'), v. 94 ('curled flames'); *Troia Britannica*, 64, 92, 167; *Hierarchy*, 422, 440, 560.

The following usages are also worthy of note.

Ed. Bullen, ii. 14: *Boracho* (= drunkard): cf. *Philocothonista*, 44.

40: *Jovial*: cf. Pearson, iii. 50, 131, 164, 174, 180, 198; *Troia Britannica*, 147, 327.

45: *Purchase* (= prize, achievement): cf. Pearson, ii. 350, vi. 413, 414; (=gain, acquire), Pearson, ii. 263, iii. 188.

64: *Frenchify*: cf. *Life of Merlin*, 360; 'Hispanified', 'Italianated'
     Exemplary Lives, 207; *Life of Merlin*, 360.
80: *Taske* (as verb): cf. Pearson, iii. 177; see 262 *supra*.
86: *Mad* (= madden): cf. Pearson, i. 217, ii. 68, iii. 98, 111; see
     262 *supra*.
87: *Confrontation*: see 297 *infra*.

The compounds are all of the Heywood pattern: 'big-limbd' and
'well-limbd', 'soldier-like' and 'lyon-like', 'long-desired' and
'sweet-complexioned'.[1] Some of these usages are no doubt common
enough Elizabethan, but others ('text', 'curled', 'he *Spanyard*',
'waft') are by no means so; and all of them and many others
occur again and again in Heywood.

Not merely is the vocabulary Heywood's, the whole of the
dialogue is in his manner. For example, i. 2, in which the elder
merchant summarizes the relations between England and Spain,
could have been written by none but our dramatist. The movement of the verse is absolutely the same as that of v of *If you know
not me*, part ii; and as in that episode Heywood's easy metre becomes
more rapid and swinging and his words more virile, so in this scene,
though it is obviously the work of the same author as the rest, the
style quickens and becomes epical:

>   any *Englishman*
> That can but read our Chronicles can tell
> That many of our Kings and noblest Princes
> Have fetcht their best and royallest wives from *Spayne*,
> The very last of all binding both Kingdomes
> Within one golden ring of love and peace
> By the marriage of Queene *Mary* with that little man
> (But mighty monarch) *Phillip*, son and heire
> To *Charles* the Emperour. . . .[2]
> *Spaines* anger never blew hott coales indeed
> Till in Queene *Elizabeths* Raigne when (may I call him so)
> That glory of his Country and *Spaynes* terror,
> That wonder of the land and the Seas minyon,

---

[1] Ed. Bullen, ii. 16, 70, 27, 57, 54, 85; for the first two cf. Pearson, iii. 135 and
Γυναικεῖον, 264, and see 266 *supra*.

[2] Cf. *If you know not me*, Pearson, i. 202:
>   Our royal marriage, treated first in heaven,
>   To be solemnized here, both by Gods voice
>   And by our loves consent, we thus embrace.
>   Now *Spain* and *England*, two populous Kingdomes
>   That have a long time been opposd
>   In hostile emulation, shall be at one.
>   This shall be *Spanish-England*, ours *English-Spaine*.

Drake, of eternall memory, harrowed th' *Indyes*. . .
                when his Ilands
Nombre de Dios, Cartagena, Hispaniola,
With *Cuba* and the rest of those faire Sisters,
The mermaydes of those Seas, whose golden strings
Give him his sweetest musicke, when they by *Drake*
And his brave Ginges were ravished; when these red apples
Were gather'd and brought hither to be payrd—
Then the *Castilian* Lyon began to rore . . .
              When our shipps
Carrying such firedrakes in them that the huge
Spanish Galleasses, Galleons, Hulkes and Carrackes
Being great with gold, in labour with some fright,
Were all delivered of fine redcheekt Children
At *Plymouth, Portsmouth* and other *English* havens
And onely by men midwives: had not *Spayne* reason
To cry out, oh Diables *Ingleses*! . . .
A Navy was provided, a royall fleete,
Infinite for the bravery of Admiralls,
Viceadmirall[s], Generalls, Colonells and Commanders,
Soldiers, and all the warlike furniture
Cost or experience or mans witt could muster
For such a mayne designe . . .
              'Twas such a Monster
In body, such a wonder in the eyes,
And such a thunder in the eares of Christendome
That the Popes Holynes would needes be Godfather
To this most mighty big limbd Child, and call it
Th' Invincible Armado.[1]

This scene is like an echo of the Armada scenes of *If you know not me*, part ii, the work of a man who had lived through that time and was still animated by the same insular but sane patriotism, still inspired by the memory of a more heroic age.[2] Again in the following we cannot fail to see the quite individual pathos of Heywood, phrased not in far-fetched or poetical figures but in the simplest of words:

Prepare to dye! An excellent bell & it sounds sweetly. He that prepares to dye rigges a goodly ship; he that is well prepared is ready to launch forth; he that prepares well & dyes well, arrives at a happy haven. Prepare to dye! preparation is the sauce, death the meate, my soule & body the guests; & to this feast will I goe, boldly as a man, humbly as a Christian,

[1] Ed. Bullen, ii. 12, &c.
[2] Prof. Schelling (*Elizabethan Drama*, ii. 424) comments on the rarity of the 'fine old-fashioned insularity' in the period to which the play belongs.

& bravely as an *Englishman*. Oh my Children, my Children! my poore Wife & Children![1]

These two samples illustrate the Heywood quality which is so pervasive as to eliminate the possibility of a collaborator. The play is in all respects and from every point of view pure Heywood, but written in that more sustained style which we find in his plays belonging to the twenties and thirties of the seventeenth century and which, no doubt from the example of the romantic Beaumont and Fletcher, he matured in the decade before in a series of plays now lost.

[1] Ed. Bullen, ii. 71.

THE JEW OF MALTA

THE degeneration of this melodrama after the first two acts, which in their admirable presentation of Barabas open the plot in a gradual way quite at variance with the helter-skelter of v, and the chaos of iii and iv, must puzzle the careful reader. Was the play always so disappointing? Did Marlowe leave it like a snake pinned beneath a heap of rubbish, with its sinister head free and a wildly lashing tail? He was ever an erratic artist, conceiving more grandly and sensationally than he could execute, and frequently forced to group loosely about his protagonists the few episodes which in moments of lyrical fervour he had been able to invent. For it was not the involution and perfect causal nexus of a plot which thrilled him to song, but the conception of a super-human character, essentially simple, as the vast abstractions of the mind must be, and shadowy from the very distance at which one must stand to take in the colossal outlines. But even so, he was the most insecure and uncritical of lyrical dramatists, one whose utterance was but intermittently articulate. So far as his conception of Barabas is concerned, the play might finish with the second act. Certainly we can imagine no addition that will not merely repeat in another way what has gone before and that will not weaken and derogate from it. Marlowe had dreamed a grand and portentous being and would seem to have taken little thought to devise five satisfactory acts once his own desire for the creation of Barabas was satisfied; like an artist who, when he had finished his statue and seen that it was good, heaped about it in most admired disorder the encumbrances of his studio. He has set Barabas in a mass of cheap incidents, the stock devices of the hack-playwright's shop, the most commonplace of dramatic expedients. In *Tamburlaine* he never tired of posing his favourite this way and that without regard to plot or consecutiveness. In *Doctor Faustus* the main incidents are magnificently imagined, only because without them the personality of Faustus would have been insignificant. It is possible, then, that in the last three acts of *The Jew of Malta* there lies concealed the bare outline which Marlowe sketched but in which he had lost all interest and which he had abandoned in such a state as to invite the sacrilege of revision. Had *Hamlet* been presented as crudely as the story of Barabas, without the amazing impressionism of the soliloquies and the skilful suggestions of psychological development, it might have seemed as absurd to us. So far as we know Marlowe invented the plot[1] and in the play we probably still have the main incidents as originally determined, but now crowded mostly into v to make room for certain ribaldry and gruesome farce, and in consequence bereft of the explanatory power of Marlowe's poetry. One of his editors has detected throughout the play passages which he cannot deny to Marlowe, even though they are almost overwhelmed with baser ore.[2] But he seems to us too generous; we can find only a little in iii, iv, and v, which a much smaller man than Marlowe might not have produced.

Despite the crudity of the plot and its breakdown, *The Jew of Malta* is not without features in poetry, general conception, and characterization which would date it later than *Tamburlaine*. In it Marlowe still shows his weakness for the superhuman hero; but his Barabas is more mature than the ranting shepherd of Scythia. The plot, too, is no longer episodic and disconnected; and the management of the verse, the toning down of the thunderous decasyllable to a more equable and generally useful vehicle for dramatic purposes, is of importance for post-dating the play to *Tamburlaine* and *Doctor Faustus*. There is a possible allusion to the defeat of the Armada,[3] and in Marlowe's prologue, which has been unconvincingly pronounced later than the first composition of the play,[4] the Duke of Guise is spoken of as dead.[5] All the evidence, then, points to the play's having been written after 1588, probably some years after.[6] Fleay assigns it to Lord Strange's men in the period 1589–94, and conjectures that it may have been one of the old plays of the Queen's men at the Theatre in the years 1587–94.[7] The first notice we have of it is Henslowe's record of its performance at the Rose, not as a new piece, on February 26, 1591/2, between which date and June 21, 1596 it was acted thirty-six times.[8] It seems to have belonged to Henslowe and was played by most of the companies which from time to time he managed.[9]

---

[1] But see J. Kellner, *Die Quelle von Marlowe's Jew of Malta, Englische Studien*, x, and ed. Tucker Brooke, 233–4. J. A. Symonds, *Shakspere's Predecessors*, 652, suggested a possible Spanish original.

[2] Ed. Tucker Brooke, 233: cf. his *Marlowe's Versification and Style, S. in Ph.* xix. 199; and his *Marlowe Canon, P.M.L.A.A.* xxxvii.

[3] Ed. Tucker Brooke, 260.

[4] Ed. Albrecht Wagner.   [5] Died Dec. 23, 1588.

[6] Ernest Faligan (*De Marlovianis Fabulis*, 164) says 1589 or 1590; Mr. Tucker Brooke, ed. 230, 1590; and Sir E. K. Chambers, iii. 424, 1589.

[7] *Stage*, 89, and ii. 61.   [8] *H.D.* ii. 151.

[9] Chambers, iii. 424–5; but cf. Fleay, ii. 61.

His son-in-law Edward Alleyn, '*the best of Actors*' as Heywood calls him, was probably the first to play Barabas and

> wan
> *The Attribute of peerelesse, being a man*
> *Whom we may ranke with (doing no one wrong)*
> Proteus *for shapes, and* Roscius *for a tongue,*
> *So could he speak, so vary; nor is't hate*
> *To merit in him who doth personate*
> Our Jew *this day, nor is it his ambition*
> *To exceed, or equall, being of condition*
> *More modest.*[1]

The 1598 inventories of the Admiral's men include 'j cauderm for the Jewe'.[2] In 1601 it was revived by the same company and 'divers thinges' and 'more thinges' were bought for it on May 19.[3] We are unable to say how the play reached Queen Henrietta's men.

As early as May 17, 1594 the melodrama was licensed for Nicholas Linge and Thomas Millington, and the day before a ballad of '*the murtherous life and terrible death of the riche Jew of Malta*' was registered by John Danter. The publication of the play, however, may have been stayed on account of the excitement over the trial and execution of Lopez for conspiring to poison the Queen;[4] certainly no edition earlier than that of 1633 which was relicensed on November 20, 1632 has survived, and Heywood would hardly have dedicated to a friend a play already in print.[5] It is to be assumed that in the course of forty-odd years and several revivals some revision would be made on this standard melodrama of crime and revenge, an assumption which receives ample confirmation from the play itself. The text is the most corrupt of all Marlowe's plays; and though

---

[1] Heywood's prologue for the Cockpit. He refers in the last four lines to Richard Perkins who had been his friend from at least 1612 when Perkins wrote commendatory verses for *An Apology for Actors*. He played Goodlack in *The Fair Maid of the West* in 1630–1.   [2] *H.P.* 118.

[3] *H.D.* i. 137. A 'Tragödie von Barabas, Juden von Malta' was acted by English actors at Dresden in 1626 (Chambers, ii. 286; iii. 425) not necessarily the same as the play 'von dem Juden' given by English actors at Passau in 1607 and at Gräz in 1608 (*ibid.* ii. 281; iii. 425); cf. Tucker Brooke, ed. 234. *The Jew of Malta* was acted by the Phoenix Society at Daly's Theatre in November 1922.

[4] Cf. Lee, *Life of Shakespeare*, 1915, 133–4.

[5] The phrase in the dedication 'now being newly brought to the Presse' merely means 'printed for the first time' and does not imply an earlier issue, as Mr. Tucker Brooke, ed., 231, and Fräulein Margarete Thimme (*Marlowes 'Jew of Malta': Stil- und Echtheitsfragen*) suppose. Mr. Tucker Brooke admits, however, that the first edition of *Tamburlaine* was 'Now first and newlie published', and the 1592 *Faustbook* 'Newly imprinted and in convenient places imperfect matter amended'. The earliest *Love's Labours Lost* was 'Newly corrected and amended'.

Bullen thought 'Marlowe . . . not less guilty of the extravagance and buffoonery in the last three acts of the *Jew of Malta* than of the grotesque and farcical additions made to *Dr. Faustus*',[1] we scarcely need the warrant of a phrase in Heywood's court epilogue, *'We onely Act, and Speake, what others write'*, for believing that more than one hand had worked at it. We can date the revisions in 1601 and 1632, without excluding the possibility of minor alterations in other years. Of the earlier revisers we can say nothing. But everything points, as we hope to prove, to Heywood's radical revision of the play in or about 1632 and perhaps also earlier.

We have already suggested that v, now packed with incident, originally filled as well a considerable part of iv, if not all of it, and that very much more space was given to making the plot plausible. The cuts, however, are by no means all late in the play. There is an obvious one, perhaps not very long, in i. 2. The Jews are offered the alternatives of paying half their estates into the common treasury or of becoming Christians, with the certainty in the event of their refusing instant compliance of losing all they possess. Barabas is angry at his fellows for agreeing to pay half their wealth:

> GOVERNOR. Why *Barabas* wilt thou be christned?
> BARABAS. No, Gouvernour, I will be no convertite.
> GOVERNOR. Then pay thy halfe.
> BARABAS. Why know you what you did by this device?
> Halfe of my substance is a Cities wealth.
> Governour, it was not got so easily;
> Nor will I part so slightly herewithall.
> GOVERNOR. Sir, halfe is the penalty of our decree.
> Either pay that, or we will seize on all.
> BARABAS. *Corpo di deo*; stay, you shall have halfe,
> Let me be us'd but as my brethren are.
> GOVERNOR. No, Iew, thou hast denied the Articles,
> And now it cannot be recalled.[2]

A rebellious speech by Barabas at the very least must have been omitted after the second last speech of the Governor's.[3] In the same scene though the officers receive no order to seize the Jew's wealth, their entrance on their return from having done so is marked and the Governor asks,

> Now Officers have you done?
> OFFICER. I, my Lord, we have seized upon the goods
> And wares of *Barabas*, which being valued
> Amount to more then all the wealth of *Malta*.
> And of the other [sic] we have seized halfe;[4]

---

[1] Ed. i. xli.   [2] Ed. Tucker Brooke, 249.
[3] Cf. *Merchant of Venice*, iv. 1.   [4] Ed. Tucker Brooke, 250.

all of which has been done while some thirty lines have been spoken on the stage. A minor point is that Barabas calls his wealth

> the labour of my life
> The comfort of mine age, my childrens hope;[1]

yet he has already told us he has

> no charge, nor many children,
> But one sole Daughter.[2]

Again in ii. 3 when Barabas instructs Abigail to feign love to Lodowick she protests

> Oh father, Don *Mathias* is my love.
> BARABAS. I know it: yet I say make love to him;
> Doe, it is requisite it should be so.
> Nay on my life, it is my Factors hand,
> But goe you in, I'll thinke upon the account:—
> The account is made, for *Lodowicke* dyes.
> My Factor sends me word a Merchant's fled
> That owes me for a hundred Tun of Wine:
> I weigh it thus much; I have wealth enough.
> For now by this has he kist *Abigall*;
> And she vowes love to him, and hee to her.
> As sure as heaven rain'd *Manna* for the *Iewes*,
> So sure shall he and Don *Mathias* dye:
> His father was my chiefest enemie.[3]

The speech is certainly meant to be disjointed, but surely something is missing after the eighth line. We think we have discovered it later in the play.[4] Other suspicious features early in the action are the tame conclusion of the Governor's final speech in iii. 3, and the lines with which he ends scene 5 of the same act:

> So now couragiously encounter them;
> For by this Answer, broken is the league,
> And nought is to be look'd for now but warres,
> And nought to us more welcome is then wars.[5]

From the phrase of Heywood's prologue already quoted, '*We onely Act, and Speake, what others write*', Fleay was put on the scent of another hand, and decided that the Bellamira sub-plot (iii. 1, iv. 4, 5, and v. 1) was inserted by Heywood to bombast out Marlowe's short play; 'the prose shows it not to be Marlow's and the story is that of the friars in *The Captives*'.[6] But in fact the Bellamira scenes are quite separate from the episode of the friars

[1] *Ibid.* 251.   [2] *Ibid.* 245.   [3] *Ibid.* 267–8.   [4] *Ibid.* 283
[5] *Ibid.* 279–80.   [6] i. 298; cf. ii. 61–2.

and their authorship does not follow merely from a reattribution of the latter to Heywood. This episode of the strangling of Friar Barnardine by Barabas and Ithamore and the deception put on Friar Jacomo to make him believe himself guilty of the murder,[1] is exactly similar to the strangling of Friar John in *The Captives* by the Duke of Averne and Dennis his man, who pass the apparent guilt on to Friar Richard by a similar trick.[2] A few months before he dramatized the full story of the rival friars in the sub-plot of *The Captives*, Heywood had introduced it in racy and compact prose into Γυναικεῖον, pronouncing it a true story of a lady of Norwich 'which I have often heard related'.[3] We cannot, therefore, agree that the passage in *The Jew of Malta* is 'earlier and less carefully worked out than the other version' in *The Captives*, and that while Heywood in *The Captives* may be elaborating an earlier conception of his own he may equally well be plagiarizing from Marlowe.[4] Far from the episode in *The Jew of Malta* bearing any sign of early workmanship on a plot later elaborated in *The Captives*, it seems to be told in exactly the allusive way in which a person retells a story he has already told. That Heywood could not be plagiarizing from the ragged episode in *The Jew of Malta* is clear from his two versions in *The Captives* and Γυναικεῖον agreeing in every detail with the complete fabliau as it is found for example in the first of Massuccio's *Novellino*. He could not have reinvented the novella from a single scene in Marlowe, as a biologist can reconstruct a prehistoric reptile from a single bone. Nor can it be maintained that at one time the episode in *The Jew of Malta* must have been given more fully, since the play, overcrowded as it now is with incident, must have contained rather less than more in its first state.

The first of the courtesan scenes (iii. 1) opens with a soliloquy by Bellamira, who is indistinguishable from Mistress Mary in *How a Man may choose a good Wife*, as her bravo Pilia Borza is from Brabo, Mistress Mary's pander.[5] The rest of the scene is made up of the return of Pilia Borza who has managed to steal money from Barabas's house, the passing of Ithamore from delivering a forged challenge to Mathias, and his sudden infatuation for Bellamira, like young Arthur's fascination by Mistress Mary. This brief passage, preparatory to the later courtesan scenes, looks like an

---

[1] Ed. Tucker Brooke, 285–6.   [2] Ed. Judson, 93, &c., 118, &c.
[3] 253, &c.   [4] Ed. Tucker Brooke, 232.
[5] Her remark, 'Since this Towne was besieg'd, my gaine growes cold' (ed. Tucker Brooke, 271), is perhaps due to the reviser's forgetting that he had cut the siege scenes.

insertion at the beginning of the act. To make room for it the second scene appears to have been cut.

Enter Mathias.
MATHIAS. This is the place, now *Abigall* shall see
  Whether *Mathias* holds her deare or no.
        [*Enter Lodow[ick] reading.*
MATHIAS. What, dares the villain write in such base terms ?
LODOWICK. I did it, and revenge it if thou dar'st.
        [*Fight: Enter Barabas above.*
BARABAS. Oh bravely fought, and yet they thrust not home.
  Now *Lodowicke*, now *Mathias*, so;
  So now they have shew'd themselves to be tall fellowes.
(*Within.*) Part 'em, part 'em.
BARABAS. I, part 'em now they are dead: Farewell, farewell.[1]

In telescoping this important incident the reviser quite unneces-sarily makes Lodowick declare he sent the challenge which he himself is reading when he enters and which we know Barabas forged and Ithamore delivered. The courtesan plot does not break in again till iv. 2, in which Bellamira and her bravo are awaiting the result of the courtesan's invitation to Ithamore. When the latter arrives he is easily persuaded to extort money by blackmail from Barabas.[2] The most suspicious passage in the scene is Itha-more's speech in couplets,

        we will leave this paltry land,
  And saile from hence to *Greece*, to lovely *Greece*,
  I'le be thy *Iason*, thou my golden Fleece;
  Where painted Carpets o're the meads are hurled,
  And *Bacchus* vineyards ore-spread the world:
  Where Woods and Forrests goe in goodly greene,
  I'le be *Adonis*, thou shalt be Loves Queene.
  The Meads, the Orchards, and the Primrose lanes,
  Instead of Sedge and Reed, beare Sugar Canes:
  Thou in those Groves, by *Dis* above,
  Shalt live with me and be my love.[3]

Instead of this being Marlovian,[4] it is quite obviously an imitation, even a parody. In *The Captives*[5] Heywood quotes from *Hero and*

---

[1] *Ibid.* 272–3.
[2] Cf. Arthur's confession of his crime to Mary and Brabo in *How a Man may choose a good Wife*, sig. I 3v–I 4.
[3] Ed. Tucker Brooke, 289.
[4] Cf. *ibid.* 233; we are inclined to date *The Passionate Shepherd to his Love* after the first composition of *The Jew of Malta*, not before as does Mr. Tucker Brooke (*ibid.* 549).
[5] Ed. Judson, 69.

Leander, and in *The Brazen Age*[1] from *Venus and Adonis,* to which Ithamore also alludes. The remainder of iv is taken up with the inveigling from Ithamore of his knowledge of Barabas's villainy, the extortion of money from the Jew, and his visit in the disguise of a French musician to the courtesan's house. In v. 1 the Bellamira episode concludes with the courtesan and Pilia Borza's accusing Barabas before the Governor. The action then returns to the political affairs of Malta and runs on from iii. 4.

The argument, then, against Marlowe's responsibility for the present state of the play is that it is in two quite different keys. The one part consists of i, ii, v (with the exception of a fragment at the beginning), and scenes 2 and 4 of iii (the duel of Mathias and Lodowick, and the coming of the Turkish envoys for the Maltese tribute). But in what remains are presented two feeble plots carelessly jammed into the very middle of the play and grotesquely incongruous with the main interest; to accommodate them iii and iv have been badly mangled and v packed with the gist of them, a rearrangement which has rendered the originally extravagant plot altogether absurd. Even if Marlowe were capable of such buffoonery as fills iii and iv, he would surely never have devoted to it the very core of his tragedy and have pitched the central acts in prose.[2] Nor would he have substituted for the Barabas of i, ii, and v another of the name who is partly a vulgar and petty criminal, partly the ridiculous, Plautine father of Heywood's comedies, the mere accomplice of a Turkish clown who with his tags of Latin and bawdy quips is not differentiated from Dennis in *The Captives* or Nicholas in *A Woman killed with Kindness.* But the very incidents for the sake of which the tragedy has been ruined are closely paralleled in two plays, *How a Man may choose a good Wife* and *The Captives,* of the man who published *The Jew of Malta* and wrote prologues and epilogues for its revival in 1632. Though some of the contamination may be due to a revision in 1601—and, therefore, quite possibly by Heywood—there ought to be no doubt, in the face of both the stylistic and the structural evidence, that the chief blame for the corruption of the play must attach to its editor.

[1] Pearson, iii. 184–6.
[2] The only prose outside iii and iv is in i. 2 (the Governor's offer to the Jews), ii. 3 (a few short speeches, not absolutely certainly in prose), and v. 1 (Bellamira, Pilia Borza and Ithamore before the Governor).

APPENDIX IV

THE MARTYRED SOLDIER

It is doubtful if the author of this 'miracle play run to seed'[1] had any other source than a very hazy knowledge of the Vandal persecution under Hunneric (A.D. 477–84) of the African Catholics; what he owes to Procopius's *De Bello Vandalico* or to Victor Uticensis's *De Persecutione Vandalica* or to any of the other post-classical historians is negligible. Briefly, the plot tells how soon after the return to the dying Genzerick (= Genseric) of Prince Henrick (= Hunneric), Belisarius,[2] and Hubert from their victory over the African Christians, Belisarius is converted by an angel and Hubert is at least moved to admiration by the courage of the martyrs. But Henrick, now king, finding Belisarius proof against all arguments, throws him into prison, where he makes converts of his own wife and daughter, Victoria and Bellina. Another prisoner, Bishop Eugenius, is instructed by an angel to effect a miraculous cure of the king, who has been injured while hunting. This Eugenius offers to do provided that Henrick will agree to release all his Christian prisoners and receive baptism. No sooner is he cured, however, than he revokes his promise and orders Eugenius to be stoned, a command which it is quite impossible to obey for the stones all turn to sponges. By this time Hubert is deeply in love with Bellina; when he is put at the head of a punitive force against the Christians he promises to her to lead it instead against their persecutors. Victoria, Belisarius, and Eugenius having been tortured and miraculously sustained, and Henrick having been killed in the midst of his sins by a thunderbolt, Hubert enters with his army, claims the crown, and confesses himself a Christian; whereupon all not yet converted proclaim their acceptance of the faith and Bellina rewards the new king with her hand.

The play was no doubt in the main by Henry Shirley, who must have written it between the date of *The Virgin Martyr*, licensed on October 6, 1620[3] and published in 1622 (S.R. December 7, 1621), to which it owes not a little in outline and even phraseology, and 1627 when Shirley died. It was acted by Queen Henrietta's men and seems to have been written for them or for the Lady Elizabeth's company. With both troupes Heywood was associated as a regular dramatist, and in that capacity may have revised their new pieces.

---

[1] Ward, *D.N.B.*, article *Henry Shirley*.
[2] Not, of course, the general of Justinian. Procopius was at one time secretary to Belisarius and is the historian of his campaigns.   [3] Herbert, 29.

Be that as it may, a pamphlet which we have shown to be Heywood's[1] was entered in the Stationers' Register on the same day (February 15, 1637/8) and for the same fee as *The Martyred Soldier*. Both play and pamphlet were published by John Okes, for whom Heywood seems to have acted as a kind of literary agent. For not only did he provide his press with a series of pamphlets but, as has already been remarked, he probably wrote for him the preface to Rowley's *Shoemaker a Gentleman*, 1638.[2] Moreover, at the end of *The Martyred Soldier*, before the epilogue which is very much in Heywood's vein, is printed under the legend 'To the Reader of this play now come in Print' the prologue to *The Royal King and the Loyal Subject*, published by Nicholas and John Okes in 1637. The dedication of *The Martyred Soldier* to Sir Kenelm Digby is, it is true, signed 'I. K.', or in some copies 'John Kirke', who also published through John Okes his *Seven Champions of Christendom* in 1638. But the following sample[3] from the epistle 'To the Courteous Reader' is unquestionably in Heywood's vein:

the worke it selfe being now an Orphant, and wanting him to protect that first begot it, it were an injury to his memory to passe him unspoken of. For the man his Muse was much courted but no common mistresse; and though but seldome seene abroad yet ever much admired at. This worke, not the meanest of his labours, has much adorned not only one but many stages, with such a generall applause as it hath drawne even the Rigid Stoickes of the Time, who, though not for pleasure yet for profit, have gathered something out of his plentifull Vineyard.

The Golden Age, preface:
I was loath . . . to see it thrust naked into the world . . . without either Title for acknowledgement, or the formality of an Epistle for ornament.
The English Traveller, preface:
[I] *thought it not fit that it should passe* as filius populi, *a Bastard without a Father to acknowledge it.*
A Maidenhead Well Lost, preface:
the Criticall censure of that most horrible Histriomastix . . . *This hath beene frequently, and publickly Acted without exception.*
The Iron Age, part i, preface:
the Playes often (and not with the least applause,) Publickely Acted by two Companies, upon one Stage at once, and have at sundry times thronged three severall Theaters.

The play itself, too, clearly shows the hands of two authors, one, whom we would identify with Heywood, contributing little, but in a style so distinct from the other's that it is easy to see where he begins and breaks off.

The first fragments we ascribe to Heywood are two passages

---

[1] See 167, 179 *supra*.
[2] Unless we accept the unlikely explanation that Okes himself plagiarized Heywood's preface to *The Four Prentices*; see 166–7 *supra*.
[3] Quoted at 167–8 *supra*.

in i. 1, in which the yet unconverted hero Hubert rather pettishly expresses dissatisfaction at the amount of notice taken of his valour in the defeat of the Christians. These useless interruptions with their words characteristic of Heywood are more explicable as interpolations than as parts of the original design; the dialogue runs on better without them; they have no effect whatever on the plot, and when Hubert visits Belisarius in prison in iii. 3 he speaks, quite unjustifiably as the play now stands, as if there had never been a feud between them.

Ed. Bullen, i. 180:

> their bold troopes
> Affronted us with steele.

Affronted: see ed. Bullen, i. 182, 'this affronting brow'; cf. Pearson, iii. 317, 363, 401; Γνναικεῖον, 70, 146, 183; *Hierarchy*, 305, 427, 528; *Pleasant Dialogues*, 179, 263; *Exemplary Lives*, 160; 'give affront' (= give battle), Γνναικεῖον, 295; 'afront' (= quarrel), *Exemplary Lives*, 155; 'front' (= confront), *Exemplary Lives*, 179; see 284 *supra*.

Ed. Bullen, i. 182:

> where in texed letters read
> Each Pioner that your unseason'd valour
> Had thrice ingag'd our fortunes and our men
> Beyond recovery, had not this arme redeem'd you.
> when the maine Battalia
> Totter'd.
> had the foe but re-inforct againe
> Our courages had been seiz'd.

Texed: see ed. Bullen, i. 224, 'the Volume My Sword in bloody Letters shall text downe'; and 283 *supra*.
Unseason'd: cf. Pearson, vi. 364; 'season'd' (= seasonable), Pearson, iv. 143; 'seasonable', *True Discourse*, 11; 'seasonably', *Brightman's Predictions*, 2.
Redeem: cf. Pearson, ii. 295, vi. 388; *Sallust*, 42.
Maine Battalia: see ed. Bullen, i. 224 'the maine Battalia'; cf. Pearson, i. 101, iii. 233, v. 247; 'battles' (= battalions), Pearson, i. 102; *Troia Britannica*, 69; see 281 *supra*.
Courages: see ed. Bullen, i. 196, 'contentments'; and 263, 282–3 *supra*, 300 *infra*.

The homely scene (i. 2) in which Belisarius is welcomed by his wife and daughter and is converted by an angel is just such as would appeal to Heywood; but in spite of some of the usages we are not convinced he did more than revise it.

Ed. Bullen, i. 185:

> To gratulate his safe and wisht Arrival.
> Musick with her sweet-tongu'd Rhetorick.

Gratulate: see 282 *supra*.
Wisht: cf. Pearson, ii. 168.
Sweet-tongu'd: see 266 *supra*.

Ed. Bullen, i. 186:

> like commixed Whirlwindes.

Commixed: cf. Pearson, v. 137; Γυναικεῖον, 70, 332; *Hierarchy*, 310, 431, 517; 'commixtion', Γυναικεῖον, 3, 330; *Hierarchy*, 309, 310, 440.

Ed. Bullen, i. 188:

> Strike their weake Opposer into nothing.
> Centuple all that I have ever done.

Opposer: see 264 *supra*.
Centuple: cf. Pearson, i. 334.

The opening of ii. 3 is a detached conversation of the constable, the watchmen, and the clown who in the manner of Heywood's clowns has a smattering of Latin. Their dialogue is thoroughly in Heywood's style. 'If their testimonie will not satisfie', says the constable, 'here my Title: at this place, in this time, and upon this occasion I am Prince over these Publicans, Lord over these Larroones, Regent of these Rugs, Viceroy over these Vagabonds, King of these Caterpillars; and indeed, being a Constable, directly Soveraigne over these my subjects.'[1] With similar variations the clown in *Love's Mistress* gives us Cupid's 'stile in Folio: Hee is King of cares, cogitations, and cox-combes; Vice-roy of vowes and vanities; Prince of passions, prate-apaces, and pickled lovers; Duke of disasters, dissemblers, and drown'd eyes; Marquesse of melancholly, and mad-folkes, grand Signior of griefes, and grones; Lord of Lamentations, Heroe of hie-hoes, Admirall of aymees, and Mounsieur of mutton-lac'd'.[2] The same clown in another place declares '*Homer* was Honourable, *Hesiod* Heroicall, *Virgil* a Vicegerent, *Naso* Notorious, *Martiall* a Provost, *Iuvinall* a Ioviall lad, and *Persius* a Paramount'.[3] Another irrelevant comic dialogue is the discussion between the clown and the huntsmen at the opening of iii. 1 which is very similar to the conversation of the clown and the Welshman before the hunt in *The Royal King and the Loyal Subject*.[4] The remark in *The Martyred Soldier*, 'And that's enough in conscience to keepe men from going were his Boots as wide as the blacke Iacks or Bombards tost by the Kings Guard',[5] is probably a reminiscence of a sentence in *Philocothonista*, 'small Iacks wee have in many Ale-houses of the Citie, and Suburbs, tipt with silver, besides the great black Iacks, and bombards at the Court, which when the *French-men* first saw, they reported at their returne into their Countrey, that the *English-men* used to drinke out of their Bootes'.[6] A scene (iv. 1) of *The Martyred Soldier*, not

[1] Ed. Bullen, i. 198.   [2] Pearson, v. 113.   [3] *Ibid.* v. 144.
[4] *Ibid.* vi. 8–9.   [5] Ed. Bullen, i. 203.   [6] 45.

markedly in Heywood's manner, contains the second occurrence
in the play of the very rare verb 'text'[1] as well as the very unusual
'deaf' (= deafen)[2] and another passage which seems to show his
hand or finger.

Ed. Bullen, i. 224–5:

> Here the maine Battalia
> Comes up with as much horrour and hotter terrour
> As if a thick-growne Forrest by enchantment
> Were made to move, and all the Trees should meete
> Pell mell, and rive their beaten Bulkes in sunder

Maine Battalia: see 281, 297 *supra*.
Pell mell: cf. Pearson, iii. 361 ('Come let us breake into the battailes center, And
    too't pel mel'); *Hierarchy*, 134.
Bulkes: cf. Pearson, v. 249; *Troia Britannica*, 118, 121, 327; *Apology*, 20;
    Hierarchy, 4, 62, 390.

Another detached dialogue between the clown and two pagans
(iv. 2)—in it the clown quotes one of his Latin tags—is, like the
opening passages of ii. 3, iii. 1 and 2, probably an addition of the
editor-reviser. Lastly, in v. 1, in which Epidophorus comes to make
inquiries about the clown's prisoners, an interpolation has pretty
certainly been made in their conversation. After the three opening
blank verse lines of Epidophorus—

> Have any Christian soule[s] broke from my Iayle
> This night, and gone i' the dark to find out heaven ?
> Are any of my hated prisoners dead ?—[3]

the dialogue drops into prose which contains several phrases
reminiscent of Heywood and the compound 'He-Christians'.[4] At
the end of the prose ribaldry Epidophorus resumes his blank verse
as if nothing had intervened:

> CLOWN. You are not of my dyet: Would I had . . . two Loynes
>   of a pretty sweatie Christian after Supper.
> EPIDOPHORUS. Would thou mightst eate and choake.
> CLOWN. Never at such meate; it goes downe without chawing.
> EPIDOPHORUS. We have a taske in hand, to kill a Serpent
>   Which spits her poyson in our Kingdoms face
>   And that we speake not of; lives still
>   That witch *Victoria*, wife of *Bellizarius* ?

From one or two words it might seem that Heywood had touched
the rest of the play here and there also.

---

[1] See 283, 297 *supra*.
[2] Cf. Pearson, iii. 322, 337, and *Philocothonista*, 81; and see 262, 284 *supra*.
[3] Ed. Bullen, i. 239.   [4] *Ibid.* 239; see 281 *supra*.

Ed. Bullen, i. 196: *Contentments*: cf. *Phoenix of these Times,* sig. D 2; see
    263, 282–3, 297 *supra.*

    200: *Stellify*: cf. Pearson, iv. 291; *Hierarchy,* 123, 125, 126; *True
        Description,* 27; 'constelled', *Life of Merlin,* 349; 'stellation',
        Hierarchy, 138.

    201: *Ingirt*: cf. *Pleasant Dialogues,* 188, 198.

    200, 243: *Imposures, Impostures*: see 264 *supra.*

    234: *Out-brave*: see 263 *supra*; cf. 'out-face', *Hierarchy,* 259, 577, 586;
        'out-live', *Philocothonista,* 14.

    236, 251: *Supernal*: cf. Pearson, v. 148; *Hierarchy,* 272, 311, 455.

    246: *Infatigable*: cf. *Hierarchy,* 256.

A YORKSHIRE TRAGEDY AND THE MISERIES OF ENFORCED MARRIAGE

THE authorship of *A Yorkshire Tragedy* is one of the most interesting problems that the Elizabethan drama presents. A. F. Hopkinson, who in his important but uncritical prefatory essay decides without a peradventure for a Shakespearian origin, an assurance somewhat impaired by his assigning to the master *Arden of Feversham* and *Edward III* as well, gives the following apparently formidable list of authorities who have reached the same conclusion as himself with regard to the powerful little play: Steevens to whom he attributes all the virtues of a scholar and a critic;[1] Collier who was so firmly convinced of Shakespeare's responsibility that he reluctantly left the tragedy out of the first two or three editions of Shakespeare which he superintended, but later included it among the authentic plays;[2] Ward;[3] Swinburne;[4] and Fleay;[5] and others of less authority. 'The opinion of such men as these', says Hopkinson, 'is of more value than the opinion of a whole regiment of dull-witted critics or biographers.'[6] But Steevens, of whom Courthope declared that only a scholar so devoid of critical insight could have imagined *A Yorkshire Tragedy* was Shakespeare's,[7] found Shakespeare's hand proved by nothing more convincing than 'his quibbles, his facility in metre, and his struggles to introduce comic ideas into tragic situations'.[1] Collier's opinion was that the tragedy should rank with *Pericles* and *The Two Noble Kinsmen* as a play in which Shakespeare had 'had a main finger'.[2] Ward can discover Shakespeare only in the best prose passages;[3] and Swinburne, after rejecting altogether any theory of Shakespeare's collaboration—a critical judgement no less worthy of note than is his later opinion—finally pronounced 'this lurid little play' a genuine work of the master.[4] As for Fleay, who too often allowed his aesthetic judgement to be overruled by external evidence, his first theory was that the author was Edmund Shakespeare under his elder brother's direction;[8] then he ascribed it to Drayton;[9] and at last, protesting his 'intense difficulty to admit that Shakespeare wrote this little play about the zenith of his power', he unwillingly fell back, in face of the external evidence, on the

---

[1] Malone's *Supplement*, ii. 675.
[2] *Athenaeum*, Mar. 7, 1863: cf. *The History of English Dramatic Poetry*, ii. 438–9.
[3] ii. 231.   [4] *A Study of Shakespeare*, 143–4, 232.   [5] ii. 206.
[6] Ed. Hopkinson, xxviii; reprinted in *Essays on Shakespeare's Doubtful Plays*.
[7] ii. 240.   [8] *Shakespeare*, 303.   [9] i. 138.

conclusion that *A Yorkshire Tragedy* was Shakespeare's ending for
The Miseries of Enforced Marriage, though he refused to abandon
his search for a more likely claimant.[1] Hopkinson's authorities,
therefore, are scarcely so formidable as he had imagined; and in
spite of his malicious suggestion we can cite critics quite as distinguished from among the anti-Shakespearians. The list might
almost begin with the names of Ward, Swinburne, and Fleay; then
would come Pope, who thought the tragedy 'a wretched play';[2]
Malone hesitatingly admitted Steevens's ascription in the preface
to his *Supplement*, but later confessed his inability to believe that
Shakespeare could have written *Macbeth, King Lear*, and *A Yorkshire Tragedy* during the same period;[3] and Farmer could not
imagine the mature Shakespeare producing 'so mean a performance';[4] Hazlitt who knew as well as most men the true Shakespearian note could not detect it in *A Yorkshire Tragedy*;[5] and to
these may be added the names of Halliwell-Phillips,[6] Tyrrell,[7]
Knight,[8] J. A. Symonds,[9] Courthope,[10] F. W. Moorman,[11] Sir
Sidney Lee,[12] Messrs. Tucker Brooke,[13] Dobell,[14] Sykes,[15] and Sir
E. K. Chambers.[16] The balance of modern critical opinion is at
least decidedly against Shakespeare's authorship.

Other quite tentative attributions have been made by Hazlitt
to Heywood,[17] by Bullen to Tourneur,[18] by Sir Sidney Lee to Heywood or Tourneur,[19] and by Mr. Dobell to Wilkins,[20] whose claims
have been more adequately urged by Mr. Sykes.[21]

Of the last-mentioned dramatist comparatively little is known,
and his work is so inextricably involved with that of other men,
except in his prose pamphlets, that it is impossible to pronounce any
particular passage to be pure Wilkins. What was probably his first
appearance in print was a tract on *The Three Miseries of Barbary*:

---

[1] ii. 206–8.   [2] *Shakespeare*, 1728, i. xxiv.   [3] *Supplement*, ii. 675.
[4] Malone's *Supplement*, ii. 675.
[5] Ed. Waller and Glover, i. 356, v. 289, x. 117.
[6] *Outlines of the Life of Shakespeare*, ed. 1887, i. 223–4.
[7] *Doubtful Plays of Shakespeare*, 81–3.   [8] *Pictorial Shakespeare*, viii. 253–4.
[9] *Shakspere's Predecessors*, 422.   [10] ii. 240.
[11] *Plays of Uncertain Authorship attributed to Shakespeare*, C.H.E.L. v. 243.
[12] *Transactions of the New Shakspere Soc.*, 1887–92, 34; *D.N.B.* article *Walter
Calverley*; and *Life of Shakespeare*, 1915, 404.
[13] *Shakespeare Apocrypha*, xxxiv–v; and *The Tudor Drama*, 365–6.
[14] *The Author of A Yorkshire Tragedy*, *N. & Q.* 10th Series, vi. 41.
[15] *Sidelights on Shakespeare*, 76, &c.   [16] iv. 55.
[17] Ed. Waller and Glover, i. 356, x. 117; cf. Tyrrell, *op. cit.* 83.
[18] Cited by Hopkinson, xxxii.
[19] *Transactions of the New Shakspere Soc.* 1887–92, 34.
[20] *Op. cit.* 41.   [21] *Op. cit.* 77.

Plague, Famine, and Civil War, about 1606–7. His *Miseries of Enforced Marriage* was written in 1605 and printed in 1607 (S.R. July 31). In the same year he collaborated with Dekker in *Jests to make you merry* and with Day and William Rowley in *The Travels of Three English Brothers* for Heywood's company.[1] In 1608 he produced his romance, *The Painful Adventures of Pericles, Prince of Tyre*, based on the play. Mr. Sykes finds traces of his work, too, in Day's *Law Tricks*, 1608,[2] and, as other have done, in *Pericles*;[3] and he would attribute to him the first part of *Two unnatural Murthers*, 1605 (S.R. June 12), which is dramatized in *A Yorkshire Tragedy*, though it is by no means clear why so undistinguished a piece of journalism required two authors. The style of the first part, according to Mr. Sykes, 'is that of *The Painful Adventures of Pericles*, the author revealing his identity by his frequent antitheses and his trick of balancing one clause of a sentence against another, with more regard to sound than sense'.[4] Even if we grant a resemblance between the styles of the two prose pamphlets, it does not in the least follow that the same author wrote *A Yorkshire Tragedy*. The prose of *Two unnatural Murthers* is a kind of degenerate euphuism, one of the contemporary varieties of journalese; it is totally different from the virile, idiomatic, and dramatic prose of *A Yorkshire Tragedy*. Wilkins was never more than a hack with very little talent. The dramatic sense revealed in *The Travels of Three English Brothers* or in the parts of *Pericles* probably his is childish and the characterization feeble. He had some command over realism, as can be seen in the brothel scenes in *Pericles* or the tavern scenes in *The Miseries*, but his characters are only animated puppets. It is curious that Mr. Sykes, who holds that *A Yorkshire Tragedy* was probably on the same subject as the 'foure plaies in one' mentioned in the heading of *The Tragedy*, supposes the first three to have been lost; but as *The Miseries* is on the same theme, 'It would therefore not be strange', he adds, 'if [Wilkins] should be found to have had a hand in another play dealing with the later and concluding episodes of Calverley's career'.[5] It is highly improbable, however, that Wilkins handled the same

[1] Fleay, ii. 207–8, accounts for Wilkins's transference of his services to the Queen's men by surmising a quarrel with Shakespeare. Hopkinson, x–xi, is of the opinion that *The Miseries*, despite the title-page, was written for the Queen's men.   [2] *Op. cit.* 79, 86, 145, 169.

[3] *Op. cit.* 78, &c., 143, &c.; cf. Lee, *Life of Shakespeare*, 1915, 404, 407–8; Delius, *Über Shakespeares Pericles, Prince of Tyre, Shakespeare-Jahrbuch*, 1868, 175, &c., and R. Boyle, *On Wilkins's Share in Pericles, Transactions of the New Shakspere Soc.* 1880–5, pt. ii. 323, &c.

[4] *Op. cit.* 97.   [5] *Ibid.* 77–8.

subject three several times; that is to say in a pamphlet and in two plays acted by the same company. Nor do we consider adequate Mr. Sykes's explanation of the differences between the styles of the *Tragedy* and *The Miseries*, that the former was written too hurriedly for Wilkins to luxuriate in his cheap antitheses.[1] There is an obvious duality of style in the surviving fragments of the *Four Plays in One*, as Mr. Sykes admits. He is not certain, therefore, 'that Wilkins was the sole author of the *Tragedy*, for it contains one or two passages . . . that would seem to be beyond the power of the hand that wrote *The Miseries*':[2] and what more natural than that Shakespeare, who had worked with Wilkins on *Pericles*, should have added 'the few magic touches that have dazzled the judgement of so many of its critics'?[3]

The sensational crime dramatized in *A Yorkshire Tragedy* took place on April 23, 1605 at Calverley Hall, when Walter Calverley, the representative of a highly respected county family and an ancestor of Charles Stuart Calverley, murdered his two elder children and dangerously wounded his wife, but was himself fortunately taken before he could reach his youngest child. On June 12 the reading public was offered a narrative of *Two most unnatural and bloody Murthers: The one by Master Coverley, a Yorkshire Gentleman, practised upon his wife, and committed upon his two Children, the three and twenty of April 1605. The other, by Mistress Browne, and her servant Peter, upon her husband, who were executed in Lent last past at Bury in Suffolk. 1605.* This crude effort appeared before the trial, at which Calverley, in order to save the family property for his surviving child, stoically refused to plead, though he was aware that the inevitable consequence of his refusal would in his case be death by pressing. On August 24, three weeks after the sentence had been carried out, Nathaniel Butter, the licensee of the first pamphlet, entered at Stationers' Hall another, *The Arraignment, Condemnation, and Execution of Master Caverley at York in August 1605.* The crime was also worked up into a ballad licensed for Thomas Pavier on July 3 and was narrated by Howes in his continuation of Stowe's *Annals*.[4] The dramatic version, which follows the first-mentioned pamphlet very closely, was evidently ready before the trial,[5] as can be inferred from the fact that no use was made of Calverley's fortitude in refusing to plead.

The registration of the play, however, was delayed till May 2, 1608 when Thomas Pavier received a licence for 'A booke Called

<hr>

[1] *Op. cit.* 77.　　[2] *Ibid.* 77.　　[3] *Ibid.* 93.　　[4] Ed. 1615, 870–1.
[5] Cf. Collier, *Athenaeum*, Mar. 7, 1863. Hopkinson, ed. ii, dates the play early in September and at any rate not later than the end of the year.

A Yorkshire Tragedy by Wylliam Shakspere', which appeared soon
after as *A Yorkshire Tragedy. Not so New as Lamentable and true.
Acted by his Majesty's Players at the Globe. Written by W. Shakespeare.* Neither the theatre nor the company is mentioned in the
1619 quarto. On August 4, 1626 the widowed Mrs. Pavier made
over the copyrights of her husband's share in Shakespeare's plays
or any of them to E. Brewster and R. Bird, including apparently
A Yorkshire Tragedy, which Bird on November 8, 1630 resigned
with the copyrights of some other plays to R. Cotes. Now Pavier
was probably the most rascally publisher of his day, and Hopkinson's
attempts to whitewash him are not successful.[1] He was William
Jaggard's partner in the abortive project to issue in 1619 a collected
edition of Shakespeare's plays, for which were printed quartos of
The Merry Wives, Pericles, and *A Yorkshire Tragedy,* all dated 1619,
and of *A Midsummer Night's Dream, The Merchant of Venice,
Sir John Oldcastle* (ascribed for the occasion to Shakespeare), *King
Lear, Henry V,* and *The Whole Contention of York and Lancaster* with
false dates and bearing in some cases the names of publishers and
stationers quite innocent of the fraud. There is the irrefutable
evidence of Henslowe's *Diary* that one of these plays, *Sir John
Oldcastle,* was the work of Drayton, Hathway, Munday, and
Wilson. Hopkinson's explanation of the ascription to Shakespeare,
that it was probably made by Drayton or the company, ingeniously
shifts the blame from Pavier, whose good faith he is concerned to
defend.[2] But as the 1600 quarto appeared without Shakespeare's
name and with the statement that the play had been acted by the
Admiral's men with whom Shakespeare had no connexion, and as
by 1619 neither Drayton nor the Admiral's men would be much
interested in the venture, we must convict Pavier of a deliberate
forgery. The other attributions of *Pericles, The Whole Contention,*
and *A Yorkshire Tragedy* were sufficiently uncertain for the editors
of the first folio to reject these plays from the Shakespeare canon.
Apparently Pavier found it profitable to deal in pseudo- or doubtfully Shakespearian pieces; and we cannot think that he was acting
with any better faith as regards *A Yorkshire Tragedy.* As for the
peculiarity in the licence, it was undoubtedly very unusual to give
the names of the authors of plays entered in the Stationers' Register;
only in nineteen cases are the authors mentioned between 1584
and 1616 although 188 plays were licensed during that period.
Hopkinson notes that three of the nineteen, *Henry IV,* part ii, *King
Lear,* and *A Yorkshire Tragedy,* were ascribed to Shakespeare, which

---

[1] Ed. xiii–xiv.   [2] *Ibid.* xiv.

he takes to be a strong argument for Shakespeare's authorship of the last play, since the ascription, if untrue, 'would be senseless and to no purpose, as the entries in the registers were not made public'.[1] But an examination of the three licences proves that the scribes merely copied the title-pages of the quartos. Besides, if the addition of the author's name to the licence was exceptional, the pro-Shakespearians must show why it was entered in the licence for *A Yorkshire Tragedy*. Surely it might reasonably be maintained that Pavier was taking no risks and deliberately inserted the name of the poet to whom the proposed quarto was to be attributed on its publication; once the play had been so attributed the ascription would stick. As an important offset to its inclusion in the 1664 and 1685 folios may be set its exclusion from the folios of 1623 and 1632. The publishers of the later folios, like the cataloguers and compilers of the seventeenth and eighteenth centuries, cannot be regarded as witnesses at all; their evidence is merely hearsay. If *A Yorkshire Tragedy* was omitted from the first folio because Heming and Condell failed to come to terms with Pavier, it is curious that they nevertheless were able to print from Pavier's quarto of *A Midsummer Night's Dream*. In fact of course if the editors of the first folio had wanted to include *A Yorkshire Tragedy*, they could have used the acting version or even the author's manuscript, as they must have done for the twenty plays published for the first time in 1623, as well as for several of the others. In any case Pavier was associated in 1619 with William Jaggard, one of the parties to the publication of the 1623 folio. The fact is that to Heming and Condell must be given the credit of publishing nothing as Shakespeare's in which he had not an important share, and of omitting nothing except *Pericles* in which every one agrees he had a hand. Why they did not include that romance is quite another problem and does not concern us here.

It was not customary to write short plays such as *A Yorkshire Tragedy* except as one of a group like Beaumont and Fletcher's *Four Plays or Moral Representations in One*; and indeed the headtitle of the tragedy now under discussion is *All's One, or, One of the four Plays in one, called a Yorkshire Tragedy: as it was played by the King's Majesty's Players*. It is not clear from this whether *A Yorkshire Tragedy* was the name of the group. But P. A. Daniel noticed that the 'yong Mistrisse' in scene 1 of *A Yorkshire Tragedy*, who is said to deplore her absent lover, is not the Wife of the piece and is not referred to again; that this first scene has nothing to do with the rest of the play; that *The Miseries of Enforced Marriage*

[1] Ed. xii–xiii.

dramatizes the earlier history of Walter Calverley; and that the aforesaid scene 1 of *A Yorkshire Tragedy* should occur in *The Miseries* between scenes 1 and 2 of ii.[1] *The Miseries of Enforced Marriage. As it is now played by his Majesty's Servants,* licensed on July 31, 1607 and printed the same year as by George Wilkins and again in 1611, 1629, and 1637,[2] tells how Scarborow (= Calverley), already betrothed to Clare, daughter of Sir John Harcop, is forced by his guardian Lord Faulconbridge and his uncle Sir William Scarborow to marry Faulconbridge's kinswoman Katherine; in the company of his dissolute friends he learns to neglect his wife; when, shortly before his arrival in Yorkshire, Clare hears from him of his marriage she dies of a broken heart; Scarborow then renounces his wife and returns forthwith to London; his extravagances there soon force his two younger brothers, John and Thomas, and the family butler to turn footpads and rob Sir John Harcop; the butler tricks Sir Francis Ilford, one of Scarborow's worthless companions, into marrying Scarborow's sister; meanwhile Scarborow has gone from bad to worse; but to end the play happily the dramatist, without any preparation, introduces Ilford and his wife reconciled, whereupon Scarborrow as suddenly repents and receives his wife again. But *The Miseries* had been registered as a tragedy, and there is little reason to doubt that, together with *A Yorkshire Tragedy,* it constituted the *Four Plays in One.* William Scarborow and Katherine are respectively the Husband and Wife of *A Yorkshire Tragedy.* Dr. Baxter, who pleads with Scarborow to mend his ways, is the Master of a College in the playlet. The 'yong Mistrisse' of the *Tragedy,* scene 1, is of course Clare, and Sam, who brings news of the Husband's marriage in the same scene, is the clown in *The Miseries* who carries Scarborow's letter to Clare. The uncle whom the Wife visits in London is evidently the Lord Faulconbridge of *The Miseries.* The Knight of scenes 8 and 9 of the *Tragedy* appears to be Sir William Scarborow, though the First Gentleman in scene 9 also speaks to the Husband with avuncular authority. The Butler of *The Miseries* is probably the

---

[1] *Athenaeum,* Oct. 4, 1879.

[2] Fleay, *Shakespeare,* 49, 148–9, absurdly dates *The Miseries,* 1603–4; but in ii. 275, he dates it as not earlier than 1605. According to Collier (*New Particulars regarding the Works of Shakespeare,* 44), there is a ballad derived from the play in Jordan's *Royal Arbour of Loyal Poesy,* sig. Dd 2v–Dd 3. Mrs. Aphra Behn's adaptation, *The Town Fop,* was published in 1677. *The Fatal Extravagance,* acted and published in 1720, and republished much enlarged in 1726, used the plot of *A Yorkshire Tragedy;* the real author was Aaron Hill, who allowed the needy Joseph Mitchell to publish it as his own. A (?) translation of the original play was staged in 1904 at St. Petersburg.

lusty Servant who wrestles with the Husband in the *Tragedy*, scenes 5 and 6. John Scarborow is the university brother of the Husband in the *Tragedy*. Perhaps Sir John Harcop, Thomas Scarborow, Sir Francis Ilford, Bartley, and Wentley correspond to the various Gentlemen in the short play. Further certain motifs in the *Tragedy* are begun in *The Miseries*. Thus the Husband's repeated abuse of his wife as a whore and his children as bastards results from Scarborow's protest against marrying Katherine after a pre-contract to Clare:

> I have done so much, that if I wed not her,
> My marriage makes me an Adulterer,
> In which blacke sheets, I wallow all my life,
> My babes being Bastards, and a whore my wife.[1]

In *A Yorkshire Tragedy*, scene 2, the Husband accuses a Gentleman of being his Wife's paramour; in *The Miseries*, v. 1, the same charge is levelled by Scarborow against the Butler. The idea of demoniacal possession is first suggested in *The Miseries*, and Scarborow whips himself to the same anguish as the Husband in *A Yorkshire Tragedy*, till he is in the mood to commit the murders, instead of repenting of his wrongs to his wife at the mere sight of Ilford and his lady reconciled.

As we have already remarked, P. A. Daniel did something to disintegrate *A Yorkshire Tragedy* by showing that scene 1 ought really to occur in *The Miseries* immediately before Clare's reception of Scarborow's fatal letter, that is between ii. 1 and 2. We would continue the process of disintegration and suggest that scene 2 of the *Tragedy* should follow Sir William Scarborow's delivery of a letter in *The Miseries*:

> Great busines for my soveraigne hasts me hence,
> Onely this Letter from his Lord and *Guardian* to him,
> Whose inside I do gesse, tends to his good.[2]

It apparently summons Scarborow's wife to London, whence in the third scene of the *Tragedy* the Wife has just returned with the good news that her uncle is

> reddy to prefer him to some office
> And place at Court, A good and sure reliefe
> To al his stooping fortunes: twil be a meanes, I hope,
> To make new league between us, and redeeme
> His vertues with his landes.[3]

It seems clear, moreover, that all the work of Wilkins's collaborator has not been removed from *The Miseries*. The author of the vigorous but unpleasant brothel scenes in *Pericles* might have drawn

---

[1] Sig. B 3v.   [2] Sig. K.   [3] Ed. Tucker Brooke, 255.

Thomas Scarborow and Ilford and his companions, and have conceived the realistic tavern scenes, the robbing of Sir John Harcop,
and the gulling of Ilford by the Butler. But in the 'little gem of a
play within a play—which might fittingly be called Love's Tragedy'
Hopkinson finds traces of another than Wilkins,[1] to whom we
certainly find it difficult to credit such a passage as this:

> O but good uncle could I command my love,
> Or cancell oaths out of heavens brazen booke,
> Ingrost by God's own finger, then you might speake.
> Had men that lawe to love as most have tonges
> To love a thousand women with, then you might speake.
> Were love like dust lawful for every Wind,
> To beare from place to place, were oaths but puffes,
> Men might forsweare themselves, but I do know,
> Tho sinne being past with us, the acts forgot,
> The poore soule grones, and she forgets it not.[2]

But be this Wilkins's or not, the clown Robin, whom we identify
with Sam in scene 1 of the *Tragedy* and whose only other appearances are in i. 1 and ii. 1 of *The Miseries*, is, we feel sure, not
part of Wilkins's contribution to the *Four Plays in One*. In the first
scene in which he appears in *The Miseries* he merely presents
Harcop's letter to Scarborow and is sent back with Scarborow's
reply to Clare. In ii. 1 to Sir John Harcop, John, and Thomas
Scarborow, and Clare the clown enters singing:

> From London am I come, tho not with pipe and Drum,
> Yet I bring matter, in this poore paper,
> Will make my young mistris, delighting in kisses,
> Do as all Maidens will, hearing of such an ill,
> As to have lost, the thing they wisht most,
> A Husband, a Husband, a pretty sweet Husband,
> Cry oh, oh, oh, and alas, And at last ho, ho, ho, as I do.[3]

Though the characters already on the stage had been wondering
when Scarborow would return, no notice is taken of the clown
except by Clare, who in an aside to him whispers,

> I would not have my father nor this Gentlemen,
> Be witnes of the comfort it doth bring.[4]

When Thomas speaks—is he 'this Gentlemen'? and why is John
the elder not mentioned?—his words are a continuation of the
conversation and run on from the line before the clown's entrance.
Now this clown has the peculiarities of Heywood's clowns, including a smattering of Latin.[5] After the delivery of the letter he dis-

[1] Ed., viii.   [2] Sig. B 4.   [3] Sig. C 3ᵛ.
[4] Sig. C 3ᵛ.   [5] See 256–7 *supra*.

appears from the play, even though the robbing of Sir John Harcop (a later addition to bombast out Wilkins's share in *Four Plays in One* to five acts) supplied an excellent excuse for his reappearance. The collaborator most likely to have written the clown's part was the author of *A Yorkshire Tragedy*, in scene 1 of which most of it is actually found; and the dramatist whose clowns are indistinguishable from this one was Heywood.

Fleay and Hopkinson take the four movements of the *Four Plays in One* to have been the tragedy of Clare (i. 1, 2; ii. 1, 2), the debauchery of Scarborow (iii. 1, 2, 4), the comedy of Ilford and Scarborow's sister (iii. 3; iv. 1, 2; v. 1), and the tragedy of Scarborow.[1] But the second of the four plays probably presented as well the episode of the younger brother's bond for Scarborow. The comedy of Ilford and Scarborow's sister is closely bound up with the robbing of old Harcop, which is certainly a patch to fill one of the gaps caused by the disruption of the *Four Plays*. There are indications in the first place that when the composite play was drafted Scarborow was to have only one brother, as in the pamphlet on Calverley's crime, and secondly that Thomas Scarborow was at first Thomas Harcop. In accordance with *Two unnatural Murthers*, the husband in *A Yorkshire Tragedy* declares that 'In my seede five are made miserable besides my selfe: my ryot is now my brothers iaylor, my wives sighing, my three boyes peniurie, and mine owne confusion';[2] and in the same scene the Master of a College informs the Husband how 'that hopefull young gentleman, your brother, whose vertues we all love deerlie . . . lies in bond executed for your debt . . . a man who profited in his divine Imployments, mighte have made ten thousand soules fit for heaven'.[3] But in *The Miseries* John Scarborow, somewhat of a moralizer at the beginning of the play, has not signed any bond for his elder brother, is not cast into prison, and is not at all a 'hopefull young gentleman', but plays the footpad with Thomas and the Butler. John, however, is the more seriously minded of the two younger brothers; 'From Oxford am I drawne', he says, 'from serious studies'.[4] Thomas is a jester and a wit. It is worth noticing that when anything has to be done or any remark of importance has to be made it is always John who acts and speaks. As has already been pointed out, Clare in ii. 1 says to the clown,

I would not have my father nor this Gentlemen,
Be witnes of the comfort it doth bring;

[1] ii. 207; and ed. vi.   [2] Ed. Tucker Brooke, 257.
[3] *Ibid.* 256.   [4] Sig. C 3.

the 1637 quarto has 'these Gentlemen'.[1] Again in ii. 1 Scarborow says, apparently to Thomas,

> For Charity have care upon your father,
> Least that greefe, brings on a more mishap;

in the 1611 and 1637 quartos 'your father' is awkwardly altered to 'that father'. It seems, then, that Wilkins for the sake of the addition of the robbing of Harcop to the plot had to alter entirely John Scarborow's character and make Harcop's son Scarborow's younger brother. The gulling of Ilford has also been rehandled and rather maltreated; it was probably at first another illustration of the miseries of enforced marriage with a more effective *dénouement* than the sudden reconciliation of Ilford and his wife. At present iv and v are very awkwardly divided; but if scene 1 of iv, which belongs to the episode of the footpads and is, therefore, a later addition to the plot, were removed, the gulling of Ilford would all fall into iv and we should no longer have the Butler, the prime mover of the action, in Yorkshire in iv. 1 and suddenly transferred to London in iv. 2. The whole of the last act, moreover, would thus be left for scenes 3-10 of *A Yorkshire Tragedy*. The present fifth act of *The Miseries* is in the main an unintelligible plagiarism of the *Tragedy* with an incongruous happy ending.

It is on the whole likely that *A Yorkshire Tragedy* was never performed separately, even though its head-title promises the piece 'as it was plaid'. On the other hand, *The Miseries* was almost certainly acted in its present form. The explanation of the disruption of the *Four Plays in One* is probably the fact that Mrs. Calverley was the grand-daughter of the actor's old enemy, Lord Cobham, whose family, despite his attainder in 1603, would still be influential enough to secure the inhibition of the more offensive parts of a play on so lurid a piece of their private history. Wilkins thereupon made his share of the composite play tolerable to the authorities and disguised its reference to Calverley 'by introducing throughout a large admixture of romance, giving fictitious names to the personages of the story, discarding the final scenes dealing with the circumstances of the crime and converting his tragedy into a "comedy" by substituting the brief scenes of reconciliation with which it now closes, using only such of the material of the three short plays formerly introductory of the final tragedy as was adaptable to his purpose'.[2] Then Pavier, laying his hands on the manuscript of the discarded fifth act and one or two of the other scenes as well, suppressed the names

---

[1] Sig. C 3v; cf. sig. Kv 'Ile aske him Whether a Cormorant may . . . see his brother [*sic*] starve.'   [2] Sykes, *Sidelights on Shakespeare*, 95.

and published the fragment as one of the *Four Plays in One* 'called A York-shire Tragedy as it was plaid'. *The Miseries* and the *Tragedy* are now poles apart. The latter is domestic, sensational, homely, terrible, pathetic, vivid, and careless of outward grace. *The Miseries* opens as a kind of city comedy with three needy gallants in the foreground waiting to pluck a pigeon and airing satirical views on women; and in the admirable tavern scenes, in the duping of Ilford, and in the robbing of Harcop it is anything but domestic and sentimental. None of the characters is really suitable for domestic drama; Clare is too lively and voluble, too much a figure from high comedy, and the rest are all out of place in a tragedy of the home. Even Scarborow is a domestic protagonist only through the misfortunes which overtake him, while the wife, instead of being a central figure as in the domestic drama proper, is kept entirely in the background.

In rebutting Heywood's claims to *A Yorkshire Tragedy* Hopkinson makes the most of Fleay's stock argument in such cases that our dramatist as a member of the Queen's company could not have written the play for the King's.[1] But Heywood wrote for Derby's men while he was still a covenant servant of Henslowe and the Admiral's company.[2] Even after he had become a sharer in Worcester's company he wrote *The London Florentine*, part i, in collaboration with Chettle for the Admiral's.[3] His *Rape of Lucrece* and *The Silver Age* were performed at court by the King's and the Queen's men in conjunction, and *The Iron Age*, if not also all the other *Ages* as well, was acted by two companies 'uppon one Stage at once'.[4] There is no reason, therefore, why Heywood in 1605 should not have assisted Wilkins in the composition of the *Four Plays in One*. Domestic tragedy was not in Shakespeare's line nor, so far as we can judge, in Wilkins's either; Heywood, on the other hand, was an acknowledged master of the *genre*.

The internal evidence for Shakespeare's authorship Hopkinson admits to be less weighty than the external. Nevertheless, he believes the style, thought, expression, and phraseology to be Shakespearian.[5] It is another Shakespeare, then, one with whom we are not familiar. Where in *A Yorkshire Tragedy*, we would ask, is the Shakespearian διάνοια, the depth and variety of his comments on life? Where are the searching glances into the springs of conduct? that web of shot figures in which every word is verily a picture? and where the unparalleled diversity, plenitude, and soaring poetry? Hopkinson

---

[1] Ed. xxxi.   [2] See 13 *supra*.   [3] See 35–6 *supra*.   [4] See 48, 64–5 *supra*.
[5] Ed. xix–xxi.

would make good his case by the Wife's opening speech in scene ii, 'What will become of us? all will awaie'[1] and compares the doubtfully Shakespearian *Timon of Athens*, ii. 2:

> No care, no stop! so senseless of expense,
> That he will neither know how to maintain it,
> Nor cease his flow of riot.[2]

The Wife's speech, it should be noted, is merely a versification of the prose of *Two unnatural Murthers*. So also are the two speeches of the Husband, 'If mariage be honourable, then Cuckolds are honourable'[3] and 'Oh thou confused man! they pleasant sins have undone thee',[4] which Hopkinson bids us compare with the prose in *Hamlet* and *As You Like It*. 'No reader', he says, 'moderately conversant with the plays of the great dramatist can fail to recognize the unmistakable style, thought, and expression of the Master. The same kind of thing is rampant throughout the play.'[5] It is nothing of the kind; after these occasional flashes the style is decidedly awkward, as in the Husband's speech in the last scene, also marked out by Hopkinson for commendation:

> Heer's weight enough to make a heart-string crack.
> Oh, were it lawfull that your prettie soules
> Might looke from heaven into your father's eyes,
> Then should you see the penitent glasses melt,
> And both your murthers shoote upon my cheekes;
> But you are playing in the Angells lappes,
> And will not looke on me,
> Who void of grace, kild you in beggery.
> Oh that I might my wishes now attaine,
> I should then wish you living were againe,
> Though I did begge with you, which thing I feard:
> Oh, twas the enemy my eyes so bleard.
> Oh, would you could pray heaven me to forgive,
> That will unto my end repentant live.[6]

'How say you, reader,' asks Hopkinson, 'do not these samples smack of the witchery of the great Master who wrote *Romeo*, *King Lear*, and *Cymbeline*?'[7] Let us set beside them, then, a passage in prose from *Hamlet*, ii. 2, and another in verse from *King Lear*, v. 3:

I have of late—but wherefore I know not—lost all my mirth, forgone all custom of exercises: and indeed it goes so heavily with my disposition that this goodly frame, the earth, seems to me a sterile promontory, this most excellent canopy, the air, look you, this brave o'erhanging firmament, this

---

[1] Ed. Tucker Brooke, 252. [2] Ed. Hopkinson, 38.
[3] Ed. Tucker Brooke, 252–3. [4] *Ibid.* 256–7.
[5] Ed. xix. [6] Ed. Tucker Brooke, 260. [7] Ed. xx.

majestical roof fretted with golden fire, why, it appears no other thing to me than a foul and pestilent congregation of vapours. What a piece of work is man! how noble in reason! how infinite in faculty! in form and moving how express and admirable! in action how like an angel! in apprehension how like a god! the beauty of the world! the paragon of animals! And yet, to me, what is this quintessence of dust?

> No, no, no, no! Come, let's away to prison:
> We two will sing like birds i' the cage:
> When thou dost ask me blessing, I'll kneel down
> And ask of thee forgiveness: so we'll live,
> And pray, and sing, and tell old tales, and laugh
> At gilded butterflies, and hear poor rogues
> Talk of court news; and we'll talk with them too,
> Who loses and who wins; who's in, who's out,
> And take upon's the mystery of things,
> As if we were God's spies: and we'll wear out,
> In a wall'd prison, packs and sects of great ones,
> That ebb and flow by the moon.

There is not much here of the true but conventional and predictable sentiment of the Husband in *A Yorkshire Tragedy*, with which we would rather compare this from *A Woman killed with Kindness*:

> Away, be gone.
> She is well borne, descended Nobly;
> Vertuous her education, her repute
> Is in the generall voice of all the Countrey
> Honest and faire; her carriage, her demeanor
> In all her actions that concerne the love
> To me her husband; modest, chaste, and godly.
> Is this all seeming Gold plaine Copper?
> But he, that *Iudas* that hath borne my purse,
> And sold me for a sin: Oh God, oh God,
> Shall I put up these wrongs?;[1]

or this:

> A generall silence hath surpriz'd the house,
> And this is the last doore. Astonishment,
> Feare, and amazement beate upon my heart,
> Even as a madman beats upon a drum:
> O keepe my eyes you heavens before I enter,
> From any sight that may transfix my soule:
> Or if there be so blacke a spectacle,
> Oh strike mine eyes starke blinde. Or if not so,
> Lend me such patience to digest my greefe,
> That I may keepe this white and virgin hand,
> From any violent outrage, or red murther.[2]

---

[1] Pearson, ii. 120–1.   [2] *Ibid.* ii. 137.

It is a failing of those who claim the play for Shakespeare that they seem to allow no poetry to any of his contemporaries. But even the minor dramatists constantly surprise and delight us. Much has been made of the fine prose in *A Yorkshire Tragedy*, and some who refuse the whole play to Shakespeare attribute to him a few sentences. But in fact the prose is not better than Heywood could command; it is poetical and even imaginative, but by an economy of means foreign to Shakespeare; it has the restraint, almost the stammering conquest of a less sure artist than Shakespeare of the difficulties of appropriate utterance. And the poetry of the play, pure and limpid as it is, is never more than a trickle.

If one were asked how Shakespeare would have treated such a theme, the reply might be that if he chose such a subject 'the less Shakespeare he'. *Othello* is a domestic tragedy of a sort, based on a sordid story of real life. But there could scarcely be imagined a drama of domestic infelicity so different from *A Yorkshire Tragedy*. *Othello*, with its political background and the music of the distant drum, is poetic, ennobling the sordid not merely by the wonders of its style but even more by its magnificently tragic conception of life; it is unsentimental yet poignant as the grief of a strong man, full of incident and complex in causation and characterization. *A Yorkshire Tragedy*, on the other hand, is poetic only intermittently, and with the poetry of naïve realism, the poetry of a '*prose* Shakespeare'. It is bare in outline, simple in structure and tragic causation, not transcending life but rejecting all save the irreducible data, and this not on artistic grounds but from the obvious inability of the dramatist to deal effectively with the many facts of a complex existence; it is childish in its philosophy and tragic exegesis, sentimental and moving us by pathos not by tragic intensity, commonplace in language and provincial in significance.

So far from *A Yorkshire Tragedy* being Shakespearian in the evolution of the plot, the conduct of the action, and the characterization, it is thoroughly Heywoodian or Heywooden. It was not Shakespeare's practice to tell a story in this forthright and downright manner, but it was Heywood's, who was fearful of omitting any step. Shakespeare as a rule avoided short scenes containing only a few curt speeches and abundance of action; there is much in the *Tragedy* which we are sure he would have excised to leave room for his entirely different methods. The play is not 'a model of constructive skill . . . and in that respect well worthy of standing beside those plays of Shakespeare's which preceded and succeeded it'.[1]

[1] Ed. Hopkinson, xx.

Such effect as the plot has depends entirely on its close following of the prose narrative. If the various scenes had been interrupted as in Heywood's other plays by a more or less incongruous secondary plot, no one would have discovered any extraordinary excellence in the conduct of the action. And the ramshackle *English Traveller* or *A Woman killed with Kindness* would appear as skilfully constructed, rapid, and dramatically logical as *A Yorkshire Tragedy* if their underplots were bodily removed. The characterization never once reminds us of Shakespeare, whereas it constantly recalls Heywood. Ralph, Oliver, and Sam are the typical, gossiping servants of Heywood, bawdy in talk, good at heart, and intensely interested in their master's affairs, with nothing much to do but provide the broad humour. The loyalty of the nameless Servant of scene 3, his intimacy, his confidential allusion to the Wife's unhappiness are as characteristic of Heywood's domestics, Pipkin in *How a Man may choose a good Wife*, Jockie in *Edward IV*, and the clowns in *If you know not me*, part i, *Dick of Devonshire, A Challenge for Beauty, The Rape of Lucrece*, and other plays. The quaintly expressed sympathy of Pipkin for Mrs. Arthur might almost be substituted for that of the Servant in *A Yorkshire Tragedy*, scene 3: 'Whither Mistresse, to the Chaunge? . . . I will Mistresse, hoping my M. will goe so oft to the Chaunge, that at length he will chaunge his minde, and use you more kindly, ô it were brave if my Maister could meete with a Marchant of ill ventures to bargaine with him for all his bad conditions.'[1] The Master of a College, the various country gentlemen, the Knight, and the maid are the usual supernumeraries of Heywood's plays. Like Heywood and unlike Shakespeare the author, intent only on the Husband and the Wife and with no surplus attention to bestow elsewhere, leaves the subordinate figures to appropriate what characters they can from the parts they have to play. Like Heywood and unlike Shakespeare he gives us no facts that reveal each figure as a human being looking before and after, having a history and existence before he is called into the circle of the play. Except the mention of the Husband's university brother, which in any case was suggested by the pamphlet, the drama takes place in a system of its own, air-tight and self-contained. There are no ramifications which link it to the outside world. We are not tempted to wonder how any of the persons in it lived before. Hamlet, the companion of Yorick, the fellow-student of Horatio, the lover of Ophelia, the courtier, soldier, scholar, or Maria, the youngest wren of nine, or Falstaff, the page

[1] Sig. A 4.

to Thomas Mowbray, Duke of Norfolk, and the once slender law-student—these are characters whose histories before they appear on the stage we sometimes try to invent. But *A Yorkshire Tragedy* is so complete in itself as to have no need of the three other plays on Calverley's earlier history. This, as we have said, is Heywood's dramatic method; he leaves no loose ends from which the imagination flies off; his plays are not, as Shakespeare's are, like a cobweb that joins the solid earth and the horns of the moon.

Of the Husband and the Wife more must be said, for such characterization as there is is concentrated in them. Their striking resemblance to young Arthur and his wife in *How a Man may choose a good Wife* is itself almost proof of Heywood's authorship. The Husband's character is made up of the same ingredients as young Arthur's, coarseness, pride, selfishness, and brutality; and though the earlier play ends happily, his progress is the same from debauchery and irrational hatred of his wife through an attempt on her life to sudden repentance and reconciliation in the end. The Wife is another of Heywood's loving, submissive women of whom Mrs. Arthur is the best example. Like her and like Luce in *The Wise Woman* she is the patient wife, even as the merciful Frankford, Matthew Shore, and Mr. Generous in *The Late Lancashire Witches* are forgiving husbands. Like Mrs. Arthur she bears all her husband's insults with a quiet dignity and restraint; like her she pleads if not for his love, at least for a show of it, a few kind words; like her she resents the interference of others in the domestic turmoil and loyally denies the charges of officious friends against her husband; like her she pursues him with her love even after the attempted murder, and as do Mrs. Arthur, Luce, Shore, Generous, and Frankford, she wins her erring spouse to a complete repentance:

> HUSBAND. How now? kind to me? did I not wound thee,
>   left thee for dead?
> WIFE. Tut, farre greater wounds did my brest feele:
>   Unkindnes strikes a deeper wound then steele;
>   You have been still unkinde to mee.
> HUSBAND. Faith, and so I thinke I have:
>   I did my murthers roughly, out of hand,
>   Desperate and suddaine, but thou hast deviz'd
>   A fine way now to kill me, thou hast given mine eies
>   Seaven woonds a peece.[1]

Surely this is *A Husband killed with Kindness*.

Heywood specialized in themes of domestic discord, especially the infidelity of a husband or a wife to a loving partner with whom

[1] Ed. Tucker Brooke, 260.

the erring one is reconciled at the end of the play. In *Edward IV*
the husband reclaims the wife; in *How a Man may choose a good
Wife* the wife wins back the husband. A year or two later Heywood
in *A Woman killed with Kindness* gave us the classical instance of the
unfaithful spouse forgiven. *The English Traveller* and *The Late
Lancashire Witches* are variations on the same theme; *The Wise
Woman* is a lighter treatment of it; in *The Rape of Lucrece* it is an
innocent adultery in which both husband and wife are blameless;
in the sub-plot of *The Captives* the wife's loyalty is proof against
temptation and in consequence the action is grimly farcical; in
Dick of Devonshire the husband-to-be violates his future wife; in
A Challenge for Beauty the unjust suspicion cast on Bonavida's
betrothed nearly leads to his death; lastly in *The Iron Age* and *Love's
Mistress* the ancient stories are domesticated to suit Heywood's
homely talent. The whole conception of *A Yorkshire Tragedy* and
the spirit which animates the play are utterly different from the
work of any other dramatist but Heywood; his plays are nearly
all in one way or another domestic, for he looked at life from
the family circle and to him the greatest thing in the world was the
home. The reconciliation in the last scene of the *Tragedy* has no
parallel except in Heywood's own theatre, the reconciliations of
Matthew and Jane Shore, of Frankford and his wife, of young
Arthur and his wife, of Master and Mistress Generous. The
simple pathos, so elemental, so independent of the choice of words,
so true even in its baldest simplicity, is not finer than Frankford's
heart-rending repetition of his wife's name 'O *Nan*, O *Nan*', or
Mrs. Frankford's moving words to her lute 'We both are out of
tune, both out of time'.[1]

Hopkinson devotes a great deal of attention to metrical and
kindred tests but makes less capital out of them than his patience
deserved. According to his unprofitable metrical survey 'the 409
blank verse lines place it before and near to "King Lear"; the 200
prose lines would class it with the same play, although there would be
a nearer approach to "Measure for Measure"'. The proportion of
rhymed lines 'places it between "Romeo" and "Richard II"'; so,
adds Hopkinson, 'the prose test and the rhyme test clash'. But the
unstopped-line test dates *A Yorkshire Tragedy* at the end of
Shakespeare's second period and the feminine ending 'restore it
to its original place near "Macbeth" and "King Lear"',[2] where of
course somehow or other it must be dated. Mr. Sykes, on the
other hand, finds proof of Wilkins's authorship in the proportions

---

[1] Pearson, ii. 140, 149.   [2] Ed. xxii.

of end-stopped lines and rhymes, the repetition in the second line of a couplet of a word in the first, the partiality for lines ending in -tion, pronounced as a dissyllable, and in other mannerisms which may more properly be called syntactical.[1] In his examination of *Pericles* Mr. Sykes gives as other characteristics of Wilkins the mingling of blank verse and prose, the introduction of rhyme into blank verse, and the frequent use of the same rhymes.[2] As good a case as this for Wilkins might be made out for any Elizabethan dramatist. The verse of *A Yorkshire Tragedy*, capable, flexible, serviceable, not particularly delicate, but never harsh, strongly iambic but otherwise undistinguished, not markedly enjambed, not noticeably end-stopped, frequently interrupted by prose, is such as can be found anywhere in Heywood. Heywood was always partial to rhyme and introduced it even within the limits of a speech, a practice which all but a few playwrights abandoned after the turn of the century[3] and which is well illustrated in *A Yorkshire Tragedy*. More characteristic of Heywood, as well as of the author of the *Tragedy*, than of most of the other dramatists is his habit of breaking up verse between two or more speakers. Another trick of Heywood's is to finish a speech with a rhymed couplet followed by an unrhymed line, sometimes defective in the number of feet; it occurs frequently in the *Tragedy*. Mr. D. L. Thomas notices how often Heywood rhymes a decasyllabic line to a shorter;[4] there are at least six examples of this in the *Tragedy*. Wilkins, we notice, uses prose, not according to the matter discussed, but according to the characters speaking; thus Thomas Scarborow, Ilford and his companions, and the Butler all but invariably use prose, whereas the other characters in *The Miseries* speak in verse. But in the *Tragedy* prose and verse are used indifferently, so far as we can tell from the corrupt text, by all the characters except the servants in scene 1. Moreover, the author seems to prefer verse in the very passages which are nearest to his prose source. Similarly in *Dick of Devonshire*, which follows its source with the same fidelity, Heywood versified what he took from the prose pamphlet. Lastly, Wilkins rhymes words in -m with words in -n, and always appears to be counting the beats of his verse on his fingers; needless to say Heywood was too experienced a metrist to exhibit any such awkwardnesses, and the author of *A Yorkshire Tragedy* was as accomplished.

Other characteristics of Wilkins's style are, according to Mr. Sykes, certain elliptical constructions including the omission of the

---

[1] *Sidelights on Shakespeare*, 80-3.   [2] *Ibid.* 150-9.
[3] D. L. Thomas, *On the Play Pericles, Englische Studien*, xxxix. 232-3.
[4] *Ibid.*

relative pronoun, the frequent use of 'tricks', 'dust' (= money), 'this voice' (= this opinion), and 'why' to preface a speech;[1] to which may be added from the same critic's essay on *Pericles*[2] the immoderate use of antitheses, especially of 'soul' and 'body', and the repetition of a word within a line. We are not convinced by Mr. Thomas's ingenious argument that Heywood had a hand in *Pericles*;[3] but far from his being ruled out, as Mr. Sykes supposes,[4] by the infrequency of the omitted relative in his work, his claim would rather be reinforced. In fact, however, the suppressed relative is characteristic of the whole period. The other ellipses alluded to above are quite common and the words cited by Mr. Sykes are all frequent in Shakespeare and his contemporaries, while the repetition of a word within a line is of no consequence. The verbal antitheses, we are told, 'run riot all through *The Miseries of Enforced Marriage* and the Wilkins part of *The Travels*, and they crop up every now and then in *A Yorkshire Tragedy*, obviously a hasty production which Wilkins had not the leisure to trick out'.[5] But these cheap graces are surely the *clichés* of the rapid writer, not flowers of rhetoric demanding time for their elaboration. Moreover, *The Miseries* was written in as great a hurry as *A Yorkshire Tragedy* and *The Travels* surely as hastily as either, for it was entered at Stationers' Hall (June 29, 1607) as having been acted only three weeks after the pamphlet on which it was based.

The relation of *A Yorkshire Tragedy* to *Two unnatural Murthers* is not uninteresting in this connexion. Unlike *The Miseries* the short play follows the prose narrative slavishly. Mr. Sykes finds the relation between play and source 'as close as that between the play of *Pericles* and the prose *Painful Adventures of Pericles*'.[6] But as a matter of fact, the *Tragedy* bears quite a different relation to *Two unnatural Murthers*; for in the one case the play was based on the prose pamphlet, whereas the romance of *Pericles* was based on the play. It was easy for Wilkins to throw the dialogue of the play *Pericles* into prose, but it demanded far greater skill to adapt the narrative of *Two unnatural Murthers* for the dialogue of *A Yorkshire Tragedy*. Again, though the pamphlet gives the earlier history of Calverley, the dramatist of *The Miseries* not only refrains from incorporating passages in his play but departs completely from it; and this not because the pamphlet did not lend itself to dramatization but because Wilkins's methods were entirely different from those of his collaborator. The latter's faithfulness to his source,

---

[1] *Op. cit.* 80–5, 150–2.
[2] *Ibid.* 153–6.
[3] See 333 *infra*.
[4] *Op. cit.* 150, note 1.
[5] *Ibid.* 152.
[6] *Ibid.* 98.

his inclusion of every picturesque detail, his insertion of passages with but little change, and the skill with which the essentials are detached from the accessories are characteristic of Heywood's dramaturgy. Even so he treats the novellas dramatized in *The Captives* and *The English Traveller*; even so he condenses Plautus or Caxton in *The Ages*; and, most striking of all, in exactly the same way he extracted the marrow of Richard Pike's *Three to One* for *Dick of Devonshire*.

It is not strange that Mr. Sykes finds a number of parallels between the *Tragedy* and *The Miseries*; the wonder would rather be if there were none. Let us compare, however, the much more remarkable parallels to Heywood's acknowledged work. *A Yorkshire Tragedy* and *How a Man may choose a good Wife* are both plays of matrimonial discord and in both we see the results of early injudicious marriages

> This tis to marry children when they are yong,
> I said as much at first, that such yong brats
> Would gree together, even like dogs and cats.[1]

A Yorkshire Tragedy, ed. Tucker Brooke, 252–3:

WIFE. What will become of us? all will awaie.
My husband never ceases in expence,
Both to consume his credit and his house;
And tis set downe by heavens iust decree,
That Ryotts child must needs be beggery.
Are these the vertues that his youth did promise?
Dice, and voluptuous meetings, midnight Revels,
Taking his bed with surfetts: Ill beseeming
The auncient honor of his howse and name!
And this not all: but that which killes me most,
When he recounts his Losses and false fortunes,
The weaknes of his state soe much deiected,
Not as a man repentant but halfe madd,
His fortunes cannot answere his expence:

How a Man may choose a good Wife, sig. B:

My husband hath of late so much estrang'd
His words, his deeds, his heart from me,
That I can sildome have his company:
And even that sildome with such discontent,
Such frownes, such chidings, such impatience,
That did not truth & vertue arme my thoughts,
They would confound me with dispaire & hate,
And make me runne into extremities.
Had I deserved the least bad looke from him,
I should account my selfe too bad to live,
But honouring him in love and chastitie,
All iudgements censure freely of my wrongs.

Sig. C^v:

My husband in this humor, well I know

---

[1] *How a Man may choose a good Wife*, sig. A 3.

He sits and sullenly lockes up his
    Armes,
Forgetting heaven looks downward,
    which makes him
Appeare soe dreadfull that he frights
    my heart,
Walks heavyly, as if his soule were
    earth:
Not penitent for those his sinnes are
    past,
But vext his mony cannot make them
    last:—
A fearefull melancholie, ungodly sor-
    row. . . .
He saies I am the cause; I never yet
Spoke lesse then wordes of duty, and
    of love. . . .
Good sir, by all our vowes I doe be-
    seech you,
Shew me the true cause of your dis-
    content.

Plaies but the unthrift, therefore it
    behoves me
To be the better huswife here at home,
To save and get, whilst he doth laugh
    and spend:
Though for himselfe he riots it at
    large,
My needle shall defray my housholds
    charge.

254–5:

        but, alasse,
Whie should our faults at home be
    spred abroad?
Tis griefe enough within dores. At
    first sight
Mine Uncle could run ore his prodi-
    gall life
As perfectly, as if his serious eye
Had nombred all his follies:
Knew of his morgadg'd lands, his
    friends in bonds,
Himselfe withered with debts: And in
    that minute
Had I added his usage and unkindnes,
Twould have confounded every
    thought of good:
Where now, fathering his ryots on his
    youth,
Which time and tame experience will
    shake off,
Gessing his kindnes to me (as I
    smoothd him
With all the skill I had) though his
    deserts
Are in forme uglier then an unshapte
    Beare,
Hee's reddy to prefer him to some
    office
And place at Court. . . .

Sig. D 2:
Father you do me open violence
To bring my name in question, and
    produce
This gentleman and others here to
    witnesse
My husbands shame in open audience:
What may my husband thinke when
    he shall know
I went unto the Iustice to complaine.

Sig. E 3:
You are deceiu'd he is not unkind,
Although he beare an outward face
    of hate,
His hart and soule are both assured
    mine.

Sig. E 4:
Admit my husband be inclin'd to
    vice,
My vertues may in time recall him
    home,
But if we both should desp'rate runne
    to sinne,
We should abide certaine distruction.
But hee's like one that over a sweet
    face
Puts a deformed vizard for his soule,
Is free from any such intent of ill:

Oh, heaven knowes
That my complaintes were praises, and best wordes
Of you and your estate: onely my friends
Knew of our morgagde Landes, and were possest
Of every accident before I came.
If thou suspect it but a plot in me
To keepe my dowrie, or for mine owne good
Or my poore childrens: (though it sutes a mother
To show a naturall care in their reliefs)
Yet ile forget my selfe to calme your blood.

Only to try my patience, he puts on
An ugly shape of black intemperance.
Therefore this blot of shame which he now weares,
I with my praiers will purge, wash with my teares.

253–4:

Still doe those loathsome thoughts Iare on your tongue?
Your selfe to staine the honour of your wife,
Nobly discended! . . .
But of all the worst:
Thy vertuous wife, right honourably allied,
Thou hast proclaimed a strumpet.

Ibid. 252–3:

Oh! most punishment of all, I have a wife. . . .
Ha done, thou harlot,
Whome, though for fashion sake I married,
I never could abide; thinkst thou thy wordes
Shall kill my pleasures? Fal of to thy friends,
Thou and thy bastards begg: I will not bate
A whit in humour! midnight, still I love you,
And revel in your Company. Curbd in,
Shall it be said in all societies,
That I broke custome, that I flagd in monie?
No, these thy iewels I will play as freely
As when my state was fullest. . . .
I will for ever hould thee in contempt,

Sig. A 2:

Oh M. *Arthur*, beare a better thought
Of your chast wife, whose modesty hath wonne
The good opinion and report of all:
By heaven you wrong her beautie, she is faire:
Is she not loyall, constant, loving, chast,
Obedient, apt to please, loth to displease,
Carefull to live, chary of her good name,
And iealous of your reputation?
Is she not vertuous, wise, religious?
How you should wrong her to deny all this?

Cf. also sigg. B, B 2, and G 4.

Sig. A 2:

I tell you true Sir, but to every man
I would not be so lavish of my speech,
Only to you my deare and private friend,
Although my wife in every eye be held
Of beautie and of grace sufficient,
Of honest birth and good behaviour,
Able to winne the strongest thoughts to her,
Yet in my mind I hold her the most hated
And loathed obiect that the world can yeeld.

And never touch the sheets that cover thee,
But be divorst in bed till thou consent,
Thy dowry shall be sold to give new life
Unto those pleasures which I most affect. . . .
    shal I want dust & like a slave
Weare nothing in my pockets but my hands
To fil them up with nailes?
Oh much against my blood! Let it be done.
I was never made to be a looker on,
A bawde to dice; Ile shake the drabbs my selfe
And make em yeeld. . . .
I hate the very howre I chose a wife: a trouble, trouble! three children like three evils hang upon me. Fie, Fie, fie, strumpet & bastards, strumpet and bastards!

Sig. B 2:

If thou wilt pleasure me, let me see thee lesse,
Greeve much: they say griefe shortens life,
Come not too neare me, till I call thee wife.
And that will be but sildome. I will tell thee
How thou shalt winne my hart, die sodainly,
And Ile become a lustie widower:
The longer thy life lasts the more my hate,
And loathing still increaseth towards thee.
When I come home & find thee cold as earth,
Thē wil I love thee: thus thou knowst my mind.

253:

Sir, doe but turne a gentle eye on me,
And what the law shall give me leave to do
You shall command.

255:

Consume it, as your pleasure counsels you,
And all I wishe eene Clemency affoords:
Give mee but comely looks and modest wordes.

Sig. I 2:

Not have my will, yes I will have my will,
Shall I not goe abroad but when you please?
Can I not now and then meete with my friends,
But at my comming home you will controule me?
Marrie come up . . .
Why you Iacke sauce, you Cuckold, you what not,
What am I not of age sufficient
To go and come still when my pleasure serves,
But must I have you sir to question me?
Not have my will? yes I will have my will.

Sig. A 3:

All you perswasions are to no effect,
Never alledge her vertues nor her beautie,
My setled unkindnes hath begot
A resolution to be unkind still,
My raunging pleasures love varietie.

Sig. B:

Sweet husband, if I be not faire enough
To please your eye, range where you list abroad,
Only at comming home speake me but faire.

Sig. I 3:

Be unto me as I was to my wife,
Onely give me what I denied her then,
A little love, and some small quietnesse.

260–1:

Heer's weight enough to make a heart-string crack.
Oh, were it lawfull that your prettie soules
Might looke from heaven into your fathers eyes,
Then should you see the penitent glasses melt,
And both your murthers shoote upon my cheekes;
But you are playing in the Angells lappes,
And will not looke on me,
Who void of grace, kild you in beggery.
Oh that I might my wishes now attaine,
I should then wish you living were againe,
Though I did begge with you, which thing I feard:
Oh, twas the enemy my eyes so bleard.
Oh, would you could pray heaven me to forgive,
That will unto my end repentant live. . . .

Dearer then all is my poore husbands life:
Heaven give my body strength, which yet is faint
With much expence of bloud, and I will kneele,
Sue for his life, nomber up all my friendes,

Sig. B 2:

But that my soule was bought at such a rate,
At such a high price as my Saviours bloud,
I would not sticke to loose it with a stab.
But vertue banish all such fantasies.
He is my husband and I love him well,
Next to my owne soules health I tender him:
And would give all the pleasures of the world,
To buy his love if I might purchase it.
Ile follow him, and like a servant waite,
And strive by all meanes to prevent his hate.

Sig. Iᵛ–I 2:

And yet, and yet, and still, and ever whilst I breathe this ayre:
Nay after death my unsubstantiall soule,
Like a good Angell shall attend on him,
And keepe him from all harme.
But is he married, much good do his heart,
Pray God she may content him better farre
Then I have done: long may they live at peace,
Till I disturbe their solace; but because

To plead for pardon [for] my deare
husbands life. . .

Was it in man to woond so kinde a
creature?
Ile ever praise a woman for thy sake.

I feare some mischiefe doth hang ore
his head,
Ile weepe mine eyes drie with my
present care,
And for their healths make hoarse
my toong with praier.

The Captives, ed. Judson, 148:

My self in person posted to the Kinge
(In progress not farr off), to him
related
The passadge of your busines, neather
rose I
From off my knees till hee had sign'd
to this.

How a Man may choose a good Wife,
sig. Iv–I 2:

Art sure she is a woman: if she be,
She is create of Natures puritie. . . .
O yes I too well know she is a woman,
Henceforth my vertue shall my love
withstand,
And on my striving thoughts get the
upper hād.

The parallelism between *A Yorkshire Tragedy* and *How a Man may choose a good Wife* is the more sustained because of the similarity of their plots; but had space permitted we might have cited the equally striking likeness between scene 10[1] and the reconciliations in *Edward IV, A Woman killed with Kindness,* and *The Late Lancashire Witches,* or, to choose a parallel of a different kind, between scene 1[2] and the welcome of Ganymede, disguised as Socia, by the servants in *The Silver Age.*[3] To account for the next parallel Steevens and Hopkinson[4] had to postulate an earlier edition of *Philocothonista,* which, however, was licensed on May 26, 1635 and published for the first and only time the same year:

A Yorkshire Tragedy, Tucker Brooke, 252:

SAM. But, Ralph, what, is our beer sower this thunder?
OLIVER. No, no, it holds countenance yet.
SAM. Why, then, follow me; Ile teach you the finest humor to be drunk in. I learnd it at London last week.

Philocothonista, chap. xii:

Of a new order of drinking lately come up amongst us, call'd a drinking Schoole or Library. The degrees taken in the Schoole: The Tongues and Bookes which they studdy, with the severall titles proper to the Professors of that Art.

[1] Ed. Tucker Brooke, 260–1.
[3] Pearson, iii. 99–100.

[2] *Ibid.* 251–2.
[4] Ed. 37.

AMBO. I faith, lets heare it, lets heare it.

SAM. The bravest humor! twold do a man good to bee drunck in't; they call it knighting in London, when they drink upon their knees.

AMBO. Faith, that's excellent.

SAM. Come, follow me: Ile give you all the degrees ont in order.

Ibid. 256:

Had not drunkennes byn forbidden, what man wold have been foole to a beast, and Zany to a swine, to show tricks in the mire?

Chap. xiii.:

Their phrases borrowed from severall Courts, with the places of dignity usurpt by them, both Civill and Martiall.

Cf. also chap. xiv -xvi.

The explanation of the frontispiece:

Calves, Goates, Swine, Asses, at a Banquet set,

To graspe Health's in their Hooffs, thou seest here met;

Why wonder'st thou oh Drunkard, to behold

Thy brothers? In whose ranke thou art inrowl'd,

When thou (so oft, as toxt at any Feast)

Can'st bee no better held, then such a beast,

Since, like *Cyrcæan* Cups, Wine doth surprise

Thy sences, and thy reason stupifies.

6:

These are most ridiculous and nasty, . . . who oft times stumbling, lie wallowing, in the kennells, and so appeare no other then *Hoggs* and swine, newly come durty and dawbed out of the puddles, and such may be called . . . *Scrophæ,* and *Scrophi pasci. i.* Sowes, or sowe-feeders.

Still more interesting is the fact that the fifth chapter of Heywood's *Curtain Lecture,* 1637, is on *The miseries of enforced contracts*: 'Others will enforce them', he says, 'to marry where themselves like, and not where their children love; the effects of which are commonly discontent and misery (for inequality either in yeeres, fortunes, or affections, is the roadway to spouse-breach and divorce): for where there is disunion of hearts there must needs be disorders in the house. . . . How often have forced contracts been made to add land to land, not love to love? . . . which hath beene the occasion that men have turned monsters, and women devills . . . I forbeare to instance any for in nomination of the dead I might perhaps give distast to such of the kinred who yet survive . . . . Further, who shall but follow the Circuit in the Countrey, besides these trialls here in the City, shall seldome find a generall Assises without some evidence or other given upon the like tragicall accidents.'[1] Only two years before in *The Hierarchy* he had alluded to various domestic tragedies in which 'the husband had killed his wife, the wife slaine her husband, and both of them their children';[2] and in *Philocothonista*, 1635, he actually alludes to Calverley and the play: 'One Master *Coverlee*, a gentleman of quality and good discent, in the like distemper wounded his Wife and slew his own Children; whom I am bolder to nominate, because the facinerous act hath by authority bin licensed to be acted on the publicke Stage.'[3]

The phraseology of *A Yorkshire Tragedy*, as can be seen from the passages quoted above, is absolutely in Heywood's vein, simple and direct but with the usual sprinkling of unfamiliar usages, all of which are common in our dramatist's authenticated work.

We have, then, no hesitation in awarding Heywood the full credit of *A Yorkshire Tragedy*, and in addition a share in the earlier episodes of *Four Plays in One*, of which share there survive perhaps only the two appearances of the clown in *The Miseries of Enforced Marriage* and in scenes 1 and 2 of *A Yorkshire Tragedy*. Perhaps the tragedy of Clare Harcop is better than Wilkins usually achieved; but whether for once he surpassed himself or another securer poet assisted him in it, we are on the whole not inclined to attribute any of it to Heywood.

---

[1] 99, &c.   [2] 34.

[3] 87. *A Yorkshire Tragedy* is full of verbal reminiscences and echoes of Shakespeare, which of course Hopkinson, xix, takes as confirmations of his general argument. But in fact they carry no more weight than the line from the *Sonnets* (xciv. 14) quoted verbatim in the pseudo-Shakespearian *Edward III* (ed. Tucker Brooke, 79). In reference to the Husband's quotation (*ibid.* 257),

> Divines and dying men may talk of hell,
> But in my heart her severall torments dwell,

from Nashe's *Pierce Penniless* (ed. McKerrow, i. 157), Simpson (*On some Plays attributed to Shakespeare, Transactions of the New Shakspere Soc.* 1875, pt. i, 163) notes that five different plays exhibiting Greene or Peele or Nashe in a ludicrous or offensive way have been attributed to Shakespeare. But surely the author of *A Yorkshire Tragedy* was, if anything, rather paying Nashe a compliment. The same couplet occurs with slight modifications in Nicholson's *Acolastus* and Marston's *Insatiate Countess*, ed. Bullen, iii. 225.

PLAYS MISATTRIBUTED TO HEYWOOD

Captain Thomas Stukeley, 1605 (S.R. August 11, 1600), was almost certainly based on 'stewtley', a new play of the Admiral's men on 11 (10) December, 1596,[1] and may indeed be that piece with less alteration than has sometimes been assumed.[2] The most recent suggestion is Mr. J. Q. Adams's that the 'magnificent Stukeley scenes' are Heywood's,[3] a theory which Miss Bates[4] and Miss Otelia Cromwell[5] find convincing. 'Stewtley' was certainly produced soon after the Admiral's men bought 'hawodes bocke' in the autumn of 1596.[6] But in reading the play carefully we could not catch the unmistakable sound of Heywood's voice.[7]

The Cunning Lovers; see under *George a Greene*.

The Life of the Duchess of Suffolk, 1631 (S.R. November 13, 1629), a degenerate chronicle of which the incidents are fictitious though many of the characters are historical, seems to have been written, if we may judge from the parallels, in sincere admiration of *If you know not me*, part i, after its revival in or about 1623.[8] The author of the play was undoubtedly Thomas Drue or Drew,[9] of whom such facts as are known are given by Mr. W. J. Lawrence in *The Times Literary Supplement*, March 23, 1922. The misattribution to Heywood, begun by Archer in 1656 and Kirkman in 1661 and 1671, was repeated by Winstanley and Langbaine, beyond whom Mr. Lawrence does not trace it, and so passed on to their successors until Collier corrected it in the 1825 edition of Dodsley.

George a Greene, 1599 (S.R. April 1, 1595) and *The Cunning Lovers*, 1654, have been tentatively claimed for Heywood by Mr. E. H. C. Oliphant[10] because in the 1639 list of plays confirmed to Beeston's Boys the first occurs immediately before *Love's Mistress* and the second between *Love's Mistress* and *The Rape of Lucrece*. As *George a Greene* was an old play when presented by Sussex's

[1] *H.D.* i. 44, 50–3; ii. 181. [2] Cf. Chambers, iv. 47.
[3] *Captain Thomas Stukeley, Journal of English and Germanic Philology*, xv.
[4] xii. [5] *Thomas Heywood*, 205.
[6] See 10 *supra*. [7] For other attributions see Chambers, iv. 47.
[8] See 33, 89 *supra* and S.R. Dec. 14, 1624 and Aug. 4, 1626 for a ballad of the '*Duchesse of Suffolke*'.
[9] The play was licensed to the Palsgrave's men as by 'Mr. Drew', Jan. 2, 1623/4 (Herbert, 18, 27; cf. S.R. Nov. 13, 1629).
[10] *Problems of Authorship in Elizabethan Dramatic Literature*, M.P. viii.

men on 29 (28) December 1593,[1] Mr. Oliphant has to suppose that the quarto was a recasting by Heywood of early work, or else that his revision was made after the play had been printed. Alexander Brome, whose birth in 1620 Mr. Oliphant unhesitatingly accepts from *Biographia Dramatica*, we are to assume was very precocious in his *Cunning Lovers* or merely patched an old play by Heywood. But the initial fact from which Mr. Oliphant argues is of itself quite insignificant.[2]

Hoffman, 1631 (S.R. February 26, 1629/30). Few students of the drama, if any at all, have been convinced by Fleay's dogmatism that Heywood had any part or lot in *Hoffman*. Fleay's inclusion of it among the plays Heywood wrote alone or in collaboration for Worcester's men about January or February 1602/3[3] conflicts with his placing it[4] in Chettle's list for the Admiral's men with the remark 'but simultaneously with the latter part of them he [Chettle] was writing for Worcester's men at the Rose also under Henslow'. Fleay's sole piece of external evidence is a payment by Henslowe on January 14, 1602/3 to Heywood and Chettle for an unnamed play for Worcester's men.[5] But 'Howghman', for which Chettle received five shillings in part payment on December 29, 1602, was for the Admiral's men.[6] As early as July 7, 1602 Chettle had received £1 in earnest of 'a danyshe tragedy'[7] for the Admiral's company, and on August 24 and September 7, 8, and 9[8] further sums, some of which were probably for the same play. This could hardly have been *Hoffman*;[9] rather it may have been, like 'spanes comodye donne oracoe'[10] which probably dramatized the events leading up to *The Spanish Tragedy*, an antecedent to *Hoffman* which presupposes some sort of introduction.[11] 'Rode-Ricke'[12] was probably the story of Roderigo Borgia, Pope Alexander VI.[13] For another suggestion of Fleay[14] that 'the [devell] licke vnto licke' of October 28, 1600[15] was *Hoffman* see Dr. Greg's proof[16] that it was Fulwell's *Like unto Like*. In dedicating *Hoffman* to Richard Kilvert, the publisher declared it wanted '*both a Parent to owne it, and a Patron to protect it*'. Now, says Fleay, in no

---

[1] *H.D.* i. 16.

[2] For *George a Greene* see Fleay, i. 35, 51, 264, ii. 158–9; *H.D.* ii. 158; Chambers, iv. 15.

[3] i. 291.   [4] i. 70.   [5] *H.D.* i. 173, 187; see 36 *supra*.

[6] *H.D.* i. 173; cf. ii. 226 and Chambers, iii. 264.

[7] *H.D.* i. 169.   [8] *Ibid.* i. 179, 181; cf. ii. 229, 231.

[9] Cf. Fleay, i. 71 and *H.D.* ii. 125.   [10] *H.D.* i. 13–15, ii. 150.

[11] Cf. *H.D.* ii. 223, 226, 229.   [12] *Ibid.* i. 131.

[13] See S.R. Oct. 16, 1607; but cf. Fleay, ii. 308 and *Stage*, 101.

[14] ii. 308.   [15] *H.D.* i. 131.   [16] *Ibid.* ii. 228.

instance 'did Heywood sanction the publication of plays not entirely his'.[1] But this proves nothing, for apart from editing *The Jew of Malta, Greene's Tu Quoque,* and perhaps others,[2] Heywood did not sanction the publication of plays which were not his at all; and as a matter of fact he did approve of the publication of *The Late Lancashire Witches,* in part Brome's, and of *The Royal King and the Loyal Subject,* which may contain work by Smith. Besides, if Perry had known of Heywood's share, would he not have preferred to issue the tragedy in 1631 with the better guarantee of a living author's name, the more so since Chettle had died in 1607? But in any case the play shows no sign of composite authorship and no trace of Heywood's hand or finger. According to Fleay, Heywood was responsible for iii. 2, and iv. 3 'in which Charles and Sarlois occur instead of Otho'.[3] The name Sarlois perplexed Fleay, for he ascribed another play, *The Trial of Chivalry,*[4] to Heywood, partly because of the occurrence in it of the character Sarlabois, there being one Sarlebois in *The Captives* which is undoubtedly Heywood's. It is by no means clear what Fleay means by iii. 2 and iv. 3. Presumably the former begins on sig. F recto with '*Enter Stilt, and a rabble of poore souldiers*' and continues to the end of the act; but act iv consists of one scene only. As for Sarlois, the only occurrence of the name in the dialogue—later it is used in the contraction 'Sarl.' for speech-headings—is in a passage on sig. F verso:

FIBS. Yes; noble, ancient Captaine *Stilt,* ye have remov'd mens hearts I have heard that of my father (God rest his soule,) when yee were but one of the common all souldiers that serv'd old *Sarloys* in Norway.

OLD STILT. I then was, and *Sarloys* was; a gentleman wou'd not have given his head for the washing; but hee is cut off, as all valiant cavaleroes shall; and they be no more negligent of themselves.

This nonsense is unintelligible enough to be fitted into any theory; it has no reference to anything else in the play. From an examination of the use of 'Charles', 'Otho', and 'Sarl.', we find that the first two are used indiscriminately by the other characters for the murdered Prince whom Hoffman impersonates, while 'Sarl.' occurs only in speech-headings for the masquerading Hoffman. We suggest, therefore, that 'Sarl.' is a printer's error, due perhaps to the occurrence of the name Sarlois, for 'Charl.' (= Charles) and that the use of both 'Charles' and 'Otho' for the one person is due, as Dr. Greg thinks,[5] to revision, not to collaboration. It must be

---

[1] i. 291.   [2] See 84, 116–17, 165–8, 287–94 *supra.*
[3] 1. 291.   [4] See 336–7 *infra.*
[5] *H.D.* ii. 226; cf. Chambers, iii. 264.

obvious, in any case, to the candid inquirer that Heywood was innocent of any share in the tragedy.

In *The Merry Devil of Edmonton*, 1608 (S.R. October 22, 1607), another piece from the Shakespeare Apocrypha, Hazlitt[1] and Ulrici[2] thought they detected Heywood; and more recently Miss Bates[3] discovered 'touches of the Heywood vocabulary . . . as well as the Heywood flavour', with which Mr. J. Q. Adams[4] agrees, though he cannot regard Heywood as the chief collaborator and finds 'the unmistakable hand of Thomas Dekker . . . in most of the scenes'. But this delightful comedy of the King's men—'a very merry play', says Pepys, 'which pleased me well'[5]—is far too spontaneous in its fun, too lyrical in its poetry, altogether too airy and fanciful to have been written by the sober and rather stolid Heywood; nothing else of his bears any likeness to this exquisite thing. Perhaps those who discern Heywood in it are, in part at least, influenced by the association of it in T. M.'s *Black Book*[6] with Heywood's masterpiece, *A Woman Killed with Kindness*, and by its allusions to reading long 'the liberall arts' at Cambridge and to watching o' nights 'on the top of Peter-house highest tower'.[7] But T. M. mentioned the two plays together because they were recent dramatic successes. The allusions to Cambridge prove nothing; we have shown elsewhere[8] that Heywood was not, as Cartwright declared, a fellow of Peter-house but an alumnus of Emmanuel.[9]

A New Wonder, A Woman never Vexed, 1632 (S.R. November 24, 1631). Fleay attempts to show, by no means plausibly, that Rowley's comedy was 'altered from an old rhyming play, the part from iii. 2 onward being slightly changed. . . . I think the original author was Heywood'.[10] Dr. Greg then suggested[11] that if there is anything in Fleay's theory '(the) wonder of a woman', a new play of the Admiral's men on 15 (16) October, 1595[12] may have been Heywood's original version. But there would be as much reason for supposing *The Wonder of a Woman* the original of Marston's *Wonder of Women or the Tragedy of Sophonisba*. Fleay has by no means proved that the state of *A New Wonder* is due to its being a

---

[1] Ed. Waller and Glover, v. 293.

[2] *Über Shakspere's dramatische Kunst und sein Verhältnis zu Calderon und Göthe*, 1839, 473.

[3] xiv. [4] *M.P.* xvi. 274.

[5] Aug. 10, 1661. [6] Sig. E 3.

[7] Ed. Tucker Brooke, 269. [8] See 6–7 *supra*.

[9] For other attributions see Fleay, i. 150–1, 157, ii. 117, 313–14; *Shakespeare*, 130–1; Tucker Brooke, *Shakespeare Apocrypha*, xxxvi–xxxviii; and Chambers, iv. 30.

[10] ii. 102–3. [11] *H.D.* ii. 177. [12] *Ibid.* i. 25–8.

revision of an 'old rhyming play'—Heywood was no fonder of rhymes than Rowley—rather than to the carelessness of the printers. The crabbed style, even allowing for revision, is quite foreign to Heywood, with whose mannerisms Fleay does not elsewhere display such an acquaintance that we can trust to his recognizing them when buried under the peculiarities of Rowley. Fleay may have got a hint for the ascription from Malone's assigning the play at first to Heywood and Rowley, a mistake which he later corrected.[1] It was, of course, natural enough to guess that Heywood had to do with a bourgeois comedy in which two of the city worthies figure, and which has among its characters a clown with a taste for Latin tags and a general resemblance to Heywood's clowns; but the play is both more naïve and more virile than any of Heywood's and in quite another style. No light is thrown on the subject by Mr. C. W. Stork's remark[2] that he once thought from the childish evolution of character and moral development in *A New Wonder* that Heywood had a hand in it, but was later convinced that the aforementioned features were due to Rowley's collaboration with Heywood in *Fortune by Land and Sea*.

Pericles, Prince of Tyre, 1609 (S.R. May 20, 1608). Mr. D. L. Thomas made out a case for Heywood's collaboration with Shakespeare in *Pericles*, which must have been very convincing for any who did not know their Heywood, though no one who does will give the theory a second thought.[3] The suggestion which depends entirely on internal evidence and is counter to all the external was rejected by Mr. Adams,[4] who undertook a long and careful study of the play for the very purpose of discovering Heywood. We can gather from *The Captives*, the plot of which is not unlike that of *Pericles*, how the prose Shakespeare would have treated the latter. If there are resemblances in *Pericles* to Heywood's manner, is it not possible that Wilkins, whom the consensus of opinion makes Shakespeare's jackal, caught something from a partnership with Heywood which our discussion of *A Yorkshire Tragedy* may have made clearer?[5]   John Tatham, who belonged to Heywood's circle, in commending *The Jovial Crew* of Heywood's collaborator Richard Brome, speaks of a literary faction that thought

> *Shakespeare* the *Plebean* Driller, was
> Founder'd in's *Pericles*, and must not pass.

[1] Bodley: Malone B 104.
[2] Ed. of *All's Lost by Lust* and *A Shoemaker a Gentleman*, 28.
[3] *On the Play Pericles, Englische Studien*, xxxix.
[4] *M.P.* xvi. 273-4.   [5] See 302-28 *supra*.

The Downfall and The Death of Robert, Earl of Huntingdon, 1601 (S.R. December 1, 1600), were respectively by Munday and by Munday and Chettle.[1] Kirkman, however, in his 1661 and 1671 catalogues, began the misattribution to Heywood which was repeated by Winstanley and Langbaine and their successors, and by the earlier editors of Dodsley, as well as by Warton[2] and Dilke.[3] Malone at first on the strength of Kirkman's assertion bound his copies with Heywood quartos, but later added a note in correction.[4] Collier in his edition of Dodsley[5] was the first to make the real authors generally known.

Thomas Lord Cromwell, 1602 (S.R. August 11), bore the initials 'W. S.', no doubt to imply Shakespeare's authorship. The waif was bestowed by Farmer[6] on Heywood, not without a show of reason, for the mixture in it of history and fiction has a slight resemblance to If you know not me, part ii, and old Cromwell might be taken by those who dimly remembered Heywood's old fathers as another sketch by him of the same type. But though we know to what Heywood could descend, we agree with Malone[7] that 'The poverty of language, the barrenness of incident and the inartificial conduct of every part of the performance, place it rather perhaps below the compositions of even the second-rate dramatick authors of the age in which it was produced'. Swinburne is even severer: 'Thomas Lord Cromwell is a piece of such utterly shapeless, spiritless, bodiless, soulless, senseless, helpless, worthless rubbish, that there is no known writer of Shakespeare's age to whom it could be ascribed without the infliction of an unwarrantable insult on that writer's memory.'[8]

The masque in The Tempest, iv. 1, has been credited by the disintegrating Mr. J. M. Robertson to Heywood, c. 1612, for reasons that will not commend themselves to many students of the drama.[9]

The Thracian Wonder, 1661. It would never have occurred to any but Fleay to accuse Heywood of this wretched tragicomedy. It was first printed for Kirkman along with A Cure for a Cuckold,

---

[1] H.D. i. 83–5, 99; ii. 190–1. Chettle 'mended' both parts.
[2] Cf. Old English Dramas, 1825, ii.
[3] Old English Plays, 1814–15, vi.
[4] Cf. Malone's Shakespeare, v. pt. ii, 308.
[5] Cf. Old English Plays, 1825, ii.
[6] Malone's Supplement, ii. 446.
[7] Cited by Tucker Brooke, Shakespeare Apocrypha, xxix.
[8] Study of Shakespeare, 232. For more recent views see Tucker Brooke, op. cit. xxvii–ix and Chambers, iv. 8.
[9] T.L.S. Mar. 31, 1921.

both plays being ascribed to Webster and William Rowley.[1] It was Collier's belief,[2] which has generally been accepted, that Kirkman confused John Webster with a certain William Webster, who in 1617 published his *most pleasant and delightful History of Curan, Prince of Danske, and the fair Princess Argentile, Daughter and Heir of Adelbright, sometime King of Northumberland,* an expansion of the story in *Albion's England,* iv. 20, from which the plot of *The Thracian Wonder* is also but not directly derived. The dramatist owes his theme to Greene's *Menaphon,* 1589.[3] Therefore Fleay's dating of the play in 1617,[4] apparently in the temporary belief that its plot was derived from William Webster's poem, can be dismissed. But the fact that it was a dramatization of a romance published in 1589 does not make more likely Fleay's identification of it, on the strength of the phrases 'You never shall again renew your suit',[5] though the love is returned at the end without suit, and 'Here was a happy war, fought without blows',[6] with *War without Blows and Love without Suit (Strife),* written by Heywood for the Admiral's men in December–January 1595/6;[7] Fleay adds 'It was probably, like many other of Heywood's plays, revived for the Queen's men c. 1607, when W. Rowley and Webster were writing for them; whence the absurd attribution . . . to them by Kirkman'.[8] Fleay's first quotation is from the pastoral sub-plot of Serena and Palemon, and the renewing of the latter's suit which he is under oath not to revive until Serena sends for him could not possibly have given a name to the play; as for the main plot, it has nothing to do with love without suit and, though it is concerned with a war happily averted, the title of Heywood's lost play would most naturally fit a wordy war without blows, followed by a marriage, in short a kind of Benedick and Beatrice courtship.[9] Moreover, *The Thracian Wonder* has not the suspicion of a savour of Heywood in it. Only in *Amphrisa, or the Forsaken Shepherdess* in *Pleasant Dialogues* did he attempt the pastoral style, and the fashion of that

---

[1] For Webster's and Rowley's shares see *The Retrospective Review,* 1823, pt. i. 119; C. W. Stork, ed. of *All's Lost by Lust,* &c., 62; E. E. Stoll, *John Webster,* 34, 36; and Rupert Brooke, *John Webster,* 206-7.

[2] *Poetical Decameron,* i. 268.

[3] Cf. J. Q. Adams, *Greene's Menaphon and The Thracian Wonder, M.P.* iii. 317, &c.; J. Le Gay Brereton, *The Relation of The Thracian Wonder to Greene's Menaphon, M.L.R.* ii. 34, &c.; and O. L. Fletcher, *The Sources and Authorship of The Thracian Wonder, M.L.N.* xxii. i. 16, &c.

[4] ii. 332; cf. Stork, *op. cit.* 14.   [5] i. 2.   [6] iii. 2.   [7] See 12 *supra.*

[8] i. 287; cf. ii. 107 where he gives Rowley a share in it; ii. 99 where he assigns it to Rowley and Middleton; and *Stage,* 104, 156.

[9] Cf. *H.D.* ii. 200.

brief idyll has no resemblance to *The Thracian Wonder's* vulgar, stupid amalgam of courts and sheep-cotes, kings and shepherds. It is absurd to make Heywood the creator of the ogrish Pheander who becomes so sheepish among the polite shepherds, or of Ariadne and Sophos, Serena and Radagon and Eusanius, all of whom might have walked straight out of the pages of Greene. Though the play has some pleasing lyrics, the style shows an alacrity in sinking that is portentous; at its best it is undramatic and like an inexperienced playwright's imitation of a fashion that had gone out before Heywood's arrival.[1]

There is even less reason, if possible, for attributing to Heywood *The Trial of Chivalry*. This amateurish romance, entered in the Stationers' Register on December 4, 1604 as '*The Life and Death of Cavaliero DICK BOYER*', appeared in 1605 with two curiously different titles, namely *The History of the trial of Chivalry, With the life and death of Cavaliero Dick Bowyer. As it hath been lately acted by the right Honourable the Earl of Derby his servants*, and *This Gallant Cavaliero Dick Bowyer, Newly acted*. But Dick Bowyer figures very little in the play, and the death of that worthy is not given at all. Apparently there was some motive for advertising the role of this minor personage; and the likeliest explanation is that in 1604 another version of the play had been staged and much more space given to Dick and his death. But the publisher, unable to lay hands on the copy of the play as recently acted, did get hold of the discarded older version, as is clear from the excellence of the text, and palmed it off on the public. *The Trial of Chivalry* remained anonymous till Phillips[2] gave its author as William Wager, apparently relying on the fact that in Kirkman's 1661 catalogue W. Wager was the last-mentioned dramatist before the entry of *The Trial of Chivalry*.[3] Fleay would identify the play through Bourbon, whom he curiously calls the chief tragic character,[4] with 'burbon', acted by the Admiral's and Pembroke's men at the Rose, November 2, 1597.[5] The original author he makes Chettle, while the reviser he supposes was the author of *Edward IV*.[6] Elsewhere, however, though he distinctly says it is not the same play as

---

[1] Cf. Chambers, iv. 49.   [2] *Theatrum Poetarum*, 194.

[3] See W. W. Greg, *Notes on Dramatic Bibliographers, Malone Society Collections*, I, iv. 325–6, for the persistence of this error, and for 'William Wayer', a name due to Langbaine's expansion in *Momus Triumphans* of a misprint in Kirkman's 1671 catalogue.   [4] ii. 318.

[5] *H.D.* i. 54, ii. 187; S.R. April 15, 1641 for '*A Tragedy called Charles, Duke of Burbon*'.

[6] i. 289, ii. 318–19; cf. *Stage*, 154 for a theory of authorship by Heywood and Smith for Derby's men.

'burone', for which Worcester's men bought properties in September and October 1602[1], he attempts very unsatisfactorily to identify them and more than usually contradicts himself.[2] His other identification of *The Trial of Chivalry* with *Cutting Dick* need not be discussed.[3] Swinburne seems to have been slightly impressed by the attribution to Heywood.[4] Our own guess is that the serious plot may be the work of William Stanley, Earl of Derby, who was 'busy penning comedies' about June 1599.[5] It is certain that Heywood at least—the name Sarlabois is no more significant than the spellings 'Sentynell', 'Sentronell', 'mordu', 'mort dew' (though Fleay thought differently[6])—did not write this symmetrical story of the kings of France and Navarre, their sons and daughters. The end-stopped verse, the long set speeches, and the entire difference in style and vocabulary rule out any theory of his responsibility for the romantic plot. Indeed, the general failure to employ or to understand the resources of the popular stage at the end of the sixteenth century points to another than any of the journeyman-playwrights and professional dramatists. The play has the improbability of plot in which situations are invented without reference to the puppet-like characters, the parallelism and balancing of parts, the tricks of style, the use of the third person for the first and second, the classical instances, the pastoralism, the lack of humour and all the other features of *Mucedorus* and the romantic plays of Greene and his school. We conclude, then, that it was either written more than ten years before its publication or was the work of one, like William Stanley, without any professional knowledge of the stage and the methods of obtaining plausibility and dramatic effect which make even inferior dramas about 1600 so much more competent than the bulk of the work of five years earlier. The detachable comic portions were obviously by some one other than the author of the serious plot; their breezy style with its constant echoes of *The Merry Devil of Edmonton* and *Henry IV* is in marked contrast to the stilted manner of the rest. If the author of *The Merry Devil of Edmonton* and Dekker be not one and the same, we are doubtful to which of the two the Rabelaisian Dick Bowyer, overflowing with energy, quips, and puns, ought to be credited. Bullen[7] would identify *The Trial of Chivalry* with Chettle and Smith's 'Love parts frendshipp'.[8]

A Warning for Fair Women, 1599 (S.R. November 17), was

[1] *H.D.* i. 181–2.   [2] i. 56, 64, ii. 306, 318–19.
[3] See 28–9 *supra*.   [4] To Edmund Gosse, Nov. 14, 24, 1892.
[5] Cf. Chambers, iii. 495, iv. 50–1.   [6] ii. 318–19; see 331 *supra*.
[7] *Old English Plays*, iii.   [8] *H.P.* 58.

supposed by Fleay[1] to have been produced by the Chamberlain's men at the Globe not long before its publication because of the prologue's allusions to 'this faire circuite' and 'this Round'. But the earlier houses of this company were probably also round,[2] and though we cannot agree with Mr. Farmer[3] that the play dates from 1589–90, yet we are inclined to put its composition several years earlier than 1599. It has been ascribed incredibly to Lyly by Phillips[4] and Wood,[5] still more incredibly to Shakespeare by Bernhardi,[6] to Lodge by Fleay 'less on positive evidence than on the method of exhaustion',[7] and to Yarington by Bullen.[8] Finally, Mr. Adams[9] bestowed it on Heywood, making out, in Miss Bates's opinion,[10] a strong case. But we remain quite unconvinced; the characters, if such they can be called, are not drawn in Heywood's manner at all; the structure of the plot, without sub-plot or comic relief, is without parallel among his acknowledged works; and the prosy, lifeless style and the featureless vocabulary are not his. He may, however, have derived from the tragedy an anecdote he tells in *An Apology for Actors*:[11]

> A woman that had made away her husband,
> And sitting to hehold a tragedy
> At Linne a towne in Norffolke,
> Acted by Players travelling that way,
> Wherein a woman that had murthered hers
> Was ever haunted with her husbands ghost:
> The passion written by a feeling pen,
> And acted by a good Tragedian,
> She was so mooved with the sight thereof,
> As she cryed out, the Play was made by her,
> And openly confesst her husbands murder.[12]

On the other hand, the tale may have been a theatrical commonplace.

Work for Cutlers. Or, a merry Dialogue between Sword, Rapier and Dagger, 1615 (S.R. July 4), is not a play but an academic dialogue, produced at Cambridge. Mr. A. F. Sieveking, who edited it in 1904 after a Cambridge revival, is a *maître d'escrime*, scarcely a critic, and his attribution of the dialogue to Heywood was based

[1] ii. 54.   [2] Cf. Chambers, iv. 52.
[3] Ed. preface.   [4] *Theatrum Poetarum*, 113.
[5] *Athenae Oxonienses*, ed. Bliss, i. 676.
[6] *Hamburger Litteraturblatt*, No. 79, x.
[7] ii. 55.   [8] *Old English Plays*, iv. 1.
[9] *The Authorship of A Warning for Fair Women*, P.M.L.A.A. xxviii.
[10] xii.   [11] 57–8.   [12] Sig. H 2.

on nothing more than the dramatist's voluminousness and his residence at Cambridge. As Miss Bates says, 'subject, manner, phrasing, all are against him'.[1] Indeed we are surprised that Mr. Sieveking's guess, which Sir A. W. Ward in his prefatory note politely passed over, has received so much attention. It is likely, as Professor Moore Smith says,[2] that it was by the same hand as *A Merry Dialogue, between Band, Cuff and Ruff*, 1615 (S.R. February 10), called in its second edition *Exchange Ware, at the second hand, viz. Band, Ruff, and Cuff, lately out, and now newly darned up.* They were both Cambridge shows, and as the second appears in B.M. Add. MS. 23723 among dramatic pieces for visits of James I to Cambridge, Professor Moore Smith supposes both to have been interludes in the course of longer plays before James on his earlier visit in 1615.

[1] xiii: cf. J. Q. Adams, *M.P.* xvi. 274.
[2] *'Victoria'*, *'Exchange Ware'*, and *'Work for Cutlers'*, *M.L.R.* iii. 373.

NON-DRAMATIC WORKS MISATTRIBUTED
TO HEYWOOD

IN 1614, probably because of the popularity of Heywood's *Ages*, especially *The Iron Age*, but also no doubt of *Troia Britannica*, there was published *The Life and Death of Hector. One, and the First of the most Puissant, Valiant, and Renowned Monarchs of the world, called the Nine worthies. Written by John Lydgate Monk of Bury, and by him dedicated to the high and mighty Prince Henry the fifth, King of England.* There has been a conspiracy from Winstanley downwards to attribute to Heywood this 'most extraordinary instance of useless patience, unwearied perseverance, and distorted taste in an editor'.[1] Thus Dr. Farmer in a MS. note[2] says, 'This modern versification . . . is generally attributed to T. Heywood: Fuller and other writers mistaking it for the original, are amazed that the language is so much more intelligible than that of Chaucer'. Subsequent writers have become more dogmatic, and Dr. Franz Albert, who gives a list of them, produced an Inaugural-Dissertation[3] to prove Heywood's authorship. Dr. Albert was evidently impressed by the unanimity of his predecessors, or rather by the absence of dissent; which, however, loses its force when one realizes that, the book itself being unimportant and not very accessible, the 'statement has been handed down and taken on faith, largely by mere compilers, though also by well-known scholars'.[4] Mr. Tatlock shows that where both Heywood and the anonymous modernizer of Lydgate drew passages from Ovid and Virgil, they did so because these episodes were too famous to omit, or because the author of *The Life and Death of Hector* had Heywood's poem before him. There are practically no other striking parallels in contents or language; indeed, when we remember the subject and the extent of *The Life and Death of Hector*, even if it were not by the author of *Troia Britannica*, the scarcity of parallels is surprising.[5] As for the supposed general resemblances in versification and style,

---

[1] Brydges, *Restituta*, ii. 395; cf. Ellis, *Specimens of the Early English Poets*, 1845, i. 241, and R. Watt, *Bibliotheca Britannica*, 1824, ii, article *John Lydgate*.
[2] *c.* 1760; quoted by Allibone, *Dictionary of English Literature*, article *John Lydgate*.
[3] *Über Thomas Heywoods The Life and Death of Hector, eine Neubearbeitung von Lydgates Troy Book*; more fully in *Münchener Beiträge zur romanischen und englischen Philologie*, no. xlii.
[4] Tatlock, 692.   [5] Cf. Tatlock, 693 and note.

they 'are of the most trivial and commonplace kind'.[1] The metrical inequalities Dr. Albert attributes to Heywood's attempt to keep as close to the original as possible. But why, then, did he modernize at all? As Mr. Tatlock remarks, no one familiar with Heywood's work will believe that *metri gratia* he wrote 'Cassandera', 'pataron' (= pattern), 'sacared' (= sacred), 'Palladiowne' or 'Palladowne' (= Palladium), &c., or that he produced lines a whole foot short. Heywood, too, was an educated man; he would not substitute familiar for unfamiliar classical names, or, when his printer allowed him, misspell them (e. g. 'Ditus' for Dictys), or call Petrarch 'Patricke Francke' because Lydgate has 'Petrack fraūceis'.[2] Moreover, Heywood had already written a series of plays, half of which dramatized the same myths as are told by Lydgate, besides a long poem on which the plays are based; and he had deliberately kept from the press the two plays of the pentalogy which were nearest in theme to the modernized *Troy Book*. But even if Heywood had taken the tremendous trouble of retelling what he had twice told within five years, no printer would have suppressed the name of so famous an historian of Troy. The attribution in the B.M. catalogue of *The Life and Death of Hector* to 'T. H.' seems to be due to a misreading of the catch-letters 'TH' or 'THe' at the end of the dedication; indeed it is not improbable that the ascription to Heywood originated in an expansion of the same supposed initials.

A reading of the title-page of *Eromena, or, Love and Revenge. Written originally in the Thoscan tongue by Cavalier Gio. Francesco Biondi, gentleman Extraordinary of his Majesty's Privy Chambers. Divided into six Books. And now faithfully Englished, by Ja. Hayward, of Gray's Inn, Gent.*, 1632 (S.R. February 22, 1631/2) would have prevented the ascription of it to Heywood.[3] Collier pointed out the error in his edition of Dodsley.[4]

A Preparative to Study or The Virtues of Sack, a copy of verses with a pronounced Royalist bias, which appeared in a single sheet in quarto in 1641, and in a new edition in 1651 *Whereunto is added the valiant Battle between the Norfolk and the Wisbech Cock*, has been repeatedly fathered on Heywood. *A Preparative to Study* has also been attributed to Francis Beaumont, Richard Brathwaite, and John Taylor.[5] *The Valiant Battle* and *The High Commendation of a Pot of Good Ale* were printed together in 1642 as by 'Thomas

[1] *Ibid.* 693.   [2] *Ibid.* 693.
[3] Reed's Dodsley, 1780, vii. 259; *Old English Plays*, 1815, vi. 104; and Sharp, *Dictionary of English Authors*, 132.
[4] 1825, vii. 218.
[5] *Catalogue of the Ashley Library*, ii. 186.

Randell';[1] but in a manuscript miscellany in the Huth Library the combat of the two cocks is said to have taken place on June 17, 1637, more than two years after Randolph's death. *A Preparative to Study*, renamed *On the Virtues of Sack*, was included in *An Antidote against Melancholy*, a song-book of 1661 in which the author's initials are given as D. R. H. E.[2] Perhaps the note in the Bodleian copy of the 1651 edition, 'by Thos. Heywood who was b. in Lincolnsh.', is the source of the erroneous attribution to Heywood; Wisbech, it may be noted, is in Cambridgeshire. The Anacreontic, cavalier swing of both *A Preparative* and *The Valiant Battle* bears no resemblance to Heywood's heroic couplets; and Heywood, who died on August 16, 1641, could not have referred, as did the poet of the former, to the death of John Leslie, sixth Earl of Rothes, which took place on August 23, and to other incidents of Charles's expedition to Scotland in the late summer of 1641. Brome has the phrase, 'Give me a Preparative of Sack. It is a gentle Preparative before Meat', in *A Jovial Crew*, 1641.[3]

---

[1] W. C. Hazlitt, *The Poetical and Dramatic Works of Thomas Randolph*, i. xviii. According to Mr. G. Thorn-Drury (*Poems of Thomas Randolph*, xxii), this ascription is 'due to nothing but careless reading of the title-page'; he assigns *The Valiant Battle* without question to Robert Wild.

[2] Bates, lxxxi.   [3] Pearson's *Brome*, i. 418.

INDEX